FILM/LITERATURE/ HERITAGE

A Sight and Sound Reader

D0219297

FILM/LITERATURE/ HERITAGE

A Sight and Sound Reader

Edited by Ginette Vincendeau

 Publishing

First published in 2001 by the
British Film Institute
21 Stephen Street, London W1T 1LN

The British Film Institute is the UK national agency with
responsibility for encouraging the arts of film and television
and conserving them in the national interest.

Cover image: Nicole Kidman in *The Portrait of a Lady* (Jane Campion, 1996)
Set by Design Consultants (Siobhán O'Connor)
Printed in Great Britain by St Edmundsbury Press,
Bury St Edmunds, Suffolk

British Library Cataloguing-in-Publication Data
A catalogue record for this book is available from the British Library

ISBN 0–85170–841–2 (paperback)
ISBN 0–85170–842–0 (hardback)

Contents

Preface

This collection brings together articles written in *Sight and Sound* over the past ten years on the relationship between film, literature and 'heritage'. The book was initially planned as a reader on film and literature, a topic which turned out to be as rich as it is elusive. Rich, thanks to the extraordinary popularity of literary adaptations over the past ten to twenty years and the wealth of material written about them. Elusive, because of the theoretical difficulties involved in comparing two different media and because the material ranges widely, from Shakespeare to contemporary cult thrillers. While this collection spans such diverse areas, the most sustained debate within literary adaptations relates to 'heritage cinema', a term which has come to define the lavish costume adaptations of canonical literature typified by *Howards End*. Thus, although film and literature remains the basic rationale of this book, a third term was added to its title and contents, to reflect the growing importance of heritage cinema both as a 'genre' and as a concept in film studies.

While most writers gathered in this volume share film as their specialism (this is worth mentioning because of the literary bias of much writing on film and literature), they speak from many different vantage points. The aim of the following introduction is to place their contributions within the wider debates on film, literature and heritage cinema.

Acknowledgments
My thanks to all the *Sight and Sound* contributors whose work I much enjoyed reading and re-reading, and who have taught me a lot about the relationship between film and literature. I am only sorry I could not include more of them in the book. Thanks also to José Arroyo, Ed Gallafent, Andrew Lockett, Julianne Pidduck and Valerie Orpen, who read a draft of the introduction and made useful comments and suggestions.

Introduction

The topic of 'film and literature' is almost limitless. Most films originate in some form of writing: a novel, short story or a play, and/or a script. As soon as cinema emerged from its fairground phase and the narrative fiction film became the dominant mode, writers were drafted in by studios to adapt existing works or write original scripts. The coming of sound increased this inter-dependency with the added importance of dialogue (in France, there is even a category of *dialoguiste* in addition to the script-writer). Conversely, there has been a steady stream of publications emerging from films, from the 1920s cheap 'novelisations' and *ciné-romans* to film scripts and today's coffee-table book-of-the-film, not to mention reissues of source books with film stills on the cover. In terms of personnel, the boundaries between film and literature (and drama) are frequently blurred and, as Ian Christie points out (page 71), film-makers such as Max Ophuls were at once literary, theatrical and filmic. Names of such crossover figures include Orson Welles, Joseph Mankiewicz, Marcel Pagnol, Ingmar Bergman, Jean Cocteau, Christopher Hampton, Alain Robbe-Grillet, Woody Allen, David Mamet, Catherine Breillat and many others. In the 'film and literature' constellation, the impact of literary classics on film has attracted most attention. It is enshrined very early on in a celebrated article by Sergei Eisenstein on the influence of Dickens on his, and Griffith's editing techniques (Eisenstein 1949). Also crucial is the importance of American crime fiction for thrillers, from James M. Cain to Elmore Leonard (see Matthews and Wootton in section 3). Arguments have also convincingly been made about the convergence in the late nineteenth/early twentieth century between modernist literature and cinema – for instance Flaubert's alternating technique, Conrad, James and Woolf's emphasis on 'mental images', the use of cinema as metaphor for time and speed, etc. – and the fact that twentieth-century literature is itself profoundly influenced by the cinema (see McFarlane 1996, for a summary of these arguments; see also Vray 1999). In this book, Philip Horne argues that 'cinematic techniques began influencing Jamesian metaphor', and film-maker Sally Potter remarks on the 'visual qualities' in Virginia Woolf's *Orlando* (both in section 2).

Film and literature, however, are self-evidently different media and some have argued that the very comparison of a film with its literary source is meaningless. As Robin Wood pithily puts it in the introduction to his book on *The Wings of the Dove*, 'film is film, literature is literature' (Wood 1999, 7). Yet the books and the films themselves, the publicity around them, statements by film-makers and our own experience as readers and spectators, all compel us, if not to pass comparative judgment, at least to see one in the light of the other. *Sense and Sensibility* cannot be watched in ignorance of Jane Austen, even by a spectator who has not read a line of the novel. Equally, every best-selling contemporary book – from *American Psycho* to *Harry Potter* – raises expectations about its movie adaptation; in fact, it may well have been written in anticipation of it. Even if critics are still searching for a specific theoretical framework to understand the relationship between film and literature in general, there are plenty of things to be said about particular cases. This is the approach taken by many of the writers on the topic at large and one of the organising principles of this book.

Literary adaptations: the 'fidelity issue'

As mentioned above, there are many ways to envisage the relationship between film and literature. However, the most common understanding of the term, shared by the writers in this collection, is that of adaptations of famous novels and plays. Because of the high cultural capital of a source book in the case of classics, but equally because of the fetishistic attachment of readers in the case of cult books (e.g. *Crash, High Fidelity*), the critical reception of literary adaptations has been plagued with the urge to assess how 'faithful' the film version is to its 'original'. As Brian McFarlane says, 'Discussion of adaptations has been bedevilled by the fidelity issue' (McFarlane 1996, 8). In the introduction to their recent collection *The Classic Novel from Page to Screen*, Robert Giddings and Erica Sheen (2000) recognise the pitfalls of the fidelity approach yet admit that, 'All the essays in [their] volume take the question of fidelity as their primary critical point of reference.' Inevitably, given that, as in the Giddings and Sheen book, writers on the subject often come from literary criticism, 'fidelity' becomes a negative yardstick with which to beat film. 'Great literature has always been traduced and eviscerated on screen' typically complains a recent *Guardian* article on an adaptation of Nabokov's *The Luzhin Defence*.[1]

The writers in this book, by contrast, mostly come from film journalism and film studies, or write for the screen, and most draw comparisons with a view to enriching their appraisal of the film, not the opposite. Thus they show themselves specially attuned to the filmic elements of the adaptations: decor, camerawork, costume, performance. In the process, they illustrate McFarlane's point that critics should judge on the basis of 'the kind of adaptation the film aims to be' (1996, 22), rather than on the assumption that there is only one way to adapt a book. Modernist books seem especially to beg this question, as their very nature is to elude fixed meanings (see Romney on Raul Ruiz's adaptation of Proust's *Le Temps retrouvé* (pp. 37–43), a book whose status comes close to combining that of classic and cult), but the same can be said of any adaptation. Indeed, throughout this book, directors and screenwriters reflect on the joys, difficulties and sheer variety of adaptation and show that there is no 'formula'. The received wisdom that long novels are more difficult because they need cuts and that short stories or novellas are easier to adapt, is on the whole confirmed. So is the notion that the better (and the better known) the book, the more difficult the adaptation – thus Michael Eaton on *Great Expectations*: 'It is arguably his best constructed story, so there's little latitude for an adapter to uncover new dimensions' (p. 287).[2] On the other hand, Peter Matthews challenges the view (put forward, among others in this book, by novelist Iain Sinclair) that pulp fiction is easier to adapt: 'It's as if [Elmore] Leonard's thrillers are already movies, with the brevity of language and exteriority a screenwriter is supposed to aim for. But almost without exception the films based on his work [...] have been duds.' (p. 241). Larry Gross (pp.

277–9) and Adrian Wootton (pp. 232–5) also talk of the difficulties of adapting quirky noir writer Jim Thompson. Several writers and directors emphasise the importance of an 'osmosis' between themselves and the material they are adapting: see Scorsese on Wharton, Altman on Carver, Cronenberg on Ballard ('A lovely fusion', according to the director of *Crash*), Thompson on *The Secret Garden*, and finally Tarantino on Leonard: '[*Jackie Brown*] doesn't take place in my universe – this is Elmore Leonard's universe [...] I found he writes like I write.' (pp. 236, 240). It is also clear how, the stronger the director's agenda, the more he or she pulls the adaptation towards their own concerns: see for instance Pam Cook's review of *The Age of Innocence*, in which she argues, 'Once again Scorsese creates a dark pessimistic vision of male desire in which woman is never more than an alibi' (p. 163). (Taubin also notes how underwritten the women's parts are, p. 65.) At the same time, several writers in this book note the irreducible differences between book and film, especially in terms of depicting interiority. See, among others, Nick James on *American Psycho* and Cronenberg on *Crash* (pp. 227–32 and 208–17).

Opinions are equally divided about what makes a 'faithful' adaptation, from Sally Potter who says, of *Orlando*, 'You have to be cruel to the novel in order to be kind to the film', to Jane Campion's irreverent attitude to Henry James in *The Portrait of a Lady* (starting her film with contemporary adolescent girls), to Scorsese's 'totally fetishistic' relation to Edith Wharton's novel (all in section 2). Philip Horne runs through Henry James adaptations, showing that the good and the bad can be found in all categories, from the most faithful to the most distant, praising 'Jamesian' films not based on James, such as *The Fallen Idol* (Graham Greene), and *The Age of Innocence* ('the most Jamesian dialogue') (p. 91), while Jonathan Romney celebrates Ruiz's *Le Temps retrouvé* as being 'as near as anyone could have hoped to the holy grail of Proustian cinema' (p. 43).

Yet, despite the immense variety of possible relationships between a source book and its film adaptation, fidelity stubbornly remains the critical criterion, as can be found both in the general literature on the subject and among articles and reviews in this book. Even *Sight and Sound* authors are not immune to the occasional 'film is not as good as the book' attitude, but interestingly, they show in the process how unstable a category fidelity is. The case of Coppola's *Dracula* – on which three articles and an interview with the scriptwriter are included in this book – is instructive. While Iain Sinclair claims that 'What we do not have, alas, is Bram Stoker's *Dracula*' (p. 102), Kim Newman argues that the same film tries to follow the novel too closely, and thus 'fails' as an adaptation (pp. 97–101). Meanwhile, scriptwriter Hart, while insisting on 'loyalty-through-reinterpretation', altered the ending and transformed the book 'from horror story to fairy tale' (p. 272).

In what still remains, fifty years later, one of the most incisive texts written on the relationship between film and literature ('In Defense of Mixed Cinema'), André Bazin addressed the issue in terms which are worth quoting at length:

> It is nonsense to wax wroth about the indignities practiced on literary works on the screen, at least in the name of literature. After all, they cannot harm the original in the eyes of those who know it, however little they approximate to it. As for those who

are unacquainted with the original, one of two things may happen; either they will be satisfied with the film which is as good as most, or they will want to know the original, with the resulting gain for literature. This argument is supported by publishers' statistics that show a rise in the sale of literary works after they have been adapted to the screen. No, the truth is, that culture in general and literature in particular have nothing to lose from such an enterprise. (Bazin 1967, 65).

Bazin's arguments remain as true today as when he wrote them in the 1950s. A little earlier, Margaret Thorp in her book *America at the Movies* (1946) also discussed the beneficial effects of literary adaptations on book sales: 'More copies of *Wuthering Heights* have been sold since the novel was screened than in all the previous ninety-two of its existence' (Thorp 1946, 142). She also astutely pointed out that 'The comparison of book and picture is for a vast audience the beginning of film criticism' (143). So why the obsession with negative comparative value judgments between literature and film?

Film and literature: critical warfare in the (post)modern age

Cinema's youth relative to the other arts is a crucial consideration when assessing the relationship between film and literature. As Bazin also said, 'If the cinema were two or three thousand years old we would undoubtedly see more clearly that it does not lie outside the common laws of the evolution of the arts.' (Bazin 1967, 55). Nobody indeed worries about the relative fidelity of operas, novels and plays – good case studies would include *Carmen* and *La Dame aux camélias/La Traviata*. However, as the Nabokov example quoted above shows, the derogatory attitude towards the cinema also operates in relation to twentieth-century books when they have reached a certain level of canonicity. For instance, Iain Sinclair derides David Cronenberg's version of *Naked Lunch* in the following terms: 'You want prestige? Buy a good title, then throw away the book. [...] The elitism of [Burroughs'] hierographic vision is not accessible through the efforts, however well intentioned, of a democratic art form'. (pp. 206–7) Literature, classical, cult or modernist, it seems, still shares the high cultural ground with opera, ballet and theatre.

This traditional cultural hierarchy is, however, increasingly at odds with societal and institutional changes, making literary adaptations symptomatic of interesting power struggles. The role of new technologies and the rise of film and media studies as academic disciplines have produced radical shifts, with film increasingly functioning as a teaching aid to a range of literacy and literary activities. In the United Kingdom, the Film and Literacy project aims to teach reading skills to primary school children, 'tak[ing] advantage of a child's visual literacy to refine how they read a text' and acknowledging the role of film as an enticement to get children to work.[3] The teachers' packs contain video and written material on adaptations such as *The Railway Children* and *The Wind in the Willows*, as well as Shakespeare films (e.g. Kenneth Branagh's *Love's Labour's Lost*). Similarly, literature and modern languages syllabuses in secondary schools and universities increasingly incorporate film, but the relationship there becomes more complex and less candid. Whether teachers and lecturers use film as an object of study in its own right, as illustrative material or as a window on a past or foreign culture, film encroaches on the supremacy of the written word. This is welcomed by some and resented by others, but in the light of these shifts the complaint that students sometimes fail to distinguish between a book and its filmed version appears disingenuous. For example, a recent *Guardian* article on Patricia Rozema's *Mansfield Park*[4] laments the growing blur in students' minds between books and films, but makes no mention of the extent to which students of English are exposed to both in classrooms and lecture halls. Could it be that the purist rejection of literary adaptations allegorises these deeper institutional shifts?

Meanwhile, film studies are not free from their own purism. Film history sees the recourse to literature as a sign of the cinema's *embourgeoisement*, away from its true popular origins (ignoring the fact that the earliest films borrowed plots from literature). The earliest film theories in the 1920s were concerned with authorship and filmic specificity, seeking to identify the essence of cinema and distance it from the other arts, especially the novel and the theatre (see Abel 1988). In the postwar period, auteurism located authorship solely in the director and elevated *mise-en-scène* as the supreme definition of the cinematic. François Truffaut's famous 1954 article 'A Certain Tendency of the French Cinema' (Truffaut 1954), one of the building blocks of the *politique des auteurs*, was mounted on the back of an excessively caustic attack on the practice of literary adaptation typical of the 'Tradition of Quality', contradicting thereby his mentor Bazin. One legacy of these strategically important polemics was to deny the writer's input into film, as several contributors to this book remark (see especially section 4).

Although auteurism has been challenged, there has been a continued drive, in film studies, to explore the specificity of film art and language. This explains, then, the conspicuous gap that exists between the abundant production of books and articles on film and literature – which derive mostly from a literary perspective and the low profile of the topic in film studies. Though we find an interest in film and literature reflected in journals such as *Literature/Film Quarterly* and in a few manuals, the fact remains that the key contemporary film studies textbooks ignore it: see *The Cinema Book* (Cook and Bernink 1999), *The Oxford Guide to Film Studies* (Hill and Church Gibson 1998), and *Film Art* (Bordwell and Thompson, first published 1979). Connections are made, but only at an abstract level, especially in terms of narrative. The work of literary analysts Roland Barthes and Gérard Genette, and Christian Metz's explorations of film language here have been highly influential (see Barthes 1977, Genette 1966–1972; Metz 1974; also McCabe 1985, Chatman 1978 and 1990). Peter Wollen drew on Russian formalist Vladimir Propp to identify structural equivalences between fairy tales and classical cinema (Wollen 1976; see also Bordwell 1985). One can also point to a few nationally specific studies which examine the connection between film and literature from a film studies perspective, such as Millicent Marcus in *Italian Cinema* (Marcus 1993), Eric Rentschler in *New German Cinema* (Rentschler 1986) and Charles Barr on early Hitchcock (Barr 1999).

What, then, of the astonishing number of books on film and literature (which it is beyond the scope of this introduction to summarise)? Acknowledged pioneers George Bluestone (1957) and Geoffrey Wagner (1975), as well as Michael Klein and Gillian Parker (1981) mapped out the field, producing useful ways of categorising the range of adaptations – 'transpositions', 'commentary', etc. – and their relative merits. As for recent work, at the risk of simplifying I will restrict my remarks to three English-language books which seem to me the most useful. McFarlane (1996) compares the way the different codes of film and literature work, 'conceptually' for literature, 'perceptually' for film (1996, 26–27). On the basis that the two media share the common ground of narrative but differ fundamentally in terms of enunciation, he proposes a distinction between what can be reasonably 'transferred' from book to screen (the narrative), and what needs to be 'adapted' (the *mise-en-scène*) (McFarlane 1996, 195). He then maps out several case studies against this framework, with interesting results. In a wide-ranging study, Tim Corrigan examines literary adaptations within four comple-mentary frameworks: precise historical contextualisation, the questioning of traditional cultural hierarchies, the actual process of adaptation, and interdisciplinarity, and he gathers articles and documents on the topic (Corrigan 1998). James Naremore (2000), in a structure similar to McFarlane's, brings together an excellent selection of articles on the 'theory' of adaptation – the 'field' of film and literature, the issue of fidelity, etc. – followed by case studies. What these books agree on, then, is the necessity for a detailed and historically grounded comparison that is aware of the specificity of each medium. The fact that these recent works emanate from film studies may signal yet new departures in the field from the patterns discussed above.

Most contemporary writers on film and literature, including several contributors to this book, also acknowledge the importance of postmodern theory to the topic. As seminally analysed by Fredric Jameson (1991), postmodernism refers to a nostalgic turn to the past (twinned with a denial of history) and a delight in allusions, self-referentiality and pastiche, aspects clearly relevant to literary adaptations. Postmodern theory certainly discredits the idea of a pure originating text spawning debased copies. Careful historical work and a wider understanding of intertextuality, as opposed to strict influence, also show that there is rarely one source for any given work. Postmodern theory here dovetails with Barthes' influential work on 'the death of the author' (Barthes 1977). As several contributors to this book acknowledge, literary 'sources' themselves are slippery: see Newman and Sinclair on the various antecedents of *Dracula* (pp. 97–104), and Michael Eaton (p. 286), who points out that 'There were pirated versions of *The Pickwick Papers* playing on the London stage while the serial of Dickens' first book was still appearing.'

Beyond the question of sources, the postmodern game of recycling, pastiche and allusions which literary adaptations foster, is highly controversial, and divides writers and critics, including in this book. Some view it pessimistically, as a sign of decadence, a failure of imagination and a loss of affect. Thus, like Sinclair, Richard Dyer finds that Coppola's *Dracula* is evidence of 'postmodern allusionism, a welter of things to make reference to without any of them mattering much' (p. 94). Pessimism becomes a doom-laden sense of 'the end of cinema' for Serge Daney, who qualifies postmodern French cinema as 'vacuous', made of 'ever more rhetorical and consensual simulations', and Jean-Jacques Annaud (who directed the adaptation of Marguerite Duras' novel *L'Amant*) as an ignorant 'post-filmmaker' (p. 24). A more optimistic view is offered by Scorsese, who sees contemporary cinema as inevitably 'Mannerist', and film-makers as 'condemned, like the artists who followed the High Renaissance, to echo and embellish the great unselfconscious works of the past' (p. 66). Others, such as Claire Monk, are more open to embracing the 'post-modern pleasures: of the performative, of self-referentiality and irony' (p. 9) offered by modern literary adaptations (for instance Thompson's tongue-in-cheek attitude to romance in *Sense and Sensibility* – p. 181). And José Arroyo praises Baz Lurhmann's *William Shakespeare's Romeo & Juliet*, which transposes Verona into Mexico and LA gang culture, mixing real and imagined, past and present, for enabling past conventions of story-telling to be made understandable to present-day audiences (pp. 120–25).

For Arroyo, but also for Julianne Pidduck on *Elizabeth* and *Shakespeare in Love* (section 2), modernisation – postmodern or not – is viewed as democratic enabling rather than betrayal or failure of the imagination. Perhaps, as Horne argues in the context of the Henry James films (pp. 85–91), literary adaptations simply conform to the dominant cinematic genres of their times. In the 1990s, one important trend is, as in *William Shakespeare's Romeo & Juliet*, the youth-oriented postmodern updating of classics, which include comic elements (Jonathan Coe notes the 'sitcom elements' in *The Madness of King George* and Pidduck comments on the comedy in *Shakespeare in Love* (pp. 135–8 and 130–35)). Another trend is the adaptation of modernist texts as well as thrillers and dystopian best-sellers into the violent and sexually explicit films in section 3 (*Trainspotting, Crash, American Psycho, Jackie Brown*). Here a particular twentieth-century literary sensitivity, which spans 'high' and 'low' literary forms, dovetails with Hollywood genres – thriller, sci-fi, gore – which increasingly incorporate sub-cultural tastes into the mainstream. Important (and critically recognised) as these film genres are, by far the most prominent type of contemporary literary adaptations falls within heritage cinema, a 'genre' which is subject to the debates about film and literature sketched out so far, but which also raises a different, specific, set of issues to which it is time to turn.

A new genre: the heritage cinema

'Heritage cinema' emerged in the 1980s with the success of European period films such as *Chariots of Fire, Jean de Florette* and *Babette's Feast*, followed by many others, including E. M. Forster adaptations by the Merchant-Ivory-Jhabvala team (usually referred to as 'Merchant-Ivory'), such as *A Room with a View*. A fuller, though by no means exhaustive list would include the British quality television adaptations of the 1980s: *Brideshead Revisited, The Jewel in the Crown* and *Pride and Prejudice*, and continue with films such as *A Passage to India* and *Maurice*. Success continued in the 1990s with *Cyrano de Bergerac, Howards End, La Reine Margot, Sense and Sensibility, Elizabeth, Shakespeare in Love, The House of Mirth, Les Destinées sentimentales*, and others, many of which are discussed in this book.

Heritage cinema thus refers to costume films made in the past twenty years or so, usually based on 'popular classics' (Forster, Austen, Shakespeare, Balzac, Dumas, Hugo, Zola). The large majority are European, though in the 1990s productions evolved towards a greater internationalism, either pan-European, such as *Orlando*, or with large American participation. Emblematic are films such as *1492, Conquest of Paradise*, made by British director Ridley Scott, and a Euro-American cast including Gérard Depardieu and Sigourney Weaver, and *Sense and Sensibility*, which was jointly created by Taiwanese director Ang Lee, British scriptwriter Emma Thompson and a British cast starring Thompson, Hugh Grant and Kate Winslet. Heritage films also draw on a wider popular cultural heritage that includes historical figures and moments, as well as music and painting, which is why articles on *Artemisia* (on painter Artemisia Gentileschi), *1492, Conquest of Paradise* (on Columbus) and *Rob Roy* (on the mythical Scottish character) are included in here even though they are not directly (or not only) based on a book. Heritage films are shot with high budgets and production values by A-list directors and they use stars, polished lighting and camerawork, many changes of decor and extras, well-researched interior designs, and classical or classical-inspired music. Their lavish *mise-en-scène* typically displays the bourgeoisie or aristocracy (*Germinal*, set among northern French miners, is an exception). Richard Dyer defines heritage *mise-en-scène* as using 'conventional filmic narrative style, with the pace and tone of "(European) art cinema" but without its symbolisms and personal directorial voices' (in Vincendeau 1995, 204). In this context, with classical Merchant-Ivory-Jhabvala productions as paradigmatic, the fact that avant-garde film-maker Sally Potter (*Orlando*), feminist auteur Jane Campion (*The Piano*) and Hollywood ex-'movie brat' auteur Martin Scorsese (*The Age of Innocence*) have made heritage films has attracted considerable attention.

Heritage films constitute a 'genre' only in a loose sense. Except for the presence of period costume, they are neither defined by a unified iconography (unlike the thriller and the western), nor a type of narrative (unlike romance and the musical), nor an affect (unlike horror, melodrama and comedy). Films referred to as heritage may in fact include elements of other genres, for instance comic moments, musical interludes, as well as gothic, and/or romance features. Despite this variety, heritage cinema has become a meaningful critical term which has elicited important debates.

Before sketching the main lines of the debate as reflected in this book, a further word of definition is necessary. Costume films have always existed, as have literary adaptations, yet the term 'heritage cinema' only emerged in the past fifteen to twenty years. What is the difference? Clearly there are continuities with earlier costume dramas, in the literary sources and the costumes. But there are two at least equally important differences. Firstly, there is a change of emphasis from narrative to setting. Earlier costume dramas tended to feature romantic, adventurous or melodramatic stories against a period background, without bothering too much with fidelity. Heritage films, by contrast, concentrate on the careful display of historically accurate dress and decor, producing what one might call a 'museum aesthetic'. Secondly, the 1960s modernist New Waves had a radical impact on classic narrative cinema, and hence heritage films. Where costume dramas up to the late 1950s exhibited a certain 'innocent' verisimilitude within the conventions of classical cinema, those of the late 1970s onwards can only be highly aware of retracing earlier grounds (in this sense they are automatically mannerist and postmodern, as discussed above).

As its name indicates, the concern of heritage cinema is to depict the past, but by celebrating rather than investigating it. Herein lies its 'problem'. Arising at the same time as the expansion of museum culture and theme parks in the 1980s, heritage cinema has been linked to retro fashion, interior decoration and tourism, provoking derogatory comments such as the 'Laura Ashley school of filmmaking', 'The

Merchant-Ivory "Furniture Restoration" aesthetic'; '[Merchant Ivory's] stately brand of adaptation', the 'white flannel' school.[5] It has been condemned as conservative aesthetically and ideologically, promoting an idealistic view of the past, and turning its back on contemporary issues (*Rob Roy* as opposed to *Trainspotting*). This argument has especially fuelled the British debates, where the films have been accused of offering a narrowly English, middle-class and imperialistic world view epitomised by the repeated recourse to Edwardian writers such as E. M. Forster (*A Passage to India*, *A Room with a View*, *Maurice*, *Howards End*). *Sight and Sound* played a vital part in these debates, beginning with Cairns Craig's trenchant criticism of Forster adaptations, 'Rooms without a View' (pp. 3–6). For Craig, the 'England these films validate is a theme park of the past' and they function as 'conspicuous consumption'. Outside *Sight and Sound*, Tana Wollen (1991) and Andrew Higson (1993) also saw, like Craig, the nostalgia of heritage films – and television – as guarantee of their conservativeness, their lavish *mise-en-scène* obliterating potentially subversive narratives. Higson thus argues that 'Even those films that develop an ironic narrative of the past end up celebrating and legitimating the spectacle of one class and one cultural tradition and identity at the expense of others through the discourse of authenticity, and the obsession with the visual splendors of period detail.' (Higson 1993, 119; see also Hill 1999) and Geoffrey Macnab's review of *The Remains of the Day*: 'On screen, however, the sheer visual relish with which the place is depicted can't help but undermine the mordant irony in Ruth Prawer Jhabvala's script' (p. 160). This line of thinking is echoed by Jonathan Coe on *The Madness of King George* which 'may have started out, many years ago, as an accurate recreation of an episode in British political history' but 'now reaches the screen as a handsome piece of Heritage Cinema, chock full of English pageantry and stately homes.' (p. 138). I could go on. The conservativeness of the 'genre' is sealed by the fact that Craig, Wollen, Higson and others all see a direct correlation between the rise of heritage cinema in the 1980s and Thatcher's Conservative government.

If Cairns and Higson are aligned with Patrick Wright's critique of the nostalgic turn to the past in his book *On Living in an Old Country* (1985), a defence of heritage as democratic 'history from below' championed by Raphael Samuel in *Theatres of Memory* (1994) can be seen at work in the counter-arguments about heritage cinema. In a letter to *Sight and Sound*, Alison Light criticised what she saw as Craig's 'killjoy dismissal of the viewer as the simple dupe of bourgeois ideology' and argued that we should read 'the return to Edwardian England in the 80s as much as a rejection of Thatcherism and its ethics as a crude reflection of it.'[6] I would add that the Thatcher–heritage correlation is an insular one. French heritage films (see Vincendeau, pp. 27–32 , and Forbes, pp. 104–9) rose to prominence also in the 1980s, during the first phase of Mitterrand's socialist government. Although French writers such as Daney criticised what they saw as 'academicism'[7] and nostalgia, the simultaneous success of the genre in two very different political contexts should at least make us wary of a direct, 'reflectionist' interpretation. French heritage films also tend to display different contents, focusing on historical figures and moments in pre-Revolutionary France – see *Cyrano de Bergerac*, *Tous les matins du monde*, *La Reine Margot*, *Marquise*. They tend not to present a rosy view of the past and thus differ significantly from the turn-of-the-century bourgeois domesticity of the British films, indicating that the debate would benefit from a broadening out to a wider national sample. Unfortunately, apart from some French films, very few non–English-speaking heritage movies have been distributed in the United Kingdom and the United States, a fact inevitably reflected in *Sight and Sound*, and hence in this collection. As a corrective, Dyer's article on 'Nice Young Men Who Sell Antiques' (pp. 43–8) gives a tantalising glimpse of other European titles.

One major line of defence of heritage cinema has focused on the films' ability to challenge mainstream representations of gender and sexuality. For this purpose, writers have drawn on feminist and gay scholarship including work on British costume films (see Harper 1994 and Cook 1996, and their earlier work in Aspinall and Murphy 1983). These positions are represented in this book most explicitly by Monk (pp. 6–11), Dyer (pp. 43–8) and Pidduck (pp. 130–35), although others, too, emphasise the ability of heritage to widen the gender and sexual cinematic horizon. Monk and Dyer note how heritage has been surprisingly (given its apparent conservatism) hospitable to gay writers and gay subjects, while Lizzie Francke and Graham Fuller (pp. 72–6 and 77–81) among others show the part played by women, as professionals and subject matter. Caroline Thompson, adapter of *The Secret Garden*, embodies both aspects, as she talks of her experience as a woman in the industry, and of her interest in gender in the book: 'I think it is a very strong book for women [...] the metaphors are female – the garden is an undeniable womb image' (p. 275). (In her 1994 book *Script Girls*, Lizzie Francke discusses the important, and usually unrecognised, part played by women scriptwriters in Hollywood.) Emma Thompson's adaptation of Jane Austen's *Sense and Sensibility* has emerged in this respect as a key case study. Fuller (pp. 77–81) and Monk (pp. 179–82) both note Thompson's feminist revisionist adaptation which reads Austen's novel as a female empowerment text. Similarly, Robin Swicord's adaptation of Alcott's *Little Women* alludes 'to concerns [about female emancipation] Alcott could not quite spell out' (p. 73). *Orlando, Sense and Sensibility, Little Women* and *The Portrait of a Lady* are all discussed as texts which portray heroines who challenge patriarchal law. But still, controversy is not absent: Andy Medhurst (pp. 11–14) is highly critical of what he sees as the class conservatism of Thompson's version of *Sense and Sensibility*; Philip Horne (pp. 85–91) sees Campion's *The Portrait of a Lady* as a lugubrious portrayal of a masochistic woman, whereas Francke (pp. 81–5) argues that it is about female masochism.

The importance of women to the heritage genre, as practitioners and subject matter, is echoed by its address to an audience which is understood widely as feminine, if not female. Conversely, the 'feminine' identification of the genre is often allied, in reviews, to a derogatory attitude towards it. Against feminist writers who see the genre's feminine address as a strength, critical views can be disparaging: '*The Remains of the Day* is a film anybody will be able to go and see with their mother. Whether or not that is a recommendation is a moot point.' (Macnab, p. 161).

In the 1990s, the debate on heritage cinema has also speculated about whether we have reached a 'post-heritage' phase. For Monk (pp. 6–11), 'post-heritage' dates from *Orlando* (1992) and includes films such as *Century, Tom and Viv, The Piano* and *The Age of Innocence*. These films, she argues, are distinguished by being more international, more self-conscious and apparently more open to 'unconventional' sexualities. But there is room for controversy here, too. She argues that, ironically, films such as *Orlando* and *Carrington* end up less open than the earlier *Maurice* and *A Room with a View*. In this she is echoed by Dyer's view of Coppola's *Dracula* ('heterosexual business as usual') and Pidduck's analysis of the cross-dressing in *Shakespeare in Love*, which she sees as undercut by the central heterosexual romance. Pidduck, however, also puts a different slant on 'post-heritage', showing how films such as *Elizabeth, Shakespeare in Love* and *La Reine Margot*, in their use of sex and violence, and in their self-conscious, mixed casts, bond heritage to a more modern sensitivity. They target a younger audience and embody 'Tony Blair's "Cool Britannia"', mobilising violence to suggest associations with contemporary events such as the Balkans war (as do *Dracula* and *La Reine Margot*). Ironically, while post-heritage films 'sex up' and 'violence up' their sources, film versions of truly violent books have to play these elements down – as Leslie Dick says in her review of *Crash*: 'it is striking to note that some Ballard fans condemn the film for the opposite reasons: not violent enough, not extreme enough, not transgressive enough' (p. 254). Similar arguments have been made about *Trainspotting* and *American Psycho*.

Pro-heritage arguments have also sought to reclaim the films' visual and aural pleasures, their investment in old-fashioned craft. Virtually all articles and reviews in sections 1 and 2 note the visual and aural sensuality of heritage films, the glorious settings, the rich colours and textures, the painterly qualities of images, the brilliance of the dialogue, the sophistication of the music. This aspect is not without controversy, since the sumptuous *mise-en-scène* is for many evidence of conservatism. Others on the contrary see it as articulating at the level of the film text the new agendas about gender and sexuality which have been noted at plot and theme level: see Fuller on *Sense and Sensibility*, Dyer on *Wilde, Ernesto* and *Maurice* (section 1). (For a radically different view of *Wilde* from that of Dyer's article, see Tony Rayns' review in section 2).

Perhaps unsurprisingly, the most spirited defence of heritage *mise-en-scène* per se, as opposed to how it furthers or hinders particular narrative concerns, comes from film-makers such as Gillian Armstrong and Martin Scorsese (pp. 72–6 and 66–72). Against the critical argument that heritage films celebrate consumption and fetishistic detail, Scorsese expresses his admiration for the craft involved and points to the objects' narrative importance. In his own film *The Age of Innocence*, he says, the smallest detail also had a point: 'we have eight meals, and [types of china] are all different, in order to make different dramatic points', adding, 'the decor had to become a character'. While not all heritage films imbue their decor with as much significance, the notion that 'the decor is a character' is a perceptive definition of heritage cinema. For while decor may reflect and construct narrative concerns, the reverse is also true: the stories and themes of heritage cinema are often about craft, about lovingly hand-made objects – alluding both to a past era (the referent of the films) and to a past, 'classical', era of film-making. This is no doubt one of the reasons why the genre is such a popular one.

A new type of popular cinema

Throughout the 1980s and especially the 1990s, Hollywood movies have undoubtedly achieved world domination, with action/spectacle as the key genre (see Arroyo 2000).

Yet heritage films have also made a significant impact at the international box-office, their exportability crucial to non–English speaking-cinemas: especially French (*Cyrano de Bergerac, La Reine Margot, Le Bossu, Le Temps retrouvé*), but also Mexican (*Like Water for Chocolate*), Argentinian (*Camilla, Miss Mary*) and Chinese cinemas (*Raise the Red Lantern, Shanghai Triad*). As Jill Forbes points out (pp. 104–5), *Germinal* came out at the same time as *Jurassic Park* and was a key pawn in the recurrent French debates about American cultural 'imperialism'. British films or international co-productions with British subject matters such as *Rob Roy* and *The Madness of King George* (as argued here by, respectively, Lochhead and Coe), also clearly aim at an American/international audience.

Calling literary/heritage films 'popular cinema' is by no means uncontroversial, since they are often regarded as archetypal arthouse fare; see for instance Griselda Pollock on *Artemisia* (pp. 32–7). Indeed, for both Monk and Lochhead (pp. 6–11 and 14–17) many heritage films define themselves against the Hollywood mainstream. Lochhead makes a distinction between *The Madness of King George* as 'a British film' and thus 'art', and *Rob Roy* as 'a Hollywood movie' and thus 'popular'. Similarly, Medhurst compares *Sense and Sensibility* unfavourably to *Restoration*, which, in its irreverent use of costume, reaches back to earlier and more truly 'popular' costume films such as *Carry on Henry* (p. 11). I would offer two comments here. First of all, the fact that heritage films are perceived as 'art' is linked to an Anglo-American critical reluctance to conceive of a popular European cinema (see Dyer and Vincendeau 1992). Films such as *Germinal, Cyrano de Bergerac* and *Le Bossu* are popular French movies, not 'art films' or rather, in the French context, not 'auteur films'. As Romney points out, the Proust adaptation *Le Temps retrouvé* signals Ruiz's move into the French mainstream (the same is true of *Artemisia* for Agnès Merlet). Secondly, Lochhead's and Medhurst's views are not always borne out by statistics. *Sense and Sensibility* was far more successful commercially than *Restoration*, and *The Madness of King George* did excellent box-office. The 'family' and 'working-class' popular film-going audiences have all but gone, and the 'middle-class' audience which appreciates, say, *Sense and Sensibility*, has moved centre stage. What is at issue here is nothing less than a changing notion of 'popular cinema'.

Film adaptations of thrillers and dystopian novels also raise the issue of the popular in terms of clashing canonical values. For instance, the thriller has a much higher status in film than it does in literature. In film history, horror, sci-fi, the thriller, film noir are canonical genres, whereas in literary history they belong (with a few exceptions) to areas defined by terms such as pulp, cult and trash. In this respect, film adaptations may drive the source book 'up' in terms of status, notoriety and audience (think for instance of Hitchcock and Highsmith, Tarantino and Leonard), rather than 'down', as tends to be the case – from many critics' points of view – in the case of classics or modernist texts (see Sinclair's comment on the adaptation of Burroughs above). The notion of 'cult' thus can fundamentally negotiate different cultural hierarchies.

Notwithstanding the importance of thriller and dystopian novel adaptations, and despite the shift towards more sex and violence in 'post-heritage', literary adaptations generally, in their emphasis on art, quality and decorum, on women and on gay and lesbian characters, provide alternatives to the violence, speed and machismo of

Hollywood action/spectacle films. They also contrast with the pervasive bleakness – and often graphic sex – of European auteur cinema. But it is, importantly, an alternative which remains mainstream in terms of *mise-en-scène*. The popularity of heritage films thus rests on their ability to straddle art/auteur and mass cinema. The film industry accordingly treats them as valuable properties, allocating them high budgets because their generic features offer guarantees of returns: high quality craft, publicity, marketing tie-ins, stars.

Exploiting the cultural capital of a famous book's author and/or title creates a 'high concept' for the films, crucial for international trade. Though this may be viewed negatively by critics, it is an undeniable factor in attracting audiences: Daney condemned Annaud for 'Cloth[ing] himself in the cheap literary finery of a story signed "Marguerite Duras"'(p. 25), but *L'Amant* was the biggest French box-office success of 1992. Tie-ins include post-film publications, to which many contributors to this book refer. Despite the fact that he had called his film *Prospero's Books* rather than *The Tempest*, to indicate to the audience that 'it is not a straight attempt to reproduce a familiar text' (p. 110), Greenaway produced no fewer than three publications to accompany *Prospero's Books*: a companion novel (*Prospero's Creatures*), the film script and extracts from the apocryphal books featured in the film. Scorsese published a book to accompany the release of *The Age of Innocence*, and Emma Thompson published her adaptation of *Sense and Sensibility*. True to what Thorp and Bazin noted, subsequent sales of books on which films are based always increase, thus perpetuating the name of the film further. The phenomenon is not confined to classics. Recent novels, such as *High Fidelity* and *American Psycho*, also enjoyed reprints following the film's release. In France, the scandal of Virginie Despentes' *Baise-moi* ('Fuck me'), the film she made (with Coralie Trinh Thi) from her own 1994 violent pornographic novel, led to a mass paperback reprint and a much-visited website. Although the film's X rating made it virtually impossible to see, the increased notoriety of the book prepares the ground for the film's forthcoming video release. Beyond book sales, tie-ins reach into areas such as tourism. In the United Kingdom, National Trust stately homes which have been used as settings for adaptations see a significant rise in numbers of visits following screenings of films or television shot on their premises.

But one of the crucial ways literary adaptations have earned a place as 'popular' in the international market is in their use of major stars. Just as Arnold Schwarzenegger epitomises the action spectacular genre, certain stars (mainly European) have come to represent heritage. Think of Emma Thompson, Hugh Grant and Helena Bonham Carter in the United Kingdom, Gérard Depardieu, Juliette Binoche and Emmanuelle Béart in France. True, on the international scene these stars carry connotations of 'quality' and European-ness. However, heritage parts command awards – among others, Depardieu's César and Cannes award for *Cyrano de Bergerac*, Thompson's acting Oscar for *Howards End*, and thus global recognition. For non–English-speaking stars, heritage is therefore key to exportability. But here, too, there is a debate whether the recurrence of heritage stars is evidence of a strong generic feature or of lack of imagination. Helena Bonham Carter is a good example of such debates. While *Variety* points out approvingly in its review of *Howards End* that 'Bonham Carter, currently starring to strong effect in the other Forster release *Where Angels Fear to Tread*, proves again that she's the best actress today at embodying the look and spirit of period roles',[8] Craig argues that 'There is a certain incestuousness in these films. In *Where Angels Fear to Tread*, Helena Bonham Carter again plays the repressed young English woman', such repetition 'giv[ing] the feel almost of a repertory production' (p. 3). Similarly, Sinclair finds that in Cronenberg's *Naked Lunch*, 'Even the cast has been hired like props, because they have a proven heritage pedigree. Julian Sands steps seamlessly out from his *A Room with a View*' (p. 207).

The importance of stardom for heritage, but equally of heritage for contemporary stardom, cannot be overstated. The films showcase acting skills, with theatrical settings, scintillating dialogue and flattering costume. Reviewers frequently note performance as a special, pleasurable feature of the films, such as Lizzie Francke on *Howards End*: 'The trademark period accessories and engaging acting ensemble are once again in evidence.' (p. 148). Literary adaptations and biopics also further stardom because they emphasise strong, heroic, characters who are already in the public domain, giving ideal opportunities for star turns: Depardieu as Columbus and Cyrano, John Malkovich as Valmont, Nigel Hawthorne as George III, Isabelle Adjani as Camille Claudel and Margot, Emma Thompson as Carrington, Judi Dench as Queen Victoria, etc. Furthermore, as Jonathan Romney argues about *Le Temps retrouvé*, in such highly self-conscious productions, the stars themselves are part of the 'heritage' the films are about: '[Ruiz] casts stars in order to highlight the film's self-reflexivity, to make it clear that this isn't simply an adaptation, but a dialogue with the novel' (p. 42). He points to the significance of casting Catherine Deneuve and Marie-France Pisier and, among others to that of director and novelist Alain Robbe-Grillet, 'whose name now belongs to a bygone literary era almost as much as that of the diarist Goncourt whom he plays in flashback'. Romney's argument can legitimately be extended to a wider sample of heritage films which use both the star system and the confrontation of specific acting traditions. As Pidduck argues, about the mix of British stage actors and Hollywood stars in *Shakespeare in Love*, this casting practice 'suggests the pleasures of make-believe so central to costume drama and historical fiction' (p. 133).

Literary adaptations and especially heritage films, then, emerge as a pervasive and popular mode of film-making, in tune with both a *fin-de-siècle* passion for 'museum culture' and a postmodern recycling of an increasingly mixed literary repertoire. For this reason they have been widely viewed as conservative, explaining why 'heritage' has become in many instances a term of critical disparagement. Yet paradoxically, under their overt nostalgia, the films respond to changes in social and cultural mores, re-interpreting texts in ways which echo new agendas, be they of politics, gender or ethnicity. In this respect, they have also attracted significant positive critical attention. The many nuances of these opposed critical positions are reflected in this book.

Despite the high profile of individual titles – *The Age of Innocence, Cyrano de Bergerac, The Portrait of a Lady, Howards End, The Piano, La Reine Margot, Elizabeth* – and despite being an economically very significant 'genre' of film-making, literary/heritage films have been somewhat marginalised critically. This is partly, of course, because they are judged on the disputable yardstick of fidelity – as a poor copy of a literary original, rather than something that requires to be evaluated on its own merits. But it is also no doubt because many of the films are European (and 'popular' European at that), and because their cultural image is predominantly 'feminine'. It is hoped that this collection will help to redress the balance by surveying a decade of this increasingly important and enjoyable filmic production and by engaging with the key issues that it raises: the nature and modalities of literary adaptation, the representation of culture, memory, history and national identity, and the specificities, as well as the pleasures, of heritage cinema *mise-en-scène*. The book will also enable the reader to enjoy a decade of diverse, opinionated but always illuminating and stimulating critical writing on cinema.

Notes

1. Steven Poole, 'The Nabokov gambit', *The Guardian*, 25 August, 2000 (G2, Screen supplement, p. 6).
2. Although this book is restricted to film adaptations, as opposed to television, Mick Eaton's short piece has been included here as it makes points that are valid for both film and television.
3. Film Education packs are published by Film Education, Alhambra House, 27–31 Charing Cross Road, London WC2H 0AU.
4. John Mullan, 'Have you read any good films lately?', *The Guardian*, 28 March (G2, p. 7).
5. First quote: in Graham Fuller, 'Shots in the dark', *Interview*, vol. 22, no. 3, March 1992, p. 40; second quote: Chris Darke's review of *Surviving Picasso*, *Sight and Sound*, January 1997; third quote: Geoffrey Macnab's review of *The Remains of the Day*, *Sight and Sound*, December 1993; fourth quote: Jonathan Romney's review of *Where Angels Fear to Tread*, *Sight and Sound*, July 1991.
6. Alison Light, 'Englishness', *Sight and Sound*, July 1991, vol. 1/issue 3 (NS), p. 63.
7. The charge of 'academicism' is the standard position among auteurist criticism to be found in France, in *Cahiers du cinéma*, but also *Positif* among others. Interestingly, *Cahiers du cinéma* recanted recently in its defence of Olivier Assayas' heritage film *Les Destinées sentimentales*. See *Cahiers du cinéma*, July/August 2000.
8. Lawrence Cohn, review of *Howards End*, *Variety*, 24 February 1992, p. 247.

Note to the Reader

The largest part of this book focuses on literary adaptations that fall within 'heritage cinema'. Section 1 sets the terms of the debates, with articles that are sometimes openly polemical. The debates then reverberate throughout the case studies and the reviews in section 2, designed to show both patterns (for instance, the 1990s craze for Shakespeare, Jane Austen and Henry James) and diversity among the films. Section 3 covers literary adaptations which are the antithesis of heritage, namely thrillers and stories of dystopian societies such as *Crash* and *Trainspotting*. Section 4 gathers interviews with screenwriters in order to give a voice to this essential, yet often ignored profession, famously dismissed by 1930s studio boss Jack Warner as 'Schmucks with Underwoods'. Today Apple Macs replace the Underwoods, but, as

James V. Hart, screenwriter of Coppola's *Dracula*, remarks, the film industry still 'doesn't look on the writer as even a third-class citizen', feelings that are echoed by several writers and film-makers in the book. While interviews with screenwriters are grouped under section 4, interviews with directors (such as Sally Potter, Martin Scorsese, Gillian Armstrong and Quentin Tarantino) on the other hand are to be found under case studies in sections 2 and 3 because they made more sense in relation to individual films.

The articles in this book were all published in *Sight and Sound* in the 1990s, with the exception of Richard Dyer's 'Nice Young Men Who Sell Antiques', and Julianne Pidduck's 'Screening the Elizabethans', which were specially commissioned,* and of Adrian Wootton's article on Jim Thompson adaptations and Philip Strick's review of *Cyrano de Bergerac*, which were published in the *Monthly Film Bulletin*, before the *Sight and Sound* new formula started in May 1991, whereby the *MFB* was amalgamated into *Sight and Sound*.

The authors gathered in this book are film critics, journalists and academics, as well as film-makers and writers. The selection of articles and reviews was hard to make, given both the extremely high level of critical writing to be found in *Sight and Sound* and the vast number of films that fall within the 'genres' of literary adaptations and heritage cinema. My final choice, within the basic remit of film, literature and heritage, was motivated by the import and resonance of both the film(s) discussed and the arguments offered about them, and by the quality of the writing. My choice of reviews was limited by the films distributed in the United Kingdom and therefore reviewed in *Sight and Sound*. Thus my desire to extend the field to national cinemas other than British, American and French was somewhat frustrated (the few Spanish films reviewed act as a token, rather than a representative sample and other national cinemas are sadly unacknowledged).

The bibliography offers a wide selection of works on film and literature, and on heritage cinema. Also listed are references to texts quoted in the introduction (where name of author and date of publication are given in brackets). I have included few books on adaptations of specific writers (except for some on Shakespeare), as this would have made the list truly unwieldy. Throughout the introduction, where reference is made to authors from this volume, the page numbers are indicated.

* A longer version of Richard Dyer's article will be published in Richard Dyer, *The Culture of Queers* (London: Routledge, 2001).

References

Abel, Richard (ed.), *French Film Theory and Criticism, A History/Anthology*, Vol I 1907-1929, Vol II 1929-1939 (Princeton New Jersey: Princeton University Press, 1988).

Andrew, Dudley, 'The Well-Worn Muse: Adaptation in Film History and Theory', in S.M. Conger and J.R. Welsch (eds), *Narrative Strategies* (Macomb, Illinois: West Illinois University Press, 1980).

Arroyo, José (ed.), *Action/Spectacle: A Sight and Sound Reader* (London: BFI, 2000).

Aspinall, Sue and Robert Murphy (eds), BFI Dossier No 18: *Gainsborough Melodrama* (London: BFI, 1983).

Aycock, Wendell & Michael Schoenecke (eds), *Film and Literature: a Comparative Approach to Adaptation* (Texas: Texas Tech University Press, 1988).

Barr, Charles, *English Hitchcock* (Moffat: Cameron & Hollis, 1999).

Barthes, Roland, *Image-Music-Text: Essays Selected and Translated by Stephen Heath* (Glasgow: Fontana/Collins, 1977).

Baskin, Ellen and Mandy Hicken (compiled by), *Enser's Filmed Books and Plays* (Aldershot: Ashgate, 1993).

Bazin, André, *What Is Cinema?* (Berkeley: University of California Press, 1967) (translated by Hugh Gray; originally published in *Qu'est-ce que le cinéma?*, vol 2, (Paris: Editions du Cerf, 1959).

Beja, Morris, *Film and Literature: an Introduction* (New York: Longman, 1979).

Bignell, Jonathan, *Writing and Cinema* (London: Pearson Education/Longman, 1999).

Bluestone, George, *Novels into Film* (Baltimore: John Hopkins University, 1957).

Blum, Rich, *Television and Screen Writing: From Concept to Contract* (New York: Focal Press, 1995).

Boose, Lynda E. and Richard Burt (eds), *Shakespeare, The Movie: Popularizing the Plays on Film, TV, and Video* (London: Routledge, 1997).

Bordwell, David, *Narration in the Fiction Film* (London: Methuen, 1985).

Bordwell, David and Kristin Thompson, *Film Art: An Introduction, Reading* (Mass.: Addison-Wesley, 1979).

Boyum, Joy Gould, *Double Exposure: Fiction into Film* (New York: New American Library, 1985).

Brady, John, *The Craft of the Screenwriter* (New York: Touchtone, 1982).

Cartmell, Deborah, I.Q. Hunter and Heidi Kaye (eds), *Pulping Fictions: Consuming Culture Across the Literature/Media Divide* (London and Chicago: Pluto Press, 1996).

Cartmell, Deborah, I.Q Hunter, Heidi Kaye and Imelda Whelehan (eds), *Alien Identities: Exploring Differences in Film and Fiction* (London and Chicago: Pluto Press, 1999).

Cartmell, Deborah and Imelda Whelehan (eds), *Adaptations: From Text to Screen, Screen to Text* (London and New York: Routledge, 1999).

Chatman, Seymour, *Story and Discourse: Narrative Structure in Fiction and Film* (Ithaca, NY: Cornell University Press, 1978).

Chatman, Seymour, 'What Novels Can Do That Film Can't (and vice versa)' in W.T.J. Mitchell (ed.), *On Narrative* (Chicago: Chicago University Press, 1980).

Chatman, Seymour, *Coming to Terms: The Rhetoric of Narrative in Fiction and Film* (Ithaca, NY: Cornell University Press, 1990).

Clerc, Jeanne-Marie, *Ecrivains et cinéma* (Paris: Klincksieck, 1985).

Clerc, Jeanne-Marie, *Littérature et cinéma* (Paris: Nathan Université, 1993).

Cohen, Keith, *Film and Fiction: the Dynamics of Exchange* (New Haven: Yale University, 1979).

Cook, Pam, *Fashioning the Nation, Costume and identity in British Cinema* (London: BFI, 1996).

Cook, Pam and Mieke Bernink (eds), *The Cinema Book* (London: BFI, 1999) (2nd edition; first published 1985, edited by Pam Cook).

Corliss, Richard, *The Hollywood Screenwriters* (New York: Avon Books, 1972).

Corrigan, Timothy, *Film and Literature: an Introduction and Reader* (New Jersey: Prentice Hall, 1998).

Costello, Tom (ed.), *The International Guide to Literature on Film* (London: Bowker-Saur, 1994).

Durgnat, Raymond, 'The Mongrel Muse' in *Films and Feelings*, (London: Faber and Faber, 1967).

Dyer, Richard and Ginette Vincendeau (eds), *Popular European Cinema* (London: Routledge, 1992).

Edgerton, Gary R., *Film and the Arts in Symbiosis: a Resource Guide* (New York: Greenwood Press, 1988).

Eidsvick, Charles, *Cineliteracy: Film among the Arts* (New York: Random House, 1978).

Eisenstein, Sergei, 'Dickens, Griffith, and the Film Today', in Jan Leyda (ed. and trans.) *Film Form* (New York: Harcourt, 1949).

Ellis, John, 'The Literary Adaptation: An Introduction', *Screen* vol. 23, no.1, May-June 1982.

Fell, John, *Film and the Narrative Tradition* (Norman: University of Oklahoma Press, 1974).

Francke, Lizzie, *Script Girls: Women Screenwriters in Hollywood* (London: BFI, 1994).

Garcia, Alain, *L'Adaptation du roman au film* (Paris: Editions diffusion, 1990).

Gaudreault, André, *Du littéraire au filmique* (Paris: Méridiens, Klincksieck, 1988).

Geduld, Harry M. (ed.), *Authors on Film* (Bloomington: Indiana University Press, 1972).

Genette, Gérard (1966-1972) Figures I, Paris, Le Seuil [1966]; Figures II, Paris, Le Seuil [1969]; Figures III, Paris, Le Seuil [1972].

Giddins, Robert, Keith Selby and Chris Wensley (eds), *Screening the Novel: the Theory and Practice of Literary Dramatization* (New York: St Martin's Press, 1990).

Giddins, Robert and Erica Sheen (eds), *The Classic Novel From Page to Screen* (Manchester and New York: Manchester University Press, 2000).

Goldman, William, *Adventures in the Screen Trade* (New York: Warren Books, 1983).

Goodwin, James, 'Literature and Film: A Review of Criticism, *Quaterly Review of Film Studies*, vol. 6, no. 2, Spring 1979.

Griffith, James, *Adaptations as Imitations: Films From Novels* (Newark: University of Delaware Press, 1997).

Harper, Sue, *Picturing the Past, The Rise and Fall of the British Costume Film* (London: BFI, 1994).

Harrington, John, *Film and/as Literature* (New Jersey: Prentice Hall, 1977).

Hawkins, Harriet, *Classics and Trash: Traditions and Taboos in High Literature and Popular Modern Genres* (New York: Harvester Wheatsheaf, 1990).

Higgins, Lynn A., *New Novel, New Wave, New Politics: Fiction and the Representation of History in Post-war France* (Nebraska: University of Nebraska Press, 1996).

Higson, Andrew (1993) 'Re-presenting the National Past: Nostalgia and Pastiche in the Heritage Film', in Lester Friedman (ed.), *Fires Were Started, British Cinema and Thatcherism* (Minneapolis: University of Minnesota Press; London: UCL Press, 1993).

Hill, John and Pamela Church Gibson (eds), *The Oxford Guide to Film Studies* (Oxford: Oxford University Press, 1998).

Hill, John, *British Cinema in the 1980s* (Oxford: Clarendon Press, 1999).

Holderness, Graham, *Shakespeare Recycled: The Making of Historical Drama* (Brighton: Harvester, 1992).

Horton, Andrew and John Magretta (eds), *Modern European Filmmakers and the Art of Adaptation* (New York: Frederick Ungar, 1981).

Horton, Andrew, *Writing the Character-Centered Screenplay* (Berkeley: University of California Press, 1994).

Jameson, Fredric, *Postmodernism or The Logic of Late Capitalism* (London: Verso, 1991).

Jorgens, Jack J., *Shakespeare on Film* (London: Indiana University Press, 1977).

Jost, François, *L'oeil-camra: entre film et roman* (Lyon: Presses Universitaires de Lyon, 1987).

Kamps, Ivo (ed.) *Shakespeare Left and Right* (New York: Routledge, 1991).

Kittredge, William and Steven M. Krauzer (eds), *Stories into Films* (New York: Harper & Row, 1979).

Klein, Michael and Gillian Parker (eds), *The English Novel and the Movies* (New York: Frederick Ungar, 1981).

Larson, Randall D., *Films Into Book: an Analytical Bibliography of Film Novelisations, Movie and TV Tie-Ins* (London: The Scarecrow Press, Inc, 1995).

MacCabe, Colin, *Theoretical Essays: Film, Linguistics, Literature* (Manchester: Manchester University Press, 1985).

Magill, Frank N. (ed.), *Cinema: The Novel into Film* (Pasadena: Salem Press, 1980).

Manvell, Roger (1971) *Shakespeare and the Film* (New York: Praeger, 1971).

Marcus, Fred H., *Film and Literature: Contrasts in Media* (Scranton: Chandler, 1971).

Marcus, Millicent, *Filmmaking by the Book: Italian Cinema and Literary Adaptation* (Baltimore: John Hopkins University, 1993).

Mast, Gerald, Marshall Cohen and Leo Braudy (eds), *Film Theory and Criticism: Introductory Readings* (New York: Oxford University Press, 1992).

Mayne, Judith, *Private Novels, Public Films* (London: University of Georgia Press, 1988).

McDougal, Stanley Y., *Made into Movies: From Literature to Film* (New York: Holt, Rhinehart and Winston, 1985).

McFarlane, Brian, *Words and Images: Australian Novels into Film* (Melbourne: Heinemann Publishers Australia, 1983).

McFarlane, Brian, *Novel to Film: an introduction to the theory of adaptation* (Oxford: Clarendon Press, 1996).

McKernan, Luke and Olwen Terris, *Walking Shadows: Shakespeare in the National Film and Television Archive* (London: BFI, 1994).

Metz, Christian, *Film Language: A Semiotics of the Cinema* (trans. Michael Taylor), (New York: Oxford University Press, 1974).

Michalczyk, John J., *The French Literary Filmmakers* (Philadelphia: Associated University Presses, 1980).

Miller, Gabriel, *Screening the Novel: Rediscovered American Fiction in Films* (New York: Frederick Ungar, 1980).

Morrissette, Bruce, *Novel and Film: Essays in Two Genres* (Chicago: University of Chicago Press, 1985).

Naremore, James (ed.), *Film Adaptation* (New Brunswick: Rutgers University Press, 2000).

Nichols, Bill (ed.), *Movies and Methods: an Anthology* (Berkeley: University of California Press, 1976).

Nichols, Bill (ed.), *Movies and Methods, vol. II: an Anthology* (Berkeley: University of California Press, 1985).

Orr, Christopher, 'The Discourse on Adaptation', *Wide Angle*, vol. 6, no. 2, 1984.

Orr, John and Colin Nicholson, *Cinema and Fiction: New Modes of Adapting, 1950-1990*, (Edinburgh: Edinburgh University Press, 1992).

Peary, Gerald and Roger Shatzkin (eds), *The Classic American Novel and the Movies* (New York: Frederick Ungar, 1977).

Peary, Gerald and Roger Shatzkin (eds), *The Modern American Novel and the Movies* (New York: Frederick Ungar, 1978).

Phillips, Gene D., *Fiction, Film and Faulkner: the Art of Adaptation* (Tennesse: University of Tennessee Press, 1988).

Pirie, David, 'The Novel and the Cinema', in Martin Seymour-Smith (ed.), *Novels and Novelists* (New York: St Martin's Press, 1980).

Rentschler, Eric (ed.), *German Film and Literature: Adaptations and Transformations* (London: Methuen, 1986).

Reynolds, Peter (ed.), *Novel Images: Literature in Performance* (London: Routledge, 1993).

Richardson, Robert E., *Literature and Film* (Bloomington: Indiana University Press, 1969).

Ropars-Wuilleumier, Marie-Claire, *De la littérature au cinéma: génèse d'une écriture* (Paris: Editions Klinksleck, 1978).

Ropars-Wuilleumier, Marie-Claire, *Ecraniques: le film du texte* (Lille: Presses Universitaires de Lille, 1990).

Ross, Harris, *Film as Literature, Literature as Film: an Introduction to and Bibliography of Film's Relationship to Literature* (London: Greenwood, 1987).

Rothwell, Kenneth S. and Annabelle Henkin Melzer, *Shakespeare on Screen: An International Filmography and Videography* (New York and London: Neal-Schuman Publishers, 1990).

Ruppert, Peter (ed.), *Ideas of Order in Literature and Film* (Florida: University Presses of Florida, 1980).

Samuel, Raphael, *Theatres of Memory - vol 1: Past and Present in Contemporary Culture* (London: Verso, 1994).

Seger, Linda, *The Art of Adaptation, Turning Fact and Fiction into Film* (New York: Henry Holt, 1992).

Selby, Keith, Robert Giddings and Chris Wensley, *Screening the Novel: the Theory and Practice of Literary Dramatization* (New York: St. Martin's Press, 1990).

Shaughnessy, Robert, *Shakespeare on Film* (London: Macmillan, 1998).

Sinyard, Neil (1986) *Filming Literature: the Art of Screen Adaptation* (New York: St Martins Press, 1986).

Simons, John D. (ed.), *Literature and Film in the Historical Dimension: Selected Papers from the 15th annual Florida State University Conference on Literature and Film* (Florida: University Press of Florida,1994).

Spiegel, Alan, *Fiction and the Camera Eye: Visual Consciousness in Film and the Modern Novel* (Charlottesville: University Press of Virginia, 1976).

Stam, Robert, *Reflexivity in Film and Literature From Don Quixote to Jean-Luc Godard* (Michigan: UMI Research Press, 1985).

Stoltzfus, Ben, *Alain Robbe-Grillet and the New French Novel* (Carbondale: Southern Illinois University Press, 1964).

Thorp, Margaret Farrand, *America at the Movies* (London: Faber and Faber, 1946).

Tibbets, John C. and James L. Welsh, *The Encyclopedia of Novels into Films* (New York: Facts On File, Inc, 1998).

Toles, George E., *Film/Literature* (Winnipeg: University of Manitoba Press, 1983).

Truffaut, François (1954) 'A Certain tendency of the French Cinema' in Bill Nichols (ed.), *Movies and Methods: an Anthology* (Berkeley: University of California Press, 1976).

Turner, Graeme, *National Fictions: literature, film and the construction of Australian narrative* (Sydney: Allen and Unwin, 1986).

Vanoye, Francis, *Récit écrit, récit filmique* (Paris: Editions Cedic, 1979).

Vincendeau, Ginette (ed.), *The Encyclopedia of European Cinema* (London: BFI/Cassell, 1995).

Virmaux, Alain et Odette, *Le ciné-roman: un genre nouveau* (Paris: Edilig, 1983).

Vray, Jean-Bernard (ed.), *Littérature et cinéma: Écrire L'Image* (Saint-Etienne: Publications de L'Université de Saint-Etienne, 1999).

Ward, John, *Literary Criticism and Cinema Criticism* (London: BFI Education, 1969).

Wagner, Geoffrey, *The Novel and the Cinema* (New Jersey: Farleigh Dickinson University Press, 1975).

Welch, Jeffrey Egan, *Literature and Film: an Annotated Bibliography, 1909-1977* (New York: Garland, 1977).

Welch, Jeffrey Egan, *Literature and Film: an Annotated Bibliography, 1978-1988* (New York: Garland, 1993).

Winkler, Martin M., *Classics and Cinema* (New Jersey: Associated University Presses, 1991).

Winston, Douglas Garrett, *The Screenplay as Literature* (Rutherford: Fairleigh Dickinson University Press, 1973).

Wollen, Peter, (1976) 'North by North-West: A Morphological Analysis', Film Form, I, reprinted in Peter Wollen, *Readings and Writings: Semiotic Counter-Strategies* (London: Verso, 1982).

Wollen, Tana, 'Nostalgic Screen Fictions', in Corner, John, and Sylvia Harvey (eds.), *Enterprise and Heritage: Crosscurrents of National Culture* (London: Routledge, 1991).

Wood, Robin, *Personal Views: Explorations in Film* (London: Gordon Fraser, 1976).

Wood, Robin, *The Wings of the Dove* (London: BFI, 1999).

Wright, Patrick, *On Living in an Old Country: The National Past in Contemporary Britain* (London: Verso, 1985).

Zants, Emily, *Chaos Theory, Complexity, Cinema and the Evolution of the French Novel* (Lewiston/Queenston/Lampetr: The Edwin Mellen Press, 1996).

A Room with a View (James Ivory, 1985)

Section I:
A 'New Genre' –
The Heritage Cinema

The British Heritage Cinema Debate

ROOMS WITHOUT A VIEW

Cairns Craig

Imagine a film rich with scenes shot in Cambridge colleges and lush English countryside, set to an accompaniment of horse-drawn carriages with the occasional punctuation of bursts of steam at railway stations. This far from imaginary work is part of a cinematic genre which has had a remarkable prominence in the 1980s: a genre which focuses on the English middle and upper classes at home and abroad before they were drowned by the flood of the World War I and the end of the Empire. Its source is often literary – and most often E. M. Forster.

And two new examples are currently under way: Charles Sturridge's adaptation of Forster's *Where Angels Fear to Tread* had its world premiere as a Royal Charity Performance attended by the Princess of Wales at the end of May; *Howards End* is in production with Merchant-Ivory.

Indeed Merchant-Ivory – who also made the film adaptations of Forster's *A Room with a View* (1985) and *Maurice* (1987) – might claim to have originated the genre, though Sturridge and Derek Granger could equally assert that they established the territory back in 1981 with their television production of Evelyn Waugh's *Brideshead Revisited*. There is a certain incestuousness in these films. In *Where Angels Fear to Tread*, Helena Bonham Carter again plays the repressed young English woman struggling with her desire to escape conformity that she played in *A Room with a View*. Rupert Graves, who plays the cowardly brother, was in *A Room with a View*, *Maurice* and Sturridge's adaptation of Waugh's *A Handful of Dust* (1987). The same cast in the same period costumes gives the feel almost of a repertory production, with actors who know well each others' strengths and limitations, and directors who know perhaps too well their audience's expectations.

But the writer toiling away at the script for the next adaptation should take heed – this genre is in danger of turning into a parody of itself. And perhaps the backers, too, should take note. It may be that the genre was viable only in the decade we have just left.

The dominance and success of this particular brand of film-making in the past ten years is symptomatic of the crisis of identity through which England passed during the Thatcher years. It is film as conspicuous consumption, the country houses, the panelled interiors, the clothes which have provided a good business for New York fashion houses selling English country style to rich Americans. Then there are all those shots of crystal decanters (Lucy Honeychurch carries two as she breaks off her engagement), of glasses glinting on silver salvers.

We are indulged with a perfection of style designed to deny everything beyond the self-contained world the characters inhabit. The Italian lover in spotless white in *Where Angels Fear to Tread*, for instance, would fit perfectly into the Cambridge world of *Maurice*; the unity of style denies the difference of culture. We feast vicariously on a luxuriant world in which whatever the turmoil of the characters' inner lives, the issue of affording a room is never in question, only the quality of its view.

The films also reflect the conflict of a nation committed to an international market place that diminishes the significance of Englishness and at the same time seeking to compensate by asserting 'traditional' English values, whether Victorian or provincial. If for an international audience the England these films validate and advertise is a theme park of the past, then for an English audience they gratify the need to find points of certainty within English culture.

Forster and Waugh have proved popular because the world in which their works are set – the world just before film became the dominant modern medium, just before the modernist experiment in literature – is the last great age of the English *haute bourgeoisie*. Here the death of inheritance that the plotlines assert (the death of the son in *A Handful of Dust*, the destruction of Brideshead, the death of Gino's baby in *Where Angels Fear to Tread*, the disappearance of the wife in *Heat and Dust*) is counteracted by the seeming permanence of the architecture, landscape and possessions that fill the screen. And it is this secure world of an earlier Englishness – the antithesis of the fissiparous relativism of the present – that the films re-create, rather than what the novels acknowledge: that England must change, or has already changed beyond recognition.

Forster knew only too well that the life he described depended on £800 a year and that beyond it was an abyss which he did not understand and therefore could not write about. His narrator is always given an ironic awareness of the extent to which the spiritual concerns of the characters are dependent upon their financial security, but that sense is entirely elided in the films. In the film *Maurice*, there are visual allusions to it (the porter scrubbing the stairs, for instance), but they do not disrupt the dominant iconography of the young men framed by Cambridge colleges. And, in the end, the middle-class hero, despite differences in class, education and wealth, is able to depart with the gamekeeper into a world whose difficulties – how are they going to survive? – the film does not even gesture towards.

The authenticity of these films to the literary is also fundamentally flawed in the relationship they set up between the historical and the contemporary. The audience is invited to understand the plot of the film as though we are *contemporary* with the characters, while at the same time indulging our pleasure in a world which is visually compelling precisely because of its *pastness*.

If these were films whose content was as much of today as yesterday, their translation into our own time would challenge us with the modernity of the issues raised. But they never do: instead we are placed back in a world whose evasions and silences are accepted as natural. The irony in *Where Angels Fear to Tread* is that the audience is invited to view the English tourists of the film in the same way as they view the Italians, certain that, whatever is done to them, they will come out unchanged at the end. For example, Gino, who marries an Englishwoman and then, after she has died in childbirth, loses his child because of the interference of her English relatives, will, we are assured, be laughing again tomorrow: the Italians are childlike, they do not take suffering seriously. And the audience plays a similar double game with the English characters: though their lives are caught up in dilemmas which demand our involvement, we are made aware that they are part of a world that has changed so much it doesn't matter any more.

Yet on another level these films elide this distance. *Where Angels Fear to Tread* ends with the two young English people (Bonham Carter and Graves) on the edge of some revelation, ready to accept some entirely new set of values. There is a close-up of their faces looking out at the audience, towards the future – a characteristic device in these films (*Maurice* concludes with a negative version of the same shot).

This encourages us to identify with them and so deny our historical knowledge of the future they are facing. For though the issues with which the characters in *Where Angels Fear to Tread* are engaged may well, as Sturridge has said, be 'love, fear, death, insincerity, a lack of truth and appreciation ... as relevant tomorrow as yesterday and today', we know that the revelation they are standing on the edge of is the World War I – a war that silenced Forster because it destroyed the secure world to which his comedy of manners was tied.

These are films in which the past is treated as though it existed in isolation from all that went before and after it, just as all those objects and possessions exist in isolation from any sense of grubby thing-making. (Who made them? Where? With how much sweat?) It is a cinema focused on a class that could pretend to be insulated from the world outside. In this it is very much in tune with our contemporary consumerist view of the world as a place in which objects exist only in acquisition, not in the labour of their creation.

'Only connect' was Forster's theme in *Howards End*, and his stories are about trying to connect across cultural and class boundaries. But Forster's trite little phrase could only have come to have such weight because of the deep inhibition against communicating with other classes and cultures that had developed in middle-class England in the course of the nineteenth century.

English identity was threatened by anything which broke through its barriers, anything which suggested it was not autonomous and self-sustaining. As Forster comments on the Wilcoxes, the archetypal middle-class businesspeople in *Howards End*: 'Though presenting a firm front to outsiders, no Wilcox could live near, or near the possessions of, any other Wilcox. They had the colonial spirit, and were always making for some spot where the white man might carry his burden unobserved.'

The plots of these films show characters struggling to cross boundaries (across class in the homosexual relationship in *Maurice*; across cultures in the Italian films). But their effect is precisely the opposite: they situate us firmly in the barricaded room of an English identity from which the outside world is viewed from above and without, not engaged with. They take us back into a world for which 'others' (the Italians, the working class) may seem alluring in their apparent openness, but are always, in the end, proved to be both unstable and untrustworthy.

So the role of these outsiders becomes that of reinforcing the superiority of the characters the films initially mock. In *Where Angels Fear to Tread*, for instance, it is the stuffy English, prepared to make the passage across the boundaries of their culture, who are in the end seen as admirable, not the Italians already liberated into a moral laxness that requires no journey to fulfilment.

This strategy of apparently satirising values which are in the end endorsed because everyone else's prove even more unacceptable is typical of the 1980s. It is a game played by Tom Wolfe in *The Bonfire of the Vanities*, where the upper-class WASP, whose essential emptiness the book and film set out to reveal, turns out to be the only worthwhile human being in a world of self-interested hypocrites.

In effect, these films engage with the idea of crossing the border between cultures, but in the knowledge that there is a safe haven to retreat into. They can allow their audiences to experience the tensions of an interrelatedness which contemporary British culture – *pace* Mrs Thatcher and the Bruges group – will have to live with, but within the profoundly safe context of the past. They can confront the need to build a new identity through open relations with other cultures only by reinforcing the values of a world which allowed its borders to be crossed one way only, at its own discretion and in the direction of its choice.

SEXUALITY AND HERITAGE

Claire Monk

Pastoral Sussex, 1915. A vintage locomotive, framed in its own steam, draws into a pretty rural station. The sole passenger to alight is an effete figure with a shapeless tweed hat, wire spectacles and the kind of huge, rigid beaver's-tail beard once attached to George Bernard Shaw. Instantly unburdened of his luggage by a porter, the bearded eccentric is offered the choice of a taxi or a horse-drawn fly. 'I don't think I need to make too hasty a decision, do you?' he responds camply, weighing up the respective charms of the two specimens of rustic rough trade on offer as his drivers. Meet Lytton Strachey, author of *Eminent Victorians* and famous Bloomsbury Set queer.

Carrington is the directing debut of playwright and Oscar-winning *Dangerous Liaisons* screenwriter Christopher Hampton, from his own script. It takes as its subject the intense, complex, sexually open seventeen-year relationship between Strachey and the ambiguously gamine painter Dora Carrington, thirteen years his junior, whom on their first meeting Strachey mistakes for a 'ravishing boy'. The film's central focus is the sexual and emotional life of a woman who rejected her female first name and wore male clothes. *Carrington* suggests she preferred an almost sex-free and often lonely intimacy with Strachey (someone who liked knitting and boys better than women) to the thrusting and tantrums of phallic heterosexuality. Though Carrington remained emotionally detached from her numerous young male lovers, her attachment to Strachey can be measured by the fact that she shot herself shortly after his death from cancer in 1932.

The above opening scene sets the tone for the film. *Carrington* treats its audience to the visual, literary and performative period pleasures associated with that critically despised but highly exportable British product, the heritage film, while pointedly seeking to distance itself, through various strategies, from the supposed conservatism these films were so often condemned for in the 1980s and early 1990s: particularly their innate escapism and their promotion of a conservative, bourgeois, pastoral, 'English' national identity. These distancing strategies range from archly explicit dialogue ('Ah, semen,' Strachey sighs. 'What is it about that ridiculous white secretion that pulls down the corners of a man's mouth?') to a camera which restlessly circles its human subjects, as if under pressure to prove that it is not lingering on period spectacle. But above all, there's *Carrington*'s choice of subject: the explicit preoccupation with 'unconventional' sexualities – gay, bisexual and active female heterosexual – and the specific focus on the Bloomsbury Set, a nexus of modernist writers, artists and thinkers whose polysexual, aesthetic and political experimentations signified a deliberate break with Victorian values. The political significance of this has not gone unnoticed by the *Daily Mail*: back in June this year [1995], it used *Carrington*'s upcoming release as the hook for a two-page propaganda piece blaming the Bloomsbury Set for everything from non-monetarist economics to the break-up of the family.

Carrington's preoccupations locate it as the latest in an emerging strand of period/literary films with a deep self-consciousness about how the past is represented: the implied reaction against heritage suggests they be termed 'post-heritage'. The strand can be dated to early 1993 and the international success of Sally Potter's *Orlando*, which perhaps helped destigmatise the pleasures of costume and period spectacle; by 1994, the trend had been consolidated not only in Britain (with the release of Stephen Poliakoff's underrated *Century* and Brian Gilbert's less successful *Tom & Viv*), but also globally, with the appropriation and renewal of the costume/literary film by Jane Campion (*The Piano*) and Martin Scorsese (*The Age of Innocence*), both non-European directors not previously associated with such projects.

What most unites the post-heritage films is undoubtedly an overt concern with sexuality and gender, particularly non-dominant gender and sexual identities: feminine, non-masculine, mutable, androgynous, ambiguous. In an increasingly international production context, in which the label 'British film' becomes ever more meaningless, the insistence on filming left-field sexual narratives can simply be seen as a strategy of product differentiation – from other European cinemas, even other European heritage cinemas, as much as from Hollywood. But nonetheless the transgressive sexual politics of the post-heritage film places it in genuine opposition to a 1990s Hollywood-defined mainstream. From *Orlando*'s transportation of its hero/ine through two genders and four centuries, the preoccupations of the post-heritage films would be found unthinkably deviant, both sexually and commercially, by the Hollywood of *Basic Instinct* and *Disclosure*, the Hollywood of predatory and punitive sexual politics, of Sadeian women and pro-family messages. (Indeed, Hampton's script for *Carrington* was written seventeen years before it finally found finance.)

But, paradoxically, the post-heritage films revel in the visual pleasures of heritage, even as they seem to distance themselves: one of *Carrington*'s ironies is the respectful conservationist 'authenticity' with which it reconstructs the home and clothes of a group of bold modernist experimenters. Similarly, the post-heritage film's upfront sexuality owes rather more to its heritage predecessors than the post-heritage film-maker may like to think. *Carrington*'s reception at Cannes earlier this year highlights this: awarded the *Prix Spécial du Jury à l'unanimité* not for Hampton's (directionless) direction, but for his (highly literary) script, the film has so far been praised not for its specifically cinematic qualities, but for its 'fidelity' (though to biographical fact, rather than literary source) and above all for its acting. Serial award-winner Emma Thompson is good as the androgynous tomboy *fatale* Carrington, but it's Jonathan Pryce's screen-stealing performance as Strachey, fussy, selfish and waspish, that brought home the Cannes Best Actor award.

However, Pryce's triumph is at the expense of the narrative's ostensible focus on Carrington herself. Hampton not only simplifies the tortuous bisexual entanglements of the Bloomsbury Set, but also – by an irony – heterosexualises them. The fact that Carrington had important and pleasurable affairs with women as well as men is completely ignored, while precedence goes to a series of rough screen couplings between Thompson and this year's pick of young male British acting 'talent' (Rufus Sewell, Jeremy Northam, Steven Waddington, Samuel West). In contrast, the physical details of Strachey's relationship with Carrington are treated with such ambiguous discretion that their relationship might never have been consummated – though historically we know it was. Likewise Strachey's physical relationships with men: there is one moment where Strachey and Ralph Partridge (the army major Carrington reluctantly marries, played by Waddington) seem to be lovers – and another where it seems equally certain they are not. It is strange that so sexually explicit a film should leave us so uncertain who is sleeping with whom: this was never so, for example, in James Ivory's not-so-explicit gay love story (and heritage film) *Maurice*.

Nevertheless, the film hardly portrays male heterosexuality sympathetically: Carrington's screen lovers are a typology of its archetypal flaws (the aggressively phallic and rabidly jealous working-class Jewish painter Mark Gertler, played by Sewell; the self-absorbed romantic travel writer Gerald Brenan, played by West, and so on). Unfortunately, Carrington's own sexuality and psyche remain opaque throughout. The camera's lingering focus on Thompson's empty gaze during each sex scene only highlights the fact that we know nothing of what she thinks or feels, while hinting at a woman caught, unsatisfactorily, between the Bloomsbury creed of polymorphous sex as liberation and the emotional need for a reciprocity Strachey cannot give. The pair's relationship seems most truthfully encapsulated in the peculiar moment when she hands Strachey a gift of a pen-wiper embroidered with the words 'use me' and tells him – *happily* – 'That's how I feel, Lytton.'

Carrington is not the first post-heritage film to fall short of its radical sexual ambitions; even the infinitely more imaginative *Orlando* ultimately failed to cinematise the playfully oscillating sexual and gender indeterminacy of its hero/ine, though this was the precise quality that made Virginia Woolf's novel so captivating and so sexy a fantasy. The irony is that the richest pleasures of ambiguity lie not in the upfront thematisations of the post-heritage film, but in two (perhaps *the* two) quintessential 1980s heritage films, James Ivory's first, low-budget adaptations from E. M. Forster, *A Room with a View* (1985) and *Maurice* (1987). Untouched by the post-heritage urge to make an issue of their self-consciousness, these two films nevertheless treat the journeys of personal and sexual identity which are their centres with an unpretentious humanity that itself constitutes a serious (and, to state the obvious, Forsterian) politics of sex and self, while offering plentiful postmodern pleasures: of the performative, of self-referentiality and irony.

Perhaps it is because these are the personal journeys of a very young woman (Lucy in *Room*) and a gay man (the eponymous Maurice) that anti-heritage critics (predominantly male and, as far as can be deduced, straight) have been able to ignore the sexual politics and pleasures of these films. That sexuality is central to their appeal has nevertheless been long understood by those who do enjoy them. 'Vintage car, vintage train, vintage plane … Vintage boys,' the *Tatler* noted of Charles Sturridge's Evelyn Waugh adaptation *A Handful of Dust* as early as 1988; and a 1990 edition of Channel 4's gay magazine *Out on Tuesday* had great fun editing together suggestive imagery and yearning gazes between boys from *Maurice*, *Another Country* and elsewhere.

The rarity of the spectacle of the male body, outside films specifically aimed at a gay audience, clearly places these movies somewhat outside the mainstream; it also makes them likely sites of anxiety for straight male spectators. It will surprise no one that *Maurice*, a gay love story, offers the audience such a spectacle, but the idea that *A Room with a View* is simmering with feminine, queer and ambiguous sexualities will seem strange to many. This is, after all, a film that was once recruited by the *Daily Mail* for one of its periodic attacks on 'permissiveness': the paper crowed proudly, but with sorry inaccuracy, that the film's 'overt sex is restricted to a single screen kiss exchanged by fully clothed lovers'. However, *Room*'s PG-certificate display of penises makes it something of a cinematic landmark: in hetero sex scenes in mainstream movies, it is *still* a near certainty that extravagant measures will be taken to conceal the male organ at all times (*Carrington* being no exception). The comic horseplay of the context of the penis display encapsulates the friction between innocence and codified suggestiveness through which the film's sexual subtext is played out: it's in the famous nude bathing scene, where the confused heroine Lucy (Helena Bonham Carter) and her snobbish, sexually unsuitable fiancé Cecil (Daniel Day-Lewis) find her uninhibited brother Freddy (Rupert Graves) and the local vicar, the Reverend Beebe (Simon Callow), romping in a pond with her rival suitor George (Julian Sands) – the suitor whose kiss, during the visit to Italy which comprises the first part of the film, prompted her erotic awakening.

Lucy's double in the film is her brother Freddy, who repeatedly acts out her unspoken desires; she may fiercely rebuff George and his physical advances, but Freddy invites him to bathe the moment they are introduced. This doubling endows the narrative with a bi-sexed androgyny and implicit homoeroticism, opening up multiple viewing pleasures. The transgressiveness of the bathing scene is sealed by Beebe's participation (Callow being famously *gay*); his only logical motivation for accompanying the two young men to the pond is voyeurism, a trait not only already established for him in the Italian section of the film, but also generally rife among the English characters on the Italian trip, most notably the 'Lady novelist' Miss Lavish.

In contrast to *Room*'s queered, gender-scrambled, deeply ambiguous celebration of female desire, *Maurice*'s corresponding perversity is the *straightness* of its treatment of the sexual and emotional self-discovery and transformation of its young gay Edwardian protagonist (James Wilby). Coupled with *Maurice*'s restrained and even dour aesthetic, this straightness seems to me to be a political strategy, as if Ivory considered the 'normalising' of gayness, by removing its visual and behavioural codes, to be the duty of a liberal-humanist campaigning film. However quaint this tactic may seem, it is not without some currency – in making gay men seem 'just like everyone else', *Maurice* seeks to demonstrate beyond argument that the same human rights apply to them as to everyone else.

Maurice was sneered at by some critics for its softly-softly approach to gay physicality, and its eloquent focus on gay *emotions* and *desire* was memorably dismissed by *Time* magazine as 'twits twittering'. Nevertheless, this focus gradually accumulates and unleashes a far more intense erotic charge than the sexually explicit but emotionally evasive *Carrington*. Recall the potent layers of fantasy appealed to by Maurice's seduction by the gamekeeper Alec Scudder (Rupert Graves): it's the fantasy of sexual release (Maurice's first with another human being) at the hands of a near stranger who appears single-mindedly through your bedroom window as if summoned by your own unconscious in the midst of a dream, 'like a genie out of a bottle', as one commentator put it. Consider, too, the S&M charge of the pair's subsequent game of cat and mouse: love letters that could be blackmail notes; the way Maurice's emotional sadism and Alec's humiliation ('You shouldn't treat me like a dog') function as a perverse courtship.

Maurice's most radical ingredient, though for many improbable, may be its near-magical happy ending – eight years after its release, there is little reason to challenge its co-screenwriter Kit Hesketh-Harvey's claim that it is 'the only time in a major film that the homosexual hero is allowed the chance of happiness'. Yet, amazingly, even this aspect of the movie has been widely misrepresented. While most reviewers had concentrated on the more platonic first half of the film, the majority of film reference guides give the impression – usually by omission – that Maurice's story ends, as tragic gay narrative convention leads us to expect, in tears. One synopsis even bizarrely claims that Maurice descends, like Dorian Gray, into promiscuity and depravity!

Perhaps it is such gross misrepresentations and failures to appreciate their intent that have led Ivory, his producer Ismail Merchant and their regular screenwriter Ruth Prawer Jhabvala into a seeming retreat from such complex and polymorphous sexual politics in more recent period films. Awkward non-hetero sexualities likely to stir ambivalent feelings in critics were notably absent from their two subsequent British literary adaptations, *Howards End* (1992) and *The Remains of the Day* (1993). The torrent of praise which greeted *Howards End*, in particular – some of it from sources previously noted for their loathing of heritage – may have had more to do with fashion than politics. Straining towards a post-heritage aesthetic in its melodramatisation of the spectacles of property and landscape, *Howards End* seems to me to turn Forster's most critical novel into a complacent Tory tract on the pleasures of property – a more conservative transformation than its derided heritage predecessors ever managed.

1995's *Jefferson in Paris* marks Merchant-Ivory-Jhabvala's first foray into (variously) the eighteenth century, big politics, big history, the French Revolution and (most problematically) the psychology and sexuality of slavery in America. It is an oddity with such complex ambitions that it would be unwise to rely on it to draw conclusions about the future shape of heritage cinema, post-heritage cinema or even Ivory's next film. Alleging that US president Thomas Jefferson had a sexual relationship with one of his slaves, Sally Hemings, who bore him children from the age of fifteen, Ivory's most (theoretically) transgressive film is hindered by its near-total lack of convincing sexual chemistry – but it may nonetheless be the most intellectually ambitious film he has made. Neither heritage nor post-heritage, but a throwback to an earlier, colder art-film aesthetic which offers little easy gratification, *Jefferson* fluffs its treatment of its black characters appallingly, but puts gender aggressively on the agenda. Its coup is to draw parallels between Jefferson turning a blind eye to carnage in his support of the revolution in France and his championing of 'universal' freedom in the abstract, while withholding *liberté*, *egalité* and *fraternité* from blacks and women – his teenage daughter, as well as his slaves. Needless to say, *Jefferson* has been dismissed in Britain as nothing but period spectacle. If *Carrington* is taken more seriously than this flawed but demanding political think-piece, the anti-heritage critics may have missed the point yet again.

DRESSING THE PART

Andy Medhurst

'I've had quite enough of dark things. I want bright things, decorative things,' says the seventeenth-century doctor Robert Merivel near the beginning of *Restoration*, justifying his decision to swap the grim squalor of medicine for the sumptuous playfulness of the court of Charles II. It's a sentiment that might confirm the worst suspicions of those who like to damn costume drama as retrogressive, blinkered escapism, a bolt-hole for contemporary audiences to shut out troubling topical concerns. This critique does have some validity: witness the hungry gratitude with which certain audiences devoured the decorous palliatives of Merchant-Ivory films while Thatcher-driven policies fractured the culture beyond the art houses – but the story of costume in British cinema history is more than the noise of rustling bustles. It encompasses other, broader, more irreverent traditions, too – the heaving cleavages and swished capes of Gainsborough and Hammer, the gutsy Dickens adaptations made by David Lean before he declined into distended epics, the swooningly overdressed refusals of restraint favoured by Michael Powell and Ken Russell, the raspberries blown at history by Sid James' Henry VIII and Kenneth Williams' Julius Caesar. For every British film concerned with respectful, meticulous reconstruction of the past, there are a dozen more which treat history as a great big dressing-up box, where a genteel commitment to period verisimilitude is discarded for the romping joys of frocking about. The potential diversity of the costume film, its flexible openness to a multiplicity of interpretations, is underlined by the release this year of three quite distinct variants: *Sense and Sensibility, Restoration* and *Richard III.*

Of course, a cavalier approach to costume has always dismayed the puritans. In the 1940s, the Gainsborough melodramas were crucified by critics for their magpie borrowings from history's wardrobe, blurring periods and mixing styles. Audiences, less constrained by such librarian-like fussiness, rolled up every time, besotted by how the sweep of the skirts drove the sweep of the stories. Costume in a Gainsborough film was central (as Pam Cook has argued in her recent study *Fashioning the Nation*) to the way they offered their predominantly female audiences the chance to imagine themselves into cultural identities beyond the confines of everyday Englishness. Costume functioned as a means to become both 'other' and 'elsewhere', as a passionate manifestation of the wish to be different. A decade later, Hammer made similar use of the expressive potential of the past, recognising that the ripe, surging emotions of its horror cycle would be all the more alluring if encased in Victoriana.

Acting as underside and counterpoint to these strategies was British vulgar comedy's love of parody. A fool's chronicle of history took in the Crazy Gang's mockery of British imperialism in *O-Kay for Sound* (1937), Tommy Trinder in Nero's Rome in *Fiddlers Three* (1944), Sid Field annoying the Roundheads in *Cardboard Cavalier* (1949), the Carry On team's frequent excursions into historical drag and Morecambe and Wise's costumed spoofs: a Golden Mile of send-ups to scandalise National Trust-type aspirations to heritage cinema.

Still, the conservative use of costume continues to flourish, hard though it is when sitting through the inexplicably BAFTA-garlanded *Sense and Sensibility* not to wonder where Morecambe and Wise are when you need them most. This is a film where dress functions primarily as distraction, where the careful period authenticity, sugary tourist-board visuals and just-right outfits act as guarantees of quality, material substance designed to hide the slightness of the narrative. As with the period verbiage the characters talk ('trow', 'ascertain' and 'ruination' hardly being the speech of everyday multiplex folk), costume serves to dignify, to assure audiences that there is profundity present when there is scarcely enough story to sustain an average episode of *Hollyoaks*. The soap parallel is apt, since the film is female-centred and entirely concerned with relationships, and proceeds primarily through gossip, but such a comparison cannot be admitted, and costume is used to hoist things several cultural notches above mundanity, to invest meaning while displaying the investment of money. The clothes that fill the screen are sartorial Polyfilla, judiciously smeared over cracks in the text.

If the original novel had not been so sacrosanct, perhaps a full-blooded Gainsborough-style *Sense and Sensibility* might have been possible. Certainly Fanny Dashwood's scheming villainy, encased in suitably elaborate, usually jet-black gowns, belongs there, while John Willoughby's first appearance – the wild stud of the moors in a flowing coat, Heathcliff meets Superman – comes straight from Stewart Granger's nonchalant heroics. Yet both these characters are eclipsed, rejected as too melo-dramatic, too vulgar, lacking the requisite Austen-esque decorum manifested in Elinor Dashwood's more demure frocks and Colonel Brandon's less flamboyant, less (if you'll pardon the expression) packet-friendly menswear. In Gainsborough terms, it's all too Patricia Roc and not nearly Margaret Lockwood enough.

Sense and Sensibility also caters for conservatively nostalgic tastes in the way it uses clothes to signify class. All the praise heaped on Emma Thompson's gently feminist adaptation of the novel seems to have ignored the fact that the class hierarchies of the period remain unchallenged. In an early scene, two of the gentry ride through the fields, individuals with a purpose and the dialogue to prove it, while a smocked shepherd trails through the background like dehumanised decor. Servants and peasants, dressed in all-purpose lower-orders outfits, are simply breathing backdrops, lumped in with the meals they serve or the animals they tend. This may accurately mirror the hierarchies of the time, but it is noteworthy that Thompson felt no need to introduce a more modern perspective here as she did with the film's sexual politics – though she's hardly the first university-educated feminist to have no grasp of the political dynamics of class.

Restoration is an altogether more interesting film. Not as smoothly concocted, it asks questions and takes risks that *Sense and Sensibility* shuns, in its single-minded quest to be the BBC 1 Christmas Day film for 1999. *Restoration* worries away at issues such as authenticity, feeling and meaning, and explores the seductions of luxury and the politics of pretence. Its image of the past is a world away from the gentilities of Jane Austen, preferring instead to depict (albeit sometimes threatening to topple into Terry Gilliam-style mediaevalist burlesque) a past caked in filth, a past that teems, a past that stinks. In such a context, costume becomes a refuge, the obscenely lavish enclave of the King's court a response to dirt and disease outside. Fanciful dress is a talisman to ward off the realities of corporeal decay, artifice a postponement of mortality.

The film begins to fall apart, however, as a result of the contradictions it sets up for itself. As Merivel is forced to leave luxury behind and return to deal with the poor and the needy, *Restoration* leans on us to applaud his altruistic sense of responsibility. But the problem is that we, like he, had much more fun in the world of gluttony, and finery and costumes that defy belief. The narrative urges us to share its switch to moralising, but the absurdly engorged compositions of the earlier part (imagine a Greenaway film in which people enjoyed themselves) refuse to give way, leaving *Restoration* a film torn between its ideological project and its semiotic repertoire. Its scenes set in plague-ridden London also flirt with a questionable AIDS subtext (a hedonistic subculture forced by the onset of illness to realise that the party might be over), which it should have thought through more fully or omitted. But it does at least call into question some of the staple ingredients of its genre, insisting that we don't just lap up costume, but think about its consequences.

At first glance, *Richard III* seems to be taking this agenda further, consciously breaking the rules of period fidelity by transposing Shakespeare's play to a 1930s England decked with fascist trappings. Here, surely, is an unapologetically political use of costume, suggesting both a twentieth-century relevance for the play's analysis of power and (more discreetly) mounting an attack on institutions central to traditional notions of Englishness. It makes bold moves (when did you last see a Royal at a urinal?) and the fast-paced, pared-down narrative refuses to mummify the text with excessive reverence. *Richard III*'s need to distance itself from the Olivier version is understandable, and avoiding Plantagenet drag is a way to achieve this: yet is anything gained by the 1930s setting, once the initial impact wears off? The gangster/Nazi parallels (gestured at throughout and made explicit at the *White Heat*-derived climax) were done better by Brecht's play *The Resistible Rise of Arturo Ui* (1941), and the attempt to stir the signifiers of British heritage pageantry into the mix only confuses the issue (Maggie Smith's Queen-Mary furs and Ian McKellen's SS boots are not compatible iconographies).

But perhaps this all steers *Richard III* much nearer to those British costume films where the past serves as playground, where a costume earns its place through impact not accuracy. (The play is, after all, sheer melodrama, with excesses of plot and polarities of character that even Gainsborough might have had trouble swallowing.) So it should probably be seen less as a contribution to literary-based cinematic culture and more as a descendant of those less respectable traditions of British dressing-up films. It's just a pity James Mason or Kenneth Williams weren't available for the lead role.

THE SHADOW

Liz Lochhead

In Tony Roper's very popular 1980s play *The Steamie* – very popular here in Scotland, that is – three Glasgow women at the communal laundry in the mid-1950s are discussing Saturday night culture: 'They're a pain in the arse, yon bloody British Pictures. Ron Randall leaning up against a lamp post, smoking a fag. He tells you the bloody story afore ye've seen it, then flicks the fag away, supposed to be tough. They cannae fight right!' The consensus: James Cagney could obliterate the lot, one punch.

Quentin Tarantino has Clarence pontificate in *True Romance* on all that 'Merchant/ Ivory claptrap. They ain't plays, they ain't books, they certainly ain't movies, they're films. And do you know what films are? They're for people who don't like movies.' Well, I'm not sure about Clarence – maybe his prejudice against cowboys in skirts would be too great – but I thought Michael Caton-Jones' new release *Rob Roy* was a movie, not a film. And I'm positive the women in the steamie would have been very taken with it as the Big Picture any Saturday night. Back then in the 1950s, the frank and free talk and the mildly raunchy private endearments would have thrilled them as much as the old-fashioned swashbuckling did me today.

> *Honour made him a man.*
> *Courage made him a hero.*
> *History made him a Legend.*

This is the kind of enjoyable hokum on the marquee that sets the tone for the *Big Country*/ John Wayne style of *Rob Roy*, even if all the love stuff would have The Duke blush.

I can't remember if *The Madness of King George* had anything so vulgar as a slogan. If it did, I don't remember it, so it must have been something as tasteful and muted as the film itself. Because it's interesting to compare these two recent works. One, I'm afraid, very much a British film, the other a Scottish-American movie. Both of them with very 'historical' sources, and both with self-conscious references to America: as if to say, 'This is about you, really, you should like this, honest, even if it's funny accents and olden-days costumes.'

The Madness of King George is about a real historic figure with absolutely no mythic presence in the national consciousness. *Rob Roy* is about a genuinely mythic figure with a very tenuous relationship to the historical man born three centuries ago. One is predicated on the not very startling aperçu that, if you're royal, your life 'tis not your own, and a king is not just an ordinary man. The other, that an ordinary man – if he is a man of honour – is a king.

For all the depth and excellence of Nigel Hawthorne's performance and how affecting he made this individual human predicament; for all the humane and empathetic wit of Alan Bennett's script; for all the sumptuous panning across heritage landscapes and tracking through heritage interiors past acreages of gorgeous costumes, *The Madness of King George* was finally reductive.

Madness abated, we see Mr King restored to Mrs King, rather better but still perhaps not quite the full shilling, and probably not yet accepting in his heart of hearts that the American colonies are really and truly gone. 'I have always been myself even when I was ill. Only now I seem myself. That's the important thing: I have remembered how to seem.' This is gentle and touching, and may make us smile. But in terms of filling a big screen with big-screen emotions, it's not a patch on this:

Rob Roy to Wee Son: 'Men have honour.'
WS to RR: 'Do women have honour, Daddy?'
RR to WS: 'Women are the heart of honour and we cherish and protect it in them. You must never mistreat a woman or malign a man, nor stand by and see another do so.'

Men have and men act. Women are. We may be astonished to hear such old-fashioned sentiments uttered without irony, but we are quite likely to admire Alan Sharp's epic nerve. In both senses of the word.

Sharp (author of *Ulzana's Raid* and *Night Moves*, among others) is one of the very few internationally known Scottish screenwriters. Producer Peter Broughan was determined from the word go that Sharp was the man who must write *Rob Roy*. So I imagine for Sharp it was a case of first-the-phonecall, rather than a burning, personal desire to explore the 'Rob Roy Highland Rogue' myth. This was an unashamed genre piece – and yet it reveals a very particular take on a subject which to date has spawned more than half a dozen screen adaptations.

Daniel Defoe was the first to make use of the legend in a literary work. Later Sir Walter Scott simply appropriated Rob Roy for his own romantic purposes. (Scott was a Lowlander, remember, who lived a couple of generations after the Jacobites and, in his novels, conveniently elided from memory their truly disastrous legacy for the Highlands, by inventing a mythic, tartan-and-sublime, noble past, a gloriously misty

Other, out of the failed attempt to reinstate a Catholic, feudal, absolutist monarchy.) Wordsworth wrote a poem about an equally romanticised version of this real-life cattle thief, protection racketeer, free-booter and pragmatist: Rob Roy MacGregor [*sic*] was a man said to boast that he 'was neither for King Shamus nor King Shordie but for King Spulzie'. (*Spulzie* means 'loot'.) It seems agreed that the MacGregors were Protestants whose surname was proscribed for Jacobite sympathies. Obviously Rob Roy was a man of many contradictions. But contradictions are not the stuff of major motion pictures.

Liam Neeson plays a hero on a heroic scale. He's a gentle giant of a man who, as befits his star status, makes no discernible effort to modify his Irish accent into Scots, who loves his wife, teaches his sons about honour and is scrupulous, indeed fanatical, about being a 'man of his word' and who, just when even the most sentimental of us in the audience are beginning to sicken of this pan-Celtic paragon, wakes us up by truly amazing escapes, wily if emetic concealments, and thrilling, single-hand combat, against the odds.

Jessica Lange plays Mary MacGregor beautifully, which must be very difficult as Mary is the ultimate male fantasy. As permanent as the land itself – indeed she is the land, wild, lovely, the place he must come back to – she is eternally desirable and desirous, murmuring sweet nothings about standing stones as she clambers astride her man in the slanting shadow of one magnificent specimen, urging him to 'make a silk purse out of my sow's ear again'.

Now I was nineteen the first time I read that line in Sharp's novel *A Green Tree in Gedde*, in 1967, the Summer of Love: I remember being very impressed. But what thrilled me most about the novel was that it took place in a very recognisable Greenock and Glasgow – why, the assignation was actually round the corner in Kelvingrove Street! Imagine, somewhere I knew, in a book! It would take a while – till *That Sinking Feeling* or *Comfort and Joy* – until I saw places I recognised in a film.

Now, in *Rob Roy*, I was looking at a very familiar landscape (although piled-up cairns are rather more familiar than standing stones on hilltops, truth be told) that I absolutely did not recognise, so successfully had it been transformed into a romantic dreamland. Of course, we must dream on celluloid, but we need to dream more, different and varied dreams, to ask ourselves what truths about the present we are hiding from ourselves by lying about the past. It's obvious why *Brigadoon* is such a perfect metaphor for Scottish culture. If you only come alive for one day every 200 years, or you only flare out on film once every decade, then it's hard not to stay frozen in static, heroic but hopeless representations of necessary myths. As Eddie Dick says, in the editorial to *From Limelight to Satellite*: 'The imagined Scotland is not imaginary.'

Rob Roy is somehow successful because it has the nerve to be a tartan-and-the-heilans picture by Clydeside men. These mountains are made with girders. The film critic John Caughie says (apropos the 1982 *Scotch Reels* analysis of 'representations of Scottishness') that there are 'three governing discourses': 'tartanry', 'kailyard', and 'Clydeside'. Well, I don't suppose, Scotland being Scotland, that *Rob Roy* will be immune from criticisms that it's 'kailyard keech': cabbage-patch trash. Which is exactly inaccurate: a cabbage-patch reductiveness is one thing you cannot justly accuse it of. Rather there is a grandiosity, a swagger, an unconscious blokishness that you might deplore, but cannot but enjoy watching, truth be told. The homophobic relish with which the crude clansmen taunt the foppish Cunningham that he 'can't tell arse from quim' is itself portrayed with a homophobic relish just about justified by the fact that they are patently wrong on both counts. Cunningham is *extremely* dangerous, both in sex and war, and provides Tim Roth with a role to steal the movie from under the noses of the stars. Everybody, surely, would rather watch Roth be a hiss-the-villain (and it's a performance of subtlety and dark vulnerability, as well as enormous bravura) than watch Neeson and Lange in their sentimental idealised married love.

I can't help feeling the writer and the director probably thought all the love stuff would make it a woman's picture, too. But what they reveal is a deep male yearning for an ideal: the woman as impossibly wise (she told him so!) and forbearing (she doesn't remind him she told him so!), as well self-sacrificing, natural, full of unlikely mother love, which seems to well up in any circumstances – and as hot as a honeymoon to boot.

Couldn't she have resented, just a little, being left alone to be raped? Couldn't she have hated the fruit of the rape, just until it was born? Couldn't he, however unreasonably, have reacted with immediate human revulsion which he'd have to fight against in himself? No, it was a big movie, brave enough to be black and white, and, in the end, after a bit of a dip – the film is maybe half an hour too long – it engages in a genuinely thrilling fight to the death.

The swordfights are the best I've seen. There are compelling secondary performances from Vicki Masson, Brian McCardie and the wonderful Andrew Keir, as well as John Hurt as Montrose, who may or may not have reason to love Cunningham; there is heartstopping Gaelic singing (though filmed a little too reverently) from Karen Matheson, which provides a good antidote to the clichéd antique movie score by Carter Burwell; there is a great joke about the 'Calvinists no' approving of shagging standing up, because it might lead to dancing'.

But I'm left wondering what this not-very-burdened-with-history Historical Movie tells me about the current myths and dreams and longings in this small country…

For most of us Lowland Scots, Rob Roy MacGregor represents the lost one, the shadow, the Highlander with his own fey red-haired otherness and honour. If we are the dominant culture, then he is in the same position as woman is to man: feared, revered, romanticised and put on an impossible pedestal.

In *Shallow Grave*, the dead nerd accountant in his voiceover tells us, 'This could be any city, anywhere.' Not without irony, as we're just about to be hauled at high speed (to techno music) through the certainly unique cityscape of Edinburgh's New Town: later we go to a hospital tartan fundraiser ball inhabited by types only found, in my experience, in that fair city. 'This could be any city, anywhere.' And then unfolds the perfect chilly little morality tale of greed, murder and bad faith.

Oh, no, it couldn't happen here, we think. Not while Rob Roy is ours and he is for us the heart of honour. No wonder the villains get all the best lines.

La Reine Margot (Patrice Chéreau, 1994)

Heritage, History and Spectacle

CINEMA'S CONQUISTADORS

Peter Wollen

Ridley Scott's film about Columbus, *1492: Conquest of Paradise*, revolves around the first sight of land after the long voyage. The screen is covered in clouds, which drift slowly away, like gauze curtains, to reveal a lush green tropical landscape, filled with trees, foliage and plants. Later in the film, Columbus recalls this image as one that will stay with him in all its vividness until his death. It is an aesthetic image, one designed to appeal to our delight in seeing. It is also an image with connotations of unspoiled nature, awakening in the viewer a presentiment of the destruction of the Amazon rainforest or the North American redwoods. It is an image which is certainly true to Columbus' own experience – his diary is full of expressions of wonder at the proliferation and verdancy of trees on the Caribbean islands. On the other hand, when he saw pine trees, which could be used for shipbuilding, he immediately switched into a different register, that of practicality and exploitation.

Although the curtain has drawn back to reveal the first image of America, we are aware that this image, too, is like a curtain. Having contemplated, Columbus is fated to land, to rip apart the curtain and to penetrate the interior in search of gold and slaves, and sites for forts and towns. From the start, there is a tension between the aesthete and the conquistador. Moreover, we are aware that this gaze will be returned by the native inhabitants. What will they see? At the time, they thought they saw extraterrestrials, men who came from the skies, as the Spaniards noted. But they soon learned to see these men from the skies in a more terrestrial light.

In his classic article, 'The Western: Or the American film *par excellence*', André Bazin attributed the power of the Western, and by extension of Hollywood cinema itself, to its epic grandeur and historic roots. Westerns reminded him of Corneille's *El Cid* or the Homeric classics – 'The migration to the West is our Odyssey'. At the heart of Hollywood cinema lay the myth of the West, the evocation of a world in which 'knights of the true cause' were set against the forces of evil and 'pagan savagery' represented by the Indian. 'The white Christian on the contrary is truly the conqueror of a new world. The grass sprouts where his horse has passed. He imposes his moral and technical order, the one linked to the other and the former guaranteeing the latter… Only strong, rough and courageous men could tame these virgin lands.'

Two years later, in 1955, Eric Rohmer developed Bazin's ideas even more radically. In an essay in *Cahiers du cinéma*, 'Rediscovering America', he argued that the classical elegance and efficacy of the American cinema came precisely from the historic role of the Americans as a colonising people like the Ancient Greeks, that there was a clear parallel 'between the first colonisers of the Mediterranean and the pioneers of

Arizona'. Typical American heroes are members of 'a race of conquerors, which opens up the land, founds cities, is in love with action and adventure, and in spite of or perhaps because of this is more determined to preserve its religious or moral tradition'. Thus, like their Greek predecessors, Hollywood film heroes are preoccupied not simply with action and conquest, but also with the underlying problems of destiny, violence, morality and law.

Neither Bazin nor Rohmer was much concerned with the historical record. They were concerned with the creation of a new form of 'myth'. The concept of 'myth', of course, gave some credibility to their neo-classical interpretation of Hollywood. Yet, in effect, they were talking about what E. J. Hobsbawm has called 'the invention of tradition'.

During the nineteenth century, the major powers of Europe and North America set about inventing an array of ancient traditions to support the official nationalism they promoted. Nationalism depends crucially on the creation of an invented national history, with its monumental heroes, dramatic climaxes, narrative goals. The myth of the West – the ever-expanding frontier, the manifest destiny that underlay America's westward dynamic, the civilising mission of the settlers, the taming of the wilderness, the appropriation of the land in order for it to be cultivated – stands alongside other national myths that justified the unification of Germany, or the expansion of Tsarist Russia to the Pacific, or the scramble for Africa, or the imposition of the British Raj in India.

Christopher Columbus is just such a monumental hero. As the historic initiator of the cycle of conquest, plunder and colonisation which was still playing itself out four centuries later in the American West, he plays a more crucial mythic role than even the heroes of the West themselves. To pursue the classical analogy, Columbus was the Theseus who founded Athens or the Aeneas who left Carthage to found Rome. Columbus was the originator without whom the national narrative could not have taken place and who inevitably symbolised the destiny which validated it. Along with Washington and Lincoln, he was an indispensable lynchpin of the invented tradition that America produced within and for itself. Columbus was the first adventurer, the first immigrant, the first prospector, the first pacifier of savages, the first missionary to the heathen, the first lawmaker, the first town-builder, the first merchant and entrepreneur, the first slave-taker, the first modern American.

The Columbus myth evolved in three successive periods, reaching a peak every hundred years, at the time of the centennial celebrations. The first significant stirrings of the cult were felt with the advent of American Independence, as the new nation began to construct its new identity and history. Patriotic anthems celebrated the rise of 'Columbia'; poets wrote book-length epics chronicling the exploits of 'the new Moses'; King's College in New York was renamed Columbia University; the new national capital, still unbuilt, was assigned its place in the new District of Columbia; and the anniversary of 1792 was marked with dinners, toasts and fervid orations. The capstone was put in place in due course, when Washington Irving wrote the decisive popular biography of Columbus, published in three volumes in 1828, in the immediate aftermath of Walter Scott's great romantic project of history creation. This first-wave Columbus was both a romantic genius and an embattled underdog, harried by flat-earthers and envious hidalgos, betrayed by perfidious royalty.

The second wave, which began with the expansion west and was given new impetus by Italian immigration into America, brought Columbus Day and Columbus Circle, and culminated in the lavish celebrations of 1892, foremost among which was the World's Columbian Exposition in Chicago, a commemoration so ambitious that it finally opened in 1893. At the exposition, Kwakiutl and Haida people from British Columbia performed in their painted cedar houses, complete with thunderbirds and totem poles, along with an Apache craftsman, a Navajo family in a hogan, four families of Penobscots in birch-bark wigwams, and Iroquois in a traditional bark house. Most significant of all was the presence of Arawaks from British Guiana in a thatched hut. Presumably these were the best available stand-ins for the Arawak-speaking Taino who were encountered by Columbus on the Caribbean beach that fateful day in 1492. The Taino, who once numbered millions, had vanished from the Earth within a few decades of Columbus' arrival, destroyed by forced labour, famine, slavery, slaughter and disease.

This was also the period in which Buffalo Bill was at the peak of his success and in which American Indians first entered show business as performers. The whooping and circling warriors of the Wild West show, ritually defeated and massacred by the white conquerors, were soon to transmute into the whooping and circling extras and stuntmen of the Hollywood Western. The Western, in turn, gave America two great twentieth-century masters of the invention of tradition in Cecil B. DeMille and, of course, John Ford. Andrew Sarris, in the record of his own voyage of discovery, *The American Cinema*, describes DeMille as the last Victorian, while Ford is cast as a director flexible enough to avoid becoming faded and dated. Today Ford's reputation has crystallised around *The Searchers* (1956), the darkest of his films, which, in its desperation, hovers on the edge of a renunciation of the very tradition Ford had dedicated himself to inventing.

Finally, a third wave of re-examination of Columbus has arrived with 1992. This time there is no grandiose official celebration, even if a life-size replica of the *Santa Maria* is tethered to the river bank in front of the State Capitol in Columbus, Ohio, not far from the life-size topiary reconstruction of Seurat's *La Grande Jatte*, which adorns a nearby park. Even this small gesture seems ironic when we remember that the original *Santa Maria* went aground on a reef while Columbus was asleep and that, after the timber and nails were ferried ashore in canoes by friendly Taino, it was cannibalised to build the first fort in the New World. The reticence of 1992 reflects, however, not a diminution of Columbus' mythic role, but a re-evaluation. Columbus as bearer of civilisation is gradually exchanging roles with the Taino; he is becoming the savage, while they become the civilised, living in harmony with nature and at peace with each other.

It is into this third-wave treatment of Columbus that Ridley Scott's film uneasily fits. The subtitle, *Conquest of Paradise*, follows the lead of Kirkpatrick Sale's major revisionist book on Columbus, *The Conquest of Paradise: Christopher Columbus and the Columbian Legacy*, published in 1990. Sale was a founder of the New York Green Party, and his exactingly researched work arraigns Columbus for his deeds and his legacy, drawing a clear connection between Columbus' own fanaticism and the pollution, plunder, massacre and destruction that followed in his wake. The Taino, in contrast, are presented as pacific, respectful of their environment and balanced in their economic practices. At the same time, Columbus is placed within an historical context that sees his arrival in the Americas as an epochal moment of culture clash, in which Columbus, as protagonist, is little more than the representative of already tainted European values.

In fact, as Tzvetan Todorov notes, there was something 'Quixotic' about Columbus. His ideas and theories were often completely crazy and wildly inaccurate and, although he changed the course of history, he was dogged by fiasco and failure – he ran his ship aground, he abandoned his crew, his chief lieutenants repeatedly mutinied, he found hardly any gold worth speaking of, he was quite unable to find any spices, his settlements failed, and he was finally dragged back to Spain in chains and, in his view, cheated of the honours and rewards he deserved. In many ways, he turned out to be the Admiral of the Mosquitoes that his detractors dubbed him. Like others of his kind, he appears hopelessly simple-minded in his encounter with the unknown, sticking with irremediable stubbornness to his preconceptions and wrong guesses. Despite his amazing adventures, he was not an interesting person and his diaries are exasperatingly tedious and uninformative. As *1492* notes, neither he nor anyone around him learned to speak Arawak or understood anything much of who his interlocutors were. At first, he mainly wanted them to point him towards gold, and later simply to bring it to him as a tribute. He could be indulgent while things were going well, but turned cruel at the scent of trouble.

The film of *1492* is only incidentally dependent for its effect on the exposition of Columbus' historic role – which might have required either a Brechtian approach alien to mainstream cinema or a voiceover of the kind forced on Ridley Scott with *Blade Runner* (1982) and then removed in the newly released director's cut. Essentially, 1492 is a traditional biopic and, like all good genre films, it follows the well-tried conventions, elaborated over the years in 300 or so Hollywood movies. As George F. Custen observes in his newly published study, *Bio/Pics: How Hollywood Constructed Public History*, the biopic occupies a particular niche within the invention of tradition, one which codes public events according to a pattern of individual success through triumph over adversity. The hero, according to this pattern, has an innovative and visionary scheme which necessarily disturbs entrenched interests and conservative ways of thinking. Eventually, with help from family and friends, the hero's project is realised and his or her achievements enter the public domain, where he/she survives counterattack or betrayal before being vindicated.

Darryl Zanuck recognised the essential dynamic of the story in a letter he despatched to the author of *The Story of Alexander Graham Bell* in 1938: 'The drama of the story does not lie in the invention of the telephone any more than the drama of Zola's life was his writing. Our main drama lies in Bell's fight against the world to convince them he had something great, and then to protect his ownership.' Thus, in Ridley Scott's *1492*, the drama of Columbus' life lies not in his epochal voyage to America, or even in his landfall on an island of the Bahamas or his meeting with the Taino, but in his efforts to get his scheme off the ground by debating with dogmatic clerics at the University of Salamanca, pulling strings to reach Queen Isabella, winning her over by his straightforward and immodest ways (a *soupçon* here of the secret love affair between them imagined by the Cuban novelist Alejo Carpentier in his *The Harp and the Shadow*). And then, after the voyage, there is his struggle to hold on to his power, his reputation and the public recognition of his achievement.

In fact, as Custen notes, this model closely resembles the struggles of a film-maker to get a project realised, although in the case of *1492* the protagonist is a director, rather than a producer. Towards the end of the film, Columbus is confronted by his aristocratic patron and told he is nothing but a dreamer: 'I did it!' he retorts. 'You didn't.' This is the traditional cry of the director against the producer and the critic. The director is easily conceived of as a hero with a vision who finds it difficult to get funded, difficult to execute his or her dream and difficult to control the final products after it is finished. Indeed, in a way, this is the story of *Blade Runner*: the story of an adventure, a voyage, carried out by a perfectionist, a tough captain, even a slave-driver, whose work is distrusted and sabotaged, and taken from him, before the original, director's version is finally and triumphantly released. In this sense, *1492* falls into the tradition of *The Barefoot Contessa* or *The Big Knife* or even *The Player* – history refracted into Hollywood on Hollywood.

Within this basic biopic framework, *1492* attempts to mellow the biographical record by presenting Columbus as something of an egalitarian, an appreciator of Indian ways, an admirer of nature and a victim of reactionary churchmen and vicious hidalgos whose penchant for violence wrecks the idyll of his newly conquered Paradise and turns the New World into catastrophe: a vision not unlike that of *Dances with Wolves*, the set-piece revisionist Western. It would have been easier had the film been unabashedly fictional, like a Western. Again, Zanuck fearlessly pointed the way, in a message wired to a replacement writer six months later, after difficulties had been created by Bell's family: 'Appreciate difficulties and am relying on you and Lamar [Trotti] to settle same without destroying story because rather than destroy present dramatic structure I would be willing to forget name of Bell and other real names and make same plot with fictional names stop They must realize that from time immemorial there has existed dramatic license which was practised when I made Disraeli House of Rothschild Lloyds of London Suez and when Warners made Pasteur and Zola stop.' This telegram brusquely encapsulates the Hollywood view of history, ruthlessly prepared to subordinate the shadowy events of the real world to the hard facts of Hollywood and its own 'time immemorial'. Ridley Scott's film remains a compromise formation, caught between the revisionist history of a Green intellectual like Kirkpatrick Sale and the truly Columbian vision of a conquistador like Darryl Zanuck.

FALLING OUT OF LOVE

Serge Daney

There is an expression in French which people use, apologetically, to describe a film during which they have had difficulty staying awake: *Ça m'est tombé des yeux*, literally, 'It fell from my eyes'. A rather nice phrase, which seems to register the fact that every film is simultaneously projected twice: once onto the cinema screen and once onto our retinas. It is almost as if, when we 'take in a movie', we have to hold it in the depths of our eyes, and cannot do so – cannot make it stick – without the 'clothes pegs' which constitute our appreciation of that beautiful thing we call cinema.

A film which 'falls from your eyes' is one where you have to keep readjusting your retina, just as circus clowns keep pulling up their trousers. The tears it produces are fake tears, caused by conjunctivitis not emotion. And the anger it provokes is also fake, born of irritation not revolt. It is in this sense that bad films are fake films.

L'Amant (*The Lover*) is a film which falls from your eyes. As a production, it is somewhat less alarming than the campaign of intimidation which accompanied its launch, and it would merely inspire pity were it not for the realisation that with Annaud we now have the prototype – fully operational at last – of a new breed of film-maker: the 'post-film-maker', in other words, one who knows nothing of what cinema once knew.

But he didn't start yesterday. Annaud found his Road to Damascus a decade ago, when he had the truly blinding intuition that everything which had for so long been 'natural' in cinema – the fact that there were men and women, bodies and characters, emotions and experiences, *stories* in short – was destined to fall into a kind of 'dark continent' which henceforth we could only reach *from outside*, with the help of ever more rhetorical and consensual simulations (of which US 'reality shows' represent the televisual pits).

Annaud is thus the chief usherette who was present at the birth of humanity (*La Guerre du feu*) and its middle age (*The Name of the Rose*), at a young animal's introduction to life in the wild (*The Bear*) and a young girl's introduction to eroticism (*The Lover*). So it was that he put his stamp on several media events of the 1980s, years which – let us not forget – were inevitably marked by the regrettable revival of old mythologies in our televisual villages. Mythologies which needed a new aesthetic matrix (advertising and its kitsch imagery) and, eventually, a new kind of communicator, devoid of feeling (Annaud, for example).

For, unlike Besson and Beineix, who are more talented or are still consumed by the passion of cinema, Annaud has always made films in complete ignorance of the fact that there had *been* any cinema before him. By dint of imagining himself to be the guiding light shining on the first faltering steps of anything which moves, by dint of watching over the prehistory of our species and our origins as *Pithecanthropus Erectus*, Annaud forgot that there were others before him who had played with this marvellous device; with cinema and those clothes pegs which hold its images on our inflamed retinas.

To judge by the way *The Lover* has been promoted, it may well be that audiovisual barbarism has at last found its own Vandals. Will we ever convert them to Cinema? Who will save us from them? Will they put us to the sword? And who are 'we' anyway? Let's just say that 'we' are the fans of clothes-peg cinema, people who have the increasingly distinct feeling of being other, other than Vandals.

Annaud, too, isn't just anyone; he is the first non-cinephile robot in the history of cinema. In the manual he mugged up in the space capsule which carried him through time to us, 'The Human Species in Twenty Storyboards', he read that cinema consisted of 'telling a story in pictures'. And one feels that he will never get beyond that particular cliché, that he will always know what cinema should look like, that it should be a 'summary' of human feeling and human behaviour. But that is indeed all he knows: his knowledge is that of the robot who doesn't know that he doesn't know everything.

He doesn't know, for example, that there are things which you see without really seeing them, and others which stare you in the face, but don't reflect any real experience; that there are moments when you must not make too much noise; that there are things which are omnipresent but insignificant, and others which are absent but powerful; that there are collective lies and partial truths – in short, that there are experiences which cinema sometimes finds it hard to approach (yet its dignity lies in the attempt). This is hardly surprising. It wasn't in the manual, because the manual – well produced though it was – was written by advertisers, during the 1980s.

Let us go back to the cinema, to our retinas and clothes pegs. Why does this film fall from our eyes? Because something essential – essential to cinema – has disappeared. Cinema has always depended on a simple fact: the knowledge that something communicates itself from one frame to the next, one image to the next, one moment to the next, one shot to the next, and that these all end up constituting a logical and entangled fabric, full of twisted threads; one where the viewer doesn't have to be continuously 'grabbed' in order to be implicated, involved, delighted and caught up in new configurations of space-time. That is why all the great manipulators of the audience – from Hitchcock to Tati, from Chaplin to Leone – have also been great logicians, who gambled on the pride which we had every right to feel – as viewers – when we had learned to see, to deduce, to imagine, on the basis of the rebus they offered us.

That pride vanished some time ago, to be replaced by mere enjoyment of the effects of 'filmed cinema'. It is undoubtedly to *faire cinéma* – to put on a show – in the manner of all the *parvenus* who seem to have acquired *droit de seigneur* over the entire world – to clothe himself in the cheap literary finery of a story signed 'Marguerite Duras' (a story where essentially there is nothing but moisture, heat haze, nervous flux and contagious sensuality), that Annaud accepted the very costly challenge of giving 'his' interpretation of a best-selling colonial novel. Which only makes all the more obvious the way that, for him, the manufacture of images has replaced cinema.

Let us take an example. Let us take a single bad cut (there are quite a few in *The Lover*). If my memory serves me well (and I have no intention of seeing the film again to check), the first thing we see of the lover is one of his shoes. The shoe, extremely fashionable and expensive, is pointed towards the viewer, rather like a face, in a long, vacant close-up. A close-up which lasts long enough for the viewer to reach the following conclusion: these shoes don't come from Dolcis and the feet which are wearing them aren't just any old feet. And, indeed, in the following image we see the elegant, finely dressed form of the Chinese lover straightening out before us as he steps from his luxury car. The problem is that between the way the shoe is positioned in relation to the viewer and the movement of the actor's body there is, dare I say it, a degree of awkwardness, of clumsiness, which results in the image 'falling from the eyes' for lack of clothes peg. In short, the tragedy of the bad cut.

Of course, I appreciate that a bad cut isn't a crime and doesn't shock anyone. But this time it's not because – as in the days of *A bout de souffle* – cinema is trying to overturn the dusty old rules which say 'how' one should cut. No, it's because Annaud's work no longer has *anything at all* to do with memory, sequence, time, montage. This is cinema where there is no communication, because everything is communicated. The shoe is an item from the script which has turned into a surreptitious little advert for an attractive, marketable object, a kind of Indochinese Bally, just like all the other promotional objects in the film, from the virgin car to the designer girl.

But readers will point out, of course, that the vast majority of the press and television has endorsed the thing. That is true, unfortunately. And, they will add, the film is a success and no one has complained. Only too true. So it is now that I must show myself worthy of this publication and introduce someone very important to the life and death of films: nothing less than the viewer. Let us return – I'm afraid we must – to our shoe.

For if the scene is so long, so badly cut and so insulting to the viewer's intelligence, it is not only because Annaud has a poor notion of his audience's critical faculties, it is also because he assembles his 'film' as a series of orphan images, images which must, *one by one*, be seen, recognised and, so to speak, *ticked off* by the spectator-consumer.

In this aesthetic, an image never finds its sequel, its mystery or its elucidation in another, more or less contiguous image. Henceforth, images are to be 'scanned' twice, once by the post-film-maker who signs them and once by the post-public who endorses them. They are only presented to the audience (and no longer articulated with other elements in the film) as a kind of preview, a run-through of *visuals*, not the sharing of a *vision*. ('You saw nothing in Cholon, nothing.') [Cholon is the Saigon suburb in which *The Lover* is set. The reference is to *Hiroshima mon amour*: 'Tu n'as rien vu à Hiroshima, rien.'] The images queue up on a waiting list, to be submitted for public approval, for instant endorsement, for God knows what kind of mark of confidence.

Let us be serious. Many people have talked about contemporary individualism and its paradoxes. One of these paradoxes is nothing less than a certain eradication of taste among a public who are more adult, that is, better informed, less naive, better off, easily bored, happily cruising among the various lifeless luxuries which the market tosses in their direction. These spectators, proud of their independence and well aware of their power, nonetheless have to face the rather comic obligation to adopt as 'theirs' all the latest clichés and the conformism of their social group, with the proviso that they can feel they are living and 'organising' these on *their own behalf.*

And nothing makes them angrier than pointing out that, for all their individuality, their independence, their refusal to follow fashions and formulae, they are still trotting out the same stunningly conformist idiocies as their closest neighbours. Which is why film critics, and indeed critics in general, for the simple reason that they dislike clichés and off-the-peg ideas, are an endangered species. In a world where the *personal appropriation of clichés* is a condition for the spread of cultural tourism, that's hardly surprising.

What, then, is this close-up of the Chinese shoe? Nothing less than a cry. The shoe cries out to be recognised, recognised in its advertising essence as solitary shoe, in its radical *shoeness* (Heidegger's celebrated *Schuhekeit*). It cries out that it means something. It cries out that it's been selected by Annaud for the spectator, in the same way as bingo numbers are called out for players to cross of their cards. Too bad for anyone accustomed to cinema, who waits impatiently for the next scene to follow, irritated by the way this film falls from his eyes. For there is no scene to follow, merely another image which in turn will demand approval and authentication by the spectator.

What was bound to happen has happened. From now on the spectator-consumer is confronted by an image *which resembles him*, which, like him, proclaims it has no need of others (other images, but also sound and duration) in order to create social and domestic kitsch (in this case, a kind of *Emmanuelle* with a bit of literary gloss).

The result, of course, is lamentable. For having become master of all he surveys in a film which is communicated to him image by image, the spectator is trapped by his own feeble status as consumer-decoder. He hasn't time to understand anything which he didn't already 'know' – which leaves him with nothing, with the already seen or the scarcely seen at all, with ads and logos, visuals and kitsch, in short, with banalities and platitudes.

How utterly pointless it was for Annaud to have shot the film in the real Vietnam. Hadn't the unfortunate man already ensured there was no danger of his camera accidentally recording a few seconds of unprocessed reality? But in an age of synthetic images and synthetic emotions, the chances of an accidental encounter with reality are remote indeed.

UNSETTLING MEMORIES

Ginette Vincendeau

As seen from Britain, *La Reine Margot*, *Le Colonel Chabert* and *D'Artagnan's Daughter* form part of the growing and (for some) tediously predictable body of costume dramas known as 'heritage' cinema. This term has gained currency on account of the films' opulent re-creation of the past and use of canonical literature, and by analogy with the heritage industry (retro-fashion, theme parks and so on). To this genre also belong such films as *Jean de Florette*, *Howards End*, *Cyrano de Bergerac* and *Babette's Feast*, premiered, typically, at the Curzon Mayfair cinema in London (as were *Margot* and *Chabert*) and targeting a middle-class and 'middlebrow' audience. Being among the few European films to penetrate the world market, they increasingly define European/French cinema as an international luxury product with high audience appeal (if low critical status).

But while *Margot*, *Chabert* and *D'Artagnan's Daughter* fit such a genre, their concentration on precise periods, events and/or characters from French history suggests quite a separate category. Indeed, what has dominated French heritage films over the past fifteen years is neither idyllic rurality (despite *Jean de Florette* and a few others) nor the celebration of grand-bourgeois domesticity and public school rituals in the British tradition, but a revisiting of history; for example, the Revolution and its aftermath (*Danton*, *Chouans!*, *La Révolution française I* and *II*, *Chabert*). World War II and the German occupation have also been a rich field, as well as the colonial past (this in common with Britain). This historical focus draws on a rich French filmic tradition which includes such auteur films as Abel Gance's *Napoléon*, Raymond Bernard's *Les Misérables* and Jean Renoir's *La Marseillaise*, but also dozens of melodramas, erotico-romantic comedies and swashbucklers. Its two golden eras were the German occupation and the 1950s 'tradition of quality': a version of *Chabert* was made in 1943 starring Raimu; a version of *Margot* in 1954, with Jeanne Moreau. Nineteenth-century historical literature is clearly central to these films: Alexandre Dumas (*père*) and Balzac, together with Victor Hugo, Eugène Sue, Paul Féval and Edmond Rostand.

Balzac, who considered himself 'more a historian than a novelist', published *Chabert* in February–March 1832; Dumas' *Margot* was published in instalments (*feuilletons*) in La Presse in 1845, and staged in February 1847 at Dumas' own Théâtre Historique, with performances running from 6.30 p.m. to 3 a.m.(!). His *Les Trois Mousquetaires* and sequel *Vingt Ans après* (to which *D'Artagnan's Daughter* is a further, 'imaginary' sequel) came out in 1844 and 1845. All these appeared under the July Monarchy (1830–1848), a period which witnessed an explosion in historiography, libraries and museums, and a parallel development of the popular historical novel linked to both new press freedom and the fashion for Walter Scott. Equally, this revisiting of the past was part of a collective stocktaking and renegotiation of national identity in the aftermath of the Revolution and Empire. The contemporary recourse in films to Balzac's and Dumas' mediations of the past must also be seen in the light of struggles over French national identity, which a conflation of factors are destabilising: the passing of the last great populist leader (de Gaulle), the end of the *trente glorieuses* years of economic boom, the demise of the colonial empire and the rise of multiculturalism. While battles rage over national identity in the political arena (among them the rise of the National Front), the present concentration on historical fictions begs the question of how representations of history are mobilised in films to engage with it.

Margot, *Chabert* and *D'Artagnan's Daughter* are stylistically different: respectively, an auteur-inflected rewriting of Dumas (Patrice Chéreau the auteur), a classic Balzac adaptation directed by Yves Angelo (ex-cinematographer on such heritage classics as *Tous les matins du monde*) and Bertrand Tavernier's pastiche of Dumas swashbucklers. But they share an awareness of their antecedents, as do industry and audience: 1994 saw the video release of the 1943 *Chabert* and the 1954 *Margot*, as well as reissues of Dumas'; *Margot* and Balzac's *Chabert* in many paperback editions, some available in supermarkets for as little as FF10 (£1), the latter neatly timed for the beginning of the school term; indeed, a veritable Margot industry was fed by new or reissued biographies of Marguerite de Valois, debates in the press and television chat shows. The genre is of course particularly conducive to such industry practices, but their appearance also emphasises the place of fictional representation within a constellation of historical knowledge, which mixes the learned and the popular, the school manual with the romantic novel, the specialist historical magazine with cartoons (the 'famous love affairs of French history' kind): it's a circulation of what might be called 'memories of history'. As *Cahiers du cinéma* famously noted, all historical films are set in the 'future perfect' tense, setting up questions the spectator already knows the answers to: thus Catherine de Medici in *Margot* consults a horoscope about her three sons, Mazarin in *D'Artagnan's Daughter* mutters 'I forgot to tell [Louis XIV] not to revoke the Edict of Nantes,' (he did, in 1685), and the triumph of the ultra-aristocrats in *Chabert* is known to be short-lived. While this trope reinforces existing myths rather than questioning them, it is also one of the pleasures of such films, throwing spectators back to childhood history books and literature.

Plots and poisonings

Where Balzac saw himself as a historian, Dumas was candid about authenticity's poverty before romance and drama. Yet his choice of periods was not accidental. The end of the Valois dynasty (1589) was conveniently eventful for a writer (plots, curses, mysterious deaths); it was also a transitional era, allowing for dramatic contrasts between 'medieval' practices – massacres, superstition, poisonings – and the refinement of the Renaissance, displayed in costumes, music and parades. The late sixteenth century (*Margot*) and early to mid-seventeenth century (*D'Artagnan*) also provided wars of religion and other conflicts (with rulers struggling to hold the country together), presaging the deep splits in French society which surfaced, for example, during the Revolution and the German occupation. It is perhaps not surprising that the 1954 *Margot*, made when the traumatic divisions of the Vichy period were most repressed, gives the St Barthélémy massacre of the Huguenots nine minutes of screen time and treats it almost as a jolly romp. Chéreau, by comparison, greatly expands the massacre and spreads violence throughout the film, reinforced by claustrophobic *mise-en-scène* and intensely physical performances. Parallels are made with contemporary religious wars (Bosnia) and with the Holocaust, with images of bodies thrown into a mass grave, images with an added resonance at a time when the French role in the Holocaust is at last being exposed. Interestingly, however, Chéreau retains the demonisation of Italians common to many earlier French historical films set during this period. His poison-maker René le Florentin may not speak with the fake Italian accent his 1954 counterpart had, but the characterisation of Catherine de Medici as evil black widow and perverted mother lurking behind pillars is stupefying. She is played magnificently, by Virna Lisi in 1994 and Françoise Rosay in 1954, but these roles belong in a tradition combining hatred of powerful women and of foreigners (as do images of the 'Austrian' Marie-Antoinette in countless Revolution dramas).

Chabert begins in 1817, as the Restoration ultra-aristocrats are busy reclaiming their *ancien régime* privileges. The new *Chabert* greatly develops the contrast between this new élite (an amalgam of old aristocracy and new money) and the poor. At the same time, it reinforces the consensual narrative resolution of the original text. Class divisions are bridged in the narrative by the new professional bourgeoisie (Derville, the excellent Fabrice Luchini), and transcended symbolically by Chabert, the hero of the Napoleonic army who bypasses the class struggle instead of fighting it. The '10,000' dead of the French army are embodied in *Chabert*'s 'unknown soldier', a destitute on the high moral ground who is reborn to claim the imperial war as revolutionary heritage. A foundling raised to the ranks of *noblesse d'empire*, Chabert also represents the meritocracy that was to build Republican France (comparable to *Les Misérables'* Jean Valjean). His courage is, as he puts it, his 'only patrimony'. But in actual fact, his *memory* is his patrimony, the memory that enables him to claim the

positive legacy of the Revolution and Empire, one that is inscribed in law. Their evil
legacy on the other hand is concentrated (by book and films) in the new class,
represented by the Comtesse Ferraud. Greedy for money, she is, as we soon learn,
tainted by her past as a prostitute, her identity thus shifting from social to sexual. The
1994 *Chabert* chooses to punish her more than Balzac does (in his *oeuvre* she continues
a successful social life in several novels); it adds a seduction of Ferraud to parallel that
of Chabert, as well as the scene where Derville delivers her comeuppance.

Sexual stereotyping is more overt in Dumas, with wicked ladies and evil queen
mothers surrounding the male heroes. *D'Artagnan's Daughter*, this modern sequel, pits
the ageing Musketeers – who therefore have a past – against a new 'Lady in Red', an
evil counterpart to D'Artagnan's young daughter (Sophie Marceau). On the one hand,
this places the story within the classic French father-daughter narrative, one which
director Tavernier has himself reworked (*La Passion Béatrice, Daddy Nostalgie*); on the
other, it reinforces the pattern whereby male identity is (however fancifully)
historical, and female identity sexual. In this 'gendering' of popular history, Margot
has been a particularly interesting case. A historically marginal personality, she is
given prominence through her (vastly exaggerated) romantic and sexual life over her
actual political ambitions and literary achievements. Dumas did raise her profile (she
barely appears in history books), but he did so by sexualising her, starting with her
name (Margot, as opposed to Marguerite, implying familiarity, connoting naive
femininity: in France, 'to make Margot cry' is a derogatory description of melodrama).
The 1954 Margot is a pert heroine of classical comedy; she visits her lover La Môle as
a masked courtesan and appears coyly naked (the use of a body double for Moreau was
much commented upon). Chéreau's invention of a scene where Margot cruises the
streets after her unconsummated wedding night is more explicit, though hardly
historical, and further reinforces Margot's sexual stereotyping. Isabelle Adjani's
mixture of intensity, glamour and fragility creates a highly charged Margot whose
antecedents are to be found in her own title roles in *The Story of Adèle H* and *Camille
Claudel*, rather than in the 1954 *Margot*. As a woman desired by rival men, she distantly
evokes Arletty's Garance in *Les Enfants du paradis*, an embodiment of France caught
between warring factions. If Margot's mother is demonised for entering the political
arena, Margot is elevated to the status of a national symbol (a Marianne *avant-la-lettre*)
at the price of staying out of it. Where Chabert's saintliness emerges from historical
circumstances, Margot's transcends them (the actual Marguerite de Valois unsuccessfully manoeuvred to establish a power base for herself, first with her brothers, then
her husband).

Heritage stars

As well as engaging with popular historical myths, and inserting themselves in
literary and filmic traditions, *Margot, Chabert* and *D'Artagnan* are heritage products in
an industrial sense. Their high budgets and production values (decors and costumes
are magnificent in all three), their prestige producers (Claude Berri at Renn
Productions, Jean-Louis Livi), directors (Patrice Chéreau, Bertrand Tavernier), literary
sources and stars all form part of a strategy to fight an industrial battle (against
Hollywood) and an aesthetic one (against television). Unlike auteur cinema, which

opposes Hollywood in terms of *mise-en-scène* and subject matter, the French heritage film takes a two-pronged line of attack, adopting Hollywood-style 'super-production' values while establishing its difference through historical subject matter and (not negligibly) language. At the same time, the recourse to canonical writers and historical subjects allows these Franco-centric films to address audiences both at home and internationally, by turning the house of Valois (and the *ancien régime* generally) into easily graspable French (or even European) myths.

Key to this strategy are the stars, who must map their existing personas onto fully formed (actual or fictional) identities. The historical film solves this difficulty by multiplying performance opportunities. Balzac makes Derville exclaim, after hearing Chabert's confession, 'I... have seen the most skilful actor of our time.' With Chabert played by Raimu in 1943 and Depardieu in 1994, it is easy to see why both films kept these lines in and made the confession a virtuoso display (both monologues are shot in long *plans-séquences*; especially long in the 1994 film). Both draw on the stars' personas as populist heroes (though the 'calligraphic' 1943 film, with strong lighting effects and unusual camera angles, turns the earthy Raimu into a spooky Chabert). Depardieu by 1994 has become the male 'national' star of heritage cinema, with *Danton, Jean de Florette, Cyrano de Bergerac* and *Chabert.* While such parts are clearly decided upon with Depardieu in mind, his success as a star is directly linked to his appropriateness to a specifically French literary canon. In all these films he plays 'larger than life' men-of-the-people who have climbed the social ladder while retaining 'popular' roots, chiming with his extra-cinematic identity. In the case of *Germinal,* he stressed his adequacy for the part of Maheu in terms of his own origins. His heritage roles are particularly well served by his performance style, a mixture of theatricality and naturalism, echoing the genre itself.

Though *Margot* also combines theatricality with naturalism, symbolised by the ravishing but soiled costumes, Adjani's Margot is rarely touched by the ambient squalor, except when her magnificent dresses absorb the blood of La Môle, or of her brother Charles IX. Close-ups emphasise the milky opalescence of her face, her glittering jewels, bare shoulders and *décolletés*. Despite Adjani's considerable talent for expressing intense passion, her visual treatment duplicates her narrative isolation from the surrounding maelstrom: she is the star among the actors (as her couture look isolated her from the grime of the metro in *Subway*). Adjani recently – astutely – said that she had 'always been such a French product'; here her 'French' image of beauty and glamour, though central to *Margot*'s appeal, collides oddly with the overall project.

A classic criticism of historical and heritage films is that they turn away from a difficult present in order to comfort their audience with a rosy picture of the past. But neither *Margot* nor *Chabert* present a particularly rosy picture. *Chabert* celebrates the memory of Napoleonic glory, but represents an era which has forgotten it; its general tone is one of doubt and suspicion. Violence in *Margot* permeates even the wedding festivities. Both films' dominant colour schemes are sombre. Divisions among the French come to the fore – unlike, for example, in *Cyrano de Bergerac* (written by Rostand in the more chauvinistic mood of the new Third Republic). *D'Artagnan's Daughter*'s ageing, tired heroes eventually whip up the enthusiasm to reinhabit their younger selves, but the first part of the film is rather downbeat. Yet these films remain immensely pleasurable, for their spectacular qualities and energy, but also for their evocation of the past, however traumatic that past was. It may be that, like Chabert, memory itself is all we have left as patrimony.

A HUNGRY EYE

Griselda Pollock

There is an unusually intense interaction between cinema and the art world in play at the moment. Opening in September in the United Kingdom, John Maybury's *Love Is the Devil* charts the relationship between Francis Bacon (1909–92) and his muse and model George Dyer, portraying the artist as a social sadist and sexual masochist. Agnès Merlet's *Artemisia* gives a version of an affair between Italian artist Artemisia Gentileschi (1593–1652) and her one-time teacher Agostino Tassi. Both films view their subjects through the lens of sex and sexuality; both raise issues about the representation of high art within popular culture. Yet it is *Artemisia* – on the surface a more conventional film given its heterosexual framework and costume-drama setting – that has generated a huge controversy, raising questions about the complex relationship between historical truth and story-telling, and in particular about the stories in popular circulation concerning the woman as artist.

At the film's New York premiere on 28 April 1998, feminist writer Gloria Steinem circulated a fact sheet prepared in collaboration with art historian Mary Garrard, who has written the major feminist analysis of Gentileschi. This led Miramax to withdraw the claim that the film is a 'true story' from a poster that still describes its heroine as 'sexy', 'provocative' and 'defiant'. A feminist art-history Internet site invites contributors to apply for copies of the fact sheet – entitled 'Now You've Seen the Film, Meet the Real Artemisia Gentileschi' – and to picket screenings. There has also been a New York symposium on the controversy, addressed by Garrard and Simon Schama, an exhibition of paintings by the film's major characters (Artemisia Gentileschi, her father Orazio, and Agostino Tassi) at the Richard L. Feigen Gallery, and in July Sotheby's New York auctioned one of Gentileschi's presumed self-portraits.

Controversy is no stranger to this artist whose place in modern art history has survived because of the notoriety of her life, rather than an aesthetic appreciation of her work. While Gentileschi herself has been described by two leading modern scholars as a 'lascivious and precocious girl', her dramatic, characterful images of such women as Susanna, Judith, Lucretia, Cleopatra and Bathsheba have been called 'animalistic', 'buxom' and 'sullen'.

The reason for such reactions is sex and sexism. In May 1611, Gentileschi was raped by Agostino Tassi, a minor sea painter apparently hired by her father, Orazio, to teach her perspective (a skill she hardly ever used in her closed, single-figure compositions). In March 1612, Orazio brought a suit against Tassi for injury and damage, resulting in a lengthy trial during which Gentileschi was tortured by the sibille method: fine cords wound around the fingers and progressively tightened. Tassi – also accused of the murder of his wife and incest with his sister-in-law – was never convicted and was imprisoned for only eight months. The trial (of which we have a transcript) was a sordid business in which Tassi alleged that Gentileschi was sexually active before and after his contact with her. She argued he had promised marriage after the rape. Rape, then as now, was classified as non-consensual sexual assault, but it was also used as a technical crime to force marriage or claim damages when a socially vulnerable woman was abused by a higher-class man. There is as yet no scholarly consensus on what happened between Gentileschi and Tassi, for there is evidence of a continuing sexual relationship. But it is certainly not possible to derive from the records a simple love story. Gentileschi's distressing testimony describes a violent rape and her account unsurprisingly exhibits an obsessive recall of every detail, including the excessive pain and her violent struggle, when she scratched Tassi's face and penis in her attempts to fight him off.

Merlet's film does not follow the transcript of the trial. Instead, she imagines a blossoming relationship in which the artistic frankness of the young Artemisia (Valentina Cervi) leads Tassi (Miki Manojlovic) to think she is already sexually active. In a moment of admittedly sudden and forceful sexual desire, he makes love to her – an act interrupted by the violent pain of her defloration. Confused and distressed, Artemisia hurries away. But she is subsequently shown soliciting his sexual touch in scenes of continuing intimacy at his studio – whereas all the trial documents stress that Tassi 'invaded' her domestic and artistic space with the collusion of the housekeeper, Donna Tuzia (Brigitte Catillon).

The sexual scandal, however, clung to Gentileschi's reputation, fixing her image as that of a *femme fatale* bent on sexual revenge. This image is then read into her dramatic representations – for instance of the Judith and Holofernes theme (a young Jewish widow deceives an ageing enemy general by apparently going over to his camp where, after a drunken dinner party intended for her seduction, she decapitates him and returns triumphantly with his head to her besieged hometown, causing his army to scatter in terror) – so Gentileschi herself is identified with the murderously sexy Judith. The conflation of an artist's biography and works of art functions very differently depending on whether the artist is a man or a woman. *His* art appears to give us access to the mystery of genius; *hers* merely confirms the pathology of the feminine, saturated by her sex, of which she becomes both emblem and symptom. And while a female artist's paintings are read with the knowledge of her 'deviant' femininity firmly in mind, her biography is usually twisted to hinge on a powerfully sexual male figure: think of Bruno Nuytten's film *Camille Claudel* (1988), where the tragedy of a major sculptor sectioned in her forties by her family and violently denied access to her art for the remaining thirty years of her life is reduced to the story of a young and beautiful woman (Isabelle Adjani) driven mad by her passion for and rejection by the robust genius Rodin (Gérard Depardieu), for whom she modelled in the nude. It is within this context that feminists have reclaimed Artemisia Gentileschi as a heroic figure, reinterpreting the creative dynamics between her gender, her art and her sexuality within the historical framework of seventeenth-century aesthetics and patronage. So there is widespread feminist outrage at Merlet's film – and not only because it seems to be saying that Artemisia was in love with her rapist. That's what I'd heard before I saw the film.

Now I'm not sure. Merlet has used the framework of this historical story to imagine a passionate professional and sexual relationship between a young artist and her teacher which is blocked by the condemnation of her father (Michel Serrault) and of society. Out of the pain of enforced separation, Artemisia leaves Rome and her father, and matures into the great artist she became. The film's premise is that the young woman's sexuality was part of her artistic creativity – but it's a scenario that founders on the historical reality of the inequities of gender embodied in contemporary institutions: the convent, the papacy, the academy, the law. Merlet recognises in Gentileschi's paintings a powerful sensuality, a richness of colour, a density of forms, a fleshiness that cry out for serious analysis and for an explanation of how she learned to paint the body when she was forbidden by Catholic convention to see her own body, let alone to study the male nude. So she shows Artemisia using sex to persuade a working-class male friend to strip so she can paint his naked torso and genitals, when in fact Gentileschi mostly painted women – single women whose sexuality, even lives, were threatened by men: Lucretia, the suicidal rape victim; Susanna, victim of sexual harassment to the point of a death sentence; Cleopatra, a great queen dying to save herself from the humiliation of being led in captive triumph to Rome.

Merlet's film does not accord with the records at any level. Artemisia is shown in 1610 painting a self-portrait that was produced when she was a mature woman in 1630. She is depicted as painting one of her most famous compositions of Judith and Holofernes using Tassi as a model for Holofernes when the painting (1612) postdates the trial and his imprisonment. But *Artemisia* cannot be dismissed simply on the basis of the licence it takes with chronology. It was never intended as art history. Rather, it has to be assessed in relation to cinema's mostly unhappy history of the artist's biopic – the point where ideologies of biography and the creative individual collide with the demands of fictional narrative cinema.

Films about artists (mostly men to date) are the site of a curious encounter between popular culture and its image of high art – symbolised by the personification of the artist – told from the point of view of intellectually sophisticated directors working in popular cultural forms: see painter turned Hollywood director Vincente Minnelli's *An American in Paris* (1951), *The Band Wagon* (1953) and *Lust for Life* (1956). The artist, like the writer or the musician, functions as the embodiment of an idea of creativity that renders the life significant. By making a narrative picture of this life, a biopic, the film promises to reveal to us the magical nature of genius. There is a long history of treating the artist or poet as a figure apart – melancholy, suicidal, mad, asocial. But in modern times – perhaps as a result of the increasing remoteness of artistic practice from the public in general – the artist has become paradigmatic of the pathology of creativity. Represented as a hysterical figure of difference and marginality, or tragically feminised (western society's sacrificial victim, a Christ figure), the artist can also embody a creativity born of masculine sexuality unfettered by the restraints of bourgeois ideology (Picasso) and become a heroic figure of resistance to social order like the unassimilable cowboy or wild man.

Gauguin (Albert Lewin's *The Moon and Sixpence*, 1942), Toulouse-Lautrec (John Huston's *Moulin Rouge*, 1953), Van Gogh (Minnelli's *Lust for Life*, 1956), Michelangelo (Carol Reed's *The Agony and the Ecstasy*, 1965) and Picasso (James Ivory's *Surviving Picasso*, 1996) have all been the subjects of Hollywood biopics that reveal the mythic function of the artist in twentieth-century popular culture. And though *Artemisia* is a product of European art cinema rather than Hollywood commercialism, its image of art and the artist borrows Hollywood's terms. Derek Jarman's *Caravaggio* (1986) stands completely apart as a film made by a painter as a subliminal self-portrait. Here, marginality is made political through the film-maker's identification with the subcultural status of the seventeenth-century homosexual artist, while the conventions of the biopic are subverted through the use of contemporary dress and mannerisms in elaborately staged compositions that echo the style of the paintings.

Consciously arty but without Jarman's ironic self-reflexivity, Merlet's film opens with an extreme close-up of an eye as a voice whispers a description of fragments of male nudes from Michelangelo's *Last Judgement*. Thus are we introduced to the concept of the artist as a hungry eye, desiring to see, to know, to participate in the jumble of expressively naked bodies and the mysteries of representation. The scene is a chapel in a convent and the eye belongs to a young girl who is peering through her hands folded at prayer towards the mannerist assemblage of naked men signifying this violent moment in Christian mythology. The girl steals a candle from the chapel and later that night uses its light and a mirror to examine and sketch her own naked body. Human anatomy was the grammar of seventeenth-century painting: without a knowledge of anatomy, the rhetoric of gesture and expression through which stories were told, ideas conveyed and dramas evoked was inaccessible. Women were forbidden this knowledge by the papacy and excluded from the academies. So how else would Gentileschi have gained a mastery of this fundamental element of her art if not through clandestine examination of her own body? But in the cinema the viewer watches her undress to learn this – and thus the gendered hierarchy of viewing and viewed is returned to the conventional cinematic order that the scene itself is denying through the political transgression of this artist–woman's curiosity.

Removed from the convent by her father, who realises that 'she is the daughter of a painter and has much to learn, but not here', Artemisia works in his studio, hungry for all she needs to know, but cannot access because of her sex. The film shows her on an outing catching sight of a couple making love, whom she watches with fascinated attention, later laying her own body in the imprint of their coupling in the sand and miming its gestures while the camera, of course, now watches her. It is this repeated dislocation (of which the film-maker seems sublimely unconscious) between woman-as-eye and woman-as-seen, fantasising sexual receptivity, that ultimately undoes the potential covenant between Gentileschi's historical negotiation of regimes of representation and contemporary feminist interventions in cultural languages.

With this scene. Artemisia as artist as hungry eye is sexualised for the first time. Narrative logic will take her into a passionate love affair with Tassi, whose arrival in Rome is defined by two scenes: one where Artemisia watches him paint on the beach using a perspective frame and a second where she sneaks up to his house at night and peers in at the licentious sexual revels for which he was notorious. These two moments – of Artemisia as aspiring artist and as sexually curious adolescent – converge in the critical scene where, between bouts of lovemaking, she is shown painting Tassi as Holofernes through his perspective frame in the room where the orgy took place.

The story of Judith and Holofernes has fascinated male writers down the ages, though in modern times Judith's actions have been attributed not to political and religious motives, but to some ambiguity in her sexuality. Was she a virgin who killed her seducer out of guilt (Ernst Hebbel)? Was she a frigid girl so ambitious for glory that out of love for her Holofernes offered himself to her (Henry Bernstein)? Did she yield to Holofernes' compelling ardour before again recovering her political purpose (Giraudoux)? Despite the original story's insistence on a carefully plotted trap, modern writers return repeatedly to the idea that sexual desire was Judith's undoing and she killed out of revenge for having been made to feel that desire.

Merlet's film – the tale of an ambitious and sensual young woman who entrances a dissolute older man who sacrifices himself for love of her – belongs in the long history of western meditations on and abuses of the story. Here the rape trial is purely the result of Orazio's rage and jealousy, and Tassi confesses to save Artemisia's hands – her painting hands – from the permanent mutilation of the thumbscrew torture. In the historical trial, Gentileschi, accused by Tassi of sexual promiscuity, was tortured because she insisted she was raped; in the film she is tortured because she refutes the charge.

In his appraisal of Gentileschi's 1612 painting of Judith and Holofernes, Roland Barthes argues that any painting 'checkmates' interpretation, suspending its viewers within a range of possible meanings of an event that never quite takes place. The monumentalisation of bodies captured permanently 'in the act' generates a tumult of potential resonances within each viewer and for each period. But here cinema's relentless narrativity situates the moment of the painting's coming-into-being within a story, making it a decodable reflection of the artist's life and the key to the plot that surrounds it.

For my money, Gentileschi's painting of Judith and Holofernes has nothing to do with her life experience. It was a popular and much commissioned subject, the major trope of sex and violence for the Baroque era, and had been painted by both her father and her major artistic reference: Caravaggio. What is being so calculatedly decapitated here is the art of these artistic 'fathers' in an act of aesthetic space-clearing and self-definition as a painter among painters, but 'in the feminine'. Gentileschi borrows the heroic mould of the political conspirator Judith to define, within the world of public representation, a figure of identification for woman as self-creating artist. Of course, mine is just a different story and no more 'true' than any of the others – but it is explicitly shaped by a feminist morality that intends to undermine popular cultural notions within which it has become impossible to figure the terms woman and artist outside the tropes of sex and death.

Like *Love Is the Devil*, *Artemisia* is not really a biopic, since there is no analysis of the impact of such events as the early death of the artist's mother, and no exploration of how she made a massively successful career in Italy and beyond after the horrors of the trial, of how she married and mothered several daughters who also became artists, or of how she negotiated with some of the major patrons of her time for the commissions on which she lived and which provided dowries for her daughters. No one wants to tell that story. And in ignorance of all the histories of women artists so faithfully recovered by feminist scholars, Merlet's film signs off with the mistaken phrase that Artemisia is considered the first woman painter in the history of art, again asserting that woman as artist is a rare exception, a belated oddity. So the myth is perpetuated in that huge audience of the cinema who will never be exposed to feminist revisionism: the myth that the terms woman and painter are rarely conjoined and only come together out of the heterosexual initiation of the vulnerable but precocious woman who opens herself to the big prick. We wait in vain for a film about women, sexuality and creativity that does not make the woman the sacrificial victim.

MASQUE OF THE LIVING DEAD

Jonathan Romney

For some film-makers, cinema's pressing mission at the end of the century is to provide a fitting memorial to its own past, to retrace its origins and commemorate its ghosts. But it could be thought equally pressing for cinema to perform a similar service for literary works. While film has traditionally congratulated itself on conferring immortality on the books it adapts, it also has a habit of erasing them – supplanting them, replacing their linguistic fluidity and potentiality with literalness and visual fixity. Instead of bringing books to life, film too often mummifies them.

So it's appropriate to end this century with an especially problematic and provocative literary adaptation: Raúl Ruiz's *Le Temps retrouvé* (*Time Regained*), based on the final volume of Marcel Proust's *A la recherche du temps perdu*. The encounter, in commercial terms, seems to have been hugely beneficial to both author and film-maker. Ruiz, long considered the most marginal of art-house directors, has experienced a modicum of mainstream acclaim since making *Trois vies et une seule mort* (*Three Lives and Only One Death*) (1996), a relatively accessible comedy with Marcello Mastroianni. But *Time Regained* has taken him almost into the mainstream itself: the film, budgeted at around FF 60 million, was prominent in the French box-office top ten in summer 1999, made its director a public figure and was even the subject of a glossy photo spread in the *New Yorker*. And whether or not it boosted Proust's actual readership, it ensured healthy sales for Gallimard's tie-in edition of the book.

It should be said that, for the novice reader, the final volume of the *Recherche* is no place to start, although – because of the vagaries of the Spanish translation – Ruiz as a boy in Chile allegedly read *Time Regained* first, then worked backwards. It is only in this final volume that the overall shape of the whole work becomes apparent: the narrator's lengthy account of a life seemingly wasted culminates in his realisation that he must now turn it into a novel. The decision of Ruiz and co-writer Gilles Taurand to adapt Proust end-first has fuelled unease, a common complaint being that magnificent as the film is, it can't mean much to anyone who hasn't read the original. But the film is less than transparent even to those who have read the *Recherche* end to end – it doesn't set about explaining who all its characters are, or their relationships to each other. Even though a scene at the beginning appears to offer an easy guide to the dramatis personae, it proves deceptive: the narrator passes photographs of his leading characters under a magnifying glass and obligingly reads their names aloud. But then this spoon-feeding method short-circuits itself as he plucks out an unknown figure and wonders aloud, 'What's he doing here?'

This question of recognition is a tricky one, because one criterion by which we tend to appraise literary adaptations is their degree of closeness to the text – their fidelity, as we say. That may be an especially misleading value in dealing with a book in which a key preoccupation of the jealous narrator is the very impossibility of establishing fidelity. With Proust, what exactly is there to be faithful to? Asked by *Cahiers du cinéma* whether his film would make sense to non-Proustians, Ruiz replied, 'No one has really read Proust. There's a strange effect of amnesia to it. Every time I read *Time Regained* – I must have read it twenty times – it's a different book. It's like a book of sand.'

Dream digressions

Ruiz could well be commenting indirectly on his own work. There's just such an 'effect of amnesia' with his films: striking and disquieting though they are, they don't easily register on the memory, precisely because of their fluidity. Some Ruiz films I can remember only imperfectly; from others I can't recall a single image; others I suspect I've dreamed. Watching Ruiz films, with their drifting, liquid logic, is like being in an artificial state of REM sleep, and, when they're over, you're not quite sure what you've seen or what you might retain.

Ruiz has adapted literature before, or at least appropriated texts as elastic armatures for his own fictions. He has used novels, from the popular to the arcane: from Stevenson's *Treasure Island* to Iranian writer Sadegh Hedayat's oneiric *The Blind Owl* (perhaps the most inherently Ruizian of all novels). From the theatre he has reworked Racine, Shakespeare, the absurdist playwright Arthur Adamov and, perhaps most successfully, the Spanish Golden Age drama *Life Is a Dream* – although Calderon's play ends up nested in a futuristic narrative about secret codes hidden in sci-fi 'B' movies.

But there's no precedent in Ruiz's work for what seems to all intents and purposes to be a legit adaptation of *Time Regained*. For the most part, the film adheres closely to the shape of the book, despite quintessentially Ruizian dream digressions. Visually it resembles a classic costume drama, handsomely photographed by Ricardo Aronovich using all the resources of realistic historical design and featuring a prestigious international cast. But since, with Ruiz, nothing is ever what it appears (it's practically an article of faith with him), we might call *Time Regained* a costume drama of a different kind: it's a Ruiz film in the costume of costume drama, heritage cinema as a form of travesty.

That shouldn't imply bad faith, for Ruiz's film is a serious, intrepid attempt to scale one of literature's magic mountains where so many have failed. Among cinema's legendary aborted projects are attempts on Proust by Joseph Losey (written by Harold Pinter) and by Visconti. Other film-makers have approached the author laterally, or via a fragment. Percy Adlon's *Céleste* (1981) is a chamber piece on the writer's last days as seen by his housekeeper and amanuensis Céleste Albaret. Volker Schlöndorff's *Un Amour de Swann* (*Swann in Love*) (1983) approached the challenge by using the only section of the *Recherche* that could plausibly be extracted as a self-contained, more or less naturalistic narrative – the flashback within the first volume *Swann's Way* to the love affair between socialite Swann and the elusive coquette Odette de Crécy, an episode which serves as founding myth for the narrator's subsequent agonies.

Living statues

Like Schlöndorff, Ruiz attempts only a chunk of the *Recherche*, but where *Swann in Love* is haunted by future events, *Time Regained* comes laden with the narrator's entire history. The last stretch of Proust's *roman-fleuve* is attended by the decrepit ghosts of the once-flourishing characters who inhabited the narrator's life. Bringing us into Proust by the exit, Ruiz invites us to read backwards, to follow the river back to its source. But where do we come in?

Confusingly, in mid-sentence, with the disorienting words, in voiceover: 'And then, everything changed.' We find ourselves in a bedroom: Proust in 1922, the year of his death, is dictating a passage of his text to Céleste (Mathilde Seigner). We see a haggard, supine Proust, but his voice (supplied by theatre and cinema director Patrice Chéreau) is detached. Neither of these Prousts is to be confused with the character sometimes referred to by critics as 'Marcel' – the book's hero and narrator played by Italian actor Marcello Mazzarella, an astonishing ringer for the writer himself. There's also a childhood incarnation of the narrator – 'Young Marcel' – and an adolescent Marcel. These blurred multiple layers of self find their first visual correlative in a *trompe l'oeil* effect: as the camera tracks slowly around Proust's room, the furnishings seem to swim, out of synch with the camera movement as though the fluidities of time and identity had leaked into space.

Particularly in the film's first half, Ruiz uses such seemingly creaky devices to suggest the plunges in and out of text and image, memory and the objective present. Solid walls reveal themselves as transparent scrims behind which we see other images and textures or ghostly watchers. The trees the narrator remembers from his youth are shaken by invisible stagehands. Such anti-illusionism draws our attention to a cinematic text being written very concretely in the space of the film set, just as Céleste's scratchy pen in the opening scene is concretely writing the words.

Archaic as it seems in the digital age, Ruiz is using a language appropriate to Proust's period, reminding us that the writer was a contemporary of Méliès – not to say of Max Linder, the foppish top-hatted comic whom Mazzarella also resembles. Ruiz's use of filters and optical effects comes into its own as an equivalent for the mechanisms Proust frequently evokes, as when he imagines men transformed by age as if by 'a tinted optical glass'. Though film is a metaphor absent from the *Recherche*, Ruiz expands on the key theme of the magic lantern – central to the narrator's childhood – to encompass the use of celluloid. After projecting lantern images on to the chalky faces of phantom onlookers, Ruiz's young Marcel becomes a projectionist, showing his adult self a newsreel of World War I as the two of them float suspended on cranes. Bringing Proust's biography into contact with the history of cinema, Ruiz is in a sense showing the writer what he was missing.

The film is perhaps less an adaptation than a masque – a performance of Proust not just in dramatic but also in musical, choreographed form. It's really a masque for the dead. In effect, Ruiz presents us with a gallery of living statues – famous literary characters given physical embodiment. A statue is an ambivalent thing: while it guarantees its subject immortality, it does so in calcified form, turning life into frozen dead matter – exactly what film adaptation tends to do to novels. Ruiz is well familiar with this ambivalent quality of un-deadness. His 1978 film *L'Hypothèse du tableau volé* (*The Hypothesis of the Stolen Painting*) is an exercise in *tableau vivant* – the art of bringing paintings to life by turning actors into statuary, using flesh as a bridge between two art forms. In *Time Regained*, he builds a similar bridge between novel and film, but constantly highlights the living death that is entailed. His characters are living statues – either statues to be animated or living beings prone to lapse at any moment into statue form in keeping with the Proustian dialectic of flowing time and the fixed moment. The narrator himself becomes a statue when he trips on a paving stone and is flung into a memory of a similar experience in Venice – fixed in a balletic pose, he is caught in frozen motion while a remembered Venice circulates around him. Elsewhere, the statues are more dead than alive. In what might seem a kitsch overstatement, a group of actors appear with hair and featureless faces whitened like marble. The theme of statuary reaches its apogee at the end of the film, when Marcel's several incarnations wander through Time seen as a subterranean catacomb with life/death masks protruding from the walls.

Such mineralisation is hardly Ruiz's invention. In the film's long centrepiece, based on the culminating episode of the *Recherche*, it is key. The narrator returns to Paris to attend a reception held by salon hostess Madame Verdurin (Marie-France Pisier). Late for the recital of the sonata by his beloved composer Vinteuil (pasticled by Ruiz's regular composer Jorge Arriagada as a mélange of Wagner, Saint-Saëns and César Franck), he waits in an ante-room where he experiences further flashes of involuntary memory. He then has a further insight into time's working as he realises that the young, vibrant characters he once knew are now considerably older – in some cases, decrepit caricatures of themselves. Among Proust's metaphors for ageing, mineral imagery is foremost; people become mineralised mummies of themselves.

In Ruiz's reception sequence, people as they really are – that is, in their older incarnations – appear fleetingly like phantasms while their more glamorous former selves predominate, as if plucked out of time. A simple but outrageous trick of choreography illustrates the effect. Madame Verdurin is revealed to be a doddering crone, but briefly slips behind a door and returns in the relatively youthful form of Marie-France Pisier. Here characters both are and are not themselves as identity undergoes slippages that can only be confusing for the viewer – just as they are for Proust's readers. The former Madame Verdurin has now become the Princesse de Guermantes, a prestigious title formerly carried by another character in the novel, who in turn is not to be confused with the real Duchesse de Guermantes, played here like a saturnine eagle by Edith Scob. The former Odette de Crécy (Catherine Deneuve), having become Madame Swann, is now Madame de Forcheville and so on. Identities shift as much as appearances.

How to make sense of this on screen? This is where the film takes advantage of the fact that it is a film and can provide us with recognisable star faces. It may be a cliché to point out that the aristocrats of Parisian salon society were the stars of their day, just as (and just as precariously as) film stars are the aristocracy of our own. But it's significant that, at the Verdurin reception, it should be a little-known actor who, as the narrator, walks into a living model of the star system, a shifting galaxy of role-playing figures.

Mummy complex

For followers of French cinema, Ruiz's casting itself becomes an illustration of time passing. Marie-France Pisier is far from the venerable dowager her character becomes, but her face already marks the distance from the skittish love object she played in Truffaut's Antoine Doinel films of the 1960s. Dominique Labourier as Madame Cottard is barely recognisable as the muscular investigator of Rivette's 1974 *Céline and Julie Go Boating*. The most striking example of time's effect is the casting of Melvil Poupaud as the Prince de Foix: a child actor introduced by Ruiz in his 1983 *City of Pirates*, Poupaud is now an adult star whom audiences have watched grow up.

Older figures seem like emissaries from a mythical past – for instance, director and novelist Alain Robbe-Grillet, whose name now belongs to a bygone literary era almost as much as that of the diarist Goncourt whom he plays in flashback. The casting of Edith Scob as the Duchesse de Guermantes can't help evoking Georges Franju's *Eyes without a Face* (1960), a proto-Ruizian poetic 'B' movie in which Scob's own features were concealed under an expressionless alabaster mask. Today, Scob's grandly patrician face with its piercing eyes and ancient aquiline beauty could be that mask, infused with its own slow maturing.

There are, however, grounds for controversy in the casting – though, oddly enough, not in the choice of John Malkovich as Charlus. Malkovich is mannered, of course, but so is his character, a homosexual aesthete and social provocateur who never stops performing. Charlus is both of the aristocratic world and outside it – like Malkovich, he is a mainstream figure who also crosses into the marginal underworld. Where Malkovich moonlights in European art cinema (Ruiz, Manoel de Oliveira), Charlus haunts the demi-monde of homosexual brothels – as in the sequence where the voyeuristic narrator's business with a chair illustrates the slapstick elements that Ruiz has borrowed from Max Linder, if not Jacques Tati.

More problematic is Catherine Deneuve's Odette. It makes sense that, in a world of celebrity, the scandalous, glamorous Odette should be pre-eminent – a former starlet become queen of the *beau monde*. It makes sense, too, that Deneuve should play such quasi-royalty: in recent years, she has seemed less to be playing parts than conferring patronage on the films she appears in. Ruiz even underlines Proust's theme of dynasty by having Deneuve's own children, Chiara Mastroianni and Christian Vadim, play key parts, as Albertine and Bloch (not the obvious parts, either – he might have stretched the point by casting Mastroianni as Odette's daughter Gilberte). Deneuve's obvious qualification for the role is her celebrated agelessness. Odette is the only person at the party who seems impervious to the ravages of time, her appearance described by the narrator as 'a defiance to the laws of chronology'. As such a defiance in real life, Deneuve herself becomes a figure of time's paradoxical working: she is visibly the same woman when she appears at the Verdurin reception as she is in the flashback to

Marcel's childhood encounter with her as the 'lady in pink' entertained by his Uncle Adolphe (a scene from *Swann's Way* pithily re-enacted here).

If we follow Proust to the letter, however, Deneuve seems less suited as an incarnation of Odette, a flibbertigibbet who achieves social grandeur only by making certain alliances, and who is referred to on her final appearance in the work as 'commonplace'. This vapid Odette is closer to the frothy Ornella Muti in Schlöndorff's film. But Deneuve's physical appearance and mythic status make her absolutely right in other ways. Ruiz casts Deneuve entirely for the way her aura overlaps with the character's; he casts stars in order to highlight the film's self-reflexivity, to make it clear that this isn't simply an adaptation, but a dialogue with the novel. A screen adaptation always risks spoiling our own visualisation of a novel: will it ever again be possible to read *The English Patient*, for instance, without seeing a nicely crisped Ralph Fiennes? But by using actors with strongly echoing resonances from their own histories, Ruiz in no way pretends there is an adequate invisible fit between character and performer; rather he presents famous actors as if they were self-consciously performing the choreography that belongs to the part. I think there is little danger that future Proust readers, encountering the protean qualities of the mercurial Charlus, will 'see' the fixed image of John Malkovich; instead, Charlus gains a new critical dimension by being seen as something of a Malkovich figure.

Malcolm Bowie, in his remarkable recent study *Proust among the Stars*, discusses the narrator's final realisation that his task as a writer is to give new life to the dying or dead figures of his world: 'Writing a book involves creating a mausoleum for individuals who were once alive. Living substance is enmarbled and entombed by the writer's pen; the semantic commotion of a literary text gives a false air of animation to what are now only frozen simulacra of the human form.' But if writing entails mummification, what does cinema adaptation of writing involve? For André Bazin, all representational art can be traced back to the practice of embalming: at its root is a 'mummy complex'. In cinema, that complex is usually repressed – we prefer to think not that photographic images memorialise the dead, but that cinema keeps the dead alive, indiscriminately animating the dead and the still-living, making them indistinguishable from each other. In Ruiz's film, we might imagine both the living and the dead of Proust's world as existing in a mummy-like state, neither dead nor alive, but suspended in a moving *tableau vivant* existence. The Verdurin reception is less a reception than a promiscuous séance.

Romantic necrophilia

Ruiz's film is very much a ghost story and often accentuates its traditional horror-movie elements of romantic necrophilia: the narrator's dead love Albertine appears as a transparent spectre haunting his dreams. A Buñuelian merging of time and space allows Saint-Loup (Pascal Greggory) to attend his own funeral, as the graveyard folds magically into the beach at Balbec, the narrator's beloved resort on the Normandy coast. It is at Balbec, too, that the dead past finally revives in the film's closing sequence, as the narrator resumes his youthful fetishistic investigations into the detail of a young girl's cuffs while his childhood self cavorts on the beach as the sea of time rushes in again.

'We are always feeling with Proust as if we were reading about the end of something,' remarked Edmund Wilson. We are, of course – about a dying social order and a life seen from its end – though we never fully understand that perspective until the final pages of *Time Regained*. Proust concludes by announcing that the novel of his life is yet to be written, though he fears it may never be, for his health may not hold out long enough. With Ruiz's film, the work has been completed – the terrible mountain has been scaled, at least in a satisfying part-for-the-whole adaptation of the writer's final volume. In making the film, Ruiz, too, is at the end of something: of a long-cherished ambition. He's also at the end of a century of cinema and, as the prophecies have it, on the verge of an age without celluloid. The film arrives at a moment when Proust, technically speaking, ceases to be modern literature and becomes literature of the past century. All this resounds in Ruiz's film and, whatever shortcomings may agitate particular viewers – too long, too condensed, too literal, too impressionistic – his *Time Regained* is as near as anyone could have hoped to the holy grail of Proustian cinema. It's a film that lives up to the novel's melancholy, its tragic exuberance and its conjuring of ghosts – a film that is a ceremony of re-animating and celebrating the mummies of Paris, of literature, and of cinema itself.

NICE YOUNG MEN WHO SELL ANTIQUES – GAY MEN IN HERITAGE CINEMA

Richard Dyer

In a Las Vegas nightclub in 1955, Noël Coward sang his own version of Cole Porter beginning:

> Belgians and Greeks do it
> Nice young men who sell antiques do it
> Let's do it, let's fall in love.

Quite unintentionally, it's a deliciously neat, if incomplete, summation of gays in heritage cinema: good-looking young men, well turned out in retro clothes amid period objects, fall in love and sell us the pleasures of the past.

Heritage cinema has been notably hospitable to homosexual subject matter (although I'm going to focus on male instances). Early examples include *Olivia* (France 1951), *Loving Couples* (Sweden 1964) and *Young Törless* (Germany 1966), things really taking off in the 1970s with films such as *Death in Venice* (Italy 1971), *Ludwig* (Germany/Italy 1972), *Coup de grâce* (Germany/France 1976), *A Special Day* (Italy 1977), *A Man Called 'Autumn Flower'* (Spain 1977) and *Ernesto* (Italy 1978). Heritage films and gay liberation developed side by side and some of the former – *The Affairs of Love* (Spain 1990), *Another Country* (United Kingdom 1984), *Maurice* (United Kingdom 1987), *Meteor and Shadow* (Greece 1985), *We Were One Man* (France 1979) – seem pretty clearly inspired by the latter. With possible exceptions (*Colonel Redl* (Hungary 1985), *Death in Venice, Ludwig, The Music Teacher* (Belgium 1988)), heritage films take a broadly positive view of homosexuality – which is to say that they take such a view while depicting pasts that did not.

To understand what is going on, one may make a distinction between history and heritage. History is a discipline of enquiry into the past; heritage is an attitude towards the legacy of the past. Both have to deal with what comes down to us, what is left over, from the past. However, whereas history uses an examination of the leftovers to try to understand what happened in the past, heritage values them for their own sake, savours the qualities and presence of dwellings, costumes, artworks, objects. Heritage cinema can be used as a vehicle for exploring history, as I'll discuss first, but its main impulse is towards appreciating the things of the past and telling stories of what it was like to live among them. Homosexual heritage cinema is above all about envisaging gay men among the attractions of pastness.

History

Homosexual heritage films did address issues of gay history. In part, they did what so much early gay history did: they showed that we were there. Just by having gay stories in heritage dress, gay men became part of the wider historical panorama of heritage cinema: we, too, were around in the 1910s and 1920s (*Céleste* (Germany 1981), *Colonel Redl, Coup de grâce, A Man Named 'Autumn Flower', A Month in the Country* (United Kingdom 1987), *Nijinksy* (United Kingdom 1980), *Young Törless*), there was a gay experience of World War II (*The Dresser* (United Kingdom 1983), *Europa, Europa* (France/Germany 1991), *For a Lost Soldier* (Netherlands 1992), *The Last Metro* (France 1980), *Mediterraneo* (Italy 1991), *We Were One Man*). Sometimes it's more pointed. *A Special Day* and *The Gold Rimmed Spectacles* (Italy 1988) state that gay men, too, were victims of fascism, explicitly bringing out parallels and differences between their situation and that of, respectively, women and Jews. Other films deal specifically with gay oppression (*Ernesto, Maurice, Meteor and Shadow, A Month in the Country*, the Wilde films); somewhat ambivalently, *The Conformist* (Italy 1969) relates the rise of fascism to homosexual repression, while *Another Country* links 1930s communism to rebellion against homophobia.

The last example also indicates the way that homosexual heritage cinema might point to antecedents to gay liberation itself. Sometimes this is done by showing characters inspirationally comfortable with themselves despite social attitudes (*The Affairs of Love, Carrington* (United Kingdom 1995), *The Dresser, The Last Metro, Loving Couples, Swann in Love* (France 1986), *Time Regained* (France 1999)). Elsewhere, characters discover and eventually embrace 'who they really are' (*Another Country, For a Lost Soldier, Maurice, We Were One Man, Wilde*), often involving a scene of 'coming out', which may range from the coded and indirect (*De Avonden* (Netherlands 1990)) through the private (*A Man Called 'Autumn Flower'*) to the brazen (*Meteor and Shadow*).

Of all the above, *A Man Called 'Autumn Flower'* is perhaps the most sustained treatment of gay liberation *avant-la-lettre*. Its hero, Lluis, a drag queen (stage name

'Autumn Flower'), is also a political saboteur against the dictatorship of Primo de Rivera in the Barcelona of the 1920s; he fights alongside trade unionists and anarchists, but also explicitly in the name of 'a revolution in which we can be ourselves [that is, gay] twenty-four hours a day'. He and his lover are arrested for trying to blow up de Rivera's train. Called to his execution, Lluis, with several days' growth of beard, picks up a compact and firmly, carefully applies lipstick, a gesture surely modelled on Marlene Dietrich's at the end of *Dishonored* (United States 1931); then, his arm around his lover, he goes defiantly, unambiguously gay, to his death. Lluis is a hero on the side of anti-dictatorship in a film made (1977) in the first flush of the demise of Franco (1975); he is part of the history of the struggle for democracy in Spain, but the film also insists that he be understood to be so as a homosexual and in the name of homosexuals.

Heritage

In such ways, heritage cinema can put gay men into history, but this is not its primary impulse. What is at issue is, rather, heritage, gays belonging in what is handed down as cherishable from the past.

One dimension of this is the importance of queers in the source material of the films, the literary heritage from which most of the films are drawn. Heritage cinema would be extraordinarily diminished without Paul Bowles, Colette, Rudi van Dantzig, Diaghilev, Forster, James, Agnes von Krusenstjerna, Napoleon Lapathiotis, Mann, Proust, Gerard van Reve, Rimbaud and Verlaine, Umberto Saba, Sackville-West, Stein, Lytton Strachey, Wilde, Woolf and Yourcenar. More important, though, than this affirmation of the place of queers in cultural patrimony is the look of the films and how gay men fit in, and especially how they are dressed.

Homosexual heritage may use the common perception of European men's clothes since the eighteenth century as highly restricted in terms of shape, texture and, above all, colour. This has often been interpreted as indicating emotional repression, as, in Flügel's influential formulation, a 'great masculine renunciation' in the name of the values effective in the pursuance of business and power: straightforwardness, sobriety and restraint.

Such sartorial restraint can be used in heritage cinema to express homosexual repression and liberation. Redl's many buttoned military jackets are always fully done up, squeezing his slightly podgy frame, suggesting someone ill at ease and anxious about giving himself away; the eponymous hero of *Ernesto* removes his stiff collar when he has sex with the labourer at the start of the film and thereafter, as his sexual confidence flowers, begins to wear light-coloured and, eventually, patterned waistcoats. Quite commonly, films also suggest the danger for queers of trying to draw on colours and fabrics beyond the normal male range. Wilde (in *Wilde*) in cream frock coat and purple or green buttonhole is clearly riding for a fall. *Meteor and Shadow* shows us its poet hero strolling through a public park in tight white trousers and large, loose white shirt with blowsy pink rosette at the neck, obviously queer and soon enough punished for such brazenness.

Things need not go so far as this. *Death in Venice* signals Aschenbach's decline into queerdom through slight but telling departures from the strictest of male attire that he has worn for most of the film. The erotic dimension of his fascination with Tadzio is only borne in on him when he follows Tadzio down a boardwalk and the latter, in a striped, buttock-clinging tank swimsuit, swings round the posts of the boardwalk, looking suggestively at Aschenbach on each turn. Aschenbach, dressed in standard male summer white suit, veers off the boardwalk, confused, sweating. The film cuts at once to a close-up of him looking at Tadzio in the hotel. Aschenbach now, for the first time, wears a dark bow tie with hollow spots. It is rather floppy, unlike the tightly knotted, narrow ties he has worn hitherto, and this floppiness goes along with the white handkerchief flouncing out of his breast pocket, a marked contrast to the handkerchief we have earlier seen him carefully fold and put in his pocket to show only small, sharp peaks. By the time Aschenbach has submitted to the suggestions of the barber and had his hair dyed and his face made up, his clothes have edged much closer to the queer. Furtively following Tadzio through the streets, he now wears a large red band round his beige straw hat and a red tie with a diamond pin; when he skulks in the shadow of a portico, the pin glints in the dark with something approaching vulgarity. He is now in thrall to queer desire; when he dies on the beach gazing at Tadzio, hair dye runs grotesquely down the side of his face. A move into more expressive clothes signals a decline into abject queerness.

Homosexual heritage can express through clothes ideas of the repression and the dangers of the expression of homosexual desire. However, it does not do so so very much. This is perhaps because one of the defining pleasures of the films is looking at men wearing nice clothes. If all that the clothes expressed were restriction and discomfort, they would be a lot less pleasurable to look at, to imagine yourself touching or wearing them. In any case, it is wrong to think of the restraint of male clothing as necessarily repressive and uncomfortable. As Anne Hollander suggests (in *Sex and Suits*), Western male clothing, especially the suit, can also be redolent of ease and grace. The masculine beau ideal of self-control and social conformity is one that, clothes promise, men can be at ease with, be at home in.

To have homosexual characters dressed like this was a declaration that gay men, too, could form part of a graceful, decorous masculinity. Queer masculinity had characteristically been represented as something abnormal, informed by ideas of sickness and effeminacy. In heritage cinema, on the other hand, gay men were shown as indistinguishable from other nicely turned, worth looking at (but not more worth looking at) men.

Good-looking clothes also facilitate the exploration of what men may find attractive in each other. Compare and contrast *Ernesto* and *Maurice*. Both represent relationships between an eponymous middle-class protagonist and a working-class lover – an unnamed labourer in *Ernesto*, Alec in *Maurice*. In both cases, it is the working-class character who knows what he wants, the middle-class one who has to find out. However, and centrally through the use of clothing, *Ernesto* constructs attraction between men overwhelmingly in terms of difference, while *Maurice* moves it towards sameness. In the process, both also suggest different models of gay social integration.

Ernesto opens with a systematic class contrast. As Ernesto selects those to whom he'll give employment that day, his black suit with bowler hat, stiff white collar and pale grey-blue tie stands out against the loose grey trousers and off-white, collarless shirts of the workmen. His youth also stands out, since his pretty, fine features and soft skin contrast markedly with his staid clothes. Class and age differences then take on an erotic charge in the sequences between the labourer and Ernesto. The former's clothes and appearance emphasise a rougher-textured male pulchritude: off-white, lightly stitched shirts or ribbed button-top vests, the buttons undone pulling open across his hairy chest; black hair, short on the sides, but long, wiry and unruly on top. He seems to burst out of his clothes, embodying a fully masculine, wholly unrepressed homosexual desire. Ernesto, by contrast, wears his black suits and stiff white collars; his wavy hair is pomaded into neatness; he is hairless (and we are told has not even started shaving yet) – his is the smooth, neat beauty of the feminine. That the contrast is not only of class and age, but also of gender is made explicit when the labourer refers to himself as the man (and relates this to his role as penetrator in sex).

When Ernesto becomes a man (he shaves, goes with a female prostitute, wants to penetrate the labourer), he meets a boy, Ilio, at a concert. Ilio has longish, fair hair and very soft features, and is not only younger than Ernesto, but also comes from a much wealthier family. As if this isn't enough, the gender equation (higher class plus younger equals more feminine) is reinforced by the fact that he has a twin sister, Rachele; towards the end, Ilio and Rachele swap clothes and the latter, now dressed as a boy, tries to seduce Ernesto, although he remains fixated on Ilio at a dressing table putting on make-up. If Ernesto's sexual preference is not in doubt (he continues to desire the biological male), it is also clear that he now desires the feminine man. What's more, he will probably marry Rachele because that's just what you do: the films ends with him at a party set up for him to announce his engagement to Rachele; he looks about desperately for Ilio and then turns to the camera and shrugs his shoulders. Through the use of always attractive clothes, *Ernesto* retains then an insistence on difference as a structuring principle of male homosexual desire, but implies that it can be maintained alongside conforming to the social organisation of heterosexuality.

The relationship between Maurice and Alec looks at first as if it is of a piece of that between Ernesto and the labourer. Alec's dark ruffled hair, rough-textured collarless shirts, loosely knotted neckerchiefs, heavy, cruddy boots and dirty leggings contrast with Maurice's fair, short-cut hair, stiff white collars, tightly knotted black ties and featureless dark shoes. The contrast is most marked when they meet in the garden, Alec in his gamekeeper's gear, Maurice in dinner jacket; that night, Alec climbs into Maurice's bedroom and they make love. Thereafter, however, clothing makes them look more alike: naked in bed together, then both in identical whites for a cricket match and, then, when he comes to visit Maurice in London, Alec wearing a neat blue suit of the same cut as Maurice's. As they lie in bed together in a rented room, the camera tracks over their neatly folded clothes, one man's set indistinguishable from the other's. They are thus integrated with each other and into a conventional masculinity.

Ernesto and *Maurice* both involve adapting (in different ways) to decorous masculinity. Such conformity at the level of costume makes it feels like the men can be integrated at the level of the film's social world. This is characteristic of homosexual heritage. Exceptionally, *A Man Called 'Autumn Flower'* achieves an integration of unmanly queenliness into its *mise-en-scène*, even while depicting a society that deals ruthlessly with homosexual rebellion.

The film begins by underlining the separation of the bright heritage world of assumed heterosexuality and the dark world of queers: Luis is a successful lawyer living with his mother in a very nice, large bourgeois flat; he goes at night to the dim, tacky nightclub to do his drag act. Part of the trajectory of the film is his insistence on bringing his overtly queer style into the rest of his life, which is also the film bringing it into the *mise-en-scène* of heritage.

In one sequence, Luis in drag is beaten up and left outside the door of his flat, for his mother to find him, although he runs off before she can open the door. But later, in the full drag of a smart señora (nothing vulgar or showbizzy – in other words, dressing heritage, not camp), he goes to see his mother in her bedroom in the middle of the night to tell her about himself. He insists that she keep the light off and the half-light on him as he speaks is appropriately reminiscent of the confessional. Eventually, however, she insists on putting the light on. He has by this point taken off his (woman's) hat and wig, affirming his homosexual identity as man in woman's clothes. She tells him to come to her and they embrace, the camera tracking back along her bed to where he has left the hat and wig. There has thus been a gradual progress of queer into heritage, from avoiding being seen at all when dumped outside the flat through the half-light of confession to the fully lit embrace of an unequivocally gay self-presentation amidst full, but unflashy and uncluttered, period trappings. Very homosexual, very heritage.

Heritage cinema depicts past worlds in which homosexuality was illegal, mocked, despised and persecuted, in which gay men thought of themselves as queers. Yet it depicts these worlds, including being gay in them, as attractive. Several commentators, notably Andrew Higson and John Hill, have argued that there is a defining contradiction in (British) heritage cinema between ostensible social critique and loving spectacle – the story and dialogue may condemn the worlds depicted, but the look and texture of the films celebrate them. Yet perhaps the films are doing no more than evoking the contradictoriness of the past itself. Against the odds, there were also for queers love and sex and friendship, acceptance and tolerance, and you could still dress well and look good. Beyond this, what I have been trying to show is that, especially through clothes, homosexual heritage cinema does something quite specific with the contradiction between critique and spectacle: it produces the utopian pleasure of a vision of integration even in homophobic societies of the past. In effect, it imagines queers being gay.

Prospero's Books (Peter Greenaway, 1991)

Section 2:
Adapting the Literary Canon

Case Studies

Orlando
FIRE AND ICE

Verina Glaessner

The floorshow at St Petersburg's Hotel Helen starts early. It also starts cold in every sense of the word: the only available response is cringing embarrassment. Outside, the Fontanka, one of the city's numerous canals, is frozen over. The ice, something Sobchak's sad city has in abundance, is indeed part of the reason for our visit.

Mixed pedigree

A key section of Virginia Woolf's 1928 'novel' *Orlando* is set during the Great Frost of 1604, the year the Thames froze over. For both director Sally Potter and lead actor Tilda Swinton, the novel, with its ecstatic style and open celebration of androgyny, proved revelatory when they read it in the late 1960s. Swinton was Potter's first choice for the eponymous hero-heroine from the time the idea of filming Woolf's novel was broached some four years ago. Yet, despite the author's canonical position in both English and feminist literature, finding financial backing for the project proved difficult.

'The Americans didn't understand it at all,' says Swinton, 'but the Russians from the beginning said, "Androgyny and immortality? We can handle that!"' And the first financial commitment came from them, after which British Screen came aboard with some 50 per cent of the £6.5 million budget. The rest comes from four other European sources: a purely financial involvement from Italy; sound crew and actor Charlotte Valandrey, who plays Orlando's first love, Sasha, from France; the production design team (and regular collaborators of Peter Greenaway) Ben van Os and Jan Roelfs from the Netherlands; and cinematographer Alexei Rodionov, responsible for the camera-work on Elem Klimov's seminal *glasnost* film *Come and See*, from Russia. It is a mixed pedigree indicative of a moment when notions of national cinema are dissolving and possibilities for a European cinema are being explored. It is also a point at which the nation state is a contentious issue.

It was important to both Potter and producer Christopher Sheppard that the crucial scenes on the frozen river be played as much as possible for real. (It is on the ice that Orlando meets his first love, and its melting signals his abandonment.) The frozen river is also the scene of Orlando's first 'Sapphic' encounter (to use Woolf's own term, even if, in strictly narrative terms, Orlando is at this point male).

For ice, the production had a choice between Canada, Scandinavia and Russia. Russia seemed most promising, not only because of the novel's Russian content (Sasha is a Russian princess), but because the then Soviet Union also offered persuasively oriental locations able to stand in for the book's Constantinople. The country in any case held a fascination for Potter: in 1987–88 she had made a Channel 4 documentary, *I Am an Ox, I Am a Horse, I Am a Man, I Am a Woman*, tracing the history of Russia through the use of women in film from the silent days to the present. 'I felt,' she says, 'that Russian film had a kind of faithfulness to the scene that did not allow itself to be distracted by glamour. Tarkovsky, for instance, was able to conjure a sense of mystery out of unusual juxtapositions, which is what I felt *Orlando* would need.'

'From the beginning,' says Sheppard, 'we were adamant that we weren't going to do a facilities deal. We wanted full Russian involvement on an equal-partner basis.' Protracted negotiations, during which the old Soviet Union vanished, led away from the more Hollywood-orientated Mosfilm Studios to Lenfilm, a studio with a strong reputation for innovative work. (Mosfilm has since signed a deal with Roger Corman that could signal new possibilities for mining Russia's rich seam of gothic/symbolist writing.) But, even at Lenfilm, the notion of a 'poor' western cinema needed explanation. 'It was a time when the old state-funded studio system was breaking up and large numbers of senior former employees were setting up independently with wild expectations of large dollar deals,' explains Sheppard. And he sees *Orlando* as 'the first fully fledged Russian–British co-production. Films like *Assassin of the Tsar* and *Lost in Siberia* simply lent a western gloss to what were essentially Russian projects, while films like *The Russia House* bring everything in.'

The frozen Thames turns out not to be the Neva or even the Fontanka canal, but an outdoor ice rink in a park not far from central St Petersburg. A hangar-like building serves for make-up, costumes, dressing rooms and canteen. Soldiers from the erstwhile Red, now Russian, Army sip coffee. They are in the employ of Lenfilm and, as night and cold set in, they tend the ice and dispense 'snow' as required, occasionally pausing to snap souvenir photographs. In one of the grey pavilions on the ice, the features of Tilda Swinton undergo transformation. She, too, is clad in black and steely grey. In one of the film's 'puns', Orlando, red of hair and pale of skin, resembles both the Lely minia-ture referred to by Woolf in the novel and the Hatfield House portrait of Elizabeth I, in which the young queen's frank gaze is undercut by the ever-attentive ears and eyes embroidered on her robe. In the film, Elizabeth is played by Quentin Crisp.

The longest love letter

The historical scope of the novel and the thematic role history plays within it make *Orlando* an unusually demanding project for its production designers. Each period of the book's 400-year span must be captured in essence, something van Os and Roelfs attempt by extensive use of only a few, typical objects from each period. They have also raided coffee-table books of the period (a Hamlyn book on Elizabethan England sits on top of Roy Strong's *Splendour at the Court*). 'It is not a question of historical reproduction,' they claim.

In collaboration with Potter, van Os and Roelfs have devised a 'colour coding' for each of the narrative's many historical periods, which are sharply delineated and fetishistically rendered in Woolf's prose. 'The England of Elizabeth is gold and red, that of James grey and silver, the eighteenth century is dominated by a powdery blue, and so on. We took the blue we use for Constantinople, in fact Khiva in Uzbekistan, from the blue of the tiles there, but for the moment when Orlando becomes a woman, we drape the room with white.' Van Os and Roelfs work closely with the cinematographer, Rodionov, and the lighting people as well as with Potter herself: 'It is the lighting that brings it all to life.'

Woolf's novel is about history and sexuality (despite her protests to the contrary), time and gender, androgyny and immortality. The protagonist is sixteen years old and male when the novel opens in the reign of Elizabeth I; at the age of thirty s/he becomes a woman and remains so through the eighteenth and nineteenth centuries to the book's close in 1928. It is a novel written with a heightened awareness of desire (in its almost contemporary companion piece, *A Room of One's Own*, the guiding emotion is anger). 'I am launched,' wrote Woolf in one of her letters, 'somewhat furtively but with all the more passion upon *Orlando*.'

Woolf based the central character on her friend and lover, Vita Sackville-West, and photographs of Vita as Orlando adorned the first edition. Vita's son, Nigel Nicolson, has called it 'the longest and most charming love letter in history'. In the novel, Vita is placed within a fantastic rewriting of her own and her family's history – a rewriting which erases the denial by law (because of gender) of her inheritance. Vita's wayward lover, Violet Trefusis, appears as Sasha; her husband, Harold Nicolson, as Shelmerdine, Orlando's first love upon assuming the form of a woman. Vita's own journey to Moscow, from where she wrote to Woolf of carriages crossing the frozen river as if it were a road, finds its echo in the book, as does her visit with Harold to Constantinople.

On the novel's publication, the *Daily Mail* characteristically headed its review, 'A Fantastic Biography. Mrs H. Nicolson and Orlando. 300 Years as Man and Woman' and the book outsold Woolf's previous novel. 'Sapphism is to be suggested,' Woolf had written when the project was still called *The Jessamy Brides*, 'satire and wildness.' It was to be an 'escapade' in writing.

Sally Potter has picked up the notion of an 'escapade' in her script, which conveys the spirit of fun, fantasy and caricature that Woolf applied to her subject. While acknowledging the book's origins in the life of Vita Sackville-West, and indeed drawing the idea of casting the protagonist as a woman throughout implicitly from Woolf's own 'casting' of Vita in that role, Potter sees the scope of the book as much wider. 'It is more broadly about history, identity, reading, writing and remembering. Although Woolf works in a lot of literary jokes, we are not making a film about literature. What interests me is how the book explores the way the English place themselves in the world in relation to their past. There is an addiction in English culture to mythologies of the past, which is not the same thing as having a sense of history. And many of these mythologies are rooted in the reign of Elizabeth I, which provides the origin for a particular understanding of national identity. It is a familiar accusation that the English are unable to let go of the past. In the film, Orlando gradually achieves this: she loses everything, but gains herself in the process.'

The view from the Netherlands is subtly different; to van Os, the novel explores 'the tragedy of the power of England that lasted through centuries and then ended. It is also, of course, about Vita, who was never the writer she wanted to be and became a gardener.' Not, perhaps, a notion of failure to which the British would subscribe.

Although Woolf closed the novel in 1928, the film brings the story into the present, a present that is suggested in the speed and modernism of the book's final chapter. 'It is not a historical film. Orlando is a completely contemporary character,' claims Potter.

Beyond gender

'For me,' says Potter, '*Orlando* is not so much about femininity and difference as about Woolf's notion of an essential self that lies beyond gender. She says that "Up to the age of thirty Orlando was a man and then when she became a woman she was not different but just a different sex."' If the self is so fluid, then so, too, must be biography, the literary category into which Woolf placed *Orlando*. And indeed sections of *Orlando* are devoted to considering the nature of biography and the differences between biographies of men and of women (the one predicated on action, the other on romance). Other passages play with the idea of dismantling the project entirely by 'writing herself into a corner' of inaction. (Potter's 1979 film *Thriller* pertinently rewrote *La Bohème* from Mimi's point of view.)

'Gender is turned on its head in *Orlando*,' says Potter, 'but issues of class remain unaddressed. We try to turn class on its head as well. We see Orlando as someone emerging out of a particular class in sympathetic struggle.'

Part of the struggle of making any film lies in turning the foreignness of a location to advantage. And indeed, in St Petersburg, foreignness creates tensions on both sides, exemplified by the elaborate arrangements for meals, whereby tables are booked and groups bussed to one or other of the city's private restaurants, where good food is served in surroundings of Miss Havisham-like decay at a price that ensures the exclusion of the Russians, who are unwilling to stake the equivalent of a month's wages on a meal.

The old studio system has left a well-publicised legacy of inefficiency and lack of initiative. But at the heart of some of the conflicts lie competing notions of professionalism – for example, between the unit's need to can between one and a half and two minutes of film a day to stay within budget and the divorce of time and money that allowed Klimov to take nine months to shoot a film and to spend a day where necessary thinking through a set-up.

Simon Perry waxes enthusiastic about the more positive legacy of the studio system: 'The huge pool of sheer old-fashioned technical skill refined through years of unbroken continuity of production.' And Potter delights in the impressive 'cineliteracy' of those with whom she works, the 'shared sense of irony and understatement'. She quotes the example of Powell and Pressburger, an ideal marriage between (East) Europe and Britain that 'liberated a very particular Englishness'.

Polyglot audience

Other factors mark out Russian cinema. There is the need to redefine the status and mode of address of film-makers long required to claim the high moral ground of 'art' within a monolithically structured industry. And there are the effects of an economy in which the legal structures and commercial practices that would allow the flourishing of a thousand neighbourhood cinemas (or video stores) are not yet in place and the hiatus before privatisation allows only the most primitive of commercial exchanges.

Both Sheppard and Perry are concerned about the future of Russian film. Perry sees a threat in the influx of Hollywood companies in search of cheap facilities deals who will unrealistically raise prices and expectations. With the example of 'an almost 100 per cent American occupancy of British screens' in mind, he reads the Russian fascination with Hollywood as ill-founded and destructive. He envisages a more positive future for both Britain and Russia in Europe (arguably it is the French who have made the most intelligent running so far, signing up directors who are both interesting and bold). 'Who knows, writing for a polyglot audience may even help to concentrate the minds of our screenwriters on the fact that film is after all a visual medium.'

Very different economic constraints seem to have forced a choice between hermeticism and loss of identity on both the Russian and British industries. In its modest way, Potter and Sheppard's project suggests that the choice may be a false one. Certainly, Woolf's study of the self seeking definition against a revivified history could hardly be more topical.

IMMORTAL LONGING

Walter Donohue talks with Sally Potter

In the 1970s and 1980s, Sally Potter was a controversial figure in British independent cinema, making films that blended narrative invention with theoretical and formalist concerns. Her 1979 short *Thriller* has long been a staple on film courses for its deconstruction of opera's sexual politics through a re-reading of *La Bohème*. She followed it up with her feature debut, *The Gold Diggers* (1983), with Julie Christie, and *The London Story*, a technicolour spy musical. More recently, Potter has worked in television: making *Women in Soviet Cinema* (1988) and *Tears, Laughter, Fear and Rage* (1986), a four-part series on the politics of emotions.

Potter's new feature *Orlando* is produced by her own company Adventure Pictures, which she formed with Christopher Sheppard. A free reading of Virginia Woolf's historical fantasia, *Orlando* represents Potter's first venture into more mainstream narrative, but it also continues some of her past concerns. Her Russian connection carries on in the co-production deal with Lenfilm and the use of a Russian crew that included Elem Klimov's cinematographer Alexei Rodionov. Potter also co-wrote the score with David Motion; her past work as a composer includes the song cycle *Oh Moscow*, and she has also run her own dance ensemble, the Limited Dance Company. All these diverse concerns find their way into *Orlando*, which with its elaborate staging and exuberant cultivation of artifice gives a startling new twist to the British costume drama.

* * *

Location: Blackbird Yard, Ravenscroft Road, and, like birds alighting on a field, Sally Potter and I are sitting here in her workroom in the renovated London shoe factory where one draft after another of the script of her new film *Orlando* was exposed, criticised, knocked into shape. Almost a year since the troop set off for St Petersburg to film the Frost Fair sequences, this interview took place.

Walter Donohue: It's strange to be sitting again at this table where so many of our script discussions took place. Can you describe something of the process of adapting Virginia Woolf's novel into your own film?

Sally Potter: It was a process of reading, re-reading and reading again; writing, rewriting and writing again. Cutting characters, stripping things right back to the bone. I did endless skeleton diagrammatic plots, all to find the guiding principle and then reconstruct the story from the inside out. I also went back to research Woolf's sources. And then, finally, I put the book away entirely for at least the last year of writing and treated the script as something in its own right, as if the book had never existed. I felt that by the time we were getting ready to shoot I knew the book well enough, was enough in touch with its spirit, that it would have been a disservice to be slavish to it. What I had to find was a live, cinematic form, which meant being ruthless with the novel. In other words, I learnt that you have to be cruel to the novel in order to be kind to the film.

Walter Donohue: Where did your interest in *Orlando* begin?

Sally Potter: When I first read *Orlando* as a teenager, I remember watching it as a film. And from the first moment I considered doing an adaptation, I thought I could see it, even if parts were out of focus. The book has a live, visual quality to it – which was affirmed in Woolf's diaries, where she said that what she was attempting with Orlando, unlike her other books, was an 'exteriorisation of consciousness'. She was finding images for a stream of consciousness, instead of using a literary monologue.

But the single idea that was sustaining enough for me to live with the project for so long was immortality, or the question: what is the present moment? And the second idea was the change of sex, which provides the more obvious narrative structure, and is a rich and lighter way of dealing with the issues between men and women. The more I went into this area, and tried to write a character who was both male and female, the more ludicrous maleness and femaleness became and the more the notion of the essential human being – that a man and woman both are – predominated. Clearly, here was just a character called Orlando: a person, an individual, a being who lived for 400 years, first as a man and then as a woman. At the moment of change, Orlando turns and says to the audience, 'Same person, different sex.' It's as simple as that.

Walter Donohue: But Orlando – a character who is both a man and a woman – has to be embodied in an actor. And you chose a woman to play this part. How did you deal with the maleness and femaleness of the characterisation?

Sally Potter: We worked primarily from the inside out and talked all the time about Orlando as a person, rather than as a man or a woman. Then there was a mass of small decisions which added up to a policy about how to play the part – for instance, we decided on no artificial facial hair for Orlando the man. Whenever I've seen women playing men on screen, it's been a mistake to try to make the woman look too much like a man, because you spend your time as a viewer looking for the glue, the joins between the skin and the moustache. I worked on the assumption that the audience was going to know from the beginning that here was a woman playing a man, and so the thing to do was to acknowledge it and try to create a state of suspended disbelief.

I was attracted to Tilda Swinton for the role on the basis of seeing her in Peter Wollen's film *Friendship's Death*, where she had a cinematic presence that wasn't aligned to what our cinematographer Alexei Rodionov called 'crawling realism', and in the Manfred Karge play *Man to Man*, in which there was an essential subtleness about the way she took on male body language and handled maleness and femaleness. Tilda brought her own research and experience to bear on the part; as her director I worked to help her to achieve a quality of transparency on the screen. The biggest challenge for both of us was to maintain a sense of the development of the character even when we were shooting out of continuity and with the ending still uncertain. The intention was that there would be a seamless quality about the development that would carry that suspended disbelief about maleness, femaleness and immortality.

Walter Donohue: The idea of suspended disbelief – was direct address to camera one of the devices used to maintain this?

Sally Potter: The speeches of Orlando to the audience took many forms during the writing, and during the shooting they were the hardest things to get right. The phrase I used to Tilda was 'golden thread': we were trying to weave a golden thread between Orlando and the audience through the lens of the camera. One of the ways we worked in rehearsal was to have Tilda address those speeches directly to me, to get the feeling of an intimate, absolutely one-to-one connection, and then to transfer that kind of address into the lens. Part of the idea was also that direct address would be an instrument of subversion, so that set against this historical pageant is a complicity with the audience about the kind of journey we're on. If it worked, I hoped it would be funny; it would create a connection that made Orlando's journey also the audience's journey; and, most important, it would give the feeling that although Orlando's journey lasted 400 years and was set in the past, this was essentially a story about the present.

The function of the voiceover at the beginning and end is to dispatch with certain issues as neatly as possible – for instance, the film begins with Orlando's voice saying: 'There can be no doubt about his sex.' I also wanted to state that, though Orlando comes from a certain background, which has certain implications, he is separated from this background by a kind of innocence. One is born into a class background, but that can change.

Walter Donohue: Was there any governing idea behind the transitions from one period to another?

Sally Potter: I tried to find a way of making transitions through a characteristic of the period (dress, poetry, music) that could launch us into the next section. And what I found was that you can be much bolder than I ever thought in the way you jump, cinematically, from one period to another. Ironically, the most striking transition is where Orlando enters the maze in the eighteenth century and emerges into the Victorian era, which was the one I hadn't worked out in the script and was still struggling with in the shoot. The decision to effect the transition by having Orlando enter the maze was made simply because there was a maze at the location which I knew I wanted to use somewhere; its final form was found in the cutting room.

Walter Donohue: Perhaps we could discuss one or two of the myriad aspects of the craft of film-making – such as framing?

Sally Potter: Framing is the magic key, the door through which you're looking. The quest in shooting *Orlando* was not just for a frame or possible place to put the camera, but for the only place. This became my driving visual obsession. To transcend the arbitrariness of where you put the camera became a joint process between Alexei and myself. And one of his great strengths as a cinematographer is that he won't settle for an obvious or easy visual solution. He's trying to peel back the layers and find this transparent place – and this search for the right frame became a parallel process to trying to achieve a transparency of performance.

Technically, we worked with a monitor, and every frame was adjusted – up, down, right, left – until there was a frame which he and I agreed was *the* frame. If we couldn't agree it was an unhappy moment, and a lot of energy was spent on that kind of tussling. Alexei's intention is to be a mediumistic cinematographer; he says that the greatest compliment Klimov paid him after *Come and See* was that Klimov felt as if he had shot the film himself. That's a very ego-free statement for a cinematographer to make, and for me it was an incredible gift, as well as a challenge that was initially almost too great to meet, because it put the gaze back on me: what did I really want? I didn't always know what I wanted; I was groping to start with. But by the end of the shoot I felt that Alexei and I had one eye.

Walter Donohue: You're credited, with David Motion, with the music for the film. How did that come about?

Sally Potter: A lot of people commented that sound was often mentioned in the script. And I wanted a sound effect structure and score that would mirror the scale of the film. Our policy during the mix was to make a broad dynamic range and then highlight certain evocative or pointed sounds – such as the peacock's cry when Orlando is walking down the gallery of long white drapes, or the sound of the ice cracking, or of rain taking over the soundtrack.

As far as the music is concerned, I originally wanted to use Arvo Part's *Cantuso*, which I had been listening to over and over again. I even got permission, but it became clear that to use it would create as many problems as it would solve – it was a piece in its own right that couldn't be cut or repeated. So I started on a journey to find out what it was about that piece of music that was appropriate to the film, and then to look for another way of achieving this. What I discovered was that a lot of the music I had been listening to for pleasure, and as a sort of spiritual reference for the film, was based on an A-minor triad, or the related C-major triad. This seemed too much of a coincidence, so I drew up a chart of the score and we mapped out a structure based on the A-minor triad and related keys. And the more I got to thinking about the score, the more I was hearing the music in my head. So eventually we decided to go into a studio to record what I was hearing using my own voice. I recorded an eight-track voice piece for each of the major cues and David Motion wrote instrumental parts around them. Some of the voice parts were lost, but others became the background to the cues, or were fitted around sections he had written and arranged. Fred Frith then improvised some guitar lines around the cues. The end song was written slightly differently: I wrote the lyrics and suggested the key; David provided some musical cues on tape; Jimmy Somerville wrote the vocal tune and then David arranged it. It was a score that was made possible through the use of a sampler and the editorial capacity that machine gives you. It was a score that was constructed rather than composed in the usual way.

Walter Donohue: The novel ends in 1928, but in order to be faithful to the idea of making the film contemporary, it had to finish in 1993. How did you devise the last section?

Sally Potter: It reached its final form after everything else had been shot. What became clear was that the correct way to approach it was not just to stick an ending on the story, but to think myself into Virginia Woolf's consciousness. What might she have done with the story had she lived until 1993? It was a strange game, a sort of second guessing that consisted in me re-reading what she had written after *Orlando*; her thoughts on issues post-1928. It seemed clear that I had to refer to the First and Second World Wars and the effect they had on consciousness. And because the book itself is almost a running commentary on the history of literature as the vehicle for consciousness, there had to be a cinematic equivalent of what had happened to that kind of consciousness postwar. In other words, the fracturing of that consciousness and the arrival of the electronic age.

Walter Donohue: What do you want the audience to feel when they've reached the end?

Sally Potter: I hope they are thrilled by the rush into the present, by the notion that finally we are here, now. And a feeling of hope and empowerment about being alive and the possibility of change – which comes through the words of the song and the expression on Orlando's face. I want people to feel humanly recognised, that their inner landscape of hope and desire and longing has found some kind of expression on screen. A gut feeling of release and relief and hope.

The Age of Innocence
DREAD AND DESIRE

Amy Taubin

At the close of Edith Wharton's novel *The Age of Innocence*, Newland Archer, a recently widowed 57-year-old with three adult children and a pillar of late–nineteenth-century New York society, sits on a bench in a residential street in Paris beneath the windows of Countess Ellen Olenska, the woman who was the great love of his life and who had become in the twenty-six years since he had last seen her 'the composite vision of all he had missed'. The countess has invited Archer and his son to tea. Archer gets as far as the front door and then hesitates, musing about the past and about possible futures, and about the occupant of the top-floor apartment, 'a dark lady, pale and dark, who would look up quickly, half rise, and hold out a long thin hand with three rings on it', if only he could bring himself to enter.

'"It's more real to me here than if I went up," he heard himself say; and the fear lest that last shadow of reality lose its edge kept him rooted to his seat as the moments succeeded each other.' With this, Wharton elevates Archer to the highest rank of romantic hero – one whose desire turns on an act of the imagination rather than an engagement with the world.

Martin Scorsese's remarkably faithful adaptation of Wharton's 1921 Pulitzer Prize-winning novel of manners, marriage and missed opportunities includes, through dialogue and voiceover narration, as much of the original text as possible in a 136-minute film, but conspicuously omits Archer's last exclamation and the three paragraphs of description that follow. At the last possible moment, Scorsese gambles on image alone (coloured by Elmer Bernstein's lushly old-fashioned score) to convey that Archer is lost in the movie inside his head, and that that movie is precisely the one we've been watching.

I have no way of judging whether the gamble pays off. Having read Wharton's novel some half-dozen times, I found myself supplying her text at crucial moments; and I suspect that Scorsese couldn't keep from doing the same while editing. Among the qualities we expect from great film-makers is a show of independence, that their works seem sufficient in themselves even as they offer a rich lode of material for interpretation. It's a bit disconcerting, therefore, when the director of *Raging Bull*, *Mean Streets* and *Taxi Driver* – Ur-texts for contemporary American film-makers – makes his debt to his source material so evident, refusing to define boundaries between original and adaptation.

Scorsese proffers neither an aggressive interpretation that would have made Wharton's novel his own even as it established his distance from it (as with Kubrick's *Barry Lyndon* or *Lolita*); nor is he acting as a post-modern scavenger, denying the inviolability of everyone else's texts while using them to shore up an impenetrable fortress of his own; nor is he even involved in literary grazing like such classical Hollywood directors as William Wyler or such art-house darlings as Merchant-Ivory. Rather, Scorsese's relation to Wharton's *The Age of Innocence* is totally fetishistic. 'What I wanted to do as much as possible was to re-create for a viewing audience the experience I had reading the book,' he commented when I interviewed him a few weeks after the film's US release, adding that, although he'd read many novels from or about the nineteenth century, he'd never felt about any of them the way he felt about *The Age of Innocence*. 'For me, it has to do with Archer's relationship to Ellen and his not being able to fulfil it as he *thinks* he would like to. That's what's so moving – the things you miss in life with people, or the things you think you miss,' he explained on another occasion.

Scorsese's desire was somehow 'to present' Wharton's novel, as in recent years he has presented restored prints of films from his personal canon: *The Age of Innocence* as a Martin Scorsese presentation, rather than a Martin Scorsese picture. The fetishism implicit in this approach mirrors the fetishism of the society depicted in the novel, where desire is felt as a threat that must be deflected on to objects and contained by ritual. (And it's precisely Wharton's understanding of the mix of dread and desire in sexuality that makes her work so resonant in the age of AIDS.)

Two years ago, when Scorsese announced *The Age of Innocence* as his next project, the media gasped in snobbish amazement at the prospect of the goodfella invading Wharton's drawing rooms. But class difference notwithstanding, there are striking parallels between them. Raging romantics, they can also call a spade a spade and look into the grave it digs.

In their best-known work, Scorsese and Wharton examine the cultures in which they came of age from the perspectives of insiders who were always outsiders. Ambivalence is central to their style. Aware, even as children, that they were unsuited to the gender ideals prescribed them, they each found an identity in art. Scorsese grew up in New York's Little Italy, an ethnically enclosed working-class neighbourhood. Exempted because of his asthma from the male rites that his films eroticise and critique, he spent his time going to the movies with his father and drawing comics – prototypes for the storyboards he still uses to prepare for production.

Wharton was born in 1862 into a no less rigid culture – that of the upper-class descendants of New York's original Dutch and German settlers. Her adolescent nicknames included both 'Pussy' and 'John'. Confined by a social order that viewed literary achievement with suspicion if not contempt, she nevertheless devoured her father's library and began to write when she was twelve. When her first engagement was broken off, the Newport, Rhode Island *Daily News* speculated that the cause was 'an alleged preponderance of intellectuality on the part of the intended bride'. Wharton didn't take herself seriously as a writer until she was in her late thirties and didn't consider herself a professional until *The House of Mirth* (1905) became a best-seller. Like Scorsese, Wharton, by adhering to the codes of realism, straddles the divide between art and mass culture.

New York, New York

A year after the success of *The House of Mirth*, Wharton began a move from the United States to France which became permanent shortly before the beginning of World War I. *The Age of Innocence*, which apart from its leap into the twentieth century in the last chapter is set in the New York of her childhood, was written from a position of self-imposed exile (or escape to freedom) – and from what Wharton saw as the unbridgeable distance produced by the war. Always a period piece, it satirises the society that marked its author for life, but also reveals her primal attachment to New York and its history, an attachment Scorsese shares.

If Scorsese is known for his brutal dissection of the codes of masculinity, Wharton, whom Henry James dubbed 'The Angel of Devastation', applied her scalpel to the construction of femininity that makes women complicit in their own subjugation. Her primary target was marriage; her identification of that institution as central to women's oppression makes her work fascinating to contemporary feminists. (Scorsese is similarly interested in how social institutions mould feeling into expression. He has an anthropologist's eye for the rituals of daily life and a Freudian's grasp of the dynamics of guilt, rage and repression.)

But Wharton's *The Age of Innocence*, however rich its descriptions of tribal forms and rituals, is not simply a social satire. While acknowledging that satire was 'her weapon', Wharton wrote of wanting '*The Age* to be taken not as a costume piece but a simple and grave story of two people trying to live up to something that was still felt in the blood at that time.'

Scorsese's *The Age of Innocence* also runs the danger of being taken as a costume drama, although he, like Wharton, is enthralled by the love story. Newland Archer (Daniel Day-Lewis), an eligible bachelor with intellectual leanings, meets the love of his life, the enigmatic, slightly scandalous Countess Ellen Olenska (Michelle Pfeiffer) just hours after proposing to her more conventional cousin May Welland (Winona Ryder). Although Wharton wrote *The Age of Innocence* in the third person, her focus was Archer – he is the only subjectivity to which we are given access. What we know of Ellen and May is almost entirely mediated by his not altogether reliable perception of them.

It may be that Wharton found the investment of the women characters in this love triangle a bit too hot to handle. Psychoanalysis counsels that all romantic triangles originate in unresolved Oedipal fantasies. (Wharton called the jargon of Freudianism 'sewerage', but she left unfinished at her death *Beatrice Palmietto*, a novel that would have been about father/daughter incest.) So it is perhaps no accident that Newland and May bear a certain resemblance to Wharton's own father and mother, and that there's much of Edith herself in Ellen, the exotic interloper, the Europeanised bohemian, the only successfully independent female character Wharton created. It's the unspoken fantasy of the daughter's rescue of the father from the controlling mother that gives the novel its double edge and that accounts for the amazing empathy Wharton has with Archer.

Scorsese, however, takes Wharton at her word. The film belongs to Archer, who despite differences of class and historical circumstance shares with the director's other heroes the repression and guilt that makes it impossible for him to act on his desires – and makes him desire only the impossible. Trapped between duty, his need to do what he's been bred to do, and rebellion, his longing to break free from his claustrophobic society, to discover the other worlds to which Ellen holds the key (that's why she's more than a sexual object), he vacillates, dashing from one woman to the other, until the tribe, rallying around the seemingly guileless May, decides for him.

What's new here for Scorsese is that the gap between desire and action cannot be bridged by physical violence. Not by the carnage of Travis Bickle nor by the head-banging of Jake LaMotta. The repressed does not return in this film; it merely produces the anxiety of ambivalence.

Under their hats

In the scenes between Newland and Ellen, and between Newland and May, Scorsese charts that ambivalence – the barely perceptible oscillations of desire – frame by frame. Here, rather than in the obsessively researched, baroque displays of decoration and architecture, costumes and artefacts, food and flowers, is where the film-making brilliance is located. Scorsese has always communicated a taste for anxiety, but never so much as in *The Age of Innocence* – the suffocating anxiety of waiting for the sign on which one believes one's life depends, wanting it to come and at the same time fearing it. Scorsese plays with the rhythms of anxiety and sexual guilt the way Hitchcock did in *Vertigo* – an unlikely film to reference were it not for the Saul Bass title sequence. In the titles to *The Age of Innocence*, the central image is not an eye, but the petals of a flower unfurling over and over in slow motion superimposed on a page from the original text. The image is sickly sweet – sensuality is posed as a threat, a disruption. One could be sucked into that sweetness, one could die of it. Better to keep it at a distance. A movie-going affair. A fetishistic object.

Full-blown romantic passion is a new subject for Scorsese and he has constructed some ravishing visual tropes to express it: dissolving an image into vaporous red or yellow as if perception was suffused, completely coloured by emotion; rising in on the lovers and then dropping out the sound so it seems that for each of them nothing exists but the other. For the most part, however, he allows the performances, particularly Day-Lewis', to carry the film.

In the rigidly coded society of *The Age of Innocence*, people rarely speak their minds or act on their feelings. So skilled is Archer in keeping up appearances that he fools even himself. He doesn't realise until halfway through the film that his initial feelings for Ellen of pity (because she's the victim of a bad marriage) and envy (for her freedom to come and go as she pleases) have coalesced into *amour fou*. Day-Lewis' performance is at its most extraordinary when he manages to let us know things about Newland that Newland doesn't know himself. Early in the relationship with Ellen, Newland goes to a flower shop to fulfil his daily ritual of sending lilies of the valley to May and finds his hand wandering towards some yellow roses and then writing a card addressed to Countess Olenska to accompany them. The gestures are of a man sleepwalking through a decision that will change his life. And what is moving for us is precisely the intensity of the denial.

If Pfeiffer and Ryder fare less well, it's partly because their roles are less fully written. The film provides them with no more subjectivity than the novel – and unless you're willing to probe for subtexts, that's almost none at all. May has one moment at the climax when we understand not only what she wants, but also what she has done to get it – and Ryder plays it like a demon. Ellen, however, remains a projection of Archer's imagination, an impossible part for an actress because there's no way to flesh out a fantasy without destroying it.

As 'grave' as anything Wharton could have envisioned, but hardly 'simple', *The Age of Innocence* is made for multiple viewings – the first time for the shock of betrayal in the last twenty minutes, the next few to unpack the narrative structure that gets us to that point, one more to ponder the ontological problems of adapting novels to film, and another just to look at the image. At some point in the second half of the film – meaning after the wedding that's more like a funeral – Scorsese cuts from an abortive encounter between Archer and Ellen to a slow-motion shot of a crowd of men in identical bowler hats walking towards the camera, while on the soundtrack we hear a mournful ditty about lost love. Newland is about to be engulfed by these men whose hats are a sign of the conformity he fears – the conformity of men who've learned to keep it all under their hats. The most haunting and revelatory image in the film, it's nowhere to be found in the novel.

PASSION AND RESTRAINT

Ian Christie talks with Martin Scorsese

'"England" means tea shops, lager louts and sun-drenched cathedral closes,' according to Terry Eagleton in a recent piece on the artifice of the national idiom. Its potency, however, is undeniable, even in unlikely quarters. A tea shop hard by a cathedral close (York Minster, in fact) was part of the setting which helped Martin Scorsese to decide in January 1987 to film Edith Wharton's *The Age of Innocence*, a passionately restrained tale, ironic and nostalgic in equal measure, an acerbic 'survivor's memoir' of *belle époque* New York. The lager louts might have seemed a more likely subject for Scorsese, but this is to underestimate the most ambitious and unpredictable film-maker at work in the United States today.

I was travelling with Scorsese to ask the questions for what was to become *Scorsese on Scorsese*. While I didn't notice that he was reading Edith Wharton on the long train journeys, he still vividly remembers finishing *The Age of Innocence* and thinks it was this experience – the picturesque winter landscape outside coupled with the pastness which Britain represents for an American – that helped him decide on what seems to many a bizarre choice for a film-maker still identified with the lowlife exploits of Johnny Boy, Travis Bickle and Jake La Motta.

For Scorsese, his fans' oft-repeated plea that he should make another *Mean Streets* or confine himself to the American hard-boiled genre is as mystifying as it is infuriating. His understanding of cinema is based on a respect for the idea of genre and on an appreciation of its niceties in countless local instances: not just a great gangster film or costume piece, but one made *there*, at *this* point in the national tradition, using *those* resources. It can sound to the uninitiated like a crazy scrambling of cinema history, but I think that for Scorsese the whole point is the poignancy of knowing that we are now irrevocably on the far side of classical film-making. However gifted a director is today, he or she can only be a Mannerist, condemned, like the artists who followed the High Renaissance, to echo and embellish the great unselfconscious works of the past.

And so, for Scorsese, *how* he engages with tradition isn't just movie buffery: it is a vital creative issue. Collecting films, ensuring they are preserved by studios and archives, contacting and discreetly helping the 'great directors' (Fellini, Kazan, Kurosawa, Powell), working with collaborators who belong to traditions he admires (Freddie Francis, Michael Ballhaus, Boris Leven, Saul Bass, Elmer Bernstein) – all these are part of the process of finding a place for himself in a post-classical era. Fredric Jameson thinks of Godard's recent work as 'a survivor's modernism'. Scorsese's ambition is wider: he wants to make the past – both historic and cinematic – fully visible in the present, a country we can visit and marvel at.

Set in New York in the 1870s, *The Age of Innocence* tells the story of Newland Archer, who is engaged to May Welland, of the powerful Mingott family. A 'disgraced' member of May's family, Countess Ellen Olenska, returns from a disastrous marriage in Europe and is snubbed by New York society. Archer asks the powerful Van der Luyden family to host a dinner for the countess to counter her exclusion. Archer falls in love with Ellen, but stifling social pressures prevent him from consummating their relationship and he is torn between his passion for the Countess and his life with May.

* * *

Ian Christie: You said that the atmosphere of England, where you finished reading *The Age of Innocence*, helped you to decide to do it.

Martin Scorsese: There was something about the timing of reading the book at that point in my life, after a long struggle to get *The Last Temptation of Christ* made, and having always wanted to make a romantic piece. There was also the popularity of *A Room with a View* and pictures like it, which seemed to make working in this style possible. But I think finishing the book while travelling around England and Scotland – I seem to remember a big snowstorm – had a lot to do with it. Then it was a matter of cleaning up my creative life so that I could do it.

GoodFellas was being written in 1987 and when I was in England that was going to be my next film, but then we were able to slip in *The Last Temptation*. For the next two years, I was mulling *The Age of Innocence* over in my head and scriptwriter Jay Cocks – who had given me the book in the first place – would come over once or twice a week, and we would discuss how to make it different from the usual theatre-bound film versions of novels.

Ian Christie: It is surprising to hear that you were influenced by Merchant-Ivory films. Maybe you see these differently from the way we – or at least I – see them?

Martin Scorsese: I only became aware of this attitude when I spoke to a British journalist while we were editing *The Age of Innocence*. He said something like, 'In England, we think these films are easy.' Well, it's not at all easy to make this kind of film in America, especially since we no longer have studios that have all the props and sets. In fact, we were able to find most of our interiors in Manhattan, Brooklyn and the Bronx, but the neighbourhoods that used to surround them are completely gone. It's tragic. In the Merchant-Ivory films and in Polanski's *Tess*, England looks all of a piece. These films take you out of today and put you very securely in a world that looks more civilised – at least if you had enough money. And they really give you a sense of a world where it took a day to travel from one town to the next.

Ian Christie: The foreigner's eye. Polanski shot *Tess* in France and Merchant and Ivory, foreigners both, have created an England that seems more real, certainly more attractive, than the real thing. In any case, as Terry Eagleton has pointed out, the great English writers of the twentieth century weren't English at all: 'They were a Pole, two or three Americans and a clutch of Irishmen.' Englishness seems to be in the eye of the beholder.

Martin Scorsese: I like the beautiful detail in a lot of the Merchant-Ivory films that use English settings. One wide shot says it all. When Jim Ivory shoots a period room, the eye is there. Perhaps it's more in his cultural make-up to understand the decor, so that when he places the camera, it's right for that room, you really see the room and all its detail. I feel more comfortable placing a camera in an Italian restaurant, or a church or club, or a Lower East Side tenement. I was lucky that in the novel all those details about decor and dress and food are there.

Ian Christie: You quote in your book that accompanies the film a sentence from the novel: 'They all lived in a hieroglyphic world, where the real thing was never said or done or even thought, but only represented by a set of arbitrary signs.' Is this why you paid so much attention to period detail in the film – and why you're irritated by all the talk about 'obsessive attention to detail', as if this comes from you?

Martin Scorsese: Yes, it's all in the book. What seems to be description is in fact a clear picture of that culture, built up block by block – through every plate and glass and piece of silverware, all the sofas and what's on them. All this wealth of detail creates a wall around Newland Archer, and the longer he stays there, with these things becoming commonplace, the harder it will be for him to move out of that society.

Ian Christie: Edith Wharton published the book in 1920, recalling a society that no longer existed after the war. Did you feel that you were showing Americans a period which most of them did not know existed?

Martin Scorsese: Of course. And it was even more sumptuous than we show. I felt the film had to show a modern audience the blocks they put around Newland and people like him. But there's also an irony and a sarcasm in the presentation of that lifestyle – both in the way I tried to do it and in the way Wharton did it in the book. The decor had to become a character for me.

Jay Cocks showed the film to an audience of Wharton specialists which included R. E. B. Lewis, who wrote the Pulitzer Prize-winning biography. And he told me that their reaction was extraordinary, because every time a dinner service was shown or when Mrs Mingott selected the silver plate, they laughed. They knew what the presentation of that particular piece meant. So when the Van der Luydens create a dinner for Countess Olenska, they are making a statement and daring people to go against them.

Ian Christie: In the book there's a fantastic build-up to that dinner that tells you just how important the Van der Luydens are and how everyone in New York society acknowledges their status.

Martin Scorsese: I tried to convey that by the attention given to the dinner itself – the centrepiece, the Roman punch – which is like having a triple high mass for a funeral, rather than a regular low mass. They are saying, 'Not only will we defend you, but we are going to do so on the highest level. If anyone has a problem with that, they are going to have to answer to us.'

Ian Christie: Just like in *GoodFellas*…

Martin Scorsese: Exactly. It's a matter of 'You have a problem with that? Then you have a problem with me and let's settle it right now.' Or in this case, 'Oh very well. We're going to have to bring out the Crown Derby, aren't we?' I remember in *The Razor's Edge*, when Gene Tierney throws a plate at Herbert Marshall, he says, 'My goodness, the Crown Derby.'

Ian Christie: It's the heavy artillery.

Martin Scorsese: Absolutely. And the Wharton specialists loved it because they understood better than other people what those signals meant. It was important for me that real goodfellas would like *GoodFellas* and say that it was accurate – and they did. With *The Age of Innocence*, I think that even if ordinary people don't understand fully the significance of the different pieces of china, they will at least see that a lot of pomp and circumstance goes into certain sequences. And as it's not done by me, but by the characters, they get some understanding of the ritual.

Such occasions are the most official way they can sign someone on and make them credible in that society. For instance, when Ellen Olenska arrives late at the party given for her, it's not important to her. Next day Newland says, 'You know all New York laid themselves at your feet last night.' And she answers, 'Yes, it was a wonderful party.' The audience has to understand that this wasn't just a party, lady! Newland is in effect saying, 'I'm getting married to your family, and we have agreed to take on the disgrace of your separation from your husband and we are going to do it with a stiff upper lip. So you really should know what we are doing for you by putting on a party.'

Ian Christie: There is something about social and professional ritual that fascinates you, whatever the setting or period. But now you seem to feel happier about moving away from your own experience.

Martin Scorsese: One of the lines that led me to make *The Age of Innocence* was my interest in doing different kinds of genre film. I mean, there's a major part of me that says, 'Let's do a Western,' but it's not that easy. I have to find what's important for me in order to feel comfortable enough to wallow in the making of a film. So, although this film deals with New York's 'aristocracy' and a period of New York history that has been neglected, and although it deals with codes and ritual, and with love that's not unrequited but unconsummated – which pretty much covers all the themes I usually deal with – when I read it, I didn't say, 'Oh good – all those themes are here.' I was just hit by the impact of the sequence near the end where Newland tries finally to tell his wife May he'd like to leave – and by her response.

It all came together in that scene, and I loved the way I was led by Wharton down the path of Newland's point of view, in which he underestimated all the women, and how he wound up checkmated by them, and how his wife becomes the strongest of them all. I find that admirable. Even though I may not agree with May totally, I like the growth of her character from a young girl to the person who takes control. You see how important her role is in the second opera house scene, which is the first time May has worn her wedding dress since the wedding. We see her seated between her mother and Mrs Van der Luyden – they have passed on the responsibility for continuing their lifestyle to her.

Ian Christie: Ironically there seems to be more of you – your own desires and frustrations – in this movie than in some of your other films, even though it comes fully formed from Wharton and is set in such an apparently remote and artificial milieu.

Martin Scorsese: There is. Sometimes when you fall in love you can't see what other people see. You become as passionate and obsessive as Newland, who can't see what's going on around him. That's the theme of *Taxi Driver* and of *Mean Streets* – it's a situation I've found myself in at times, and I've found the way it plays out so wonderful. But then Wharton goes beyond that and makes a case for a life that's not exactly well spent, but a life that happens to him. Newland has his children, then he finds out that his wife knew all along about his love for Ellen and even told his son about it. Basically he is what they call in America a stand-up guy – a man of principles who would not abandon his wife and children. When he really wanted something most, he gave it up because of his kid.

That's very interesting to me – I don't know if I could do the same. But I do know that there are a lot of people, even today, who would: it's about making a decision in life and sticking to it, making do with what you have. And then, of course, during the conclusion you realise that a generation has gone by. The children don't react in the same way; the First World War is looming ahead and they can't understand why everybody was angry. I don't say it's a happy ending, but it's a realistic and beautiful one.

Ian Christie: I think there was a strong emotional reaction at the screening I attended. It was at the Odeon Marble Arch, our biggest screen, and the sensory impact of the film was extraordinary.

Martin Scorsese: That's great, because the emotional intensity is very important to me. What kept me going as I was reading the book was what a writer friend of mine called 'the sweet romantic pain' of the situation, where Newland and Ellen can't consummate their relationship. A touch of the hand has to suffice for months; the anticipation of a two-hour ride to a train station is so sweet, it's almost overwhelming. That was the real reason I wanted to make the film – the idea of that passion which involved such restraint.

Ian Christie: A friend and colleague, John Gillett, told me that he thinks this carriage scene is one of the finest he has seen for a long time – and he hates *GoodFellas*! I think the films are very close: they both try to be truthful to the milieu in which they're set and to make you feel the emotion, the allure, the danger as something almost palpable.

Martin Scorsese: Like drowning in it. Actually there are elements of Rossellini in there, especially *La Prise de pouvoir par Louis XIV*, because that's where I discovered that the more detail you see, the better you know the people. Other films do that, too, but Rossellini did it in a bolder way. In *Louis XIV*, he ties up the entire story in the presentation of a meal. In *The Age of Innocence* we have eight meals, and they are all different in order to make different dramatic points. But, although *The Age of Innocence* may look lavish, the editing, the angles, the dissolves and the length of the images were all worked out way in advance to give the impression of extravagance. In fact, it only cost $32–34 million, and some of the most complicated things, like the beginning of the ball sequence, took only three-quarters of a day. But it was important to achieve the effect of a saturation of detail.

Ian Christie: *The Age of Innocence* is a very literary film – deliberately so. But it's not theatrical, except where you bring in theatre and opera as part of the period texture and a dramatic counterpoint to the unspoken story being acted out among the characters.

Martin Scorsese: One of the films that made a strong impression on me as a child was Wyler's *The Heiress*, which, though it's based on Henry James' novel *Washington Square*, was actually taken from a play. I've seen it since and it holds up well, but it is theatrical. The acting is extraordinary – Ralph Richardson, Olivia de Havilland, Montgomery Clift, Miriam Hopkins – but it's still in three acts: the conflicts are all played out in traditional dramaturgy; characters talk in a room and confront each other, all in dialogue. There is no narration, no montages, no flashbacks or flashes forward and no visual interpolations such as letters.

I'm trying to get away from this three-act approach. Over the past ten years, I've found everyone in Hollywood saying: 'The script is good, but we need a new Act Two,' or 'Act Three just isn't there.' Finally I said to a bunch of students: 'Why are we using the term "acts" when the damn thing is a movie?' I like theatre, but theatre is theatre and movies are movies. They should be separate. We should talk about sequences – and there are usually at least five or six sequences, rather than three acts – which are broken up into sections and scenes. When I screened a few films for Elia Kazan back in 1992 and we discussed them afterwards, I found that he, too, was trying to get away from conventional theatrical dramaturgy in *East of Eden* and *Wild River* – neither of which, incidentally, he'd seen since he made them!

I certainly tried to find a different structure for *GoodFellas*, though that was more like a documentary on a lifestyle. For *The Age of Innocence*, I wanted to find a way of making something literary – and you know how America is cowed by the tyranny of the word – also filmic. I also wanted a massive use of voiceover because I wanted to give the audience the impression I had while reading the book.

Ian Christie: The experience of watching a film is often closer to reading than to watching a play. *The Age of Innocence* made me think of Max Ophuls – the most literary and even theatrical of film-makers, but also the most filmic. It's about creating and manipulating the spectator's point of view, in time through voiceover and in space through those devastating camera movements.

Martin Scorsese: I adore Ophuls and we looked at the new print of *Lola Montès*. But for me, the major Ophuls film was *Letter from an Unknown Woman*. By a happy accident, it seemed to be on television practically every afternoon when I was a child – that's the wonderful thing about Ophuls having made four American films – so when I was at home sick from school there would be *Letter from an Unknown Woman*. I couldn't tell at the time about camera moves, but I loved the romance and tragedy of it.

Ian Christie: I thought that the way you move the camera so deliberately and eloquently in *The Age of Innocence* is like the way Ophuls tracks and cranes, as if you've entered into the characters' emotions and memory.

Martin Scorsese: That's what I was hoping. I'll never forget the arrival of the piano up the staircase in *Letter from an Unknown Woman*. And then the depiction of a whole life in miniature and the sense of romance in the sequence where Louis Jourdan takes Joan Fontaine to the fairground train ride, and the fake backgrounds just slide past them. Ophuls created a world that was unique. Even though I'd seen other films set in Vienna at the turn of the century, they didn't have the grace and truth that Ophuls had in that film, which stood repeated viewing. I used to have a still on my wall in Hollywood of Louis Jourdan at the end, when he decides to go to the duel – that wonderful shot of him at the desk as he's reading the letter.

Ian Christie: You have worked with a wide range of collaborators during your career: perhaps only De Niro and Thelma Schoonmaker recur regularly. But even as personnel come and go according to the demands of each film, there is a sense of 'family' about your method of working and a closeness with fellow creators that you clearly seem to seek. Thelma Schoonmaker has always insisted that the Academy Award she got for the editing of *Raging Bull* really belongs to you, too, since you planned all the incredible distinctions and distortions in that film. I've seen the de luxe new editing suite you have, and I wonder how you work together in it?

Martin Scorsese: That's where the whole creative process happens. I sit in that chair behind her and we have worked out a system of red lights and buzzers to communicate with. It's set up for the way we like to work. Although I'm not in the editors' union, I did make my living as an editor for a while in the 1970s, and I feel that working on the script and editing are my strong points, as opposed to understanding camera movement and lighting. I love editing. I love what you can do with a film, where you can cut and not cut. It's Eisenstein really.

The way I work now is that I lay out the editing pattern, and pretty much all the time I decide where to cut and what not to cut. But what Thelma does is to focus on the characters in the film. She'll say, 'Maybe we're losing some aspect of so-and-so here. Maybe we should change this performance of this one reading because it might indicate that she's not as sympathetic towards him and we want the audience to realise it at this point.'

There's a lot of that kind of editing in *The Age of Innocence*. And in *Raging Bull* some scenes were written, but there were also improvisations within the writing. So we would have ten good takes of Joe Pesci and twelve good takes of De Niro, and we would keep switching them around. 'Why don't we use Take 4 again of Joe, because I think we lost something there,' she would say. Or, 'We lost something on De Niro there so maybe we should try Take 8 again.' It has more to do with the spiritual quality of what's happening with the people in the film that she is able to perceive and help balance out for me.

The actual cutting – well, there's pure Eisenstein stuff in *The Age of Innocence*, like when the wife gets up and walks over to him, and you see three cuts of her rising. That's something I can imagine in my head, draw the pictures, and say, 'Do this one here, that one there.' Then Thelma puts it together and I ask her what she thinks, and often she'll suggest changes.

It took a little longer to edit *The Age of Innocence*, mainly because of the dialogue scenes – trying to work out how long a pause should be. But because there is such an appetite for stories about our business and I had taken between nine and ten months – working with only *one* editor! – they painted this picture of me as someone 'obsessed with detail'. But editing is the most important original element of the film-making process, so why short-change it? It's a sorry state of affairs when just doing my job properly is described as 'obsessive'.

Little Women
WHAT ARE YOU GIRLS GOING TO DO?

Lizzie Francke talks with Gillian Armstrong

When producers Denise DiNovi and Amy Pascal were casting around for directors to work for Columbia studios on a third version of Louisa May Alcott's semi-autobiographical *Little Women*, Gillian Armstrong must have seemed an obvious choice, perhaps even a little too obvious. Her debut feature *My Brilliant Career* (1979) was also adapted from an autobiographical novel: Miles Franklin's, who at the age of sixteen was writing about her life with a wonderfully audacious spirit. Alcott's March sisters, particularly the intrepid, literary-minded Jo, were nineteenth-century girls of slender means pulling together while their father is away during the Civil War. An updating of their adventures surely needed some of the mettle that Armstrong had injected into *My Brilliant Career*, with its boisterous heroine Sybylla Melvyn. Alcott, too, had had a rather unusual life: her family were transcendentalists who at one point lived in a commune, while she grew up to champion social reform and was the first woman to register to vote in her home town of Concord. Asked to come up with a 'girl's story' by her publisher in 1869, she chose to intimate the brave new world for young women in those times through the character of Jo in *Little Women* (and to some extent through the wilful youngest sister Amy, who becomes a painter). But there is also a sense of restraint in the novel, as though Alcott could not let her own experience quite bubble through. In the film, however, Armstrong and screenwriter Robin Swicord gently loosen the stays, alluding to concerns Alcott could not quite spell out. In the novel, for instance, the March mother, known as Marmee, exhorts the virtues of modesty in a young girl: in the film this speech becomes an ironic comment about a society which disenfranchises women. 'Ladies guard their modesty for one practical reason: we are not as highly valued as men. We are forbidden to govern, or vote or inherit land.'

As played by Judy Davis, *My Brilliant Career*'s Sybylla would have recognised this plight. 'This story is going to be all about me ...' announces Davis with a fiery glint, as she trudges round the dusty outback farm in her layers of calico petticoats, pen and paper in hand. Set in 1901, the film seemed to bequeath the coming century to young female audiences. Here is a bush-girl heroine, who starts out gorse-haired and slightly gap-toothed, dreaming of being a writer, battling with all, not least herself, to achieve it. *My Brilliant Career* was about optimism and opportunity, and for the late 1970s this was something of a revelation. In its final image, Sybylla is looking ahead, smiling as her head tilted towards a future that is uncertain, but also promises to be eventful. With Davis' exuberant, peppery performance and Armstrong's painterly eye, the film stamped itself on many an imagination and no doubt prompted some to speculate where their own careers might venture.

A Virago classic for the film world, Armstrong's treatment of *My Brilliant Career* brought Sybylla and Miles Franklin to wider mainstream audiences at a key moment in feminism's reappraisal of women's contributions to history and literature. Armstrong was the first woman to direct in Australia since Paulette McDonagh of the trailblazing McDonagh sisters (Paulette, Phyllis and Isobel, respectively, director, writer/producer and actress during the late 1920s and early 1930s). With her producer Margaret Fink and her screenwriter Eleanor Witcombe, Armstrong ensured that women had a high profile in the new wave of Australian film-makers that emerged in the late 1970s, a group which included Peter Weir and Bruce Beresford. (Indeed, it is interesting with hindsight to note that the two major successes of Australian cinema in 1979 were, somewhat incongruously, *My Brilliant Career* and George Miller's *Mad Max*.) In this respect, Armstrong and *My Brilliant Career* indicated a whole array of possibilities, something surely not lost on those Australian women film-makers who have since made their mark: Jane Campion, Alison Maclean, Ann Turner, Tracey Moffat and Jocelyn Moorhouse.

As Armstrong reflects on her own early career, the value of having precedents becomes clear. 'When I went to film school it had only been going for five years. I didn't go to film school to be a director. I didn't think about it because there were no women directors. I studied theatre design first at Swinbourne Technical College: it was really only by going there that I learnt about film from the practical side. I was lucky – because it was an art school, it was much more liberated than other types of education. But when we started talking about what we were going to do when we left, the lecturers viewed us with some puzzlement – as if to say 'What are you girls going to do?' Certainly, I had no idea of how I was going to make a living. My only aim at the time was to be a script supervisor in drama at the ABC TV station. That was my ultimate ambition. It was just lucky that my final year coincided with the time that the Australian government had just started to invest in the idea of a film industry as a result of various film-makers lobbying. Fred Schepisi had just got some money to make a short film and asked some of the students to work on it for experience. He was very positive and took time to look at our final year films.'

With Schepisi's encouragement, Armstrong decided to pursue a career in film. 'But it was interesting: when I first tried to get a job, all anybody could suggest was continuity, either that or neg matching.' It was only after meeting a woman editor at one production house that Armstrong was persuaded that she had more than a modicum of creative talent. 'She was quite firm about me not going into continuity, and persuaded me into editing. It is perhaps indicative that at the time even women editors were rare. But there were various changes occurring in the early 1970s: the rebirth of the industry also coincided with the arrival of the feminist movement, which was particularly strong in Sydney.' Armstrong cites in particular the Sydney Women's Film Group (SWFG), formed in 1971, who encouraged the then-nascent national film and television school to be conscious about ensuring an equal female intake, whilst also putting pressure on the government to set up a separate women's film fund. Armstrong herself sat on selection panels for the fund and also had her films screened at the numerous festivals that the SWFG organised. At the same time, however, she sat apart from the group. 'They were a political movement who were more interested in the content of the films, in that it had to be about women's issues. I was interested in the content and how it was applied and for that I was sometimes criticised. But if they were narrow, it was also their strength. The SWFG had a powerful effect which really did pay off.'

While feminism helped Armstrong redefine what professions women could do, she was very clear in interviews after *My Brilliant Career* about not being defined as a 'woman's director', seeming a reaction specifically to the typecasting she was experiencing at the time, which she claims sent her 'in the opposite way looking for completely different material. I was offered every single story that was about a young woman achieving – the first woman to climb a mountain, the first woman to fly a plane. Everyone thought Sybylla was me – that I had had a terrible struggle as a young woman, but really I had a very easy pathway.' But though she claims that she 'hasn't gone out and planned it', in retrospect her career has indeed been devoted to stories about women.

There also seems to be a consistent dedication in the fact that, interlaced with her feature film career, are a series of three documentaries, all with state backing: *Smokes and Lollies* (1977), *14's Good, 18's Better* (1981) and *Bingo, Bridesmaids and Braces* (1988), chronicling the lives as they grow up of Josie, Kerry and Diana, three working-class girls from Adelaide. Superficially similar to Michael Apted's *Seven Up* and its follow-ups, Armstrong's series has a far more considered view of class and gender, and the Australian film critic Philippa Hawker, making the comparison, has commented, '[Apted] also tracks the lives of a group of three girlfriends, but fails to get very far with them. Of all his subjects, they are the most distant, the most resistant to self-analysis; partly, one suspects, because Apted himself does not find the minutiae of their lives interesting and does not succeed in seeing them as individuals.' Meanwhile, Josie, Kerry and Diana are given the space to chronicle their lives with great precision, part of the documentary process, rather than mere objects of its scrutiny. In *14's Good, 18's Better*, for instance, there is a fierce sense of self-awareness as Josie wryly recounts how she sent an elaborate bouquet to herself after giving birth to her first child, since there was nobody else to do it. This sense of the value of such telling details is exactly what Armstrong brings to her fiction.

Her debut aside, Armstrong's features seem to come in two forms, in terms of their approach to female experience. There are the period films for Hollywood: *Mrs Soffel* (1984), based on a true story about a jail warder's wife who escapes from her own dour, prison-like marriage to run away with a lusty young convict, a suitably melancholic and atmosphere-based tale which one suspects should have been a little starker still; and now *Little Women*. Then there are the edgy, contemporary films made on low budgets in Australia: *Starstruck* (1982), *High Tide* (1987, scripted by Laura Jones who also adapted *An Angel at My Table*) and *The Last Days of Chez Nous* (1992, scripted by novelist Helen Garner), the first was a kitsch post-punk musical about a wannabe Debbie Harry, the latter two finely nuanced, sharply observed and visually alluring studies of dysfunctional family relationships (at the point where the documentarist and the woman who once aspired to be a theatre designer meet): Judy Davis' second-rate singer Lilli in *High Tide* winds up at a washed-out seaside trailer park and finds herself caught up with the daughter she abandoned years before; Kerry Fox's impetuous and greedy Vicki in *The Last Days of Chez Nous* seems intent on smashing up her elder sister Beth's already cracked family life.

It isn't that opportunities for directing contemporary stories in Hollywood haven't come her way: tellingly, she turned down both *Ghost* and *Working Girl*. She also worked on *Fires Within* (1991), which focused on the re-establishment of a relationship between a Cuban political prisoner and his family after his release (a story not dissimilar to that of Mira Nair's forthcoming *The Perez Family*, also scripted by Swicord). But *Fires Within* proved to be an intolerable experience and, after much re-editing, which resulted in a refocusing of the film around the sex scenes between the leads Jimmy Smits and Greta Scacchi, Armstrong took her name off it.

Certainly, Armstrong is very circumspect about Hollywood. Though she describes *Mrs Soffel* and *Little Women* as positive experiences, she puts this down to working with producers who share her sensibility and who are willing to fight through the studio bureaucracy to keep a film's integrity intact. It is also important that she is able to work closely with the screenwriter. 'The script is everything. But I am finding that at the moment that American scripts, of which I am reading dozens at the moment, tend to be mostly formula. Time and time again when I read something that has an extra edge to it, in which the characters have more depth, it has been adapted from a book.'

Meanwhile, she puts Hollywood's renewed interest in the literary adaptation/costume drama down to the success of Merchant-Ivory, particularly *Howards End*. The 1910 novel toyed with questions of female emancipation, which James Ivory and Ruth Prawer Jhabvala then brought to the fore. One cannot but think of how E. M. Forster's Schlegel sisters fit in with the March siblings and Sybylla: there is a return engagement, an overstitching-in-time in which women, bustling around in their layers of skirts, are perpetually poised on the brink of something else.

Fifteen years on from *My Brilliant Career*, Armstrong considers: 'I actually had a lot of doubts about doing *Little Women* when it was originally offered me because I felt that it touched on many of the concerns of *My Brilliant Career*. Basically, the arguments that were put to me were that *My Brilliant Career* was done so many years ago, enough time for a whole generation of young women and girls to be out there who had never seen it.'

It is revealing then that Armstrong is happy rather than offended when told that the film of *Little Women* reminds at least one viewer of why she liked the book when she was eight – or was it the 1933 George Cukor film version with Katharine Hepburn as Jo, or the 1948, by Mervyn LeRoy, or even the 1970 BBC series? Indeed, *Little Women* is enough part of popular culture for people to know about the death of Beth without having read or seen it. With Swicord's script, the film – along with this 32-year-old's memory – provides a selective reading as it filters out the more sanctimonious preachings of Marmee, and enhances the more obviously progressive implications on the subject of the education of women and of Jo and May fulfilling their artistic aspirations. In this respect, it is a handsomely decorated 'feminism for beginners' primer that also deftly allows for all the anticipated emotional release.

Little Women has rightfully reinstated Armstrong's reputation to a wider audience. But one hopes that she can carry the March sisters beyond the 'coming of age' through to the more complicated entanglements characterised by her Australian films. *High Tide* and *The Last Days of Chez Nous*, both centred on the shifting and perplexing nexus of female relationships in fragmented families – families only the potentially feckless Amy March could ever have imagined. These are films about the hollowing out of aspirations, the cutting down of dreams into pragmatic reality. And both end speculatively, pointing a way forward, but without making promises for the true great-grand-daughters of Sybylla and Jo.

Sense and Sensibility
CAUTIONARY TALE

Graham Fuller

'A film by Ang Lee' is what we're told we're watching during *Sense and Sensibility*'s opening credits, but are we to believe it? Emma Thompson wrote the screenplay and, although she didn't craft the film as a vehicle for herself, she ended up taking the lead role. So is hers the shaping vision behind it? In high-street terms, the answer is yes; and there's even a coffee-table book – *Jane Austen's Sense & Sensibility: The Screenplay & Diaries* (Bloomsbury) 'by Emma Thompson' – to commodify her proprietary interest. The selling points of this latest Austen movie are not Lee's reputation as the auteur of *Pushing Hands* (1992), *The Wedding Banquet* (1993) and *Eat Drink Man Woman* (1994), nor the specific fireworks he used to illuminate the hermetic social world of the English gentry in Georgian England. For many, the lure is the film's cachet as an exquisite costume romance in the vein of James Ivory's tasteful E. M. Forster adaptations, a cachet confirmed by Thompson's presence as the heroine Elinor Dashwood and of fellow Merchant-Ivory alumnus Hugh Grant as her unforthcoming suitor, Edward Ferrars.

Since Jane Austen always told variations on the same story (of delayed romantic consummation with delicate tonal shadings and faintly nuanced moral conclusions), the rarefied Austen milieu can function as a curiously state-of-the-art barometer for degrees of authorial hijinks in the cinema, if not in television. Following the 1971 Granada production of *Persuasion*, the BBC drama department knocked out largely uninspired adaptations of the other five major Austen novels between 1972 and 1987. The question of who authored them was never raised, for television was then and remains a writer's medium, despite the move toward all-film drama in the late 1980s. The scrupulously faithful-to-the-book 1980 *Pride and Prejudice*, for example, was unarguably the work of Fay Weldon; and, since its performances were execrable and its visual style negligible, there's no reason why director Cyril Coke would have wanted to claim responsibility for it anyway.

As tangibly as last year's robust, modernist *Pride and Prejudice* was composed and framed – in contrast to the 1980 electronic studio version – Simon Langton's directorial point of view was modest; the series' auteur was writer Andrew Davies, whose decision it was to allow Elizabeth Bennet to cavort around the countryside, Mr Darcy to rise from his bath, and Lydia Bennet to disarm Mr Collins with her cleavage. The big-screen assault on Austen has meanwhile served up a smorgasbord of styles: Amy Heckerling's unaffectedly post-modern update of *Emma* in *Clueless*, Roger Michell's social realist *Persuasion*, the classical *Sense and Sensibility* and let's not forget Whit Stillman's 1989 Fitzgeraldian take on *Mansfield Park* in *Metropolitan*, which pre-empted the Austen zeitgeist by five years. The imminent trio of Regency *Emmas* – one for cinema and two for television in the next two years – will at least enable auteurists to focus on a single text.

Sense and Sensibility's producer Lindsay Doran had long nurtured a wish to make a film of Austen's first published novel. As she says in her introduction to Thompson's book, she met the actress on the set of Kenneth Branagh's *Dead Again* (1991) and discovered their mutual passion for Austen. Doran then chanced on the comedy series that Thompson had written and performed for the BBC in 1988 and was impressed by two particular sketches, which shared an economy of language and a fond yet ironic appreciation of heritage culture staples. In one, a disgruntled Maid Marian offered a feminine perspective on Robin Hood's policy of stealing from the rich to give to the poor; the other spoofed the sexual ignorance of Victorian brides. Not unreasonably, they convinced Doran to commission Thompson to write the *Sense and Sensibility* script. Over the next five years, Thompson poured out 400 pages, which she rationalised, through copious rewrites, into a drum-tight blueprint for a two-hour film. Lee would cut more; mostly speeches, he says.

Consciously and unconsciously, Thompson must have identified with the material and its creator. She and her actress sister Sophie are the daughters of actress Phyllida Law and Eric Thompson, the actor, stage director, and writer–narrator of *The Magic Roundabout*, who died in 1983 when he was fifty-two and Emma twenty-three. 'My father was always ill when I was growing up,' Thompson recently told *Vanity Fair*. So, like Jane and Cassandra Austen, the Thompson sisters grew up with a permanently sick parent, and, like the Austens and the Dashwood sisters, lost their father prematurely.

It is the death of Henry Dashwood (also at fifty-two, in Thompson's script) that supplies *Sense and Sensibility* with its structuring absence, in the film as in the novel. The danger of marginalisation caused by the law of patrilineal descent prompts Elinor to assume the male position in the disenfranchised female Dashwood household and the heroic role in the narrative, which contains Austen's most feckless crew of men. (Elinor is thus a cousin to Margaret, the sensible older Schlegel sister, whom Thompson played in Ivory's *Howards End*.)

This role reversal (and her own role in facilitating it) must have resonated powerfully with Thompson. As well as playing an amnesiac in *Dead Again*, she had acted for her husband Kenneth Branagh (the two have since parted) in *Henry V* (1989), *Much Ado About Nothing* (1993) and *Peter's Friends* (1992), in roles that stand little scrutiny in terms of female empowerment. In 1993, Thompson told Robbie Coltrane in *Interview*, 'I used to do a sketch which started, "I'd like to thank my husband, the director," which got enormous laughs, but, of course, it was a virtually self-fulfilling prophecy.' Now here she is creating her own vehicle with her first screenplay, in which Elinor, the character she plays, explains to her lover the frustrations of being forbidden from earning a living. If a case can be made that Thompson is *Sense and Sensibility*'s auteur, its suffragette and heroic 'male' surrogate, then it is equally valid to suggest it is a personal psychodrama.

Sense and Sensibility (1811) was Austen's sourest look at the oppression of women through marriage, property and family. The movie relays this through Thompson's self-deprecating irony, and a brio which is in direct contrast to Michell's lowering *Persuasion*, with its achingly slow feminist awakening (and its own Thompson, Sophie, as the querulous hypochondriac Mary Musgrove). Proving a superb creator of scenes, Thompson harnesses all kinds of comic business to the story's themes: when

Elinor tries to get little sis Margaret to come down from her treehouse, which Thompson invented, their conversation leads to the awful truth, delivered in modernised Austenian dialogue, that 'houses go from father to son, dearest – not from father to daughter. It is the law.' Intentionally silly repartee (about the source of the Nile) between Elinor and Edward reveals his sympathetic feeling for her family. Nothing is gratuitous. There is even room in this script for a joke about horseshit, the vulgar Mrs Jennings (Elizabeth Spriggs) warning the Dashwood girls about stepping onto the streets of London; this is Thompson the scatologist spoofing gentility.

Thompson was clearly less interested in exacting verisimilitude than in period evocation, as with the recent *Pride and Prejudice*, and more interested in the tension between people who can't speak their feelings, or speak them too much, than in surface detail. The film embodies the dialectic between Elinor's rationality and the romantic cult of sensibility espoused by her sister Marianne (Kate Winslet), an emotional 'choice' that is more about female survival under an oppressive patriarchy than it is about mere behaviour. This dialectic is established in the scene where Elinor asks Marianne to stop playing a funeral dirge because it is upsetting their grieving mother (Gemma Jones); it manifests itself both verbally (Elinor's ironicisms versus Marianne's sarcasm; irony being the language of someone too cold, sarcasm of someone too hot) and structurally. The juxtaposition of the sequence in which the survivalist Elinor, learning that Edward is not coming to Devon, tells her mother it is better to trust the head than the heart, next to the sequence in which Marianne promotes her romantic death wish by falling for Willoughby on the hillside, is brilliantly wrought.

Thompson's finest job of characterisation, though, is her use of Margaret Dashwood (Emilie François) – a character barely present in the novel and ignored by the 1980 BBC film – as cautionary symbol. Hiding in a treehouse and under a table from the pernicious John (James Fleet) and Fanny Dashwood (Harriet Walter) when they come to take over Norland, Margaret physically personifies Elinor and Marianne's conceal-ment of their romantic secrets from each other; only when Marianne lies close to death do the older sisters achieve communion, enabling each to learn from the other's philosophy. Margaret has militated against their circumspection by blurting out Elinor's attachment to Edward to Mrs Jennings and Sir John Middleton (Robert Hardy); later she will spy on Marianne and their mother. She is both concealer and revealer. With her atlas, telescope, treehouse (crow's nest) and child's omniscience, this shock-headed sprite is the film's Puck, who reminds us what fools mortals are.

Unlike Thompson, Ang Lee was no devotee of Jane Austen, having never read any of her books before he was hired to direct Thompson's script. Yet his own films chime with it. *Pushing Hands* is the story of the uneasy coexistence of an elderly Chinese man and his American daughter-in-law, and reminiscent in its claustrophobia of the scenes between the impoverished Dashwood women and the *arrivistes* John and Fanny. *The Wedding Bouquet* is nothing if not a study in concealment and sexual repression. *Eat Drink Man Woman* concerns a widower's struggles to stay close to his three daughters, the eldest of whom is as repressed as Elinor, as they make their way in the world. The structuring absence of each entry in this ironically titled 'Father Knows Best Trilogy' is that of a mother/wife figure. Lee's appreciation of codes of social behaviour in his native Taiwan, his handling of the dangerous bottling up of feelings and presumably his craftsman's skill with interiors were what recommended him to Thompson and Doran over tried and trusted Brits.

So what did Lee make of Austen-land? How did he frame it all? Obsessively is the answer.

Watching this film, I was forcibly reminded of Camille Paglia's unfashionably neo-conservative thesis that western art is a pagan battleground between the phallocentric Apollonian quest for control and the horrors of Dionysian disorder, the chthonian female swamp. 'Cinema is the culmination of the obsessive, mechanistic male drive in western culture,' Paglia wrote. 'The movie projector is an Apollonian straightshooter, demonstrating the link between aggression and art. Every pictorial framing is a ritual limitation, a barred precinct. The rectangular movie screen is clearly patterned on the post-Renaissance framed painting. But all conceptualisation is a framing.'

Sense and Sensibility is a concatenation of fields and planes, its *mise-en-scène* a rigorous exercise in drawing straight lines around the emotionally distraught, sexually hungry and, therefore, potentially ruinous women characters. This ritual framing is as fetishistically achieved as the elaborate meals that Mr Chu prepares for his daughters to tempt them to stay at home in *Eat Drink Man Woman*. To reinforce the point, Lee shows us the ostentatious array of framed pictures on the stairway at Norland. The shot in which Marianne gives her mother the letter from Sir John inviting them to live at Barton Cottage replicates Vermeer's *The Letter* (1666), in which two women are framed by the perspective window of a doorway, and immobilised by it. A shot of Edward in a doorway silently watching Elinor in a doorway silently watching Marianne playing the piano doubles the trick. Even outdoor shots – Elinor and Marianne discussing propriety as they pass through a gate to a village field – are as discretely contained as Gainsborough's rural portraits. Thompson's script omitted Austen's detail of Elinor being a painter of decorative screens, so Lee became one himself, and with a vengeance.

A key motif in the film is that of women looking out of windows, as if seeking escape. Elinor at her desk watches Edward swordfighting with Margaret; the camera tilts from Mrs Dashwood happily watching Elinor and Edward strolling in the grounds to Fanny watching them angrily from a higher window; at different moments, Mrs Dashwood and Elinor turn away and look forlornly outside. Crucially, all these scenes were written by Thompson as gestures against confinement. It is Lee, of course, who turned them into windows within windows, a cinematic equivalent of double-glazing. The spectator is asked to identify with those characters who are passive (Elinor, Edward, Colonel Brandon) and passive-aggressive (Fanny and Imogen Stubbs' slyly watchful Lucy Steele) as they observe the damage done by the active characters (Marianne, Willoughby, and the gossiping pair, Sir John and Mrs Jennings).

In this gynaecentric universe, with its yawning doorways and portals, the measure of a male character's virility is how vigorously he enters a room, or tries to bust the frame. The romantically wounded Brandon (Alan Rickman) and the maternally emas-culated Edward enter them diffidently or hover on the threshold. The seducer Willoughby, according to Sir John a 'decent shot – and there is not a bolder rider in all England', rushes through them heedlessly. His materialisation on horseback at the site of Marianne's fall carries the film from Gainsborough to Gothic (if not to 'Gainsborough Gothic', the 1940s school of Regency melodramas).

In fact, the film depicts a wilting phallocracy. Edward fences with the eleven-year-old Margaret and pretends to be her subordinate; Brandon, who carries his hunting barrel down, timidly offers Marianne his knife to cut reeds in a Hardy-like vignette; and, when he and his rival Willoughby meet, they are shown with their riding crops tucked behind their backs (Brandon's is marginally the bigger). Masculinity is made pathetic and comic. Meanwhile, the film's two splendidly satirical Gothic sequences show how (self-)destructive female energy will not be trammelled; the first of these is anticipated when Marianne breaks from the Dashwood family group (framed in the gateway on arrival at Barton) and hurries through the cottage: and we glimpse the Edenic hillside where she will fall. There, as on the moor above Willoughby's house later, she becomes the centre of Turner-esque vortices of rain and fog, abandoning herself to Willoughby in one sequence and finding herself abandoned by him in the other.

'All conceptualisation is a framing,' said Paglia, and so it is that these Gothic sequences frame the second act of *Sense and Sensibility* and are framed in turn by the opening and closing sequences of men on horseback: John Dashwood riding to his father's sick bed; the unobserved (and by now lovelorn) Willoughby riding away from Marianne's wedding. Still, Apollo may frown on and frame Dionysus, but he cannot stop the Dionysian from blossoming. *Sense and Sensibility* is Ang Lee's classical masterpiece, but Emma Thompson's romantic triumph.

The Portrait of a Lady and other Henry James novels ON THE BRINK

Lizzie Francke

By what process of logical accretion was this slight 'personality', the mere slim shade of an intelligent but presumptuous girl, to find itself endowed with the high attributes of a Subject? – and indeed by what thinness, at the best, would such a subject not be vitiated. Millions of presumptuous girls, intelligent or not intelligent, daily affront their destiny, and what is it open to their destiny to be, at the most, that we should make an ado about it?

HENRY JAMES' PREFACE TO *THE PORTRAIT OF A LADY*

* * *

The opening few minutes of Jane Campion's *The Portrait of a Lady* are sublimely designed to disorientate any viewer corseted into certain expectations of the literary-adaptation piece. For a few moments, we may think we have wandered into the wrong movie theatre, as we watch a group of contemporary Australian teenage girls talk candidly about their romantic hopes. We seem to have caught them on some long, balmy afternoon, these joyfully open faces swaying gently with their thoughts, eyeing us wistfully, their off-screen voices delightfully calling up what love might mean for them. Young women on the brink of their lives with everything before them: it took me back fifteen or so years, to school conversations when there were hours and hours to spend on endless speculation about all our futures, romantic or otherwise. And the *otherwise* was increasingly becoming so important. For those were the years when we started cramming our heads with ideas and aspirations, reading Austen, George Eliot, the Brontës, James and others, by the yard. And we frowned as everything started becoming so much more damned complicated. Mere slim shades of intelligent, presumptuous girls, yearning to be the heroines of our own stories, we were waiting, like the clear, young faces gracing the opening minutes of Campion's film, to be written on by our own wisdom, to be filled out into subjects worth (in our arrogant but so uncertain heads) reading about.

This tangential opening scene – which one could describe as Campion's own preface to *The Portrait of a Lady* – exquisitely evoked this tender moment of youthful anticipation, and may be as much about her own green years as any: the graduation short with which she began making her own firm, auspicious mark as a film-maker, *A Girl's Own Story*, was preoccupied with the confusions of adolescence. But this chorus of young girls also helps us infer where she places this novel in her own life, which she first read as a teenager, when she was no doubt hungry to find fictional women navigating a path ahead of her.

The Portrait of a Lady bestows on the world one of the greatest heroines in fiction. As read by Campion's film, Isabel Archer (Nicole Kidman) is a gauche and difficult young American on the brink of womanhood, whose uneasy metamorphosis – emotional, moral or spiritual – takes place as she ventures through a Europe that is both glittering palace and cold, forbidding mausoleum. In the talk of those around her (and this is a film about talk, rather than the silence of *The Piano*, with the often brutal admissions of the protagonists delivered in a smartingly clipped style), she is subjected to scrutiny, dissection and ultimately terrible deception, as she befriends the intriguing sophisticate Madame Merle (Barbara Hershey) and the decadent artefact collector Gilbert Osmond (John Malkovich), two mendacious Americans with an affected – and infected – sense of their 'European-ness'. Isabel's tale, as she inherits a legacy and consequently becomes a woman of means, with seemingly more freedom to choose what to do with her life, is not just one of female individuation, but of the defining of one culture in the face of another.

In this sense, it is revealing that, at the press conference held before shooting started, Campion explained how, when she first read the novel, she identified with the naive young Isabel – that to be from the Antipodes in the twentieth century was akin to the American experience in the nineteenth century. Now Campion journeys to Europe (and Hollywood) for this film, and may at last shake the label 'best woman director from New Zealand' (she is so obviously in the world league, period). *The Portrait of a Lady* is a tale about women on the verge of journeys in many ways.

This contemporary prologue, which frames the film, succinctly conveys what kind of literary adaptation this is. Campion and screenwriter Laura Jones (who previously worked with her on *An Angel at My Table*) offer a reading that seems to hark back to the first youthful exploration of the novel, and then to elaborate on it. To purloin James' own metaphor, Campion has returned to the cold Jamesian House of Fiction that she once built in her head, has dusted down the rooms of her choosing and installed the audience.

With the type of visceral sting she executes so well, Campion launches the unsuspecting viewer slap into the tale (boldly skipping the novel's first hundred-odd pages), with us party to Isabel's early days in England, fresh off the boat from America, and fending off one of her suitors, the solemn Lord Warburton (not presented as a buffoon or prig, but just plain decent), as he makes a desperate proposal to her. The film's almost suffocatingly intense pace allows little respite as it takes its grand two-plus hour tour (even Wojciech Kilar's restrained score, quivering with repressed emotions, is sparingly used). There is no polite build-up, and no establishing long-shot introductions: rather, we come immediately face-to-face with the heroine and her dilemmas, as she looks for a way out of a tight corner. Isabel is faced with the proposal in the garden (here full of snarly trees) which so many romances build up to – for example, in the present Jane Austen vogue, Austen's novels have been read as so much bumbling pre-prandial to the jolly betrothals. Campion's film, by contrast, starts with a refusal which is mixed with a nostalgia for another time, when there could have been a simpler response, as Isabel states: 'There was one moment when I would have given my little finger to say yes.' (Though Jones' succinct script tinkers only slightly with James' own interlocution, here it seems deliberately to recall *The Piano*'s Ada, who did give her index finger to do a version of this.) This is a gruelling, hard scene, accentuated in the close-up: Nicole Kidman's scrubbed white skin fills the screen, her unruly auburn hair swept wispily on top of her head, her eyes full of trepidation, tears proudly clinging to the lower lids, not uncouth enough to fall. And having taken us up the garden path with this opening, we are snapped straight into a claustrophobic, dimly lit world, where Isabel's face often appears as luminous as an opal in the shadows around her.

Most striking about the garden sequence is the degree to which Kidman reminds us of her Antipodean sister Judy Davis, bracing herself for her future at the opening of Gillian Armstrong's *My Brilliant Career* (1979). Like Davis' boisterous Sybylla, Isabel is at first depicted as an awkward sort, with a determined stride that would have horrified the deportment tutors of the day. Worse still, she's the kind of girl wont to probe her walking boots with a hearty sniff, obviously with little regard for the niceties of 'lady-like' etiquette. No, Isabel is a cerebral type, who collects words ('nihilism', for instance, is written out in neat scroll and pegged to her wardrobe): an intelligent woman, though without Sybylla's obvious vocational aspirations, or those of her journalist compatriot Harriet Stackpole in *Portrait*.

This reference to Armstrong's film may be subconscious, but it seems a fleeting homage to a moment that would have been of great influence on Campion's career, setting out as she did as the Australian New Wave of cinema had just gathered full momentum. It is as if the director is marking out her starting points, which go on to intersect in so many ways. But one might also see *Portrait* as a rejoinder to *My Brilliant Career*; the exuberant celebration of one young woman's creative independence, so much needed in 1979, can be more circumspectly examined in 1996. As if to say, everything is just so much more damned difficult than one first hoped for.

But this is something we know that Campion has known from the start. From *A Girl's Own Story*, through *Two Friends, Sweetie, An Angel at My Table* and *The Piano*, Campion's heroines have been truculent individuals, tripped up by their desires (and one may sweepingly suggest her films can be measured by how they keep their footing among all the treading of water and land). Her work has been so deliriously uncensored that she taps into the most perverse parts of the female psyche, unafraid to deal with women who are the undoing of themselves. At the troubled and therefore fascinating centre of her work is the exploration of female masochism, the match to Scorsese's excursions into the male equivalent. Patently there in *The Piano*, this is no less present in *Portrait*, where Isabel allows herself to be ensnared by Osmond into the most emotionally sado-masochistic of relationships. Malkovich, at first apparently revamping his Valmont from *Dangerous Liaisons*, proves terrifyingly persuasive as the spiteful and contemptuous Osmond. With goatee and mesmerising look, he seems the devil, no less, the master of shades who takes her ransom in a gloomy Roman catacomb. In one of the most audacious, shocking moments (illustrating the darkness of their relationship), he forces Isabel onto a chair, piled like a throne with cushions, much as a parent might seat a fidgety child, or a collector put a doll on display. But, even after such humiliation, she is both willing and wilful victim. Her path is beset by things for her perhaps to stumble on, bringing her down to the primordial moral level of some of those around her. But (as she claims), 'I will not crawl.' The film follows this, the camera obsessed with the trailing of her skirt-train, to which new flounces are added as her financial and marital status increases. As she propels urgently forward through the beautiful and sometimes dwarfing detritus of classical and post-classical Europe, her dress is like some fin-tail, a strange remnant, reminding us of the origins of her species in this moral and emotional evolution.

And half Isabel's battle is for herself not to become a beautiful thing, an ornate bauble in Osmond's collection. Campion traces her journey, from ingénue to a woman caught up in an elaborate style (at times she wears a net-like lace veil that seems to emphasise just how snared she is). Tightly shot, this film deals mostly in close-ups: it is, after all, about portraits. And what is most striking is just how many portraits there are – with Kidman's own metamorphosing (even at one point taking on the mask-like appearance of the starkly attractive Madame Merle). In a tightly wound performance, Kidman gives very little away. But we can see her looking, her blue eyes, so proudly loath to shed tears, soaking up everything around her. And if we peer at the portraits long enough, we may discern what is going on in the headstrong head at their centre, as she peers at her reflection and finally comes to recognise herself – though such self-recognition rarely provides easy answers. In a film haunted by Eros and Thanatos, caught up in their dry embrace (snatches of Schubert's *Death and the Maiden* are heard on the soundtrack), the path to love seems one of psychotic self-destruction.

For Campion does not like easy endings – after the choppy finale of *The Piano*, *The Portrait of a Lady* is no less bracing. Coming full circle (in this and many other ways one is reminded of Max Ophuls' cinematic carousels), the finale finds Isabel back in the garden we first met her in (it's now gaunt with winter) attempting to disentangle herself from the sapping desires of her persistent suitor, Goodwood. The white lightning of the final scene seems to spring as swiftly as the opening, as Campion catches the perilous ambiguity of Isabel's destiny, beating a retreat only to find she is shut out in the cold, shut out literally and metaphorically. It is an astounding moment: a sudden cold flash in which whole audiences of presumptuous girls may find existential truths. Then, with the door of this House of Fiction closed securely behind, Campion leaves us asking of ourselves what other paths are there to be followed.

THE JAMES GANG

Philip Horne

As the craze for Hampshire's Jane Austen begins to subside, the New York-born Henry James (1843–1916), who settled in next-door Sussex in 1898, has been edging forward as the current classic literary adaptee of choice for the English-speaking film world. A little surprisingly, as many people would agree with Daphne Merkin in a recent *New Yorker* that 'There is something about Henry James that doesn't warm to the screen.'

She was reacting to *The Wings of the Dove*, the new film version of what she calls a 'majestically interior' late masterpiece of the same name, by an author 'whose greatest interest is the solitary nature of consciousness'. Which you might not guess from this bustling movie: for it translates James' elliptical narrative back to the highly dramatic story at its root – and then adds more drama, inventing scenes in pubs, bedrooms, opium dens and the Venetian *Carnivale*. As experience, the film is markedly different from the effortful intensity of reading the book – and raises questions of fidelity and betrayal not only on its dramatic action, but also in its very genesis. Can Henry James be faithfully filmed? What would a faithful James film be like?

Of course, in so different a medium, the very idea of 'faithfulness' begs all sorts of questions. The imaginative experience of watching a (two-hour) film is not like that of reading a (twenty-hour) book. If a long novel is being adapted, ruthless cuts and selections must be made and film-makers need a radical interpretation and a structure of their own to retain direction, shape or dynamics. The result must stand as a work in its own right. With absolute fidelity impossible, extreme closeness to portions of the original may be dangerous unless really thought through. Besides, James himself altered material from one form to fit another: when dramatising his novel *The American*, James changed it drastically, giving it a happy ending (a death but a marriage) and then, when audiences still weren't satisfied, an even happier one (no death and the marriage).

'The problem with James is that nothing is ever stated and film doesn't allow that kind of vagueness,' said François Truffaut. But he said this while making *La Chambre verte* (1974), a haunting film based on three James stories at once – and was defining, not ruling out, the task of filming James. 'We're going to have to explain everything, make everything clear, and we're also going to have to find a thousand ways of emphasising what I call the privileged moments,' he continues. These 'privileged moments' can be fairly fleeting impressions; in his famous 1884 essay 'The Art of Fiction', James declared defiantly that: 'It is an incident for a woman to stand up with her hand resting on a table and look out at you in a certain way.' We may think this absurd and/or unfilmable – or we may recall that in cinema it is an 'incident' for Robert De Niro to sit at a bar and, smiling to himself, flash a glance at Ray Liotta.

Born a few decades later, James might himself have written for film; his young novelist friend Hugh Walpole went to Hollywood in the 1930s. James spent half the 1890s trying unsuccessfully for a hit in the theatre and took a lively interest in the rise of the mass media. In 1900, he took his thirteen-year-old niece to a variety show including Biograph films of the Boer War. He worried that the 'rather horrid figures and sounds' would haunt her dreams. They seem to have haunted his.

Indeed, cinematic techniques began influencing Jamesian metaphor. 'Crapy Cornelia' is a 1909 story set in modern New York. Its hero is gazing out of a window when the middle-aged heroine attracts his attention: her looming head 'grew and grew… came nearer and nearer, while it met his eyes, after the manner of images in the cinematograph'. The psychological impact of altering image size had clearly registered. The hero has just been indulging a phantasmagoric vision, of a bright modern future with a *nouveau riche* wife. When he recognises Cornelia from his past, James has his imagined scene dissolve under the looming face: 'everything had altered, dropped, darkened, disappeared'. Conjured to evoke an internal reality, this suggests that cinema, with its 'thousand ways of emphasising… the privileged moments', can take on James' world.

Moreover, in twenty novels, more than 100 stories, plus plays, essays, biographies and more, there is no single Henry James. There's the social ironist, the historian of country houses, high-cultural tourism and the lives of the cosmopolitan rich, charting with wit and sensitivity the shifts from Victorian to modern values and manners in America and Europe. Then there's the James of what T. S. Eliot called 'the deeper psychology', who 'grasps character through the relation of two or more persons to each other' through a subtle chemistry tracing 'these curious precipitates and explosive gases which are suddenly formed by the contact of mind with mind'. This more 'modern' James, with his interest in experimental techniques to present a character's point of view, made excursions into psychological gothic and dramas of troubled consciousness.

Then there's an American and a European James, an 'early' (light, international, full of sharp banter) and a 'late' James (darker, more complex, full of loaded silences). For Ezra Pound, James is above all the 'hater of tyranny', champion of 'the rights of the individual against all sorts of intangible bondage'. For others, he is the arch-apologist of sacrifice, of martyr's wounds that look suspiciously self-inflicted. Some see a sensitive imaginer of women's experience, adolescence and the hard choices of whether (and whom) to marry; others see a veiled misogynist endorsing regulation of women through the imposition of false ideals. Murders, suicides, ghosts and much adultery occur in his work, as a rule indirectly: melodramatic and tragic impulses give a tense surface to his work without disrupting it.

So, although many regard James as 'difficult' – passionless, depressing, uneventful, ambiguous, impossibly inward-looking – there is much to feed cinema's voracity. I argue here that the screen has tackled James in three ways: faithful adaptations that swallow him whole (or attempt to); free variations that move further off (often with Freud as the presiding spirit); and the 'Jamesian' film, which though not actually an adaptation of any of his stories is clearly inspired by his example.

'Faithful' adaptations
THE HEIRESS (1949)
Director William Wyler, who cut his teeth on silent Westerns, believed that 'the emotion and conflict between two people in a drawing room can be as exciting as a gun battle, and possibly more exciting'. From a dramatisation of *Washington Square* by Ruth and Augustus Goetz, this may well be the best James film, showing how loves are destroyed and lives blighted. Handsome, penniless Morris Townsend (Montgomery Clift) woos Catherine (Olivia de Havilland), plain, shy daughter of the rich Dr Sloper (Ralph Richardson). Suspicious father confidently identifies Townsend as a fortune-hunter, but Catherine is in love, and defies his veto: though right about Townsend, the doctor is monstrous in his insistence. More morally harrowing than *The Innocents*, the material here, too, is pushed towards genre, hints expanded on in the service of the melodrama James avoids. Though the film's abusive Victorian tyrant father is darker, less patronisingly kind to Catherine than the book's, he is also humanised by his feelings toward the girl's dead mother, against whom his daughter can never measure up. Sloper, both lightened and deepened by a magnificently poised performance from Ralph Richardson, is the core of the film: first dominating, then defeated. The model here is the Women's Picture, with the worm turning, and a satisfying but appalling reversal. Years later, Townsend returns and is spurned back by a now frighteningly steely Catherine, de Havilland chillingly grown into her father's bitter ironies. An echo of Richardson is heard in the great (invented) line, 'Yes, I can be very cruel. I have been taught by masters.'

THE INNOCENTS (1961)
This adaptation of *The Turn of the Screw* (director Jack Clayton, screenplay Truman Capote and William Archibald, additional dialogue John Mortimer) pushes a Freudian reading of a famously ambiguous tale. Often thought the best film of a James story, it sustains a relentless high pitch, almost inducing in the viewer the hysteria it diagnoses in its heroine, a governess marooned in a country house in charge of two children she must protect against a pair of malevolent and corrupting ghosts. In James, the ghosts may or may not be products of her fevered imagination – in the film, Deborah Kerr as the governess is terrifyingly shrill, overheated and twice the age of the book's twenty-year-old heroine, an unmistakably middle-aged 'Victorian' virgin. The written story works by stealth, leaving the object of fear to suggestion. On screen, Freddie Francis' black-and-white 'Scope cinematography is beautiful and unsettling, and the ghosts terrify (especially the woman in black in broad daylight, staring malignly across the lake from the reeds). But the scares lack steady build, while the most unpleasant soundtrack prior to David Lynch's *Eraserhead* bombards us not only

with George Auric's highly explicit music, but also with constant shock sound effects: thunder, chalk-squeak on slate, rooks' wings exploding, doors and windows creaking or slamming. Exaggerated gothic is the keynote and symbols hammer at the 'privileged moments'; spiders crawl from the mouths of statues, ants from the eyes of dolls. In the last scene, as the governess confronts the ghost he can't see, the little boy shouts (as he doesn't in the original), 'It's because you're afraid you're mad!'

DAISY MILLER (1974)

In Peter Bogdanovich's cool and lovely 'Scope film, little-seen and unjustly treated, Winterbourne (Barry Brown) sees Daisy (Cybill Shepherd) seem to kiss a florid Italian companion in the Pincian Garden: their heads hidden behind her parasol, he jealously assumes the worst. I took this as a perfect visual invention by Bogdanovich, until I read James: 'She came a little nearer and he held the parasol over her; then, still holding it, he let it so rest upon her shoulder that both their heads were hidden from Winterbourne.' James' novella is a bright romantic comedy of cross-cultural misunderstanding darkening to tragedy as the American flirt of the title challenges and is ostracised by the prim American community in Italy. The original is so economical that Bogdanovich (with Frederic Raphael) can add rather than trim – and he handles it with classic Hitchcockian precision (in Truffaut's phrase, 'as though it were a thriller'). The wavering, obsessive hero watches, falls in love with and struggles to understand Daisy, in the manner of countless cinematic lover-detectives before and since (above all, James Stewart in *Vertigo*). Film's formal capacity to edit between viewer and viewed perfectly suits this tale of surveillance and suspicion; Daphne Merkin's excessive claim (that 'the true excitement of [James'] plots is all on the inside') scarcely applies.

THE BOSTONIANS (1984)

The 1979 Merchant-Ivory adaptation of James' period comedy *The Europeans* – about Europeanised cousins returning to the New England of the 1840s – was a crude if jovial 'heritage' production. Pretty sets, costumes and music pleased those attracted to James by the glamour of cosmopolitan high life, and much James material was retained – but without his sexiness, wit or edge, the result smacked largely of commercial cultural calculation. Better-remembered is the Merchant-Ivory version of *The Bostonians*. Set in the 1870s during a period of intense feminist agitation, the novel traces the conflict between rich, shy, man-hunting young spinster Olive Chancellor and impoverished, reactionary Southern lawyer Basil Ransom. They battle for the love of Verena Tarrant, an electrifying orator: Olive wants her as a companion in the cause of women's rights, Ransom as a conventional wife adorning his fireside. The film-makers' faithfulness seems transparent – but their very starved idea of both James' and the cinema's art had charmlessly primitive results. As Pauline Kael said, they 'don't dramatise the great material they selected, and Ivory doesn't shape the performances'. The plot turns on Verena's energy and value, and we must see and feel her attraction – the tepid, well-meaning Madeleine Potter merely recites long, flat speeches in long, flat takes. Christopher Reeve is amiable as Ransom, but lacks the necessary unconscious vindictiveness. Vanessa Redgrave (at forty-seven, James' 'pale girl' Olive) gives an intense, humourless performance in a void.

THE PORTRAIT OF A LADY (1996)

Jane Campion's flawed, lugubrious, often gloriously beautiful film achieves its passionate version of fidelity at a cost – its deviations from the book are notorious (the modern Australian girls discussing love and kissing in a prologue; the heroine's three-in-a-bed sexual fantasy, with her suitors dematerialising *Star Trek*-fashion at the end of it). Laura Jones' shooting script keeps scrupulously close to the original dialogue and much imagination is poured into exactly re-creating the look of James' world, yet Campion perversely allows the actors their head in gestural improvisation, with awkward, anachronistic results. More serious still is Campion's masochistic reading of Isabel's choice of husband, Gilbert Osmond.

In the novel, Isabel faces an ethical dilemma – the film empties out this debate. When, late in the film (but not in the shooting script), Isabel (Nicole Kidman) opposes the elegantly cruel Osmond (John Malkovich), she suffers physical abuse at his hands – he raps her knuckles, trips her on a marble floor and (bizarrely) grinds his head into her temples. To have him go so far beyond maliciously calculated mind games is to play up one scene at the story's expense – for, as a battered wife, Isabel is all-too justified in rebelling. In a later scene, retained from the novel, Osmond appeals insidiously to her sense of responsibility and faith – 'I think we should accept the consequences of our actions, and what I value most in life is the honour of a thing' – but the scene's force is now destroyed. In the novel, a dying Ralph can tell Isabel that Osmond 'was greatly in love with you' – the film would have been richer for this scene, but it's been made impossible.

THE WINGS OF THE DOVE (1997)

With a script by Hossein Amini, Iain Softley's film takes 'modernising' liberties with James' plot. It changes the details it doesn't altogether discard, retaining no more than half-a-dozen lines from the novel; it's even set amid the social instabilities of 1910, rather than the restrictions of the book's 1901. The original plot is morally challenging in its urbane ruthlessness – the film's variations aim perhaps to evoke sympathy for the beautiful, treacherous Kate Croy (Helena Bonham Carter), who persuades her lover Merton Densher to 'make up' to the dying New York heiress Milly Theale – to get money that will allow Kate and Merton to marry comfortably. Charlotte Rampling plays rich Aunt Maude – in the book, a manipulative but sentimental dowager – as Lady Ottoline Morrell crossed with Cruella de Vil, presumably to make Kate seem sweeter. As the plot's centre of moral value, Alison Elliott's Milly has attractive depth and animation; Linus Roache as Densher is creditable in a role Ralph Fiennes was to have played. Bonham Carter is the partner of Kenneth Branagh, whose Renaissance Films made this adaptation: with its swirling camera and relentless eventfulness – champagne is drunk, guns are fired, lords barge into girls' rooms at night – it has a crude gusto and perhaps epitomises a new, youthful, late-1990s heritage style (as did *Much Ado About Nothing*, another Renaissance Film). But to bohemianise and sex up the milieu – this Kate can kittenishly curl up on Densher's bed – is to lower the pressure of the novel's bottled-up sexual passion. Nevertheless, a daringly painful final scene of 'explicit' loveless sex unexpectedly captures, at the very last minute, some of the moral force of the original.

Free variations
THE LOST MOMENT (1947)

Martin Gabel's delirious, intelligent, weirdly compelling Freudian fairytale gives free spin to *The Aspern Papers*, James' tale of an unscrupulous editor in Venice trying to get his hands on long-dead poet Aspern's love letters to mistress Juliana Bordereau, still alive at 105 in a crumbling palazzo with only odd spinster niece Tina for company. Susan Hayward plays Tina as a buttoned-up tartar by day – but at night she becomes the young Juliana, hair down, *décolletée*, radiantly sensual. In his turn, the editor (Robert Cummings) becomes Aspern and (as in *Vertigo*) half-enters Tina's obsessive fragile world as her lover. The film plays up the gothic elements – but its bizarrest twists, such as this mirrored affair, are present as subtextual irony in the original.

THE NIGHTCOMERS (1972)

Michael Winner's nasty 'prequel' to *The Innocents* stars a bedraggled Marlon Brando, hamming but at least watchable as an evil Irish Peter Quint (the valet). What was unspeakable in James is here frontally staged. Thora Hird's turn as Victorian Repression ('You slut!') plays its part in a kinkily sado-masochistic scenario, with the corrupted children watching and imitating Quint's sexual tormenting – bondage, whipping – of the governess Miss Jessel. If less badly written (by Michael Hastings: 'Oh! You brute!') or filmed (Jessel's drowning is particularly amusing), this gothic snuff panto could have had some of the abusive power of *The Innocents*.

'Jamesian' films
THE FALLEN IDOL (1948)

Hitchcock had a predilection for torturing his heroines with uncertainties about husbands and their secrets (especially Joan Fontaine in *Rebecca* (1940) and *Suspicion* (1941)). The mannered, witty dialogue of George Cukor's *The Philadelphia Story* (1940) makes central a spoilt, undecided Katherine Hepburn, who with her fine sense of romantic possibility seems a reprise of Isabel Archer in *The Portrait of a Lady*. (And the same director's *Gaslight* (1944) inserted a prefatory calculating courtship not in Thorold Dickinson's 1940 UK version that also suggested Osmond's courtship of Isabel in *Portrait*.) But surely the greatest of the 'Jamesian' films is Carol Reed's sophisticated, tragic *The Fallen Idol* with Ralph Richardson, scripted by Graham Greene from his 'The Basement Room' (1935). Greene passionately admired James, partly for his 'sense of evil religious in its intensity'. Out of elements derived from *The Turn of the Screw*, *The Pupil* and *What Maisie Knew*, the film presents an ironic account of the dangerously innocent world of childhood and its struggle to participate in the dark adult milieu of lies and secrets, failure and pain. Repression and self-sacrifice are not endorsed, perhaps, but are at least sympathetically understood for their root in honourable feeling: Richardson's Baines, butler in a London embassy, is a marvellously delicate picture of a kind, weak man overcome by circumstance. His friend and protégé, the little boy Philip (a fine Bobby Henrey), is followed down into a deeper psychology of complex interpersonal relations, warpings and waste. Baines attempts to express this dimension with a Jamesian insight: 'We've got to be very careful, Phil, because we make one another.'

THE AGE OF INNOCENCE (1993)

Written after James' death, his lifelong friend Edith Wharton's 1920 novel pulls together Jamesian scenes, themes and plot elements from all over his *oeuvre*. Countess Ellen's situation echoes Baroness Eugenia's in *The Europeans*, Newland Archer's uncertainty about the moral worth of the woman he loves resembles Winterbourne's in *Daisy Miller*; Archer, like the hero in *The Beast in the Jungle* (the man 'to whom nothing on earth was to have happened') realises his love too late, becoming 'a man to whom nothing was ever to happen'; Wharton's May, like the betrayed American girl-wife of James' crowning achievement, *The Golden Bowl*, realises she is betrayed and manoeuvres in silence to win her husband back. Wharton's novel cannot decide on its tone: the 1870s is a past it alternately satirises and yearns for, while Archer is both mocked as a characteristically unreliable hero and allowed the poignant feelings that give the novel life. Martin Scorsese's film improves on the book by concentrating sympathetically on the emotional force of every scene for the hero, a rigorous focus on point-of-view that is highly Jamesian. It also delivers arguably the most Jamesian dialogue scenes in cinema: the agonising *tête-à-têtes* between Archer and Ellen, and Archer and May, acted and edited so tensely that every word, pause and eyebrow's motion is charged with meaning. As in James, we feel the struggle of 'two people in a drawing room', for exact expression in their emotional negotiations is crucial to their fate, and never 'just talk'.

Dracula
DRACULA AND DESIRE

Richard Dyer

The cinema was packed. Tom and I took the first two seats together we could find and I didn't take notice of whom I was sitting next to. We were in any case too engrossed in unguarded conversation to be bothered. It was freezing outside, but hot in the cinema, so we had to take off successive layers of clothing. I was just starting to struggle out of a pullover when the person sitting next to me gave my knee a sharp knock. I turned in surprise and he hissed, 'There's no need to keep rubbing your leg against mine.' I was so startled by this sudden eruption of homophobia that I immediately went into politeness overdrive, I was sorry, I really hadn't realised. And throughout the film I kept my body tensed away from him, lest my relaxed knee inadvertently touched his dreary thigh. Perhaps it was only this that made me feel alienated from the new *Dracula*, but I suspect also that Coppola's Stoker's vampires are not my vampires, not by any means queer.

There is no doubt that Bram Stoker's *Dracula*, which the new film follows so fully, is the literary *locus classicus* of the vampire. Huge though the corpus of vampire tales is, the character of Dracula dominates. His is probably the only vampire's name most people know: it sells holiday tours and images of dictatorship in Romania, it is used in the titles of films in which he does not appear (such as *Dracula's Daughter* and *Brides of Dracula*). Dracula is the vampire *par excellence*. Yet, admirable and fascinating as much of Stoker's novel is, I prefer Sheridan LeFanu's 'Carmilla', or Richard Matheson's *I Am Legend*, or, above all, Anne Rice's *Interview with the Vampire* and its sequels. Similarly, in films, I prefer non-Draculas such as the aforementioned *Daughter*, *Kiss of the Vampire, Daughters of Darkness* or *Near Dark*, or those that only take Stoker's *Dracula* as a point of departure (Murnau's *Nosferatu*, Bela Lugosi's incarnations, Peter Sasdy's *Taste the Blood of Dracula*). The new *Dracula* is not of these.

Francis Ford Coppola and scriptwriter James V. Hart have, as the credit that opens the film, 'Bram Stoker's *Dracula*', suggests, indeed gone back to Stoker. In terms of inclusion of incidents and characters, there is more left of the novel here than in any previous film versions, with the possible exception of the 1970 Spanish *El Conde Dracula* (Jesús Franco). To the now well-trod lines of Jonathan Harker's visit to Transylvania and Dracula's coming to England to wreak havoc on Harker's friends and relatives are added elements that have only occasionally appeared in previous versions (the character of the Texan, Quincy P. Morris; the pursuit of Dracula back to Transylvania finally to ensnare him). The one substantial new element added to this, a prologue explaining how Vlad the Impaler became Dracula, gives a particular inflection to the story, but remains true to the project: it is well known that Vlad was an inspiration to Stoker.

The manner of telling also owes more than usual to Stoker. The use of multiple narrative strands (Jonathan and Mina, Lucy and her beaux, the asylum, Van Helsing) is sustained, as in the novel, until two-thirds of the way through, when it is ironed out into a linear, much less engrossing stalk-and-kill climax. The film also makes a stab at retaining the novel's multiple points of view, with sequences inaugurated by voiceovers, captions and visuals that link the subsequent events to a particular character's perspective. Care is even taken with the novel's emphasis on different ways of telling, both formal modes (diaries, letters, news stories) and media (handwriting, typing, cylinder recording). To the latter is added reference to the cinematograph, not as a source of the story we are seeing, but as something that Dracula himself has recourse to in his seduction of Mina.

Coppola's *Dracula* flings itself at all this narrative material, emerging like a music video directed by Dario Argento. As in a video, narrativity comes at you in snatches, more a suggestion of connected incidents across a welter of vivid imagery than a fully presented plot. As in Argento's *Suspiria*, say, or some other post-1960s horror movies such as Sam Raimi's *The Evil Dead*, narrative, and with it the pleasures of tease and suspense, are unimportant; it's the maelstrom of sensation that matters. This means that the story may be hard to follow if you either haven't read Stoker's *Dracula* or have a less than total recall of it (I remembered who Renfield and Quincy were, but it goes so fast that I had a hard time figuring out how and why at the end Mina gets to Transylvania before her menfolk). With *Suspiria* or *The Evil Dead*, this doesn't matter too much since there's so little plot anyway, and it may not matter with this Dracula either. The point, perhaps, was not to do Stoker in full-blooded re-creation, but simply to allude to as much as possible of the book while getting on with the business of creating a particular feeling and exploring the connotations of the Dracula idea.

As to the feeling, Coppola has certainly achieved something distinctive. Always one of cinema's great colourists, he has here come up with a symphony in engulfing red and black. The prologue is shot in near-silhouette, black on red, setting the colour key signature for the film. Early sequences in Victorian England are anaemically coloured, gradually to be swallowed by red and black, vermilion and pitch, blood and the night. I am not the first to have reached for 'engorgement' as a word to describe the film. It's not just the redness of blood swelling the film's climaxes, but the fullness of the image, bursting to the edge of the frame with thick colour and dense visual texture. Most remarkably, it's in the vampires' costuming, most voluminous when they are most needy. They look bloated with lust, and yet move then with greatest speed and ease, gliding not walking, as if monitored by the desperate urgency of desire. When Lucy has become a vampire, she is dressed entirely in white, with bridal lace and fold upon fold of silk, and her face, too, is pale as death; yet her shrouded body rears up turgidly, the lace ruffs round her neck are puffed like a monstrous lizard, even her cheeks seem fuller. Even without the red, she is the embodiment of engorgement.

To this stunning – and wearying – feeling, Coppola adds many of the connotations of vampirism. The vampire motif always has something to do with the idea of a being, or way of being, that literally lives off another. It was born (in the early nineteenth century) of a society increasingly conscious of interdependency, while losing that firm sense of fixed, rightful, social hierarchy that had concealed dependency; in short, it was born of industrial capitalist democracy. The vampire idea deals in the terror of recognising, challenging or being challenged by dependency, and always registers this through the body: the dependencies of its needs and drives, especially, but not exclusively, sexuality. Like all long-lived popular cultural ideas, innumerable variations can be played on this basic concept, its vivid iconography and compelling narrative patterns. Folklorists stress the fear of the living that the dead are not well and truly dead, a fear that may also conceal a hope; Marxists liked to compare capitalists to vampires, feeding off the labour of the working class. In *Ganja and Hess* (1971), Bill Gunn used the vampire idea to explore the dependencies of race and colonialism; the British short *The Mask of Lilith* (1986) similarly explored vampirism as a metaphor for gender, sexual and racial oppression and resistance.

The possibilities are endless, and Coppola and Hart know a good few of them. You want the attraction and terror of sexuality, the attraction of the terror of sexuality? Here it is, in Dracula's metamorphosis from glowering bearded prince to cadaverous old goat to *fin-de-siècle* dandy, and in the wolf/ape thing that takes Lucy in the night. You want, more specifically, male fears of female sexuality? Here is the engorged, uncontrollable libidinous preference of Lucy and Mina for Gary Oldman's dandy Dracula over Keanu Reeves' sensitive but proper Jonathan. Or AIDS is a possibility, flung in here in a few lines ominously connecting sex, blood and disease. There's even a vegetarian reading, in a cut that has the audience groaning as at a bad pun and which is borrowed from *The Hunger*, where Van Helsing's dismemberment of Lucy's head is followed straight on by him carving with relish into a side of rare beef.

Or how about the vampire as the old world, old Europe, Eastern Europe, leeching off modern, industrialising, Western Europe (and North America)? This has in recent years been seen as one of the novel's most interesting themes, stressed not only in the references to modern means of communication (typewriters, cylinders), but also in the characters of the Texan (the new rich of the New World) and Jack Seward, the lunatic asylum director with new, rational and humane ideas about madness and its treatment. This is all there in Coppola's *Dracula*, given new inflection by a sequence at the cinematograph and by rendering parts of the final stalk-and-kill to look like a Western, the genre that encapsulates the conquering destiny of ethnically European expansion. The film is even aware of a gendered dimension to modernity, not so much, as in the book, through Mina, associated through typing with the New Woman's skill with technology and the possibility of an independent career, but in the way female nudes are interpolated into the endlessly repeated film shown in the sideshow booth where Dracula seduces Mina, a recognition of the simultaneous historical production of woman and cinema as spectacle.

The film seems to know about all the above; such themes are there not just by virtue of the completeness of its use of the novel's incidents and characters. Yet none of them is really developed or compelling. It's post-modern allusionism, a welter of things to make reference to without any of them mattering much. The most interesting and, surprisingly enough, original is a Christian interpretation. Christianity has, of course, always been part of the vampire tale, but often in a rather perfunctory way. Holy water and a cross held up in the vampire's face might put him or her off for a while, but so did a bunch of garlic; real destruction could only come about by a stake through the heart, vaguely Christian perhaps, but pretty pagan, too. The Christian possibilities seemed not to have survived the riposte of the character in Roman Polanski's *Dance of the Vampires* (1967), who waves aside a proffered crucifix with the information that he's Jewish. There are few vampire films (or pieces of writing) since in which Christianity has any force, yet it is the one theme that gets some development in the new film.

The potential for a fuller Christian reading of the vampire idea is obvious. The central sacrament of Christianity is wine drunk as blood (in the Catholic doctrine of transubstantiation, this is at the spiritual level no mere symbol, it is the actual blood of Christ); the most important icon of Christianity is a dead man who has eternal life. Most writers and film-makers have failed to exploit this, either because they depict vampires as the enemy of Christianity, or because they are not interested enough in Christianity to bother. In Coppola's *Dracula*, by contrast, Dracula is strongly associated with Christ.

The opening section depicts Vlad as a Defender of the Faith against the Turks (in other words, against Islam, though the film perhaps prudently plays that down); when he discovers that his beloved Princess Elizabeth has killed herself, thinking him dead, he believes God has deserted him (as, on the cross, did Christ); blood gushes from the crucifix on the altar and Vlad, soaking and drinking it up while railing against God, becomes a vampire, Dracula. When Dracula seduces Mina (a reincarnation of Elizabeth), he makes a cut in his breast for her to suck at; such a cut is familiar iconography in medieval and later Christian art, and the connection is insisted on by crosscutting with Mina marrying Jonathan and taking communion with him, drinking wine/blood as a sign of transcendent union. When Dracula is finally impaled, his face metamorphoses from hideous white slug to long-haired dandy via a bearded incarnation that is Vlad, but also looks like countless images of Christ. In short, although the theme disappears from view from time to time, Dracula here is an anti-Christ, not so much in the sense of being an enemy of Christ as in being an inversion of the Christ idea. Drinking Christ's blood while cursing God damns him to eternal life, dependent forever on human blood, having gorged on and rejected divine blood. He offers his eternal life by the same token as Christ offered his, the drinking of his blood.

But what do we feel about all this? Christ-like or anti-Christ, what is our relation to him? Worship or identification, pity or revulsion? The long life of the vampire idea resides in just such various possibilities. If the image started out as one seen from the outside, there was always the possibility that it could be seen and felt from within; if the vampire is an Other, he or she was also always a figure in whom one could find oneself. The image allowed that from the start of its appearance in modern Western culture (if indeed it had any life before in folk cultures, as many modern Western writers like to claim). The narrative devices used ostensibly keep the vampire at a distance: the tale is often presented as one told to the narrator by another narrator who sometimes themselves have only heard it told; even when a direct first-person narrative is used, the vampire is not the narrator. Yet he or she is always the most interesting, memorable and even attractive figure in the tale. If the narrator and all around so easily fall prey to the vampire's magnetism, nay charm, the latter must have something; the narrator often tells us little about him or her self, and other characters, for all the vampire needs their blood, seem anaemic by comparison. The vampire was always a figure to be desired as well as feared, to be identified with as well as distanced from. One of the magical things about *Interview with the Vampire* is the device of presenting the tale as a transcript of a tape recording of the hero telling his story to a journalist; not only does this give the word to the vampire himself, but it also draws attention to the fact of doing so. Jody Scott's polymorphous lesbian science-fiction variant carries this breakthrough triumphantly forward in its very title, *I, Vampire.*

In film, there is no such grammar to tell you with whom you are supposed to identify. Without voiceover or relentless subjective camera, it's much less clear who is 'telling' a film. But, like vampires in literature, film sets up distance only to have it converted to identification.

The device of the journey, taken from Stoker, often serves to put the vampire at a distance: there is a strong sense of a movement away from what the western, urban-minded audience would find familiar and towards the strangeness of foreignness. Honeymooners, the next step for the young unmarried heterosexual couples supposedly making up the bulk of the audience, might especially seem ideal identification figures to lead the viewer into the realm of the vampire other. Yet this device is even less insistently (if resistibly) distancing than the narrational devices of written fiction. It is true that few vampire films make the vampire a clear central figure whom we stay with throughout – I can only think of movies such as *Graveyard Shift*, *Nick Knight* or *To Die For*, plus films about real-life 'vampire' Peter Kürten (*Le Vampire de Dusseldorf* and *The Tenderness of Wolves*) and George A. Romero's *Martin* (the film of *Interview with the Vampire*, supposedly under contract, has not yet seen the light of day). Yet the journey motif has led in some interesting directions, often inviting involvement more than encouraging distance.

In *Kiss of the Vampire* (Don Sharp, 1965) the lacklustre honeymooning couple cannot hold a candle to the vampires who prey on them. With the wife in their thrall, their leader says to the husband, 'Now that your wife has tasted one of life's rarer pleasures, do you think she will want to return to you?' Who cannot see that he is right? Who would not rather spend time with the sister or brother, she bursting voluptuously out of her gown, he gazing with intense, melancholy eyes at you as he plays intense, melancholy music at the piano? And who would not prefer that delirious costume ball to sitting at home with this stodgy British hubby? Similarly, in *Daughters of Darkness* (Harry Kümel, 1970) a pasty pair of newlyweds wind up on a wintry night in a deserted hotel on the Belgian coast. In the circumstances, who would want to keep to the straight and narrow when you could feel queer with the only other guests, Delphine Seyrig and companion? Well, of course, many people would, including the man sitting next to me. There's undoubtedly a queer way of reading vampirism, and my neighbour knew that's what I was hoping for.

I want 'queer' here to carry as many meanings as possible. Certainly I don't just mean lesbian and gay, but any apparently marginalised, sexualised identity (which includes many perceptions of women and non-white, even non-Anglo ethnic groups). But I do mean to include the old as well as the new connotations of queer, the despicable as well as the defiant, the shameful as well as the unashamed, the loathing of oddness as well as pride in it. The vampire has played every variation on such queerness. The 1922 *Nosferatu* is a hideous outsider, driven on by his lust, eyes falling out of his head at the sight of Thomas' sturdy frame and unable to resist Mina's deadly allure; to identify with him, as one still might, is to identify with loneliness, self-hatred and loathsome desire. To identify with Bela Lugosi's Count is still to identify with isolated outsiderdom, but already with someone more refined and fascinating than the dullards ranged against him. *Taste the Blood of Dracula* (1969) is one of the most enjoyable exposés of Victorian values in all cinema, with respectable bourgeois fathers secretly randy for the sensation that only Dracula can bring their jaded palates and their daughters killing them off with glee under Dracula's tutelage; Christopher Lee's Count is as straight (and English) as can be, but how deliciously he provokes normal society against itself. And with *Kiss of the Vampire*, *Daughters of Darkness* or *Near Dark*, the vampires become the thing to be, infinitely preferable to the world they feed off.

Coppola's Dracula, like Stoker's, like Christopher Lee's, does not belong with these vampires. He's not a pervert. He might occasionally turn to male flesh (between the scenes in the film as between the chapters in the book) and have on hand female vampires mutually pleasuring each other, but there is none of the delighted and sustained homoeroticism of 'Carmilla' and *Interview with the Vampire*, or *Daughters of Darkness*, *The Velvet Vampire*, *The Hunger*, Barbara Steele in *Danza Macabra* and, a rare male example, the Dutch *Blood Relations*. He may in the end be destroyed for his disruptive desire, but it's really business as usual in terms of the representation of heterosexual male sexuality. Dracula – Stoker's, Lee's, and Coppola's – is rampant, driven, rearing sexuality, uncontainable by modern, domestic, feminised society. It is ugly – beneath the dandy veneer lurks slug-like, leech-like desire; but it's what women want, even in its ugliness: Lucy is ecstatic beneath the half-ape, half-wolf that takes her in the garden and Mina does not flinch, even when her dandy slits his chest open for her. And like Stoker's dripping prose and Hammer's thickly coloured textures and solid *mise-en-scène*, only more so, Coppola's film is full of blood, stiff with desire, a hymn to engorgement.

Yet Dracula is an outsider, without being socially marginal. One version of the vampire idea precisely presents normal male sexuality as outside of society. If 'society' resides in moral order, in marriage, in the unemotional, un-erotic workplace, then it has no place for driving randiness and uncontrollable priapism, themselves conceived as the nature of male sexuality. Normal male sexuality in this perspective accords straight men too the glamorous badge of outsiderdom. No matter that they also have unequal power over women and children, no matter the vastness of the heterosexual sex industries, no matter the ubiquity of sexual tension at work – at the level of representation, male sexuality is seen as profoundly unsocialised and unsocialisable. Thus Stoker's, Lee's and Coppola's Dracula, thus the dominant image of the vampire, so commandingly virile, so unerringly straight, also expresses the profound contradictoriness of the cultural construction of heterosexual masculinity, at once dominant and disgusting, natural and horrible, mainstream and beyond the pale.

But that's not what *I* want from vampires. For all its incidental pleasures (some of the costumes, the US stars doing English accents, picking up the allusions as a genre aficionado is bound to), the new *Dracula* was not addressed to me. Just as I held myself off from the man in the seat next to me, so I held myself off from the film. Just as he perhaps believed that all gay men are after all straight men, so the only place for me in relation to this *Dracula* would have been as alienated assistant at the spectacle of straight male engorgement. In a way, the man next to me was right: I had no place there. But with so many other vampires to feast with, I can manage without this one.

BLOODLINES

Kim Newman

Germany 1922. America 1930. Britain 1958. America 1979. America 1992. What have these times and places in common? First, they saw the appearance of major film versions of Bram Stoker's *Dracula* (1897), namely F. W. Murnau's *Nosferatu* with Max Schreck, Tod Browning's *Dracula* with Bela Lugosi, Terence Fisher's *Dracula* (*Horror of Dracula*) with Christopher Lee, John Badham's *Dracula* (British-shot, but Hollywood through and through) with Frank Langella and, most recently, Francis Ford Coppola's *Dracula* with Gary Oldman. Second, they were the site of major economic and social upheavals: the chaos of Weimar, the Great Depression, the post-Suez loss of imperial clout, the Iranian hostage crisis and the fall of Jimmy Carter, and the current recession and the replacement of Bush. Even lesser versions of *Dracula* have come at historical turning points: Jesús Franco's *El Conde Dracula* (Lee again, 1971) at the end of Franco's Spain, Dan Curtis' television *Dracula* (Jack Palance, 1973) with Watergate, Philip Saville's BBC *Count Dracula* (Louis Jourdan, 1979) with the arrival of Margaret Thatcher.

Dracula evidently appeals to nations in crisis. Though the novel draws on the nineteenth-century tradition of gothic and ghostliness, it is almost a scientific romance: indeed, Van Helsing briefly flirts with a 'rational' explanation for Dracula's existence, blaming vampirism on mineral deposits in the Carpathians. Constructed as an invasion fantasy, *Dracula* is as comparable with Sir George Chesney's *The Battle of Dorking* (1871) and H. G. Wells' *The War of the Worlds* (1898) as with post-gothic predecessors, such as Shelley's *Frankenstein* (1818) and Stevenson's *Strange Case of Dr Jekyll and Mr Hyde* (1886). Stoker's great strategist plots his relocation to London with Bismarckian efficiency, employing property rights and railway timetables as much as supernatural powers. A literal filthy foreigner, Stoker's Dracula is pitted against an emblematic array of Englishness (with tolerated Americans and Dutchmen generously included, just as Stoker the Dubliner could be included in the London society he was so taken with), before being driven back to his crumbling Third World castle to be properly dispatched.

In my own contribution to the mythos, *Anno Dracula* (1992), I chose to expand on this neglected strand, extrapolating a late-Victorian London in which Dracula has prevailed over Van Helsing and moved from the petty conquests of the wives of solicitors to become a new Prince Consort in control of the Empire. My purpose in the novel, as here, is to open *Dracula* to a variety of interpretations. For, despite the attempts of Coppola and screenwriter James V. Hart to invalidate all versions of *Dracula* but Stoker's and their own (implied in the film's opening credit to be one and the same), the strength of the fictions that cluster around Dracula lies in their diversity. In assessing the myths – ranging from the *Sesame Street* Count through Bunnicula, Deafula, Spermula, Duckula and Granpa Munster to the post-Stoker literary versions of Fred Saberhagen (*The Dracula Tape*, 1975), Peter Tremayne (*Dracula Unborn*, 1977), Brian Stableford (*The Empire of Fear*, 1988), Brian Aldiss (*Dracula Unbound*, 1989) and Dan Simmons (*Children of the Night*, 1991) – we shouldn't follow Coppola and Hart in deeming acceptability to be a matter of how closely a given work follows Stoker's text, but instead look at how effective it is on its own terms as an extrapolation from a set of material that Stoker himself co-opted, but didn't always make the best use of.

Stoker's Dracula is a brute, a barbarian, a ravager and an invader, but the cinema has preferred to portray him as a romantic, an aristocrat, a seducer and an outsider. In this, the true ancestor of most Draculas is Dr John Polidori's Lord Ruthven, central character of that odd fragment 'The Vampyre' (1819). Before the arrival of Dracula at the end of the century, Ruthven was the epitome of vampirism, appearing in as dizzying a variety of stage and novel adaptations as Dracula has in twentieth-century movies. Before Ruthven, the folkloric vampire was a mindless peasant more like cinema's flesh-eating zombies; inspired by his patron–tormentor Lord Byron, Polidori recast the vampire as a fatal aristo who wanders Europe 'ruining' the innocent daughters of virtuous but ineffectual upper-middle-class families.

Intriguingly, there have been only two attempts to film 'The Vampyre' – a 1945 cheapie *The Vampire's Ghost* with John Abbot as a pop-eyed bloodsucker running a honky-tonk in the African jungle and the BBC's new serial opera for Christmas, *The Vampire: A Soap Opera* – as if leeching of Ruthven's characteristics into Dracula's rendered further adaptations superfluous. The other nineteenth-century vampire archetype is the heroine of J. Sheridan LeFanu's 'Carmilla' (1872), which cunningly rethinks Ruthven as a girl, an apparently useless teenager foisted on *parvenu* families by her countess mother on the correct assumption that her hosts will be impressed by her title. Carmilla's tactic is to become cloyingly dependent on her female victims, making her the root of the persistent lesbian vampire image and a precursor of the cuckoos-in-the-nest of *The Hand that Rocks the Cradle, Poison Ivy* and *Single White Female* (all 1992).

When Browning made his *Dracula* in 1930, he worked not from the novel, but from John Balderston's Broadway version (1927, a revision of a British adaptation by Hamilton Deane, 1925), in which Lugosi had played. The opening reel, as Karl Freund's camera creeps around a cobwebbed Castle Dracula, shows a *Nosferatu* influence, but the remainder opts for drawing-room melodrama. Lugosi moves as elegantly in society as Ruthven (and Sir Francis Varney of *Varney the Vampyre*, 1847) did before him, hand-kissing in a continental manner that makes red-blooded British heroes seethe, politely concealing all manner of suggested improprieties behind his cape. By adopting the full evening dress associated with the Devil in pieces such as Marie Corelli's *The Sorrows of Satan* (1895) and Shaw's *Don Juan in Hell* (1903), Lugosi sets a precedent echoed by many subsequent screen Draculas ('How would you like to spend 400 years dressed like a head waiter?' George Hamilton comments in *Love at First Bite*, 1979). His sartorial style was taken up immediately by Carlos Villarias as *El Conde Dracula* in a Spanish version shot simultaneously with the Browning film on the same sets, and was followed by pale imitations such as his own Count Mora (*Mark of the Vampire*, 1935) and Armand Tesla (*The Return of the Vampire*, 1943), David Peel's Baron Meinster (*The Brides of Dracula*, 1960), Ferdy Mayne's Count von Krolock (*Dance of the Vampires*, 1967), Robert Quarry's Count Yorga (*Count Yorga, Vampire*, 1970), and William Marshall's Prince Mamuwalde (*Blacula*, 1972).

Only Murnau's *Nosferatu* plays on Stoker's actual themes of invasion, nationalism and dominance (by no coincidence is the Beast from the East's first British victim surnamed Westenra, Light of the West). Schreck's vampire (feebly echoed by Klaus Kinski in Werner Herzog's *Nosferatu the Vampyre*, 1979) creeps from primitive Wallachia to a rationalist Bremen which substitutes for London and effectively prompts Murnau to translate Stoker's Irish espousal of English values into a gay soon-to-be exile vision of the German bourgeoisie. Bringing with him a Pied Piper's swarm of plague rats, the shabbily dressed, stick-insect-thin Graf von Orlok is an invasion from shunned history, dragging stiff-collared burgers into a primal nightmare of disease and cruelty. With his bad breath and worse manners, Von Orlok presents the repulsive side of Stoker's Dracula that has invariably been sidestepped by successive generations of film-makers. And, along with Christopher Lee, *Nosferatu* is perhaps the sole adaptation that seriously attempts, as Stoker does, to be frightening.

It's a rare screen Dracula whose ambitions have the political dimension Stoker insists upon with talk of having 'commanded nations and intrigued for them'. *Jonathan* (1969) features Paul-Albert Krumm as a ranting Hitler lookalike presiding over vampire orgies staged like party rallies; Christopher Lee in *The Satanic Rites of Dracula* (1973) poses as a property developer and schemes to end his misery by wiping out the human race with a bio-engineered plague. Perhaps most ambitiously, David Carradine, succeeding his father in *Sundown: The Vampire in Retreat* (1990), works to integrate the vampire nation with humanity and, in a finale more Christian than anything in Coppola's film, earns the forgiveness of God as vampirekind is reconciled with the Church and the fear of the cross lifted from them.

The 'classical' Draculas of the period between 1930 and 1970 follow the Ruthven mode, icily romantic and ruthlessly predatory, making conquests not for their own bloody pleasure but to score off the stuffy and puritanical Van Helsings. Perhaps unique is *Son of Dracula* (1943), in which Louise Allbritton seduces Lon Chaney Jr in order to become an immortal vampire, even marrying the Transylvanian Count, although she intends to spurn him in favour of her mortal lover. In Chaney's Count Alucard, as in John Carradine's gloomy Dracula of *House of Frankenstein* (1944) and *House of Dracula* (1945) and Francis Lederer's communist-bloc refugee in *The Return of Dracula* (1958), there are traces of a perhaps sincere romanticism which will emerge fully thirty years later. This strain goes ruthlessly into remittance during Christopher Lee's long reign at Hammer films. A bluntly disdainful tyrant, Lee puts the moves on the heroines of *Dracula* (1958), *Dracula, Prince of Darkness* (1965), *Dracula Has Risen from the Grave* (1968), *The Scars of Dracula* (1970) and *Dracula AD 1972* (1972) to avenge a slight (the staking of a concubine, an attempted exorcism) and make their menfolk suffer. There is no suggestion that Lugosi or Lee feels anything for those they vampirise: their quarrels are with Van Helsing and his acolytes, and the struggles of these films are vigorously masculine.

When Hammer had exhausted the *Dracula* material, it passed out of English hands, first into such modernist American rereadings as *Count Yorga, Vampire* and *Blacula*. There followed continental mutations such as Franco's *El Conde Dracula* (first but not last to trumpet itself as the 'definitive' Stoker text), *El Saga de los Draculas* (1973) and *Jonathan* (Hans W. Geissendörfer's serious and neglected political reading of the novel), culminating in Paul Morrissey's oddly effective *Blood for Dracula* (1974), in which Udo Kier's sickly nineteenth-century man is nauseated in the 1920s by non-virgin blood and destroyed with hammer and sickle by revolutionary Joe Dallesandro. Then came a series of versions, culminating in Coppola's current entry, that come to grips with both the novel and earlier film adaptations: Dan Curtis' *Dracula*, scripted by Richard Matheson, John Badham's *Dracula*, inspired by an Edward Gorey-designed revival of the 1927 play, the BBC's *Count Dracula*, scripted by Gerald Savory and containing more of the novel than any other adaptation, Herzog's *Nosferatu the Vampyre*, a dead butterfly of a film pinned to Murnau's vivid original, *Love at First Bite*, which wittily makes of itself a sequel to the Lugosi movie, and even the Jamie Gillis pornos, *Dracula Sucks* (1979, a.k.a. *Lust at First Bite*), which re-uses almost all the 1930 script, and *Dracula Exotica* (1981, a.k.a. *Love at First Gulp*), which makes a few distinctive additions to the myth.

Blatantly in evidence is an increasing and genuine romantic feeling, first observable in Robert Quarry's fatal crush on Mariette Hartley in *The Return of Count Yorga* (1971) and in Paul Naschy's chubbily agonised and suicidal vampire in the revealingly titled *El Gran Amor del Conde Dracula* (1972). In more serious adaptations, Palance's hollow-cheeked and ethnically correct Carpathian broods over the girl he lost and pursues her 1890s lookalike (Fiona Lewis); Kinski's bitter, self-pitying

Nosferatu dotes on Isabelle Adjani; Langella's curly-haired Latino stud in open-necked romance-hero white shirt pays genuine court to Kate Nelligan; and Jourdan's aged *roué* for once seems sincere when confronted by the authentic period prettiness of flirt Susan Penhaligon and gamine Judi Bowker. The Hamilton and Gillis films are obviously more concerned with love (and, in the porno movies, sex) than bloodlust, some sort of apotheosis being reached in *Dracula Exotica* when, under the influence of true love, Dracula is transformed from a bat into a dove. This acceptance of a vampire as a deserving lover is evident among female-themed vampire movies too, as witness *Lust for a Vampire* (1971), *Le Rouge aux lèvres* (*Daughters of Darkness*) (1971), *The Velvet Vampire* (1971), *Lèvres de sang* (1975, the best of Jean Rollin's many contributions) and *The Hunger* (1983). Such interpretations doubtless contributed to the establishment of the (largely female) audience for the sympathetic/glam vampire novels of Anne Rice (*The Vampire Lestat*, 1986), Chelsea Quinn Yarbro (*Hotel Transylvania*, 1978), Suzy McKee Charnas (*The Vampire Tapestry*, 1983), Nancy Collins (*Sunglasses After Dark*, 1990) and Freda Warrington (*A Taste of Blood Wine*, 1992).

In many ways magnificent, Coppola's *Dracula* suffers from a fatal misreading of the original material, a fault it has in common with Hart's *Hook*. Like Matheson in 1973, Hart reveals Stoker's vampire as the historical Impaler and revives the most tiresome of monster motivations (cf. *The Mummy, Blacula*): the search for the reincarnation of the lost love. The character is capable of myriad interpretations, but for all the wonders of his setting, Oldman takes his place in the losers' box with weary John Carradine (*Billy the Kid vs Dracula*), desperate David Niven (*Vampira*), Frank Zappa-ish Zandor Vorkov (*Dracula vs Frankenstein*) and frankly miscast Alex D'Arcy (*Blood of Dracula's Castle*) and Miles O'Keefe (*Waxwork*). Depending heavily on the image of Dracula as a faithful lover and centuried romantic, the film has trouble when he appears as a rubberised bat – or wolf-monster. In his heart, this Dracula is less the brute of Stoker's original than the naive and sentimental Hamilton of *Love at First Bite*, but, even given that angle on the mythos, Coppola (like Badham and Herzog) comes short. Despite strenuous bosom-heaving and tears trickling down prosthetic cheeks, this Dracula, begging pity from Mina and the audience, is a whiner rather than a gallant, sadly lacking in demonic passion and, ultimately, the literal dead centre of a film so visually strong it deserves a more potent King Vampire.

INVASION OF THE BLOOD

Iain Sinclair

Blood money, liquidity. 'Dracula sucks in £21m,' thrills the *Evening Standard*. 'Money is flowing as copiously as blood.' Blood is now perceived as a commodity, a prime asset. Uninfected blood (none of that Third World stuff) is liquid gold, life-sustaining. We quake in fear of a run on the blood banks: unruly aliens threatening our hard-earned immunity from poverty. Blood weddings (thirteen-year-old script plus Winona Ryder hooks Coppola, secures funding) open untapped veins of credit. The production coagulates through each of its weird sisters: Columbia/Zoetrope/Osiris. Zoetrope being a shamanic toy, a slit drum offering the illusion of movement. And Osiris? The god of death, the scattered one whose percentage points are the privilege of stardom. 'The seventh-best opening for any film in history.'

Why not cast Sinatra?

In Hollywood, history is what a director becomes the morning after a lousy preview. It is that which can be rewritten by accountants. Dracula's selling point is that he belongs to history: his transfixion on the end of an iron toothpick has been shown more times than the assassination of Kennedy. He has become an unofficial elder statesman, a roving ambassador. He's been undead as long as Richard Nixon and has recently acquired the same kind of posthumous (but still breathing) respectability. He is even beginning to look like Ronald Reagan, after a course of *gravitas* injections.

For this latest final comeback (why didn't they cut the make-up budget by casting Sinatra?), a team of opticians grafted hard scleral shells over the Count's eyes; lenses last seen screwed into the latex mask of the youthful Orson Welles, to transform him into the power-vampire *Citizen Kane*. Raving within his Californian pastiche of a Transylvanian castle, Kane was the independent shadow, the reflection that W. R. Hearst refused to acknowledge when he looked in the mirror. Hearst's arteries of black propaganda return us to headlines proclaiming self-fulfilling prophecies of blood-money triumph. Blood treated with light transformed to loot.

F. F. Coppola, by temperament a binger, began as a celluloid junkie, sitting red-eyed at his dawn movieola to impress the exploitation-factory boss. He earned his shot: *Dementia* (1963, axe murderer attacks noble Irish family). Things are very different now: middle-European aristo bites back. It is still a controlled environment, no rogue skies, no weather. There are borrowed London streets, dizzy with the usual hyper-active extras. But prestige grants the time to prepare, squads of graduate technicians. The most expensive tent show on earth. It's more like a moon shot. The director of photography, Michael Ballhaus, has survived fifteen Fassbinders and is hot from Scorsese's *GoodFellas*. There are ample funds to take care of 'contact lenses, prosthetics, blood tubes, wolves, insects, babies'. What we have here are all the classic subterranean genre elements – with major transfusions of respectability in the form of cash. Corman plus budget, that's the spin.

What we do not have, alas, is Bram Stoker's *Dracula*, which is how this season's model has chosen to market itself. Authenticity, certificates of heritage approval. Unfortunately, the *Dracula* published by Archibald Constable in 1897 was not Bram Stoker's either. He would not have claimed sole copyright. The vampire could be traced in folklore back to, at least, the seventeenth century. Stoker constructed, from many sources, an immensely persuasive hybrid: a nightmare capable of earthing the unconscious terrors of his own time. He blended Polidori's doomed Byronic wanderer with the sexual ambiguities and pleasurable traumas of Sheridan LeFanu's 'Carmilla'. He borrowed the multi-voiced narrative dynamically exploited by Wilkie Collins in *The Woman in White*. Coppola can only pay lip service by making reference to typewriters, phonographs, letters, journals. He refuses to fracture his favoured method of orchestrated independent sequences, interspersed with seizures of moralistic crosscutting. The hieratic ironies which carried the *Godfather* saga now decay into a gamey vulgarity: we are forced directly from a vivid blood transfusion to a side of beef on the dinner table.

Stoker persuades by stealth, by the slow accumulation of arduously researched detail. Longueurs the cinema can never indulge. Coppola is most comfortable with a form of serial opera, millennial rock'n'roll with all the stops out. We are offered a necrophile *Love Story*, the 'love that never dies'. It takes 400 years, but as the sun sets over the Carpathians, Vlad the Impaler gets his girl. Aria and recitative. Climax and curtain. The thousand small deaths of visual orgasm. The nosferatu, this geriatric Valentino, moves in from the wings, where he lurks through the body of Stoker's text, to take centre stage as an absinthe-tippling masher. The focus shifts from Stoker's morbidly repressed head sex to a psychotic anatomy lesson. The action, once visited entirely on those regions between neck and brain, now runs amok. Gang rape by an animated eiderdown, top-dollar nipples rearing out of liquid bedspreads, werewolves guzzling pudenda on top of rustic sepulchres. It's wild, but it belongs to the industrial parasites whose idea of class is to add numerals after a title (just like royalty), to manufacture a spurious respectability. *Dracula CLX.*

Unspecified horrors accumulate

The most serious division between the original *Dracula* and this interpretation is the film's refusal to inhabit a true psychic geography. In compensation, Coppola provides a battery of shock effects, interesting and driven, which are perfectly tuned to the mores of late-Victorian illusionist theatre. Dry ice, gunpowder, ghost mirrors, double-exposure, forced-perspective miniatures. A world Stoker would have been happy to acknowledge, a world to which he would have been granted access through his long association with Henry Irving. (It has been suggested that Irving's emphatic sibilants and consummate stagecraft contributed to the actor/manager aspects of Count Dracula.) But behind these seductive smokescreens there needs to be a living city. Coppola, marooned on his sound stages, has nothing as evocative as the list of addresses to which Dracula's chests of earth must be delivered; 197, Chicksand Street, Mile End New Town, Jamaica Lane, Bermondsey. Unspecified horrors accumulate around such specific map references. We should not forget that the Count banked with Coutts, and was a premature investor in Docklands. From his abbey at Purfleet (currently an oil refinery), his properties circumnavigated London. Those poisoned bolt holes of mouldy soil are probably still in place, sustaining all the mushroom towers of Thatcherite folly.

The dying century incubates an anxious sleep. And who better to interpret and give form to this anxiety than the custard-pallor Gary Oldman, with his tumescent Versailles pompadour? (Let's hear it for Stuart Artingstall, stylist and wigmaker.) Oldman has shuffled the tarot pack of paranoid icons: Sid Vicious, Joe Orton, Lee Harvey Oswald. A perfect preparation for this customised plague manikin. He is the manifestation of disease, campy and fatal, a revenant elaborately made-up for an AIDS benefit. He is the needle with which Coppola immunises complacency.

But does it suffice, this *fin-de-siècle* retread? We have lost our nerve, and seem incapable of breeding our own nightmares. We live in an age of plagiarism and theft, dignified as 'post-modernist'. Victorian guilts and sweats brought forth *Jekyll and Hyde*, *The Mystery of a Hansom Cab*, *The Invisible Man*, *Dracula*: prophetic syntheses of a general trauma. Dreams that were real. Dreams whose bleakest features were soon to be enacted upon the landscape, as literature passed seamlessly into the headlines of the *Police Gazette*. Edwin Drood mutating into Montague Druitt, the Ripper suspect.

Now we are condemned to rummage through the attic, brush down Frankenstein, Sweeney Todd, all the familiar nursery ghouls. Our worst imaginings surround us. They are already on the streets, plucking at our coat tails. Coppola's account of Bram Stoker's *Dracula* succeeds best when it taps our present panic. The chaos of the Balkans, the collapse of communism, a chill wind from the east. The same invasion paranoia was lanced in the 1950s by a cycle of low-budget science-fiction quickies. Invasion of the blood is worse, red sex perverts wanting to bite into our virgin meat. 'Civilisation vs syphillisation', as Anthony Hopkins' post-Lecter Van Helsing puts it. A bad case of poacher turned gamekeeper. The cannibal residue in his pale smile is appropriate. All the garlic that Coppola once crushed into spaghetti sauce has to be nailed to the walls to keep the infection out. It's like treating AIDS with vitamin C. We fear for our investments. Dracula is raiding a depressed market. There is no mistaking his kinship with tired royal blood lines. He's off his grub, won't touch his wine. The man's obviously anorexic. This is what appals the director. Even the scumiest Mafia torpedo enjoys his meatballs and Chianti, before garrotting the competition. Vlad, with his bulimic blood-gorging, has to be decapitated, returned to the Church. We have to understand that a United Nations posse, armed with Winchester repeaters out of Buffalo Bill's Wild West Show, can take care of any upstart, vampire ayatollah.

Germinal
KEEPING IT IN THE FAMILY

Jill Forbes

Claude Berri's reputation in Britain rests almost entirely on his hugely successful adaptations of Marcel Pagnol's *Jean de Florette* and *Manon des sources*. Since then, by his own account, he has been searching for a 'big' subject in order to make a film whose impact will equal those blockbusters of the 1980s. After a false start with an adaptation of *Uranus*, Marcel Aymé's portrait of small-town life in occupied France, he has returned triumphantly with *Germinal*, his version of Emile Zola's novel of 1885. The Paris opening, fortuitously or not, coincided with the final stages of the GATT negotiations and the appearance on French screens of Spielberg's *Jurassic Park*. '*Germinal* versus *Jurassic Park*' screamed the headlines in all but the most sedate newspapers – a bellicose juxtaposition that served as journalistic shorthand for the whole postwar history of the French struggle against American media domination. Berri's film, which undoubtedly stiffened the resolve of the French negotiators, was propelled into the front line of the battle to 'save' French culture.

This was not just newspaper hype. Berri deliberately set out to insert *Germinal* into a cultural debate which has exercised France for half a century. As the global market becomes a reality and European integration draws closer, so the desire to assert cultural specificity grows stronger. Culture has always been seen as the reverse side of the economic coin, as a potential, albeit ideological, trade off. It is a notion put forward not only by politicians such as former culture minister Jack Lang, but by writers such as Alain Finkielkraut, who has denounced 'mass culture' as American, or theatre director Ariane Mnouchkine, who attacked Euro-Disney as a 'cultural Chernobyl'. The role of cinema in the defence and propagation of French culture can be traced back to the Vichy regime, when the government first intervened to protect the film industry against German domination. As in so many other walks of life, the postwar settlement did nothing to disturb this arrangement, merely substituting an American adversary for the German, but continuing to treat film imports as a Trojan horse, a war waged by other means.

This notion of cinema as both the most threatened of French cultural products and the vanguard of its cultural defences is not without irony, given the obvious resilience of the French film industry, which is by far the largest in Europe and arguably the most artistically interesting. French film producers may tell you they are on their knees, but they lie. On the other hand, as Berri emphasises, they do not seek success at any price.

The most popular film in France this season is neither *Germinal* nor *Jurassic Park*, but *Les Visiteurs*, with 14 million domestic viewers at the last count. But this is a film which, as Berri remarks, 'was not intended to be a big success': a relatively low-budget work which happens to have struck a chord with audiences, but which as a comedy bordering on farce cannot serve as a flagship for the industry as a whole. According to Berri, popular appeal can be programmed in France in much the same way as Spielberg has done in America. Indeed, the career of this most successful of French director/producers has been directed towards that end. But what is it in the Pagnol diptych and the Zola adaptation that delivers the brand of populism Berri seeks? And is it enough to base a popular national cinema on historical adaptations that are of scant relevance to present-day concerns?

The Pagnol films tell a tale of revenge built around the control of natural resources. The elemental is foregrounded in a way that proves that 'nature will out': human nature in the form of peasant cunning, divine nature in the form of a water spring. This is not so distant from Zola. The title *Germinal* recalls the idea that as we sow we reap, and just as the seeds of revenge are sown in *Jean de Florette*, so are the seeds of revolution in *Germinal*. The social vision of both authors is built on the belief that predispositions, whether moral or physical, are transmitted from generation to generation, and both affirm this continuity as 'nature' pitted against an increasingly insistent 'culture'.

Above all, these films put forward a view of French history which is decidedly anti-modernist. Alongside the visual appeal of *Jean de Florette* and *Manon des sources* – the lush colour, the sounds and scents of the countryside before it was destroyed by intensive farming, the peculiar mix of Van Gogh and Elizabeth David that so excites the British middle classes – lies a deeper message about the perenniality of the values of nature and the family. And *Germinal*, which depicts the violent industrial world that was superimposed on this Edenic garden, a world of crude industrialisation and the crude human relations it engendered, is equally nostalgic and committed to the notion of generational continuity. As we see Etienne Lantier leave the pit village in the final shots of the film, a voiceover reminds us that his legacy will germinate here in the class struggles to come.

For late-twentieth-century audiences, the mining environment of *Germinal* – like the lost countryside of the Pagnol films – is highly exotic. It is not just that the pits have closed (earlier in France than in Britain), but the culture of solidarity they generated has all but disappeared, too. The sequences that resonate with present-day concerns reflect us as though through a distorting mirror. The scene in which the pit wives castrate the grocer who refuses credit to the strikers might stand as a parodic reminder of the limits of the individualistic capitalism of the 1980s which administered the *coup de grâce* to the industrial working class in France as elsewhere, only to falter itself. And the fact that Zola's heroine La Maheude is forced to go back down the mine to feed those members of her family who have survived the debacle of the strike stands as a curious parody of women's emancipation, a statement of the right to work for a pittance in filthy, dangerous conditions.

Like *Jean de Florette* and *Manon des sources*, *Germinal* is a film whose heart is in the right place, a film which is not morally demanding. Novel and film are built around stark contrasts which alternate with insistent regularity: the toiling workers, the feckless bourgeoisie; the quarrels above ground, the solidarity below; night and day; heaven and hell; work and idleness; riches and poverty; youth and age. Zola is the master of the moral made visible – one reason, no doubt, for his appeal to film-makers. But ideologically Berri's project is more complex.

Etienne Lantier is an incomer to the pit village of Montsou, a person displaced by industrial change and forced to wander France in search of work in a hideous parody of the 'tour de la France' traditionally undertaken by apprentices to gain experience of their craft. The incomer is a favourite narrative device in the nineteenth-century novel: we find it in Stendhal, in Hugo, in Dickens, and perhaps most spectacularly in Hardy (an author who appeals to Berri, who produced Polanski's *Tess*). The incomer usually serves as both observer and catalyst, his presence precipitating often catastrophic changes. In both *Germinal* and the Pagnol diptych, however, the agents of change do not win through, but are defeated by the forces of reaction. What triumphs in both is the family as a social unit, which both authors see as the locus of values.

This emphasis is exacerbated in Berri's adaptation of *Germinal* by the virtual elimination of the political dimension of the novel. Zola's *Germinal* is a curious mixture of topical observation and anachronism. It was inspired by a visit to the Anzin mine, scene of a long strike in 1884, the development of which is recounted in the novel. However, *Germinal* purports to be set at the end of the Second Empire, in the late 1860s, when there was also considerable labour unrest in the mines which culminated in the creation of a French section of the Internationale.

The various strands of the labour movement as it unfolded are represented in the novel, with Rasseneur the pragmatic possibilist, Souvarine the anarchist, and Pluchart, who is Etienne's mentor, the syndicalist. But in the film such distinctions have all but disappeared. Early on we see a brief discussion between Rasseneur and Etienne about whether the time is ripe for a strike, but Pluchart (at least in the version released in Britain) does not figure at all, while Souvarine is not the sardonic commentator of the novel, but a watchful presence whose act of sabotage is scarcely explained by his previous attitude. Berri's adaptation focuses almost entirely on the family groups, the miners and the bourgeoisie, and on the contrast between their living conditions and mores: starvation here, indulgence there; promiscuity among the workers, adultery among the middle classes. These contrasts are of course to be found in Zola, but what Berri does is to refashion his tale as a domestic drama, and, ultimately, as a picture of female indomitability, so that La Maheude, played by Miou-Miou, becomes the film's lynchpin.

Such a movie is perhaps unsurprising given Berri's earlier career. His life is extensively documented in his first features – *Le Vieil Homme et l'enfant* (1966), *Mazel Tov ou le mariage* (1968), *Le Pistonné* (1969) and *Le Cinéma de papa* (1970) – films whose real subject is his own close-knit Jewish immigrant family (his father was Polish, his mother Romanian) and how his father's abiding interest in art and films meant that instead of going into the rag trade, Claude, his sister Arlette Langmann and her partner Maurice Pialat all embarked on careers as director/producer, writer/editor and director of films, respectively. Claude himself started life as an actor, though not a successful one, he claims, and from time to time he can still be seen in small parts in friends' films, often in unflattering roles such as that of the homosexual punter in Patrice Chéreau's *L'Homme blessé*.

Berri's *Le Cinéma de papa* takes the phrase used by Truffaut to dismiss the French cinema of the 1950s as outdated and turns it into an affectionate portrait of 'Daddy's cinema': Berri's father's influence on his son. The father's more difficult relationship with his daughter is depicted in Pialat's *A nos amours*, scripted by Langmann, in which Pialat himself plays the role of the father. Berri says the portrait is 'completely wrong', yet what the viewer retains is the impression of an extraordinarily charismatic individual. Much of Berri's subsequent career, his gradual engagement with subjects of 'national' significance, might, were one inclined to crude analysis, be seen as a way of trying to fulfil his father's ambitions. And it is surely significant that just as the daughter Suzanne dominates in *A nos amours*, so the imaginative male characters in both *Jean de Florette* and *Germinal* find their masculinity challenged by women who perform their tasks or realise their ambitions for them.

Berri sees his intimist mode as having been played out by the mid-1970s. The example of the *nouvelle vague* was ever present, and particularly of Truffaut, whom he admired extravagantly. Berri regrets he was not able to imitate Truffaut's achievement of 'speaking about himself without telling the story of his life'. An exception, born of deep personal unhappiness, was *Tchao Pantin* (1983), arguably Berri's masterpiece, in which Coluche movingly plays a defrocked policeman turned night petrol-pump attendant who witnesses the brutal murder of a North African drug pedlar and, despite his self-imposed withdrawal from society, gradually becomes involved in the hunt for the killers, losing his own life in the process.

A glance at Berri's activities in the 1970s confirms a lack of artistic direction in his own films coupled with an increasingly sure sense of what to back as a producer: André Téchiné's *Souvenirs d'en France*, Jacques Doillon's *La Femme qui pleure*, Jacques Rivette's *Céline et Julie vont en bateau*, as well as a series of hugely successful if artistically dubious comedies by Claude Zidi such as *La Moutarde me monte au nez*. But it was producing *Tess* for Polanski – a venture he embarked on out of admiration for the director's work ('Having failed with Milos Forman [Berri had produced *Taking Off*], I wanted to see if I could succeed with another technically brilliant East European') – that shifted Berri on to the terrain he now occupies. *Tess* (1979) marked Berri's first real venture into literary adaptation, and though he continued throughout the 1980s to produce selected auteurs – Demy, Forman, Miller, Rivette, Chéreau, all of whom he had worked with previously – the main thrust of his effort now went into large-scale productions. This marked a significant moment of change in the history of contemporary French cinema, for Berri was among the first producers to understand that cinema had to offer something different from television. French film-makers had been protected from competition with the small screen by the slow development of television in their country. But following the initial deregulation of 1975, and at the point when television companies were first allowed to participate financially in film production (prefiguring the massive privatisations of French television in the 1980s), Berri switched register.

Does Berri see his cinema as helping to create a popular national culture akin to that provided by television? In an interview at the end of the 1980s, he remarked that he was not interested in European cinema, but in international and national cinema, adding resignedly: 'I did not seek to become involved in the GATT debate. But it was inevitable.' Though he refuses to discuss competition with Hollywood, at least in the aggressive terms adopted by many of his compatriots, he is in favour of European quotas for television and of screening more European films. It seems clear that the mantle he seeks to assume is that of Renoir in the 1930s and Carné in the 1940s: a combination of the production values of the grand panorama and subjects that embody the 'matter of France'. This was Carné's achievement in *Les Visiteurs du soir*, inspired by a masterpiece of French medieval literature, and in *Les Enfants du paradis*, whose reconstruction of the great days of boulevard entertainment presented the people as the actors of history. Filmed under the Occupation, both these works were intended to contribute to national cultural survival. In the same way, Renoir's *La Règle du jeu* offered a critical portrait of French society just before the debacle of 1940. These works have been dismissed as 'boulevard cinema', but they could also be described as populist in the best sense, with the film-maker acting as the conscience of the nation.

Both Renoir and Carné also filmed adaptations of Zola's novels (*La Bête humaine* and *Thérèse Raquin*, respectively), but in each case it was the melodrama of Zola's narratives that dominated, the way his plots could be made to resemble those of a Hollywood film noir, and the relationship they posit between sex and death. It would appear that such subject matter is too intimist to underpin a national cinema, even in America. In this respect, *Germinal* was well chosen, since it is more obviously political and less overtly melodramatic than some of Zola's novels. It is clear, too, that Berri has attempted to recreate the moral impact of Carné's great reconstructions. Perhaps if

Alexandre Trauner, who worked for Berri on *Tchao Pantin*, had lived to design the set of *Germinal*, the machinery of the mine and the mean streets of the village might have acquired the symbolic dimension of his urban environments in *Les Portes de la nuit* and *Subway*. But the set of *Germinal* is slightly flat, lacking that organic relationship with the characters who people it which we find in the best films of the 1930s and 1940s. The design proclaims the film's large budget and the attention to authentic detail. But what it fails to do is represent the spiritual journey to hell and back – that founding moment of consciousness which transforms the exploited worker into a revolutionary – that Etienne undertakes. It is as though a late-twentieth-century film about the labour movement, because of what has happened to labour, cannot find the visual idiom in which to express its subject.

Berri's attention is now turning to the Holocaust, to what might be called the 'matter of central Europe'. At present the vaguest of projects, it obviously has the potential to embody all his concerns to date – the Jewish family, his central European origins, history, personal suffering and so on. But haven't Spielberg and the Americans got there first?

Since the demise of the *nouvelle vague*, to be the most successful and influential French producer of your generation is to be a character constantly in search of a subject. Nor does Berri get much help from contemporary novelists, whom he feels tend not to write the kind of work that can easily be adapted to the screen. His forthcoming production, Chéreau's *La Reine Margot*, due to open in Cannes next year, is another historical reconstruction. Whatever its merits, Berri's disaffection with the contemporary, his implicit view that the present is trivial by comparison with the past, that the significance, what he calls the 'emotion', he seeks can be found only through the transformation of history into spectacle, must surely point to the inevitable decline of European cinema unless history can be made relevant to the present day. It is ironic that the failure of the miners' strike in *Germinal* seems more relevant in Britain, on the tenth anniversary of our own miners' strike, than it appears in France.

Shakespeare and the Elizabethans
A TALE OF TWO MAGICIANS

Adam Barker talks with Peter Greenaway about
Prospero's Books

Flaunting their erudition and relishing their overt staginess, Peter Greenaway's films divide audiences. There are those prepared to entertain his conceits and play the game, and others for whom a Greenaway film is about as exciting as a guided tour through an ancient museum where the catalogue has been lost. What is not in doubt is

Greenaway's achievement. Producing a regular stream of low-budget movies, from early shorts such as *H is for House* (1976) to *The Cook, The Thief, His Wife and Her Lover* (1989), he has made one of the most challenging bodies of work in postwar British cinema.

In person, Greenaway is a far cry from the malicious manipulator which his work might suggest. Quiet, courteous and amiable, he speaks with practised eloquence. But despite his willingness to expound on the ramifications of his densely packed work – and to admit to its failings – it is hard to avoid feeling that his fluency is ultimately unsatisfactory. When asked to consider the personal roots of his work, Greenaway is at first unexpectedly reticent, and then skilfully guides the conversation back to safer ground.

This interview was conducted over three days in Greenaway's spartan Hammersmith production offices – more reminiscent of a workshop than a film studio. The setting reflects his artisanal approach to film-making, where as far as possible the money goes on the screen rather than on the extravagant trappings of the film industry.

Greenaway is hard at work editing his new movie in time for Cannes. *Prospero's Books*, as it is known, is a version of Shakespeare's *The Tempest* starring John Gielgud. Shakespeare's play centres on Prospero, Duke of Milan, who has been deposed by his brother, Antonio, supported by Alonso, King of Naples, and now lives on an island with his daughter, Miranda. Opening with a storm in which the corrupt brother and his courtiers are shipwrecked on the island through Prospero's magic, *The Tempest* shows Prospero's staging of an action in which he intends to take his revenge on his usurping brother.

Initially approached by Gielgud, who has cherished the idea of putting the enigmatic drama on screen for some time, Greenaway rapidly transformed the play into his own idiosyncratic vision. The film picks up on a brief mention in the text of twenty-four books from his library which Prospero is permitted to take into exile. These desert island volumes become an abstract counterpoint to the story, like the number count from one to 100 in *Drowning by Numbers*. While remaining faithful to Shakespeare's text, Greenaway has put the words of all the characters into Prospero's mouth for the first two-thirds of the film.

The results – if the unfinished editing copy I was allowed to see is anything to go by – are fascinating, and sure to polarise viewers of Greenaway's work even more than any of his previous films.

*   *   *

One of the reasons we have called the film *Prospero's Books* rather than *The Tempest* is to indicate to an audience that it is not a straight attempt to reproduce a familiar text. One of my many interests was to pursue the twenty-four books that Gonzales, Prospero's loyal courtier, supposedly put into the bottom of the leaky vessel in which Prospero was sent out into exile. That idea, I suppose, really holds the material together.

And it seemed quite logical from there to consider *The Tempest* very much as a text, as something written. So what happened in the end is that I made the twenty-fourth book *The Tempest* itself. So the whole film is structured around the idea of Shakespeare/ Prospero (Gielgud) sitting in his cell on the island writing the play that you see.

The first word of the play is 'Bosun', which is a very interesting word because it is one that is never written down. It was used by seamen who were basically illiterate, so that when they came to write the word down it was 'boatswain'. It's a nice opening point about the topsy-turvy use of oral and written language.

So the film opens with Gielgud sitting at his desk experimenting with the word 'Bosun', and you see it written up on the screen many times. The evocation of that word in conjunction with the first book of the film, which is the *Book of Water*, supposedly put together by Leonardo da Vinci, sets the film off. Right at the beginning, then, the audience knows we are at the origins of the play, and I make no attempt at straight illusionism.

At the end of the film the books are all destroyed. What happens, then, is that the apocryphal books – which of course never exist – are created in the first minute and destroyed in the last minute of a two-hour film. They are there only for the film, which I think is an intriguing idea.

Following this so far? Good. Because it gets worse. In addition to the labyrinthine complexity of its narrative, *Prospero's Books* is visually the most dense of Greenaway's films, thanks largely to the first extensive use of high definition television (HDTV) processes for the big screen. HDTV uses twice as many lines as conventional television to achieve better resolution, higher contrast and a wider range of colours. The resulting image – which also has a wide, cinema-like screen ratio – can be manipulated using all the sophisticated techniques of video editing: slow motion, superimposition, and animation.

Shot on 35mm film, *Prospero's Books* is being edited using a combination of conventional film techniques and television post-production. Greenaway has edited three separate versions of the film which run in parallel and will ultimately be mixed together into a single two-hour narrative. He has spent a month in Japan using state-of-the-art HDTV editing facilities provided by the television company NHK. In order to test the potential of the technology, NHK contributed about £2 million worth of editing time free of charge (representing more than the entire production budget of about £1.5 million).

The high definition techniques – also being used by Wim Wenders for his forthcoming road movie *Until the End of the World* – allow Greenaway to unite the sumptuous cinematography evident in *The Cook, The Thief, His Wife and Her Lover* with the sophisticated image manipulation of his television production of Dante's *Inferno*. Greenaway is wary of the film being seen as a 'technological freak', but believes he has only scratched the surface of the technical possibilities.

Working in conjunction with Tom Phillips on *A TV Dante*, there seemed to be a way through television to engender a whole series of new ways of making pictures, which I was much more familiar with in terms of painting and draughtsmanship than I was with cinema. It was an ability primarily to reorganise the screen ratio, to play with colour in a way you can't in the cinema, and to extend and reshape the elements of the pictorial imagination, which you can do easily in painting. There was a time when I believed that the cinema had an ability to use all the letters of the alphabet and TV could only use the vowels. I don't believe that to be the case any more; I think TV has its own vocabulary, its own alphabet. So what I wanted to do in *Prospero's Books* is to make the first tentative steps towards an expanded cinema which uses television vocabulary but still hangs on to the cinematic idea of creating images which are bigger, noisier, louder, more engulfing than you are.

It's a terrible admission to make, but I do feel for me that cinema has somehow ceased to be a spectator sport. I get tremendous excitement out of making it rather than out of watching it. I suppose on another level it is like trying to regain those first days of the cinema when the audience rushed out because they thought that the waves coming in were going to wet their feet.

Whatever Greenaway has done, he has been the subject of sceptical enquiry. He began his career as a painter but was always being told that his work was 'too literary'. As an experimental film-maker in the 1970s, his affection for elaborate, elusive storytelling – as seen in *A Walk through H* – led him into conflict with the prevailing non-narrative approach of structuralist film-makers such as Peter Gidal.

With Greenaway's shift into feature films in *The Draughtsman's Contract*, a new worry emerged: was Greenaway interested enough in the conventional concerns of drama – character, events and emotion?

Most of the films originate essentially as ideas – not as events, not as pieces of narrative, not as a desire to express a character. I have always admired, even if I cannot emulate, those people who manage to engender their cinema from the ground up – someone like Godard, for example, whose ideas appear in his imagination already as pieces of cinema and then simply have to be realised.

It differs from film to film, but for me the starting point is a set of ideas – or maybe ideas is too strong, a set of notions. *Belly of an Architect*, for example, came about because I wanted to consider the ideas that were current in Great Britain at that time about the responsibility of the architect. *A Zed and Two Noughts* was initially a film made to consider how man, the superior species of the world, has subjugated the rest of the animal life to his credo, his attitudes.

A good description of some of my film-making activity is 'a conversational dissertation wrapped up in an entertaining narrative form'. At the core there are a number of notions and interrelated ideas which need to be discussed, almost in a conversational way.

While Greenaway recognises his contemporary isolation in attempting to construct a cinema of ideas, drama and formal self-reflexivity, he draws inspiration from other art forms. His heroes include modernists such as the painter R. B. Kitaj and the composer John Cage, but also Jacobean dramatists such as Ford and Webster. He is especially drawn to the masque form – the courtly entertainment – where it was not unknown for the king himself to participate in elaborate stage allegories representing the power of the monarch.

Despite the metaphorical message of *The Cook, The Thief, His Wife and Her Lover* about the avarice and philistinism of Thatcher's Britain, the film borrowed its dramatic form from Jacobean drama, with Helen Mirren taking final cannibalistic revenge on her brutal gourmet husband. So what is it that draws Greenaway back to the seventeenth century?

> The masque is basically an elite private entertainment, very much to do with symbols and emblems and allegories. And anybody who has seen my cinema will know that metaphors and allegories fascinate me enormously. The other aspect of Jacobean drama I like is its extraordinary relish for risk-taking. It's very visceral, very corporeal and often plays with extremely taboo subjects like incest, for example in 'Tis Pity She's a Whore. I suppose these things were at the back of my mind when writing The Cook, The Thief. And although The Draughtsman's Contract is a Restoration drama and not a Jacobean drama, there is a lot of Jacobean concern for that hard edge of morality, sex and violence, which I think gives the film a lot of its tensions.

However, The Tempest, which begins with some of the thrust of Jacobean revenge drama, doesn't develop in the expected way. Though in Greenaway's hands the darker aspects of the play are predictably foregrounded, what is unusual is that the spirit of conciliation prevails.

> The play would certainly seem to start off as a revenge drama, with Prospero in the first five minutes ranting about his past and vowing revenge. But then two-thirds of the way through, almost without prior warning, the situation is broken open completely and there is a moment of truth when Prospero decides to forgive everybody. We have actually used this as a pivotal moment in the film, and for my purposes I am very happy with that sudden change of heart. But you must not be misled into thinking that this is psycho-drama. It is a drama of conceits and allegories and metaphors, and under these terms a sudden change of heart can no doubt be seen to be relevant to all the other concerns of the play.

Greenaway's films are littered with flawed male protagonists whose arrogance and grandiose artistic schemes are ultimately their undoing – from Anthony Higgins' conceited draughtsman to Brian Dennehy's auto-destructive architect. But Prospero is in many ways the ultimate manipulator – a magus who contrives the whole story. Does he represent a new kind of hero for Greenaway?

> There is a deliberate amalgamation or confusion between Shakespeare, Gielgud and Prospero – they are, in effect, the same person. It is Shakespeare's last play, his farewell to illusionism, his farewell to playing games, his farewell to all this anti-naturalism. Gielgud at eighty-seven is obviously near the end of his life, and he has had an incredibly long theatrical career. So in terms of English classical theatre, it is his goodbye to illusionism, to costumes, to dressing up, to playing games. And of course within the confines of the play itself this is exactly what Prospero does – in the famous last speech he actually turns to his audience and begs their forgiveness and abandons his magic before he leaves the stage.

At the same time, I don't think there is any doubt at all that when Gielgud appears in *Prospero's Books* he is an actor. He is giving in some ways a purple performance; he is a virtuoso actor and we allow him that space – this is quite deliberate. There are things about Prospero where you feel that's also true – sometimes when you read the dialogue you can see him looking at himself from the outside as he plays his various roles: patrician statesman, silly old fool, prohibitive father. It is a series of ways of breaking the character down.

Perhaps what most distinguishes *Prospero's Books* from Greenaway's previous work is its lack of strong female protagonists. In Shakespeare's play, Miranda is the only woman, and she is little more than a child; in *Prospero's Books*, Greenaway may have added Susannah, Miranda's mother, who is seen in a series of flashbacks, but neither of the women enjoys a major active role.

While Greenaway's work has often been accused of misogyny because of the extreme humiliation suffered by women characters of his films – especially the sexual abuse hurled on Helen Mirren in *The Cook, The Thief* – Greenaway professes an enthusiasm for strong female characters who, more often than not, turn out to be secretly running the show. So how did he deal with Shakespeare's most famous naïf, Miranda, Prospero's daughter, as played by Isabel Pasco?

For the first third of the play she is no more, I suppose, than the representative of the audience, the device Prospero needs to explain to the audience what the history has been. She makes no contribution to anything herself. I have to admit that in the film we have pushed that tendency even further, because we have made her constantly asleep. And even at the end she still doesn't come over as a particularly strong-minded wench.

But as a pawn, as a cipher, Miranda is essential to the play because she certainly believes, as I do, in the Darwinian evolution – she is the kingpin, or the queenpin, on which the whole drama peculiarly rests. Ultimately, Prospero does get his revenge because he manages to unite the kingdoms of his enemies through the offspring Miranda will no doubt have from her marriage to the son of Alonso, King of Naples.

But perhaps Miranda's passivity was finally too much even for Greenaway. He has written a companion novel to the film which imagines the voyage back to Naples after the play is over. Miranda becomes a constant source of irritation to the conventional courtiers around her – partly due to her enduring virginal behaviour, and partly because of the unconventional ideas which have been drummed into her by her father, from, anti-clericalism to the dangerous new ideas of scientific reason.

The provocative potential of intellect and divergent thinking is a subject close to Greenaway's heart. The vertiginous array of arcane and erudite references contained within his films is legendary. How does he justify what is, for some, the main obstacle to appreciating his cinema?

I think civilisation has got where it is not by being led by its emotions, but by degrees of rationalisation, in many complex ways. Why can't this be the subject matter and content and structure of film-making? Because of my inclinations, my cultural background, my education and my temperament, I get great delight out of the manipulation of ideas. Some people find it very difficult to understand that the mere discussion of ideas can be fantastically emotionally satisfying. I try very hard to put that into the cinema so that maybe other people can feel it as well.

Despite Greenaway's steadfast defence of the world of ideas, it is precisely this fascination which is so often the downfall of his protagonists. When pressed on this question, the personal reserve dissolves – for a moment.

Perhaps I gave myself away most in *Belly of an Architect* about what I have come to believe are the most sensitive areas – about the validity of art, about whether art is worth doing at all, and if art is worth doing, what sort of art is worth doing more than anything else.

I hadn't realised how personal that film is on lots of different levels – the older I get, the more personal I find that movie – about immortality, posterity, the significances of reproduction, both artistic and genetic. I suppose I do feel a certain optimism for art itself. Small pieces of jade from an ancient 5000-year-old Chinese tomb: we don't understand their political significance, we don't understand their religious significance, but they are able somehow to communicate to us in other ways. There seems to be some clue here, a search for doing something which in a cosmic sense would be totally and absolutely useless, but in a human sense – if we are allotted a certain amount of time on Earth – we need to engage with unless we all want to go and commit mass suicide. But if you take the other, more pragmatic view, in a Darwinian sense my purpose on earth is entirely over. I have engendered two daughters, I have passed on the genetic material, so what I do now, between their birth and my death, is just embellishing the nest a little. The spark, that piece of electricity from God to Adam, has passed on, and I am merely engaged – in a cosmic sense – in decoration.

Peter Greenaway is publishing three books in conjunction with the film – the script, a novel called *Prospero's Creatures* and extracts from the apocryphal books under the title *Ex Libris Prospero*.

DAMNING DESIRE

Mike O'Pray talks with Derek Jarman about *Edward II*

Edward II is the latest in a long line of personal 'heroes' who Derek Jarman has wrenched from history. Others include Sebastiane, the masochistic martyr of gay projections; Elizabeth I of *Jubilee*, the Virgin Queen whose qualities find their ultimate expression in Tilda Swinton's Madonna roles in *The Garden*, *Caravaggio* and *The Last of England*; Prospero of *The Tempest*, the ultimate Shakespearean conception of the artist (as film-maker); the Pasolini-like Jesus of *The Garden*; and Caravaggio, the original rough-trade lumpen artist. But behind Jarman's recent film of Christopher Marlowe's play is also a recognition of the playwright himself as an active, passionate man who was not only gay, but died in a fight inside a Deptford tavern. Marlowe must be linked here, then, with Jarman's passion for the work and lives of Caravaggio and Pasolini – both gays who died violently.

If *Jubilee*, made in the white heat of the punk movement, was Jarman's first attempt to shape the present by means of the past, then *Edward II* tries to do the same in a less schematic way. It creates a world where Edward's obsessive and tragic love for the ambitious Gaveston is exploited as a modern gay love affair set in contemporary England, while at the same time it retains a medieval simplicity to the sets. Typically, Jarman's depiction of the contemporary is determined by the emotional and dramatic demands of the play, so 1960s gangster fashions jostle with 1930s *Vogue* and the balaclava hoods of the 1970s terrorist. Edward's rebellious noblemen are transformed into the pillars of the modern British establishment – bishops, generals, businessmen.

Edward's wife, Isabella (Tilda Swinton), colludes sexually and politically with Mortimer (Nigel Terry, Jarman's Caravaggio), who, envious of Gaveston's prestige and believing that Edward is neglecting his responsibilities as monarch, violently opposes him in a civil war. Jarman's recurring themes of the intimacy of death and love, of the role of institutional violence in society (particularly by the military, of which Jarman's father was a member), and an overwrought sexuality are all reworked in *Edward II*. Images of water, especially in Edward's cell, recall the dream sea sequences in *The Garden* and the idyllic swimming sequences in *The Angelic Conversation*. The violence is characteristically brutal and ambiguous. Isabella's murder of Edward's brother Kent by biting out his throat is horrific and intensely erotic, as is Edward's murder of Gaveston's assassin.

Jarman's ambivalence towards military figures reminds us of his remark that 'if we must have troops, let's have them in bed'. It is a persistent image in his films, from *Jubilee* (where a policeman is bedded before being killed) to *Edward II*, where Nigel Terry sheds the ambiguities of Caravaggio for rampant heterosexuality.

When Jarman says of Marlowe's play that it 'touches on areas that still aggravate people', you can almost hear the relish in his voice.

The Throne

'The throne and who is fit to sit on the throne is what it's all about. I made this very clear with an image of the throne that keeps recurring. Different people get on to it in different ways. Gaveston here became a sort of chattering, evil incubus in the night, reminiscent of the Fuseli picture. The smoking was something the two actors brought into it.

I think it was supposed to be a joint to be passed between them: "We're stoned on the throne and fuck you" was what was going on in their minds. Gaveston is working class and not French, as he is in Marlowe. I couldn't get a French actor and I didn't want a fake French accent. When I was casting Gaveston one of the things I liked about him was his class; there is an element where he might become a vicious, Kray-like gangster in the beating up of the archbishop. And that has to be there, because it's in the character, it's in the way it's written. It also makes the whole thing more poignant – what you have is a situation where two people have obviously fallen in love and one can't understand just what the attraction is. Gaveston is sexuality and class merged. I wanted to have the North/South divide – so Edward has a northern accent, too. He pronounces "castle" in the northern way and whenever he did that my heart leapt because it was also against traditional verse-speaking.'

Edward and Isabella

'I have no problems with heterosexual love scenes. I usually do gay scenes, but I have this unusual scene between Edward and Isabella which is a love scene that goes wrong. Now this must have happened to everyone at some point in their life – when they go to bed with the wrong person. Or what has been passionate, in the cold of early

morning, isn't any more. I don't know many scenes in the cinema quite like that – showing two characters in bed when it's not working out and with no dialogue. I think Colin MacCabe thinks of it as my misogyny in a way. I'm not certain it is. We discussed this with Tilda. I think it's realist, in the sense that bed scenes are nearly always super-real.

Edward is preoccupied, I don't think he's impotent. It just isn't working out. And he's furious about the whole thing. I was trying to keep up this psycho-sexual tension all the way through. All these people trapped in a merry-go-round of conflicting emotion. This is what really excited me about the whole thing. You can show a range of emotion

in *Edward II* that you don't usually get in the cinema.'

Pyjama Party

'Ian said we should light this by spotlight because of Annie Lennox – and suggested we put a spotlight on Edward and Gaveston, too. It works because it restores the theatricality of the whole thing. The spotlight

is on them simply because that is where the spotlight is. In old-fashioned theatre terms, it's a good solution. The actors insisted on Marks and Spencer's pyjamas. There was a sense of humour in the whole thing. The film needed a lightness of touch in places and this has been misinterpreted as my quirky campness. But I don't think it's true; these light-hearted decisions endear you to a character or should do, and it's what we need.'

Gaveston and Edward

'Ken Butler, the associate director, shot this scene between Gaveston and Edward and about three others. Ian Wilson did the lighting. The idea was that it was very late at night. We lit people coming in and out of shadow. Every now and again we blacked out the background so we were just on faces – then the dialogue really comes up. My couple of "fucks" that everyone complains about are necessary in that sense. But I've left the dialogue intact as much as possible. The suits come from a young designer who offered us the suits for Gaveston. You might not notice them but they are rather

unusually and beautifully cut. I put Edward in a duffle coat for most of the film. How does one depict a drop-out and make him look monastic and medieval as well? The duffle coat was the answer. I didn't make him put the hood/cowl up. David Warner's 1960s Hamlet wore a duffle coat, or at least looked like the 1960s student CND radical.'

Isabella, chairman of the board

'Tilda was often in the most theatrically and powerfully composed shots, and here she really is chairman of the board, of Pepsi Cola! She's also Joan Crawford! It was obvious she had to be at the other end of the table, so we cut round to her. Although, of course, you don't know until then whether she is there or not. It's a painterly style, but the whole thing is incredibly simple film-making. I'm a naive film-maker in that sense. Early on Tom Priestly said to me that the best films are just cut – so every time the

camera goes on a move, beware! And he said, "If you've got no money, Derek, then just do a simple long-shot, close-ups, mid-shots." I've always done that because we've never had the money to set up compli-cated shots. With low-budget film-making you got what you could get. I always think of Dreyer's *Passion of Joan of*

Arc. I would be very interested if I could just press a button and see what the film would look like in black and white. It would probably look nearer to that Dreyer look. I am pleased we have colour, I wouldn't make a black and white film because I think that would be arcane.'

The string quartet

'Very Jarmanesque! It could be that marvellous picture of the cellist with the big dress on by Augustus John. I think that's where this came from, although her dress is green and she has red hair! And there is a deliberate homage to *Some Like It Hot*, when Edward and Gaveston enter and dance – which was the actors' idea. This group had done the music on other films and have worked with Simon Turner [Music]. It's along the lines of the sailors' dance in *The Tempest*. I didn't want it to be heavy; I needed to show that at some point this relationship is actually fun, they're having a good time.'

The police line

'Essentially it's just one set for the whole film. How the set changes is determined by how it is lit and it was up to Ian Wilson to invent the light to make some scenes outside, some inside, to give certain atmospheres. The set became a metaphor for the trapped country, the prison of our lives, "the closet of our heart", in Edward's words. There is no sunlight, it's deep in the earth really.'

Mortimer and Isabella

'Ken Butler directed this one, too. I was not well that day and it's done really well. I might have done it differently, but I can't think I would have done it better. I might have reframed slightly on Tilda's face, which falls out of the frame a bit on the next shot, a close-up. Or I might have put a Paganini [a wooden box] under her so that the two of them are absolutely framed up into the frame. At first, when Tilda rushes into the scene, it was funny, but we subverted that with sound. Simon Turner's music is very good with this scene. It's rather clever because Mortimer does have these disingenuous lines – "Who's this, the queen?" – but somehow you get away with it because she has a veil on. There is an element of a real horror film (Corman's *The Tomb of Ligeia*, perhaps?) – after all, we were making this in Hammer's old Bray studios. The lighting is eerie with the slats. We decided on lighting on the day. We thought this scene was probably outside, with a lattice. It's the moment when their relationship becomes passionate.'

The cage

'I wanted to turn everyone into a mannequin, as if they'd been drained of life. Tilda wanted the dead flowers in her hands, Christopher was not keen. It looked like she had received a bouquet for some perform-ance and I like that. And he's clapping, as at the end of *The Garden*, as if he's applauding some mad performance. The little boy is always there. He's a witness and a survivor. Whenever we had a spare moment I did another little scene with him to add because we had so little time. In the actual play, Edward III must be seventeen or so. When he's dancing on the top of their cage later, it reduces him to some sort of puppet. By using Tchaikovsky, I wanted to reinforce the idea of them as wind-up dolls. I was thinking of Eisenstein's *Ivan the Terrible*, when he mounts the throne, that great moment when child Ivan's feet dangle from the throne and don't reach the ground. I couldn't get a quotation in like that, it would have been too much. There is an element of young Edward being me, but everyone identifies with the child and he is the same child in all my films.'

KISS KISS BANG BANG

José Arroyo

William Shakespeare's Romeo & Juliet is a kiss-kiss bang-bang movie. It's got action, spectacle and romance and it aims to entertain. Unlike other movies of Shakespeare's plays – the ones we all get bored by on school trips to the cinema – *Romeo & Juliet* doesn't salaam to Shakespeare's language. The words are all there, as glorious as always, but they are not the *raison d'être* of the film. If most other Shakespeare films nullify the expressive power of *mise-en-scène* by subordinating it, in the service of the language, the Australian director Baz Luhrmann (who made the high-camp dance film *Strictly Ballroom*) elevates Shakespeare cinematically. He makes Shakespeare's work relevant the way it rarely has been in films, by treating his words merely as great dialogue. *Romeo & Juliet* is a moving picture. The dialogue is performed and heard as much in and through the exhilarating movement of striking images, and it is in and through motion that the film moves its audience emotionally.

Romeo & Juliet is set in a 'constructed' world, one that is different enough from a 'real' one to allow for different ways of being and knowing, but with enough similarities to permit understanding. It is a device presently popular across a variety of cultural forms. In comic books, whenever writers want to experiment with risky storylines, they place their characters in a 'parallel universe' (DC Comic Books has a whole Earth II where characters introduced in the 1940s are older and have led different lives than the Superman or Wonder Woman of 'our' world). Science fiction often constructs new worlds in which to set contemporary dilemmas, and fantasy novels brew epic potions of topical villainy by combining modern characterisation with medieval social structures, chivalry, magic, mythological monsters and, sometimes, futuristic technology. In a broader sense, every movie could be said to construct its own world (that we accept the city in which *Casablanca* is set as standing in for the real place doesn't mean it's anything remotely like Casablanca). In the narrower sense I am using here, the convention of a constructed world has traditionally been associated only with particular genres: sci-fi, fantasy, horror and – to a different degree – the musical. But it is arguably now a dominant device, not only in a great deal of action/spectacle cinema, but also in such art fare as *Orlando* or *Swoon*.

Much of *Romeo & Juliet* was filmed in Mexico City, and the topography of that millennial urban nightmare is a key component of the film's look. Verona is depicted as a massive industrial sprawl. At the centre of the city, a gigantic icon of Christ, arms outstretched, ineffectually looms over its inhabitants. Skyscrapers indicate that the Montagues and the Capulets are rich and warring corporate owners. But the skyscrapers are so rickety, dusty and old that they indicate a crumbling social structure. The city is close to sunny beaches and open skies. Its citizens sport rich clothes, fast cars and flash guns. But the city these citizens move in, its streets, buildings and institutions, are all in decay. The clothes mark caste while cars and guns may be mobilised to sudden and deadly consequence. The colour schemes change through the movie, but such bright pinks, blues and oranges are rarely to be found in nature. Verona's Prince, although powerful, is ineffectual against the anarchic gang violence that is the city's *modus operandi*. The way Verona is visualised evokes violent delights as well as violent ends. Pictorially it emphasises the ritual performance of ancient hates that is one of the film's themes.

The film's creation of this imaginary world, one like ours but different, allows us to recognise the actions depicted. We've seen that type of gang violence in news reports from Los Angeles, and the film borrows its iconography from LA gang culture (one gang member has the word 'Montague' tattooed on his scalp). Yet this imaginary construction also renders understandable a world where filial duty, religious devotion, family honour and the institution of marriage have an importance that they do not in ours. In other words, such a construction contributes not only a visual setting for the film's action, but also sets the dramatic terms for that action and therefore the conceptual schema for the audience's understanding. Constructing a world which combines the real with the imagined, the past with the present, results in a depiction of a sense of time and space which is quasi-mythic.

Fredric Jameson has argued that this is typical of the dehistoricising effects of post-modern culture. But one could counter-argue that what he calls dehistoricising can be a means of making past conventions of storytelling understandable in the present context. The construction of mythic time and place in *Romeo & Juliet*, a 'no time' that is all time, and a 'no place' that stands for any place, is built bit by bit out of previous, inherited modes of telling, showing and understanding. These operate allegorically, and involve the viewer in sophisticated strategies of interpretation. So we are required to decipher what this constructed world stands for and how it comments on our own.

Romeo & Juliet is complex, but also direct, pleasurable and easily accessible. The story is framed by a television news report. The television slowly materialises from a dark screen until it takes over the frame. A black newsreader with the *faux*-friendly attitude, regulation hairdo, and style of announcing so typical of American television begins to tell us about 'the two households, both alike in dignity'. The camera then cuts away from the newsreader, as we get to the report itself. As the voiceover continues to tell us how 'civil war makes civil hands unclean', we get a tabloid television montage of quickly edited images of chaos: some from a helicopter, some out of focus, some zooms and quick wipes. The end of the film will reverse this process and the television newsreader will fade to black as we are told that there 'never was a story of more woe/Than this of Juliet and her Romeo'.

The brawl at the beginning of the play, which ends with the threat of a duel between Benvolio and Tybalt, is filmed at a hysterical pitch. The audience seems to be assaulted by every cinematic trick in the book: impossible point-of-view shots (a huge close-up of Tybalt's silver-heeled boots); quick cutting of pans, zooms, wipes. The scene culminates in the most characteristic device in the contemporary action/spectacle genre: the moment when something potentially destructive, moving at great speed, is shown in slow motion, to evoke the beauty of anticipating the horror to come. Here, that moment is when Tybalt draws his weapon on Benvolio.

The frenzy of this first scene is so viscerally exciting that the language gets lost in the action. The intent is probably strategic: to announce that *Romeo & Juliet* will be a Shakespeare film like no other. However, one is grateful that this kind of loss is not compounded. How the language gets performed – by the director, cinematographer and other film-makers as well as the actors – is still the major attraction in seeing a Shakespeare film. Fortunately, from then on, no matter how action-packed or how excitingly filmed the scene is, the speeches will be heard.

We are introduced to Romeo via a helicopter shot in a setting that conveys his state of mind. Initially we just see something that looks like a Victorian monument with a hole apparently blasted through it. The sun is coming up over a new day, over the near-apocalypse of the past. When we get to Romeo, the camera comes to rest, as he sighingly foreshadows what will happen – the brawling love, the loving hate. When

Romeo tells us that 'Love is a smoke made with the fume of sighs' and a 'madness most discreet', the camera is in close-up. This alternation – between filming public scenes as action-packed and quick-moving, and slowing down the pace and moving the camera closer when the protagonists are expressing emotion in private – is characteristic of the film; plot is filmed intensely with a complex array of film devices; the intense emotions of Shakespeare's characters are filmed quietly and more simply.

In this version of *Romeo & Juliet*, the Prince is something akin to a Chief of Police, Mercutio is a black drag queen, the Montagues are white while the Capulets are Hispanic. This amounts to more than just the attribution of ethnic or racial characteristics to characters: it helps to restore to Shakespeare's filmed work a polyphony that has been eroded through years of respect. Having Harold Perrineau depict Mercutio as a drag queen is a delight, if not too much of a surprise; a certain bawdiness is one of the pleasures of Shakespeare, and previous film interpretations (including John Barrymore in George Cukor's 1936 version) have tended towards camp. Even a black Mercutio will not seem strange: we've become used to blind casting in Shakespeare (good though Denzel Washington was in Kenneth Branagh's version, he was still Much Ado About Nothing). But what will (I think) surprise is Perrineau's recognisably black-American inflection; and that Vondie Curtis-Hall speaks the Prince role in the usual received pronunciation and declamatory style expected of Shakespearean princes, while Paul Sorvino as Fulgencio Capulet and John Leguizamo as Tybalt speak with a Hispanic accent. The language is just as poetic; and in the sense that it adds a racial and ethnic dimension to the characterisation, arguably richer, more relevant to contemporary culture. And it is undoubtedly more 'realistic' and (perhaps because of that) more accessible. The vocal performances here aren't as attention grabbing or as theatrical as the vocally complex and rich declamatory style usually associated with Olivier (though they derive from a great British tradition): yet I find that it's a style that works beautifully in this film.

The film's attribution of ethnicity puts an interesting slant on how the film depicts gender. As in *West Side Story*, Romeo's side is White, while Juliet's is Hispanic. This device attaches to Shakespeare's characters certain modern stereotypes, which make them more understandable. Tybalt, for example, is as sleek and agile as a puma. He wears Cuban heels, tight pants, a Matador jacket and a pencil-thin moustache. Every movement he makes has the elegance and force of a flamenco gesture. His pride, temper and the importance he attaches to family honour are far more understandable to present-day viewers as Hispanic stereotypes than as the values of a Renaissance nobleman. Likewise, Juliet's refusal of her father's becomes more transgressive when read through her ethnicity.

The way the film racialises the family is intriguing. It is the woman's family which tends to be depicted as of a 'minority', thus doubly disempowering her. Within her family context here, Juliet has very limited power over her actions and her future – not only because she's a young girl, but also because she's an Hispanic young girl. Romeo's love is thus also a promise of integration, one which gets fulfilled after their death when the two families reconcile at the end. Moreover, as in *West Side Story*, which has Natalie Wood as Maria, whose family is clearly marked as ethnically Other, the heroine is played by a 'white' actress. Thus, while Paul Sorvino can personify ethnicity as Capulet, Claire Danes as Juliet doesn't even use the accent. Her ethnicity is a kind of drag impersonation imposed on her character by genealogy. This adds a certain erotic frisson to the relationship while not burdening the love story with any extra social repercussions inherent in an inter-racial romance.

Perhaps *Romeo & Juliet*'s greatest success is in its depiction of the love story. The film really captures the romance of adolescent love: sometimes flighty but also exaggeratedly and touchingly pure. When Romeo goes to the party where he will meet Juliet, he takes some drugs and all of a sudden the black sky is full of red fireworks. Something explosive is about to happen. When he does meet Juliet, everything quietens down. He sees her eye through white coral in a fish tank. We see both of them in close-up staring at each other as tropical fish in brightly beautiful colours glide over their faces. Even as they are separated by the tank, their reflections are already side by side. The private moments of Romeo and Juliet are always shown as enclosed or submerged. In the balcony scene, they kiss under water. After they are married and he sneaks into her bedroom, we see them under a sheet. The morning after, we see them through an overhead shot that finds them grounded on the bed, their adolescent bodies unprotected even by a sheet, much less from the dangers that lie ahead.

Romeo & Juliet works on many levels, but it could all have fallen apart with the wrong casting. Leonardo DiCaprio and Claire Danes not only act the parts well, but also, more importantly (an importance we can glean from the success of the rather badly acted Zeffirelli version in 1968), they look like adolescents. Danes brings a quiet resolution to her part, a maturity and pragmatism evoked by her face and figure as much as by her acting, while still looking like an adolescent. DiCaprio is skinny and gangly, seemingly all arms and legs. His walk, somewhat pigeon-toed, makes him seem very vulnerable. This version of the film places rather more onus on Romeo than on Juliet. He is the one who bears the brunt of feeling: it's his face in close-up most of the time indicating how he wants, longs, feels and sometimes, eyes hidden by tears, suffers. His performance is all raw emotion. When he's in exile in Mantua, it's not just the flat barren desert of red earth and regulation trailers that speak his desolation, but the way he moves. When he hears of Juliet's death it's not just that the camera lifts up suddenly to crush him that expresses his grief, but the way he falls on his pigeon-toed heels. It's a superb performance.

Romeo & Juliet draws on many genres. We can detect elements from *Rebel Without a Cause*. The *Dirty Harry* films are evoked, as are Fellini and Busby Berkeley. But they are all brought together through a camp aesthetic pitched at a melodramatic level. In traditional melodrama, effect tends to be in excess of cause. A one-night stand, a missed encounter or a simple misunderstanding could lead to a lifetime of tragedy. Romeo and Juliet fall in love instantly; they promise to marry one another and because of this (and several misunderstandings) they both kill themselves. Geoffrey Nowell-Smith has written of the notion of conversion hysteria in melodrama: that which the text represses on the level of plot and dialogue returns in the *mise-en-scène* as 'hysterical' moments. Though Shakespeare's text doesn't leave much unsaid, the *mise-en-scène* excessively intensifies that which the characters are saying. Every emotion is overdetermined. When the two fall in love we're told so by the film on the level of the music, the colour and the camera movement, as well as the dialogue. The function of camp in the film is to add a layer of signification to the narrative while distancing the viewer from it. When the pair meet she's wearing wings and he's wearing shining armour. She's his angel; he's her knight. When Romeo goes to the party, the acid tab he takes is imprinted with a broken heart. On one level, this campy *mise-en-scène* contributes to what we are shown about the characters' state of mind; on another, it is so knowingly excessive that it has the paradoxical effect of making the dialogue and situation seem more naturalistic.

I am not sure that the film's campness is necessarily a gay camp. True, the story of a forbidden love whose discovery brings catastrophic consequences has traditionally appealed to gay men (it's no accident that Cukor and Zeffirelli directed previous Hollywood versions). This *Romeo & Juliet* could certainly and easily lend itself to a queer reading on many levels: the focus on Romeo, the display of the male body through the film, the types of sets, props and clothes the film utilises. But I don't think it specifically addresses a gay subculture through its campness in the way, say, that Derek Jarman's *The Tempest* does. Camp is just another element that – as in so many other post-modern films – helps *Romeo & Juliet* to construct its frame of reference and particular tone.

It's a very hybrid film, one that quotes and borrows from everywhere and yet garners the requisite effects. At Romeo's death scene, Romeo and Juliet lie on top of an altar. They are surrounded by crosses of red flowers in which blue neon lights are embedded. It could have become kitsch, but it isn't. Though the film is quite knowingly referential (we see the Globe Theatre Pool Hall at the beginning of the film), there is no irony in the emotional scenes. The crosses are theatrical, but they suit the film's world, complementing the tone of the scene and Romeo's state of mind. They are part of the film's construction of a vernacular that can convey Shakespeare's story to a contemporary audience in a filmic way, eliciting a variety of feelings which, in the appropriate places, include laughter. But not boredom.

Titus
BLOODY ARCADES

John Wrathall talks with Julie Taymor

The acclaimed American theatre director Julie Taymor is best known in the United Kingdom for converting *The Lion King* into a musical, currently playing to packed houses in the West End. It might seem quite a leap from a Disney family spectacular to her feature-film debut, *Titus*. Adapted from Shakespeare's earliest and most outlandish tragedy *Titus Andronicus*, it's the bloodthirsty story of the fall of a Roman general and his family and the ruthless revenge he exacts on his trio of persecutors: Tamora Queen of the Goths, the Emperor Saturninus and Aaron the Moor. In place of the life-affirming sentiments and Elton John melodies of *The Lion King*, *Titus* offers a relentless catalogue of rape, torture, human sacrifice, mutilation and murder.

There is, however, a connection. In both instances, Taymor's distinctive achievement lies in the flair and dynamism with which she reinvents proven material for a new medium. It's a paradox she enjoys: 'I work cinematically in the theatre and I work theatrically in the cinema.'

As with Ian McKellen's *Richard III*, its closest relation in the realm of Shakespeare on film, Taymor's vision of *Titus* originated in an acclaimed stage production, off-Broadway in 1994. The cast has changed entirely (with the exception of Harry Lennix, formidable and surprisingly sympathetic as the unrepentant villain of the piece, Aaron). But in terms of costume and imagery, Taymor's two versions have much in common. Mixing eras – from ancient Rome to 1930s fascism to the present day – her film is undeniably theatrical, not in the narrow sense of stagey, but in the way she uses the word when she talks about such silent directors as Méliès, Murnau and Lang: 'They were so creative cinematically, they were theatrical. They really used the medium in a way that wasn't just to reproduce nature.'

Even the most purely visual and overtly 'cinematic' moments in *Titus* are drawn from Taymor's stage production. At intervals throughout the film, which with inevitable pruning sticks closely to Shakespeare's text, she interrupts the action with what she terms 'Penny Arcade Nightmares'. These short, surreal sequences, densely packed with superimposed images and symbols, attempt to get inside the characters' fevered imaginations, providing a visual equivalent of Shakespeare's soliloquies while at the same time making visually explicit the rich imagery of his language. See, for instance, a hallucinatory flashback from the point of view of Titus' daughter Lavinia to her rape and mutilation at the hands of Tamora's sons, who are compared in Shakespeare's text to tigers.

The Penny Arcade Nightmares are the most overt expression of Taymor's visually eclectic strategy. It's as if, in her effort to put the play across as powerfully as possible, she grabs whatever comes to hand – an unfettered, scattershot approach which is justified, in her view, by the source play's own gamut of styles, from tragedy to outrageous black comedy and surrealism. In *Titus Andronicus*, Taymor explains, 'Shakespeare mixed Greek tragedy and mythology, Ovid's *Metamorphoses*, his idea of Roman history, which is bogus, his idea of Roman ritual, and Christianity.'

Shooting largely in Rome not only gives the film a frisson of real history, but also allowed Taymor to tap into the creative well-spring of Italian cinema via two key collaborations with veteran image-makers. DP Luciano Tovoli shot *The Passenger* and *The Oberwald Mystery* for Antonioni and a couple of films for Dario Argento, while production designer Dante Ferretti, before his current long-term association with Scorsese, worked extensively with Pasolini (*Salo*, *The Canterbury Tales*) and Fellini (*And the Ship Sails On*, *Ginger and Fred*). The result is a film of extraordinary – even, if such a thing is possible, excessive – visual riches.

* * *

'We had to make the crossroads. It's plastic. And we needed these vanishing points, too, so the stones were cut out of garbage-bag plastic. These are genius people, the artists at Cinecittà. All the landscape is real. We were right next to the Via Appia Antica, the old Roman road... I had to create environments that would allow for these events to be accepted as reality but also heighten the imagery so it supports the language. You look for clues – Titus talks about "the Tribunes more hard than stones". For me the image comes from the situation and the language.'

'Shakespeare doesn't tell us who to root for. His work is so complex and disturbing and exciting because he doesn't make it simplistic like in modern movies. In the first scene we're rooting for Tamora, then look what she becomes. And so Jessica Lange changes visually from exquisitely beautiful and raw in the first scene, with no make-up and an almost modern haircut – someone we can identify with – to something extraordinarily artificial, with almost no eyebrows and that incredible crown. She has distorted visually into a monster because vengeance has eaten her up.'

'This is the turning point for Titus. He's looking at this still life of his hand made into art. It's that state when we step outside ourselves and actually see who we are. It's truly absurdist. This is the moment when he says: "For these two heads do seem to speak to me/And threat me I shall never come to bliss/Till all these mischiefs be returned again/Even in their throats that have committed them." He touches his hand very naturally. And from then on, you think he's going mad. Anthony Hopkins doesn't think he's mad at all. I do. But in madness you find truth because you see the world from a different point of view. I think *Titus Andronicus* is the first theatre of the absurd.'

'Because this play is as much about violence as entertainment as it is about violence itself, I wanted to start with the child's approach to violence, which is through his toys. The toy soldiers come from all different eras – GI Joes and *Star Wars*, Goths and Romans. He's innocently playing, but he's also like a god manipulating these characters on his table, and unbeknown to him he's almost a conjurer. The next thing you know it's a real war and the kitchen walls are shaking; a bomb goes off and the window shatters. It's amazing to me, this growth from the innocence of boys' violent play with cowboys and Indians, or *Star Wars*, into the real thing. It felt as if this could be the bookend to this extraordinary comic tragedy.'

'In productions in Shakespeare's day, they wore Elizabethan clothes and togas. Shakespeare was blending times and so am I, playing with reference points so you get a feeling about the twentieth century – this imagery of totalitarianism. Because we were mixing the times we limited

the colours: the idea was that there would only be black, white, red and metallics, which helps to make it one world. Alan Cumming's red costume was inspired by one of Tamara de Lempicka's paintings. His haircut was because he was doing *Cabaret* on

stage and there was no way we could change it. But I didn't need to.'

'There's something about the image of Marilyn Monroe with the wind blowing up her dress which is an incredible rape. This woman has to hold down her skirt and there's the roar of the subway going underneath and blowing it up. It's the most iconographic image of Monroe that exists. And so, for Lavinia, with these tigers attacking her: there's no more powerful sensual, sexual image of a woman than that. On the other hand, in the play Lavinia is always talked about as if she's a goddess on a pedestal. And a ballerina, in modern Western societies, is the pristine female image of perfection and grace. I wanted to play with the defilement of these two icons of female virtue and sexuality.'

'There's only one scene in the movie I would have cut if I could. And that's the prostitutes on the street. I shouldn't have shot it. And I know why it happened. I had a really great image for it, which was going to be Titus walking down the street and the shopowners closing those metal shutters. But we couldn't afford it. I went, "Oh right, well then just give me  three prostitutes" – instead of going the gamut, to an empty street. I looked at CGI-ing them out, but it was too expensive. And I couldn't cut it altogether because of the voiceover – I needed the space of him walking along.'

'I never got over the image of the unburying of the Chinese terracotta army and I wanted this shot of the army coming in to be like the terracotta army on the march.
It's as if the child's toys are coming alive. This coliseum is in Croatia, of all places – the irony of that. Not CGI-ed, as in other movies we know, but we got the real place where people have been slaughtered, the place that has blood on its stones. And these extras are the Zagreb Police Academy. A month later, we wouldn't have been allowed to shoot there because you had Kosovo. And that bleeds into this movie greatly.'

ELIZABETH AND *SHAKESPEARE IN LOVE*: SCREENING THE ELIZABETHANS

Julianne Pidduck

Unabashedly sexual and spontaneously ahistorical, John Madden's *Shakespeare in Love* and Shekhar Kapur's *Elizabeth* tailor the Elizabethan age to fit the current zeitgeist. In the process, they also contribute to a reinvention of British heritage cinema. These films take part in a Shakespeare and Elizabethan heritage industry marked by the reconstruction of the Globe theatre and by plans to rebuild the Rose – let alone the cinematic Shakespeare offerings from Kenneth Branagh (*Henry V*, 1989; *Much Ado About Nothing*, 1993; *Love's Labour's Lost*, 1999) and others such as Baz Luhrmann's *William Shakespeare's Romeo & Juliet* (1996). A similar renewed interest in Elizabethan biography is fuelled by David Starkey's recent book and television series *Elizabeth* and by John Maybury's forthcoming biopic *Marlowe*.

With a 'high concept' pitch combining iconic historical figures, all-star international casts, generic cross-dressing and the mystique of the Elizabethan period itself, *Elizabeth* and *Shakespeare in Love* reached far beyond heritage cinema's established audiences. Miramax's *Shakespeare in Love* grossed £20.4 million domestically and $100 million in the United States, while Polygram's *Elizabeth* netted £5.5 million and $29.4 million, respectively. For British heritage cinema exports, this level of international success is rivalled only by *The English Patient* (1996, $78.7 million) and *Sense and Sensibility* (1995, $43.2 million). What is it about the Elizabethan period, and these films in particular, that captures the imagination on the cusp of the new millennium?

To profile either a debutante Elizabeth I or a scruffy 'Will' Shakespeare afflicted with writer's block is to fly in the face of the restrained Regency and Victorian settings prevailing in British period drama. Kapur's and Madden's versions of the English Renaissance bristle with sinister plots and poisonings, religious, political and artistic rivalries, audaciously improvised plays and histories not yet written. These two films re-imagine the British past not through mannered conversation and polite realism, but rather through unformed identities, energetic craftsmanship and raw potential. These films project a bold and brash new Britishness both at home and abroad. With their freewheeling historical vision, their eyes firmly pinned on the bottom line and their vehement disavowal of repression, they embody the spirit, if not the reality, of Tony Blair's wished-for 'Cool Britannia'. But do they also suggest a special affinity between the Renaissance and the present cultural moment, or is this double cinematic event a one-off? Or, to put it another way, does this focus on the Elizabethan signal a novel, post-heritage kind of costume film?

Heritage and post-modern histories

This Elizabethan duo undoubtedly springs from earlier British period drama. Classic television serials such as *Brideshead Revisited* (1981), *The Jewel in the Crown* (1984), and *Pride and Prejudice* (1995) once served as a touchstone of national culture – 'passion plays' broadcast to millions of homes. Since the 1980s, these same television films and serials have been successfully marketed abroad to North American speciality channels, while the success of films such as *A Room with a View* (1985) and *Maurice* (1987) has spawned a lucrative chain of heritage films. With their classic literary sources, quality acting and high production values, this genre continues to appeal to an importantly middlebrow, mature, and predominantly female audience. Linked by critics such as Tana Wollen and Andrew Higson to conservative values, an Anglo-centric view of national identity and a rise in the museum and tourism industries, heritage films have also provoked fierce critical debates.

Elizabeth and *Shakespeare in Love* share a radically different attitude to the past from that displayed in these heritage films. In these new Elizabethan films, although period costumes, settings (notably the remarkably accurate reconstructions of theatres), naturalistic *mise-en-scène*, and actual historical figures gesture towards historical verisimilitude, the script has changed. Authenticity is replaced by a post-modern irreverence towards canonical narratives, be they historical or Shakespearean.

The new Elizabethan films emerged in an industrial context where preview audiences overrule filmmakers, historians and literary critics alike. With *Elizabeth*, Indian director Kapur (*Bandit Queen*, 1994) plays fast and loose with history. Michael Hirst's script freely telescopes and embellishes disparate historical events into a dramatically condensed time frame. Elizabeth's cinematic ascent to the throne becomes less the triumph of Enlightenment reason than a bloody tale of sexual and political intrigue. Kapur's Elizabethan world is a visceral spectacle incorporating hybrid influences from the cruel beauty of Derek Jarman's *Caravaggio* (1986) and *Edward II* (1991) to Akira Kurosawa's *Ran* (1985). Kapur argues that, 'Being Eastern, I could play up to the melodrama in its colours, light, behaviour patterns, storytelling and sense of chaos – I could make it a little mythic.' Of course, *Elizabeth* is not the first outsider's treatment of English culture. Taiwanese director Ang Lee's *Sense and Sensibility* offers a poetic spin on Austen, while the Merchant-Ivory production of Kazuo Ishiguro's *The Remains of the Day* (1993) gives a poignant 'downstairs' account of class relations. But these works remain very much within the traditional, restrained stylistic frame of British heritage cinema.

From his opening aerial shots of Protestant martyrs in flames to the Coppola-esque montage of executions, Black British cinematographer Remi Adefarasin (*Truly Madly Deeply*, 1990; second unit on *The English Patient*) makes *Elizabeth* brutal, larger-than-life and unpredictable. A crepuscular lighting scheme plunges the viewer into disorientating darkness and shadow with splashes of deep reds, golds and blues. Castles, cathedrals, boudoirs and torture chambers ooze an inky gloom illuminated erratically by flickering torchlight. The vast, spare *mise-en-scène* dwarfs the figures amongst the pillars and cold, dark stone of Durham Cathedral (an audacious stand-in here for Whitehall Palace).

Like the recent French Dumas adaptation *La Reine Margot* (1994), *Elizabeth*'s epic sweep exceeds specific historical reference. The river running red with blood accompanied by a dramatic vocal score, the battlefield at Leith Castle littered with the bodies of young men and boys: these images evoke a catalogue of wars from the American Civil War to Kosovo.

A waltz with the audience

Playing as much to visceral and sensual pleasures as to the mind, *Shakespeare in Love* and *Elizabeth* address the audience differently from most heritage films. The viewer is engaged in the 'game' of historical fiction, which for Jean-Louis Comolli 'requires the participation of the spectators not as consumers but as players, accomplices, masters of the game, even if they are also its stakes'. Renaissance artists gleefully pilfered earlier classics for dramatic material, and this process continues apace in the post-modern heritage film. A palimpsest of plays within plays and a sly coupling of historical and fictional figures, Tom Stoppard's script for *Shakespeare in Love* fences with audience expectation over the genre of the play and the outcome of the love affair: Is this a comedy or a tragedy? In dramatising the moment of writing, the play comes back to life. Rather than playing the petrified classic with its outcome and every word a *fait accompli*, the film casts the viewer bodily into the creative process.

Shakespeare in Love should not be confused with the pedagogical Shakespeare of the BBC and the RSC, or Branagh's safe adaptations. But neither does it venture as far afield as Baz Luhrmann's psychedelic *William Shakespeare's Romeo & Juliet*. Instead, with the sparring and mutual plagiarism of Marlowe and Shakespeare, the film imagines the Elizabethans afresh, busy making theatre and history. Madden has Joseph Fiennes constantly in motion – sprinting through the dirty streets of South London, nimbly dodging offal underfoot and slops from above, or fencing Colin Firth's Lord Wessex. Through rapid-fire editing, the theatre's physical energy and dancing wordplay are palpable on screen. Even so, choreographed grace dissolves into slapstick when Will's ardent ascent to Viola's balcony ends in a clumsy fall.

Of course, in keeping with his play and film *Rosencrantz and Guildenstern are Dead*, Stoppard's humour continues a long-standing British tradition of historical send-up including *Monty Python and the Holy Grail* (1974), *I, Claudius* (1976), the *Black Adder* series (1982–1989) and *Let Them Eat Cake* (1999). Meanwhile, art cinema (*The Madness of King George*, 1994; *The Tempest*, 1979; *Edward II*, *Orlando*, 1992; *The Draughtsman's Contract*, 1982; *Prospero's Books*, 1991) has gleefully perverted iconic texts and official history. Lacking Sally Potter's and Jarman's political edge, as well as Peter Greenaway's aesthetic innovation, *Shakespeare in Love* is cut from softer cloth. While retaining the star power and flirtation of romantic comedy, it gets dressed up as 'quality' through its historical costumes and settings, Shakespearean lineage, and a string of Oscars, BAFTAs and Golden Globes.

Many a cinephile might choke on *Shakespeare in Love*'s 'best film' BAFTA and Oscar, yet the film must be appreciated for its canny mix of sensibilities. Stoppard self-consciously evokes Shakespeare's breadth of address: from the pit to the queen's box, from the earthy humour of Bottom or *Hamlet*'s gravediggers to the sublime heights of the sonnets. History and Shakespeare buffs are left to untangle a web of historical and cultural references, while others revel in the love story, letting the beauty of the words, bodies, costumes and faces wash over them. Lowbrow–middlebrow tensions resonate in running gags about pleasing all tastes. In response to Shakespeare's lofty literary aspirations, theatre manager Philip Henslowe remarks that 'Love and the bit with the dog. That's what they want.'

'Passing': global Shakespeare

Part of the global appeal of *Elizabeth* and *Shakespeare in Love* lies with their international all-star casts. American stars Gwyneth Paltrow and Ben Affleck work beside Australians such as Oscar winner Geoffrey Rush and relative newcomer Cate Blanchett, French actors Fanny Ardant and Vincent Cassel, and the former footballer Eric Cantona. The picture is completed by the British 'quality' performers such as Judi Dench, Kathy Burke, Colin Firth, Richard Attenborough, Christopher Eccleston and Joseph Fiennes. This casting strategy combines theatre actors with popular film and television stars. For instance, *William Shakespeare's A Midsummer Night's Dream* (1999) casts Rupert Everett alongside Kevin Kline, David Strathairn, Michelle Pfeiffer, Sophie Marceau, Callista Flockhart and Anna Friel. Aside from commercial motivations, this mélange of accents, star personas and acting styles suggests the pleasures of make-believe so central to costume drama and historical fiction.

Consider, for instance, the casting of American Ben Affleck with his hunky star persona (*Chasing Amy, Good Will Hunting*, both 1997) as leading Elizabethan actor Ned Alleyn. Within the story, ironically, Shakespeare (played by Fiennes) needs Alleyn's star presence to sell his play. To his credit, not only is Affleck fetching in tights, but he also brings faultless comic timing and a dynamic physical presence to match Fiennes' own. Part of the novelty of Affleck (or for that matter, of Cantona) in period costume lies in watching a popular American, Australian or French actor perform in British heritage movies. Perhaps the ubiquitous Paltrow best illustrates the role of the American in period costume. From *Emma* (1996) to *Sliding Doors* (1998) to *Shakespeare in Love*, Paltrow's greatest asset (besides her lovely neck) might be a perfect English accent – an ability to 'pass' in British drama, while remaining Pure Hollywood.

Disguise and cross-dressing are stock tropes both in Shakespeare and in 1990s cinema (*Orlando, The Adventures of Priscilla Queen of the Desert*, 1994; *The Crying Game*, 1992; *Todo Sobre Mi Madre* (*All About My Mother*), 1999; *Ceux qui m'aiment prendront le train*, 1998; *Boys Don't Cry*, 1999). As these films illustrate, gender disguise can prompt queer or feminist social critiques. Borrowing liberally from *Twelfth Night*, *Shakespeare in Love* plays on Viola's disguise across sex and class as Thomas Kent. Sparking a romantic comedy of errors, Viola's cross-dressing also prompts a feminist critique of the long-standing historical ban on women on stage. But with its aggressively heterosexual account of Shakespeare's passions and its boy-meets-girl plotline, the film keeps to safely conventional sexual politics. The transgressive potential of seeing two 'men' embrace is undercut by the audience's certainty that Viola's moustache is false, and any 'queer' fantasies are channeled toward an anticipation of the moment when her breasts are unbound.

The Queen's bodies

Like *Shakespeare in Love*, Elizabeth is a raucously unconventional biopic. Along with Madden's own *Mrs Brown* (1997) and Nicholas Hytner's *The Madness of King George*

(1994), *Elizabeth* marks a return in British period drama to royal biography. Yet at issue here are not so much sober matters of state as the dramas of the bedchamber. With a monarchy largely confined to a symbolic function, the aristocracy seems to pique public interest for their passions and idiosyncrasies, especially in the wake of the Princess Diana craze. Commenting on the dramatisation of *Elizabeth*, Hirst remarks, 'I wanted to show her as a young woman – the young woman arrested for treason and afraid for her life; the young woman passionately in love with Robert Dudley – and not the white-faced, pearl-encrusted icon of her later years, and of historical memory.'

Clearly, a queen who is not a virgin makes for more interesting cinema. The classic 1971 television serial *Elizabeth R* starring Glenda Jackson portrayed the chaste girl and the woman against the pedagogical backdrop of Elizabeth's entire career. Kapur's film, in contrast, cuts to the chase: the impossible figure of the Virgin Queen. The film's framing of Elizabeth aligns adroitly with certain contemporary feminist dilemmas: How can a woman navigate the conflicting pressures of social decorum, sexual desire, power? Through a slippery morasse of deadly factions, the core narrative traces how the unformed young Elizabeth is propelled (and propels herself) toward Power. This process is punctuated by two moments evoking famous portraits. First, amidst the pomp and ceremony of the coronation, an impassive but frail Elizabeth tentatively adjusts the crown on her head in a shot reproducing the coronation portrait. Then, at the end of the film, to a soaring choral score, she is shorn of her flowing auburn locks and refashions herself as the Virgin Queen. Stepping out of a blinding light she reappears in court powdered, elaborately coiffed, her body crustacean-like with embroidery, lace and jewels. Immobilised for the second time as her own (older) portrait flanked by the coat of arms, Elizabeth has become Britannia.

In Tudor legal parlance, the king or queen was seen to have two bodies, the immortal 'body politic' and the mortal 'body natural'. Elizabeth chronicles how these two bodies are fused in the Virgin Queen. Yet, in the cinematic experience, there is a third body present, that of the actor, what Comolli calls 'a body too much'. Cate Blanchett's subtle performance negotiates a character who is in emphatically contemporary (an ambivalent feminist heroine) with the crusty iconography of History. Yet, even as Elizabeth presents a gothic feminist parable of power, sexuality, ambition, the outcome is ambiguous. To add yet another body to the mix, if Elizabeth has become Britannia, she has also become Margaret Thatcher.

But it would be doing *Elizabeth* and *Shakespeare in Love* a disservice to suggest that the bodies in question are merely virtual. Against a British heritage tradition premised on precise dialogue, pastoral *mise-en-scène* and subtle dramas of love and class distinction, these Elizabethan films explore the body's messy sensuality. *Shakespeare in Love* is marketed not only on the standard heritage fare of romance, but also on sex, and *Elizabeth* incorporates some of the pulsating sexual energy of *La Reine Margot*, where a masked Margot (in a very ahistorical scene) stalks her sexual prey by night. With her recurring demand 'Play a volta!' the young Elizabeth enjoys the sexual agency of absolute power. Not unlike a tango, the stylised Italian volta, with its formality, precision, and stiff poses, amplifies the sexual frisson between Elizabeth and Dudley in a public rite of foreplay.

Sex, intrigue, raw physicality and violence distinguish these Elizabethan films from a largely demure British tradition. Whether *Elizabeth* and *Shakespeare in Love* present a mere blip in a relentless diet of nineteenth-century *politesse* – I would suggest not – their crucial difference could be distilled down to costume and what lies underneath. The stiff geometrical shapes, bristling lace ruffs, elaborate gowns encrusted in gold embroidery and jewels all belie an underlying raw sexual energy. Sumptuous hems seem destined to be dragged through the mud, while tightly laced bodices are rife for ripping. And on Joseph Fiennes, Gwyneth Paltrow and Cate Blanchett, these elaborate costumes conceal some of the most lissome bodies in the biz. These films present the early modern English as creatures of passion and tragic romance, of slapstick humour and bawdy worldliness. Finally and crucially, in an affront to costume drama's tender sensibilities, the costumes *come off.*

The Madness of King George
POWER MAD

Jonathan Coe

'Transcendent' was the word used to describe Nigel Hawthorne's performance in the National Theatre production of Alan Bennett's *The Madness of George III*, not by some hyperventilating reviewer, but by Bennett himself. It was Hawthorne alone, according to the playwright, who turned the mad King from 'a gabbling bore' into 'a human and sympathetic figure'. Now the play has been filmed and retitled: *The Madness of King George*. And since we know that Hollywood is big on humanity and sympathy, Hawthorne's star performance must account for much of its transatlantic success. For a film which has the temerity even to flirt with the idea that 'the state of monarchy and the state of lunacy share a frontier', it has enjoyed a remarkably warm welcome.

Until now, Hawthorne's only major American role has been in Marco Brambilla's dystopian satire *Demolition Man*, where he played another lunatic, of sorts – an evil scientific mastermind called Dr Cocteau, who is responsible for the brainwashing of Los Angeles. By the year 2032, he has turned it into a community of clean-living, clean-talking, vegetarian, non-violent zombies. Justifying his actions to a sceptical Sylvester Stallone, and looking back to the brutal urban wars of the late twentieth century, he explains that, 'People wanted the madness to be over.' But the rhetoric of the film makes it clear that Cocteau himself is the real madman: his unforgivable crime, in the words of Wesley Snipes, is that he has taken away 'people's right to be assholes'.

Cocteau, whose sanity is also repeatedly called into question by Stallone's character, can be viewed as yet another in the long line of mad genius figures so beloved of Hollywood and so frequently played by British actors: madness, in the mainstream cinema, being commonly equated with evil. Serious attempts to deal with such conditions (schizophrenia in Ken Loach's *Family Life*, for instance) are rare exceptions to the rule. For the most part, film-makers have homed in on the area of criminal pathology, and exploited the idea of madness with its titillating overtones of absolute, uncontrollable transgression – in an attempt to provoke ever greater extremes of suspense, while justifying these extremes with a spurious recourse to pseudoscientific authority. I suppose the trend set in when Hollywood discovered Freud in the 1940s: Curtis Bernhardt's *Conflict* (1945) was one of the first films to realise that 'Funny things happen inside people's heads'. But this discovery was to stand directors in good stead over the ensuing decades, with such psychiatrically-inclined thrillers as *Spellbound* and *The Spiral Staircase*, through the 1960s excesses of *Shock Corridor* and *Twisted Nerve*, the genre reaching glossy apogee in the 1990s, with *The Silence of the Lambs*.

The best-known and most honourable bucking of this trend came in the mid-1970s with Milos Forman's *One Flew Over the Cuckoo's Nest*. Although it offered a tamer, palliated version of Ken Kesey's novel, it still managed to suggest a provocative blurring of the line between madness and sanity – something which Hollywood later did its best to develop in mainstream comedies such as *The Couch Trip* and *Crazy People*. More importantly, the film left us in little doubt that it was the zealous enforcement of a repressive power structure (in this case, presided over by Nurse Ratched) which should be regarded as the greater madness and the greater evil. Perhaps it needed a director like Forman – a refugee from Soviet-occupied Czechoslovakia, whose parents died in the Nazi camps – to bring this idea explicitly to the screen.

On one level, then, Forman's film bears out an observation made by Roy Porter: 'The history of madness is the history of power.' In the chapter on George III in his *Social History of Madness*, Porter (a friend of Bennett who was offered a walk-on part in the play) usefully reminds us that 'from the eighteenth century onwards the idea was increasingly floated that there was actually something pathological about the exercise of power itself'. As early as 1696, when Jonathan Swift incorporated 'A Digression concerning the Original, the Use and Improvement of Madness in a Commonwealth' into *A Tale of a Tub*, he had argued (with magnificent double irony) that madness had been 'Parent of all those mighty Revolutions, that have happened in Empire, in Philosophy and in Religion'. Famously defining happiness as 'a perpetual Possession of being well Deceived', he claimed that the lucky lunatic 'creams off Nature, leaving the Sower [i.e. sour] and the Dregs for Philosophy and Reason to lap up', thereby ascending to 'The Serene Peaceful State of being a Fool among Knaves'.

There are disappointments in store for anyone seeking this vein of ironic radicalism in the screen version of Bennett's play. Although Nigel Hawthorne spends most of the film behaving very much like a fool among the assorted knaves in his circle of ministers and physicians, his condition is anything but serene and peaceful: the King's insanity manifests itself as scatological gibbering, requiring him to be forcibly gagged, tied down, straitjacketed and subjected to a succession of shockingly primitive medical treatments. Finally, of course, a cure is found. The film ends with the beaming Monarch and his family waving at us from the steps of St Paul's, so that it traces an unashamedly traditional comic pattern: order, followed by chaos, followed by order restored. While this may be dramatically satisfying, it does raise questions both about the extent to which Hawthorne's performance dominates (or even hijacks) the proceedings, and about Bennett's own conception of the relationship between madness and power. In short, *The Madness of King George* seems to be asking us to do something rather peculiar: namely, to accept that the return to power of someone who was (as the film cannot help making pretty clear) an intolerant despot should be regarded as some sort of happy ending.

How, exactly, has it managed to paint itself into this corner? There's no doubt that Bennett feels a certain sentimental attachment not only to the King himself ('I've always had a soft spot for George III,' he writes in his introduction to the published play) but to the very idea of monarchy. He came clean about this in a recent essay about the making of the film for the *London Review of Books*: 'I found I was less sceptical about the monarchy as an institution than most of the production team, partly because ... I was older than most of them and more set in my ways. Certainly, I'm no republican.' His 'soft spot' finds its expression in some of the screenplay's more whimsical Bennettisms: notably the bedtime dialogues of Hawthorne and Helen Mirren (Queen Charlotte), who refer to each other affectionately as 'Mr King' and 'Mrs King' – a detail which at my screening drew the first real waves of sympathetic audience laughter.

What has been lost in the play's transfer to the screen, meanwhile, is its adroit balance between personal and political narratives. Properly mindful of the need for a clean, agile narrative trajectory, Bennett has been obliged to jettison most of his political baggage, and the sense of a teeming, complex network of unstable party and personal loyalties has vanished. Instead we have Pitt versus Fox – the former here both cold fish and good egg, the latter played with an air of dark, saturnine menace by Jim Carter. This menace makes Fox the most imposing historical heavy since F. Murray Abraham's Bernardo Gui in *The Name of the Rose*. Carter's every appearance floods the screen like a pool of inky blackness, and he prowls through the film wearing such a delicious scowl that it can't be long before Hollywood drafts him in as resident villain. As a result we barely register the fact that his character, Charles James Fox, is historically considered to be humane and progressive, struggling in the teeth of Royal opposition to introduce a programme of reform which includes the abolition of the slave trade. Instead, faced with such a gloriously sinister opponent, the King starts to look even more vulnerable and loveable.

For Nigel Hawthorne's George is loveable: so loveable that this, too, does a certain violence to history. Without doubt, it's a mesmerising and heartbreaking perform-ance, and one which holds the film together. It will surprise many British filmgoers who only know Hawthorne from his performance as the Machiavellian Sir Humphrey Appleby in *Yes, Minister*, although that character can't help coming back to haunt the memory here from time to time. Nicholas Hytner, the director, seems slightly embarrassed by the ghost of sit-com which stalks the film, and keeps trying to raise the tone with baroque camera flourishes and visual allusions to *King Lear* – Hawthorne running amok on a heath wearing only his nightshirt, and so on.

This is all very well, but as I recall, *Yes, Minister* actually offered much more insight into the distribution of power within the British establishment, largely because it was under no pressure to target itself at anything but a British audience. The really significant thing about Hawthorne's performance, after all, is the extent to which it has given the film international – for which read American – appeal. Like Hugh Grant's star turn in *Four Weddings and a Funeral*, it seems to have scored a direct hit on the G-spot for American audiences. One explanation for this might lie in Bennett's own screenplay, which lays great weight on the problematic relationship between the American colonists and their colonial masters. In their bitter struggle to free themselves from George III's sovereignty, we can see the origin of the complex American response towards the upper- or ruling-class Englishman, of which he is their villainous archetype. We gain a fresh sense of how deep-rooted the feelings are, and how thoroughly compounded of awe and contempt.

Over the last few years, Hollywood has battled to cope with these icy, autocratic figures by casting them as villains pure and simple, in the shape of Hawthorne, Alan Rickman, Jeremy Irons and others. No credible equivalent had been found for the plummy but plucky and likeable Brits (Ronald Colman, David Niven) we used to export so successfully. Recently, however, the British cinema has discovered how to market a new, friendlier variety which delivers the Americans from their memories of thraldom, offering them a delicious sensation of release which seems to translate itself immediately into box-office returns and Oscar nominations. What we have now learned, in a word, is how to demystify our ruling class for the benefit of American audiences. And so Hugh Grant manages to portray an upper-crust bachelor, not as the expected unemotional, cold-blooded enigma, but as a flustered romantic who quotes David Cassidy lyrics and says 'fuck' nine times in the first scene as if he had found himself in a BBC-accented Tarantino movie; and George III, in the hands of Bennett and Hawthorne, is no longer an unbending tyrant obsessed by tradition and protocol, but a sweet, befuddled old man who calls his wife 'Mrs King' and never breaks wind in bed without an apologetic 'Saving your presence I will try a fart.'

From what Bennett has written about it in the *London Review* and elsewhere, the making of *The Madness of King George* has been a history of compromises. The resulting film is highly enjoyable, intelligent, good to look at, beautifully acted – but there is an irony at its heart more cutting than any its author can have intended. The project may have started out, many years ago, as an accurate re-creation of an episode in British political history and an exploration of the strange affinity between madness and power; but it now reaches the screen as a handsome piece of Heritage Cinema, chock full of English pageantry and stately homes, and in its final reassuring insistence that the Royal soap opera will run and run, unequivocally committed to the status quo. The American studios now call the financial shots, and it seems that they will allow us to tell our own stories, but only on their terms. It is the terrible and continuing revenge of the colonists on their erstwhile oppressors.

Como agua para chocolate/Like Water for Chocolate (Alfonso Arau, 1991)

Reviews

CYRANO DE BERGERAC
France 1990
Director: Jean-Paul Rappeneau

Paris, 1640. A performance of Balthasar Baro's *La Clorise* at the theatre of the Hôtel de Bourgogne is interrupted when the leading player, Montfleury, is ordered off stage by belligerent poet and swordsman Cyrano de Bergerac. Outraged at the interruption, the Comte de Guiche, a nephew of Richelieu, urges one of his men, the Vicomte de Valvert, to prompt Cyrano into a duel by insulting him for the size of his nose, a subject on which he is notoriously sensitive. Although bested in the fight, de Valvert tries a sneak attack and Cyrano kills him. Later, he drives off a band of 100 assassins paid by de Guiche to attack another poet, Lignière, at the Porte de Nesle. Cyrano's cousin, Madeleine Robinot, known as Roxane, asks him to meet her next morning at the home of the poet-pastrycook Ragueneau. Although deeply in love with Roxane, Cyrano has always been too shy about his appearance to make his feelings known, and now it is too late: Roxane loves Christian de Neuvillette, a new recruit to the same Gascony regiment as Cyrano's, and begs Cyrano to ensure his safety. Meeting Christian, Cyrano finds that the handsome young man is also in love with Roxane, but incapable of expressing his feelings; Cyrano offers to write his love letters to Roxane for him and, since they express Cyrano's own passion with his own wit and skill, they are immensely effective. De Guiche, now a colonel, pays court to Roxane, who persuades him not to send the Gascony cadets (including Cyrano and Christian) to join him at the siege of Arras, a town occupied by the Spanish. Infatuated, de Guiche decides to claim her for his own, but after a torrent of letters from Christian/Cyrano, and an impassioned night-time visit to her balcony from her lover (with Cyrano doing the talking), Roxane impulsively marries Christian moments before de Guiche arrives and, in a fury, orders him to war. Soon Christian and Cyrano find themselves, along with the Gascony troops of Carbon de Castel-Jaloux, under siege in their turn by the Spanish forces. Undeterred by the blockade, and unknown to Christian, Cyrano takes letters through the enemy lines twice daily for despatch to Roxane who, desperate to see her husband, finally brings a wagonload of provisions to the starving Gascons just before a fresh Spanish onslaught. Wounded in the fighting, Christian dies in her arms without revealing Cyrano's role in their courtship; in his pocket, she finds the final love letter. Fifteen years later, Roxane lives reclusively at the convent of the Dames de la Croix in Paris, regularly visited by Cyrano. Widely unpopular for his bold and outspoken writings, Cyrano is mortally wounded in an ambush, but struggles to Roxane's side for the last time. As he recites Christian's final letter, Roxane recognises its true author as the one love of her life and watches despairingly as he dies.

* * *

In adapting Rostand for the screen, Jean-Paul Rappeneau and Jean-Claude Carrière have trimmed surprisingly little from, and added substantially to, the Cyrano legend. While admitting to having 'tidied up' the play by deleting its more obscure references, condensing whole pages to a few lines and strengthening the role of Christian to offset a less 'frantic' Cyrano, they have remained faithful to a first principle – that all speeches, film or no film, would continue to be in verse. It was Rappeneau's instinct that Rostand's flexible couplets, leaping from one character to another in mid-line and maintaining their alexandrine rhythm by an unpredictable, boldly naturalistic scattering of words and exclamations, would work as well on film as on stage. And, although the project was much delayed, nearly foundering several times because of this insistence, the film proves him right even while requiring us to appreciate a complex orchestration of speech, editing, camera movement and background music that most audiences would surely become aware of only if something went gravely wrong.

To British ears, ironically, the fine distinction between Rostand's verse and something in the Rostand style is unlikely to cause concern – indeed, the energy of the performances and the visuals is such that the unflagging pace of the language itself, a delightful, cunning, punning, witty coherence like a network of veins beneath the skin of the drama, can flow unnoticed from scene to scene except when a sudden satisfying emphasis of rhyme momentarily catches the attention. Rappeneau steers this symmetrical vocabulary with an exciting eloquence. His cast at first complained that their words and their movements were impossible to synchronise – that they had to move at one speed and talk at another – but the balance has been achieved to such an extent that the director has even been able at times to cut from one scene to the next to complete a dependent clause in quiet triumph and without missing a beat. With only Laurence Olivier to offer any serious (if intermittent) precedent for such aural dexterity on British screens, it seems unlikely, however, that this aspect of *Cyrano* will get the recognition over here that it deserves, particularly as two other factors muffle its clarity.

The first, consistent with Rappeneau's argument, is that the mannered swaggering and declamation of the seventeenth century seems a wholly appropriate context for rhetoric and oratory; amid the peculiar routines, reticences and affectations of the period, a certain extravagance of communication is to be expected. Even to the French, Cyrano and his contemporaries are near-foreigners and should logically converse in a patois of their own. That this happens to be within the quaint parameters of the alexandrine soon seems wholly normal. The second complication, against which Rappeneau could hardly be expected to prepare a defence, is that his film acquires a further, assonant rhythm with the addition of subtitles. Discreetly, humorously and sympathetically devised by Anthony Burgess, these, too, are in rhyming couplets – but divided every which way in the usual arbitrary manner of titling, constructed on the basis of a limited number of letters per line. Insofar as there is time to appreciate the Burgess patterns while trying to listen to Rostand and watch Rappeneau and admire Depardieu, they are rewarding to read, despite hints of desperation ('poet' rhymed with 'do it') and a few Burgess-isms such as 'bewitchment'.

If published as a separate translation, they could offer a better chance to compare, for instance, Cyrano's coruscating catalogue of nasal insults with the accuracy of Burgess' wit, or to notice whether any allowance can be made in English for the use of the triolet form when Cyrano introduces his Gascon colleagues. Oddly, the more dubious phrases, if noted and recalled, turn out to come direct from Rostand – such as the vivid reference to a slug crawling over a rose. But while no sensible translation of *Cyrano* is to be respected if it's not in verse, the finer points of lexicography are an unwelcome intrusion when, in the heat of the moment, the love of Roxane is being won by resounding flourishes of metaphor and hyperbole, part pure metric punctuation for its own sake, part pure self-indulgent sophistry, and part raw declaration of an unparalleled heartbreak. Better, perhaps, to know no English at all – or no French – than to be scuttling, as this version requires, between one language and the other, each scene brandishing its own alternatives.

What has been extended from Rostand in Rappeneau's reading is largely wordless. As silent witness to Cyrano's public adventures in Paris, for instance, an unidentified boy leads the camera into the opening scenes, brings Cyrano his hat after the duel and wakes beneath a sheaf of sketches of Cyrano in his room in time to wave the hero off to battle (after which, slightly dissatisfyingly, he isn't seen again). Responding warily to this speculative gaze, Cyrano can be interpreted either as boyish in his turn, consistent with his outbreaks of juvenile petulance, or as a champion admired and celebrated despite himself, without regard to the shape of his nose. It is a measure of Depardieu's performance in the role for which he seems to have been invented that the nose quickly becomes unremarkable; instead, its owner appears increasingly to carry some internal deformity that chokes his existence and must inevitably destroy him in bitter reward for so honourably betraying himself.

But Rappeneau needs to go no further than Rostand's illustrations of Cyrano's intransigence (the blow that felled the *real* Cyrano, a full year before his death at thirty-six in 1655, was said to be from an outraged patron), and concentrates on other expansions such as Roxane's tremulous reactions to her overwhelming tide of correspondence, the strange interlude with the *précieuses*, and the lively woodland skirmish in which the heroine is rescued from the Spanish amid some slapstick with a roast pig (Rostand's version, more charming, less colourful, has her riding straight through enemy lines using her smile as passport). With Depardieu's bulky vehemence at last plumed in the splendour it deserves, Rappeneau's Cyrano has become an elemental being, bursting from the confines of the theatre, where in the first scene he has already held centre stage, to do battle with all and sundry, larger than life, beneath the open skies. At odds with his tirades of academic reference – which imply a wide-ranging but cloisteredly bookish upbringing – Cyrano is filmed as a creature of the countryside, his writings, his battles and his defeats alike pursued amid forests and meadows. Hurling through the cornfields as the Spanish unleash a futile volley, or matching his frenzied inspiration to crashes of thunder during the famous balcony scene (completed in delicate tragedy with his lonely figure retreating through the rain while his rival claims the precious reward), Cyrano adds his voice to the rustle of the leaves above his dying body as the camera drifts meditatively upwards (although not quite aspiring to the Moon, his preferred destination).

Recalling *La Vie de Château* – which was also lyrically photographed by Pierre Lhomme and also told the story of the courting of a girl by two men, not quite what they seemed, against the background of war – Rappeneau continues to relish the land-scapes and seasons of history, repeatedly using trees, smoke, shadows and sunlight to externalise the moods of his characters. The crowd scenes are breathtakingly explored (the mêlée at the theatre and the shambles of the battlefield are spectacular, while the encounter with the 100 assassins, gently misting into slow motion, rightly has the spirit of a fable). But his finest orchestration is the moment when Roxane and the camera rush together to Cyrano in the garden and, for one jolting instant, the anguished champion might hope that the world has changed. This is faultless film-making and it serves Rostand, way beyond his words, immeasurably well.

Philip Strick

PROSPERO'S BOOKS
Netherlands/France/Italy 1991
Director: Peter Greenaway

The early seventeenth century. On a secluded island, Prospero, the deposed Duke of Milan, sits in his palace surrounded by a retinue of magical spirits, and begins to improvise the text of Shakespeare's *The Tempest*. As he speaks the lines, the action unfolds... A storm blows up at sea, threatening the boat carrying Alonso, King of

Naples, the king's brother Sebastian and son Ferdinand, an old courtier, Gonzalo, and Prospero's brother Antonio, who has usurped his dukedom.

As his daughter Miranda sleeps, Prospero tells her of their past: of his late wife Susannah; of how, in order to concentrate on his studies, he handed over his rule to Antonio, only to find himself being betrayed; and of how he and Miranda were driven away in a boat, equipped by his friend Gonzalo with a selection of Prospero's most prized books, from which, since landing on the island, he has derived his present power and knowledge. Prospero reminds his attendant spirit Ariel of how he freed him from servitude to the witch Sycorax, and with Miranda visits the witch's son, the savage Caliban.

Ferdinand arrives safely on the island and, when he meets Miranda, they fall in love; but Prospero pretends to take him prisoner. The rest of the party arrive on the island; while the king and Gonzalo sleep, Antonio and Sebastian plot to kill them and usurp the crown, but Ariel intercedes. Also washed ashore, Stephano, a butler, and Trinculo, a jester, encounter Caliban, who proposes that they murder Prospero and have Stephano rule the island in his place. Spirits bring a banquet to Alonso's party, but Ariel appears disguised as a harpy, to accuse them of their various crimes and to present Alonso with an image of his son's death. Prospero blesses the union of Miranda and Ferdinand by staging a masque presided over by the goddesses Iris, Ceres and Juno.

Trinculo, Stephano and Caliban try to invade Prospero's palace, but are repelled by spirits. Having witnessed Alonso's grief, Ariel persuades Prospero to have mercy on the lost party. As the king's party arrives at his palace, Prospero throws off his robes and, restoring Ariel's freedom, forgives his old enemies. Prospero proposes to leave the island with them, on the now-restored ship, and orders all his books to be destroyed; the only ones saved, rescued from the water by Caliban, are a volume of Shakespeare's plays and a smaller volume that completes it – the text of *The Tempest*. Prospero finally begs forgiveness of the audience and asks to be set free in his turn.

* * *

Just as Prospero's twenty-four volumes, which include the text of the drama we're watching, comprise a collection of all knowledge, *Prospero's Books* might itself be seen as the encyclopaedic summum of Greenaway's formal and thematic concerns to date. Certainly it alludes in one way or another to nearly all his previous films: it contains a book of mythology, a compendium of all possible narratives, like his own compendium film *The Falls*; it reprises his repertoire of water motifs, from *Water Wrackets* to the recent short *Death in the Seine*; it ceaselessly interrogates the printed word and image (echoing *A Walk through H*); and it directly transcribes visual and musical motifs from *The Cook, The Thief, His Wife and Her Lover*.

Greenaway interprets *The Tempest* as the story of a mind reviewing its entire contents. The film's own re-reading of Greenaway's oeuvre could conceivably represent an attempt on the director's part to exhaust his repertoire before embarking on an entirely new project; and in a sense, any further steps in the direction indicated by this film would be superfluous. *Prospero's Books* does suggest at least two possible paths – an elaboration of the new cutting rhythm explored here; and a further exploration of the mixing of cinema and paintbox, of the play of identity and difference between film and video, and of the new type of cinematic literariness which that playfulness opens up. This is not the composed, urbane literariness of Merchant-Ivory, or even of *The Draughtsman's Contract*, but rather film rethought as an infinitely malleable 'writing'.

It may seem curious that this near-resumé of the director's films should be derived not from his own screenplay, but from Shakespeare. However, this is only indirectly a 'version' of *The Tempest*. It would be truer to call it a variation in the musical sense, an annotated commentary (just as Greenaway and Tom Phillips annotated the *Inferno* in their *A TV Dante*), or – quite literally – a reading of it. A commentary on the play is supplied by images of the books, generated by high-definition television and computer-paintbox graphics. And there is an extraordinary amount of writing – words etched in stone, on parchment, in air, on water, in the image itself. To complete the effect, text, image and sound constantly blur into each other – the mariner's cry 'We split! We split! We split!' becomes a motto for the film's infinite fragmentation of language and image.

Prospero is at once actor, author and director of his own script, and by no means the first such *magister ludi* in a Greenaway film. Tulse Luper, the master forger of the early films, and the heroes of *The Draughtsman's Contract*, *The Belly of an Architect* and *Drowning by Numbers* all figured as projections of Greenaway's own self-questioning aspirations to transcendental authorship. At the same time, they functioned as flawed, doomed figures of the auteur as autocrat, and Prospero, too, is partly the victim of his own power. What Greenaway primarily reads in Shakespeare is a sense of awe at, but also a critique of, the autocratic imagination. Imprisoned in his guise as Renaissance doge, Prospero is prisoner of the various frames, mirrors and proscenium arches that compartmentalise the screen – until, that is, he renounces his power, and begs the audience to grant him a termination of the illusionistic contract.

Prospero's palace, like his mind – and like the film itself – resembles a labyrinthine department store, containing all possibilities in the most obscure arrangements. The film is organised so as to exhaust the viewer's perceptive capacities. This is partly because of an extremely brisk cutting speed that is something of a departure for Greenaway (although it echoes *A TV Dante* and the rhythmic editing of *Making a Splash*); and partly because of the sheer proliferation of imagery. The baroque visuals – fashioned as ever by cinematographer Sacha Vierny and designers Jan Roelfs and Ben van Os – are extravagant to the point of profligacy. When a succession of spirits present wedding gifts to the young couple, each gift is only briefly glimpsed, but each is meticulously composed and lit to resemble a Dutch still life. Greenaway is no less profligate with his erudition, and the allusions to Renaissance Italian, Dutch Golden Age, Spanish and French nineteenth-century painting are legion.

The ostentatious erudition could in itself be considered kitsch – when the script calls for a screen full of sleeping mariners, they're inevitably lit like Géricault's *Raft of the Medusa* – but then it is quite knowingly so. Tumbling underwater nymphs recall the synchronised swimmers of *Making a Splash*, but also the glaucous odalisques of French academic painters such as Bouguereau, not to mention their Busby Berkeley descendants. Indeed, the only true precursor of this filmed Shakespeare is Max Reinhardt's 1935 *A Midsummer Night's Dream*, whose turbaned princeling is briefly reincarnated here by Ariel (another *Dream* echoed is Peter Brook's production, with its trapezes).

Greenaway obscures action while displaying it, employing several internationally illustrious actors and requiring them to remain not only mute, but almost unrecognisable under ruffs, masks and vast hats. The fact that, for the most part, John Gielgud speaks all the parts jettisons the certainties usually provided by dramatis personae. Greenaway provides the elements of spectacle, but leaves the task of ordering them to the viewer, whose role as final arbiter of the film's shape is addressed in Prospero's closing speech. By presenting too much to take in at a glance, Greenaway tests to the limit his ideal of a painterly cinema. The tendency to over-emphasise points reaches a delirious apogee when the film animates textual images: an anatomy book disgorges throbbing, bloody organs, a bestiary swarms with frogs and lizards. This contributes to a general undermining of the smooth surface of the text, disturbing the (already slender) certainties of the play with evidence of words' tendency to become flesh (or water, or metal, or colour, or any of the other metamorphoses the books exhibit).

If Greenaway seems to be cramming like there's no tomorrow, there is at least a thematic justification. The images come and go, consuming themselves in a flash, just as the books finally combust or erase themselves. The film embodies a desperate awareness of the transitory, immaterial nature of images, to an extent countered by a fixation with the materiality of bodies, most disturbingly when Susannah opens up the 'book' of her own belly. The film seems impelled to take on every visual possibility imaginable, in as concrete terms as possible, before the whole 'insubstantial pageant' reverts, as it must, to 'the stuff that dreams are made on'. To the cacophony of Prospero's 'isle full of noises', Greenaway adds a visual and conceptual 'cacography' that invites reading all the more energetically for defying it.

Jonathan Romney

EDWARD II
United Kingdom 1991
Director: Derek Jarman

Imprisoned in a dungeon, guarded by the jailer Lightborn, King Edward II of England recalls his reign. Newly crowned, he writes to his lover Piers Gaveston in France, summoning him to share his kingdom. Reunited, Edward and Gaveston look forward to a life of hedonism, but Gaveston's return is greeted scornfully by the Bishop of Winchester. With Edward's blessing, Gaveston has the bishop beaten up and imprisoned.

Rejecting the love of his queen, Isabella, Edward appoints Gaveston to the nobility, despite the advice of his brother Kent. The enraged nobles, headed by the soldier Mortimer, resolve to take action and petition Edward to banish Gaveston, but Gaveston remains defiant and humiliates Isabella by feigning to make a pass at her. Faced with the risk of being deposed, Edward is persuaded to banish Gaveston. But when the rift between Edward and Isabella deepens, the queen has Gaveston recalled, intending to have him killed.

Isabella and Mortimer become lovers. Snubbed by the nobles on his return to England, Gaveston returns their insults and is stabbed by Mortimer. Edward quarrels with Kent, who joins Isabella's camp. Gaveston flees, but is caught and killed by Mortimer's troops. Edward leads the people in revolt, and kills the policeman who garrotted Gaveston. Mortimer captures Edward and his follower Spencer and kills the latter.

Mortimer and Isabella prepare to reign together and Isabella summons Lightborn, an assassin, to kill the captive Edward. Kent quarrels with Isabella and Mortimer, and is killed by Isabella. In prison, Edward envisages being murdered by Lightborn, but the latter refuses to kill him. Now deposed, Isabella and Mortimer sit in a cage lamenting their fate, while Prince Edward – Edward's son – stands triumphant guard over them.

*   *   *

Billed in the published book-of-the-script, *Queer Edward II*, as the play 'improved by Derek Jarman', this film is partly recognisable as Marlowe and wholly recognisable as Jarman. After the imagistic patchwork of *The Garden*, Jarman returns to the enclosed theatrical format of *Caravaggio*, staging Marlowe's narrative on a sparse but adaptable single set. A mud-walled dungeon stands in for the cavernous interior of Edward's castle and for exterior locations, with forbidding metalwork added for the prison. By flaunting the relative poverty of the film's resources, as well as its ability to transcend them, Jarman proclaims his adherence to the aesthetics and ethics of low-budget filmmaking, and asserts his own position as an economically and ideologically marginal director – a position he has embraced as much as he has had it foist upon him.

Jarman has shuffled sections of the play, excised its minor characters and superfluous incident, and turned the narrative inside out by having Edward review his reign from prison. Above all, the famous death-by-poker climax is staged as a lurid red-lit fantasy, with Edward reprieved for a final speech. Although such cutting-and-pasting of a sacrosanct 'classic' might seem cavalier (ironically, the film is partly funded by the BBC, arch-preserver of the tradition), this *Edward* is a close reading of the text, paying critical attention to its sexual-political meanings, sometimes tweaking them for good measure (hence, Isabella's 'Is it not strange that he is thus bewitched?' becomes 'Is it not queer ... ').

Given the play's history of conservative and bowdlerised interpretations, *Edward II* is clearly ripe to be reclaimed as a gay myth for an age of state-endorsed homophobia. Marlowe's play ends with a return to order after political and sexual turmoil; in Jarman's version, when the child prince, lipsticked and high-heeled, finally dances to 'The Sugar Plum Fairy', there can be no doubt which order triumphs. Yet this reading yields more problematic results than is immediately apparent. Rather than present a clear-cut story of gay martyrdom, Jarman overlays the play's complexities with his own thematic obsessions, producing a contradictory film which is readable less in terms of sexual politics than in terms of the code of the 'Jarman film' as a genre in itself.

For example, Gaveston's violent revenge on the bishop – carried out with a gang of scowling thugs – seems out of proportion to the offence. In the original, this transgression clearly identifies Gaveston as a villain, but it seems incongruous in a version that casts him as a victim. The violence is further complicated by its erotic overtones. In their scene with the bishop, Edward and Gaveston wear dark suits, while the leather-clad thugs similarly embody a sado-masochistic 'rough trade' fantasy. If Gaveston and Edward as his accomplice are being celebrated as glamorous hoods, it is all the more difficult to accept them later as heroes and martyrs. These quintessentially Jarmanesque images add up to a contradictory surfeit of meaning that the text cannot accommodate.

This approach entails particular problems for the treatment of Isabella. Envisaged, according to Tilda Swinton, as a composite of Margaret Thatcher, Grace Kelly, Ivana Trump and others, Isabella's nature is largely contingent on the image and wardrobe she adopts for each appearance. Until her central soliloquy – a long static shot – she is the wronged, wounded wife, but once she decides to rebel, she is caricatured more forcefully as a political monster.

In fact, it is when she becomes sexually active with Mortimer that she becomes truly monstrous, a pompous Evita-like demagogue behind a microphone. Finally, in an image that nothing in the film quite prepares for, she becomes a vampire, killing Kent by sucking at his jugular. This moment of misogynistic horror is in fact part of a more general heterophobia. Indeed, making a heterophobic film to counter an entire history of homophobic ones seems a fair polemical strategy, the logical result of reversing the terms of reference that have often been imposed on Marlowe's play. But to suggest the corruption of the homophobic state, Jarman resorts to a hackneyed image of heterosexual perversity – the sight of Mortimer being whipped by two 'Wild Girls' recalls the spanked judge of *O Lucky Man!* or the accountants in bondage of *Personal Services*, well-worn British cinema shorthand for Establishment hypocrisy.

The stigmatisation of heterosexuality is only effectively resolved in the final image of the prince's triumph, a twist on the Oedipal scene in which he at once becomes his father and appropriates his mother's sexuality. *Edward II* is finally most effective for its elaboration of the 'Jarmanesque' as a style of contradiction, but serves as a reminder that the open-ended structures of *The Garden* or *The Last of England* can accommodate a far greater disparity of meaning than Jarman is able to fit into this more rigid format.

Jonathan Romney

HOWARDS END
United Kingdom 1991
Director: James Ivory

1910. Helen and Margaret Schlegel live with their brother Tibby in London. Helen is invited to stay with the Wilcox family, with whom she has recently become acquainted, at their country home, Howards End. There she falls in love with the younger son Paul, but the affair is short-lived. Months later, Helen attends a concert and inadvertently walks off with a stranger's umbrella. The owner, insurance clerk Leonard Bast, follows her home to retrieve it. Taking the Schlegels' calling card, he returns to the house where he lives with his girlfriend, Jacky. The same day, the Wilcoxes move into the apartment opposite the Schlegels for the wedding of their son Charles to Dolly. Margaret pays a courtesy visit to Mrs Wilcox, and a friendship develops. When it transpires that the lease on the Schlegels' house is about to run out, Mrs Wilcox offers to help. She is, however, seriously ill and soon dies, leaving a note bequeathing Howards End to Margaret. Henry Wilcox and his children destroy the note.

Meanwhile, Jacky turns up at the Schlegels demanding to know where Leonard Bast, now her husband, is. The following day, Bast visits to apologise for his wife's outburst. The Schlegels decide to take an interest in the young man's affairs. By chance, the sisters learn that the company he works for is about to go bankrupt. They warn him, but he resents their interference. Henry Wilcox invites Margaret for lunch. Later, he suggests that she take over the lease on his London house. Subsequently, she accepts his proposal of marriage. Meanwhile, Helen learns that Bast changed his job, but was then made redundant, while his previous company continues to prosper.

Margaret joins Henry at his Shropshire home for preparations for his daughter's wedding. During the celebrations, Helen arrives with the Basts demanding that Henry help them. There, Jacky recognises Henry as her former lover. Humiliated, Henry refuses to help the Basts. Later, Helen and Leonard meet and end up making love. Helen then disappears to Germany, missing her sister's wedding. Hearing that she is back in England, Margaret arranges to meet her at Howards End, where Helen reveals that she is pregnant by Leonard. In a confrontation between Charles Wilcox and Leonard, who have both followed the others to Howards End, Leonard is killed. Charles is convicted of manslaughter. The following summer, Henry announces to his family that he is leaving Howards End to Margaret, who will in turn leave it to Helen's son. Henry finally explains to Margaret the secret about Mrs Wilcox's original bequest.

* * *

With only *The Longest Journey* left to film, *Howards End* is a sign that the Forster screen adaptation machine is finally grinding to a halt. Written in 1910 and considered to be the author's finest work, the novel's portrayal of moral decay and unscrupulousness in an English society shaken by economic and social change is particularly appropriate in the grey light of the present Depression. Set firmly on home ground, ironically the movie takes as its subject – as well as the issues of inheritance and disenfranchisement found in the original – the very heritage industry that 'the Forster film' has become part of.

The trademark period accessories and engaging acting ensemble are once again in evidence, but both director Ivory and screenwriter Ruth Prawer Jhabvala, whose script extracts the sharpest teeth from Forster's original dialogue, have tried to get to the heart of the novel's world view. The attempt to be faithful results in an episodic structure which crams the rise of the lower middle class and the New Woman into two-and-a-half hours. Nevertheless, this is a more troubling and rigorous inquest into a bygone era than usual. The shadow of impending modernity is to be found in references to the suffragettes, the motor car and train, echoing Forster's obsession with social and mechanical mobility (one is tempted to speculate that the novelist's plea 'only connect' refers as much to railway junctions as to personal encounters).

Their investment in maintaining the status quo makes the outwardly genial Wilcoxes, headed by Anthony Hopkins as the father, the villains of the piece. They embody all that is grasping and greedy, shamelessly buying up England with the profits of their colonial enterprises and living comfortably on a lie. By contrast, the Basts provide the moral and political standards for those around them. Signalling the arrival of the urban white-collar worker, their cramped dwelling is shaken by the thundering of a nearby railway line. Samuel West's sensitive Leonard Bast is a tragic hero whose literature-inspired reveries are an escape from his dull office routine, but even these dreams are full of shadows. If West's accent is slightly too near the nasal twang of a Mr Pooter and Nicola Duffett's flame-haired and buxom Jacky is a caricature of a Toulouse-Lautrec showgirl, these characters nevertheless provide a solemn anchor for the film.

Bast is no mere pawn in the game of Fabian *manqué* Helen Schlegel. Rather, his observations provide a cutting critique and a fitting *gravitas* to the finale. While Helen can afford to extol books as 'more real than anything… when people fail you there's music and meaning,' Bast retorts, 'That's for rich people after their dinner'. This line rests uneasily with the assumptions of the great English literary heritage, and is a far and passionate cry from the elegant witticisms for which the Forster film is usually admired.

Lizzie Francke

ORLANDO
United Kingdom/Russia/France/Italy/Netherlands 1992
Director: Sally Potter

England, 1600. The young aristocrat Orlando and his parents hold a grand banquet for the elderly Queen Elizabeth I at their ancestral home. The Queen proclaims an affection for the handsome Orlando and gives him the deeds of his parents' house. By 1610, the Queen and Orlando's parents have died. Orlando, who is now betrothed to Favilla, attends a celebration held on the frozen River Thames by King James I in honour of visiting royalty from Muscovy. Favilla is humiliated when Orlando falls in love with Sasha, a young Russian princess. They arrange to meet on the frozen river at night, but Sasha does not keep her promise. Heartbroken, Orlando goes into a deep sleep and wakes up in 1650. He decides he wants to write poetry and entertains the scurrilous poet Nick Greene, who is more interested in securing a pension from Orlando than discussing the finer points of the craft.

In the year 1700, Orlando abandons his creative ambitions and turns his attention to politics. He asks William of Orange to send him abroad and ends up as the British ambassador in Central Asia. There he befriends the Khan and happily adopts an Eastern way of life. Ten years later, the Archduke Harry is sent out to bestow Orlando with a reward for services to his country. A party is held, but, since a war has just broken out in the region, no one turns up. Orlando is caught in the fray, but cannot bring himself to fight. He escapes his duty when he wakes up one day as a woman. 1750: Orlando has returned to England and attends the literary salons. As Lady Orlando, she is informed that she has no rights to the ancestral home. The Archduke offers to marry her and help her out of this predicament, but Orlando refuses.

One hundred years later, she meets her true knight and equal in the form of Shelmerdine, a wild adventurer from America. She proposes to him; he turns her down, but they live together for a while. Orlando is visited by two of Queen Victoria's officers and told that the lawsuit against her is settled – she must forfeit everything unless she has a son. Shelmerdine decides to return to America, but Orlando resolves to stay in England, even though she has now lost her beloved and her inheritance. Time speeds up and Orlando finds herself pregnant in a war-torn twentieth century. She emerges into the present with a young daughter and a completed manuscript, fulfilled at last.

*   *   *

Sally Potter's long awaited adaptation – or, more appropriately, interpretation – of Virginia Woolf's celebrated novel (which was written as a love poem to the flamboyant Vita Sackville-West) charts a journey from one Elizabethan age to another. The mythical Orlando shakes off the fetters of biological and cultural destiny to become – as angelic songster Jimmy Somerville, complete with laurels, wigs and lyre, pipes in the finale – a reinvented being that is 'one with the human race'. Woolf's creation cannot be easily classified. S/he is not so much an androgyne, rather a person who passes from male status to female over the course of 400 years, finding a first love in the exotic, foreign Sasha which is subsequently reflected and consummated in the adventurer Shelmerdine (Billy Zane may not be able to act, but he has a smile at least as bewitching as Charlotte Valandrey's Sasha).

Sexual ambiguity no longer causes the frisson it did when Woolf was writing, so Potter has made the question of status the central point of the film – Orlando learns how a change in gender is equivalent to excommunication. Lady Orlando is faced with two lawsuits, one which pronounces her legally dead and therefore unable to own property, while the other informs her that she is female – 'which amounts to the same thing'. But this death to the world is a rebirth for Orlando, who surveys her naked female form in the mirror in an echo of Botticelli's *Birth of Venus*. Orlando is never seen naked in his male incarnation – he is never authenticated as a man, rather he remains effeminately boyish. But with Tilda Swinton – in playful mode with frequent nods and winks to the camera – in the title role, the audience knows that there is a woman underneath those clothes. As a privileged child of the aristocracy, Orlando is in any case feminised by the gorgeous finery of his age. Clothes maketh the society man and woman – and Orlando seems as uncomfortable in the frock-coats and wigs, the doublet and hose of male attire, as in the cumbersome crinolines that hamper her progress through the Great Hall. Only in Eastern robes does Orlando appear to be free – as much from the constraints of Englishness as of gender.

Indeed, *Orlando* is full of jokes about the English, whether it be the custom of talking loudly to foreigners (with knowing wit, this particular exchange is in French) or the imperialist habit of collecting countries. The film is also a romp through English history, which it presents as richly textured spectacle. Potter creates an embroidered style similar to that of Peter Greenaway (whose production designers Ben Van Os and Jan Roelfs she has borrowed) which, together with the Nymanesque score, confirms her place in a particular tradition of British European-influenced art cinema. She also flirts with the attractions of pomp and circumstance. The pageant for Queen Elizabeth I is a visual feast of autumnal russet, red and gold, while the eighteenth-century salon's pastel palette could have been devised by Wedgwood. Details such as the tea-cup shaped topiaries – perfect emblems of the clipped Victorian era – are a delight. A frozen tableau of a woman with flowers and fruit trapped under the ice of the River Thames has a cold beauty – until we realise what is entailed in the creation of that image.

While there are many ironic touches – such as the casting of Quentin Crisp as the Virgin Queen and the twentieth-century salonier Ned Sherrin as Addison – the overladen visual style perversely turns the film into a celebration of the cultural heritage that Orlando in her liberated female state must reject. In the closing scenes, Orlando, in gentrified jodhpurs and jacket, joins the tourists and takes her cherubic daughter around the home that once was hers, but which now they can only look at with wonder. In many ways, this epitomises the experience of viewing *Orlando* itself.

Lizzie Francke

EL MAESTRO DE ESGRIMA
(THE FENCING MASTER)
Spain 1992
Director: Pedro Olea

Madrid, 1868. Fencing master Don Jaime de Astarloa visits his pupils, grandsons of the banker Salanova, for their weekly lesson. Single-mindedly dedicated to his art, he takes little interest in the political crisis rocking Spain: discontent with Queen Isabella, and agitation for the return of the exiled republican General Prim. Home in his study, Jaime works on his long-planned treatise on the art of fencing. He is interrupted by Adela de Otero, an enigmatic woman who asks to become his pupil. Jaime refuses, but is won over by her beauty and skill with the rapier. As the lessons proceed, he becomes captivated and teaches her his deadly secret – a lethal thrust to the throat. Another of his pupils, the Marques Luis de Ayala, comments on the unwonted smartness of Jaime's dress, and is intrigued to hear about Adela.

Jaime takes Adela to a lecture by an Italian fencing master, where Luis introduces himself to her. Soon afterwards she cancels her lessons, and – to Jaime's chagrin – is seen in public with Luis. Calling on Jaime, Luis entrusts him with politically compromising letters; a few days later he is found killed by a rapier thrust to the throat. Jaime takes the letters to his friend, the radical journalist Carceles. Adela is reported missing: there is blood in her apartment, and a body – seemingly hers – is taken from the river. Revisiting Carceles, Jaime finds him brutally tortured and the letters stolen; he chases the thief, who escapes in a carriage bearing a heraldic device Jaime had noticed among Adela's possessions.

Paying a final visit to Salanova, who is sending his grandsons to Switzerland for safety, Jaime sees the same device on the banker's carriage. Adela, who had faked her own death, comes to Jaime's apartment seeking one missing letter, the most crucial of all. She admits killing Luis on Salanova's orders and, while making advances to Jaime, tries to stab him. They duel and Jaime – though hampered by a buttoned foil – manages to kill her. As Isabella's deposition and the return of Prim are announced, Jaime sits burning the manuscript of his treatise.

*   *   *

'Feelings are never pure,' Adela de Otero tells the fencing master Don Jaime, just before trying to kill him. 'You still believe in good and bad.' *The Fencing Master* is a study of a man out of his time, dedicated to a skill and a code of honour which, even in Spain, had by the mid-nineteenth century become laughably outmoded. During a key scene at the opera house, a soprano sings 'Addio del passato' ('Farewell to the past') from *La Traviata*. When we next hear the aria, it's over the final image of Don Jaime destroying his life's work. Contemptuously shutting out the present, he tries to cling to an idealised past, but in the end that, too, is lost to him.

The use of a Verdian *leitmotif* is apt: the film draws on operatic conventions, but plays them against the grain, with none of the high spirits one usually expects from swordplay movies. Instead the prevailing mood is elegiac, at times almost devotional, with interiors shot in a dusty, smoky light as though in some library or convent where the past clogs the very atmosphere. 'Fencing is like communion,' Don Jaime tells Luis, 'one must be in the right frame of mind.' Luis, frivolous and philandering, neglects this advice and so falls easy prey to Adela.

Though couched in the form of a period thriller, *The Fencing Master* scarcely tries to mystify us: it's fairly evident from the start what's going on, and the outcome of the final duel comes as no surprise. What concerns Olea and his screenwriters – who include the author of the original novel, Arturo Pérez Reverte – is character as fate, the way people's emotional configurations turn them and can be turned against them. Adela (a witty, acute Assumpta Serna) seizes on Jaime's predilections no less than those of Luis – and in her turn is exploited, through her taste for intrigue, by Salanova.

The film's chief fault is that it's all a little too neat and thought-out. Its greatest asset is the moving performance of Omero Antonutti, a Taviani regular, who plays Don Jaime as a man teetering on the brink of old age, faced with the belated resurgence of emotions he had long since rejected yet never subconsciously ceased to hanker after. As the turmoil of his feelings matches the turmoil of the streets outside, his stance and gait seem to shed the years. And in the coda, as he sits watching his whole life literally turn to ashes, the austere misery of his expression rescues the scene from romantic cliché.

Philip Kemp

MADAME BOVARY
France 1991
Director: Claude Chabrol

Village doctor Charles Bovary meets Emma Rouault while he is treating her father's broken leg and they marry shortly after. Emma is happy at first, but an invitation to a society ball kindles her social aspirations and she becomes discontented. Her deteriorating health leads Charles to abandon his practice in Tostes and take another in Yonville, a larger town. Emma's condition improves and she gives birth to a daughter, Berthe.

Charles falls under the influence of Homais, the local pharmacist, and Emma is attracted to Léon Dupuis, a law clerk. The attraction is frustrated when he leaves for Paris to study and, feeling stifled at home, Emma increasingly loses interest in caring for her husband and daughter. She begins an affair with the dashing Rodolphe Boulanger, a local landowner, which offers her the passion and excitement lacking in her domestic life.

Enlivened by the affair, Emma becomes more attentive to Berthe and Charles, encouraging her husband in his efforts at pioneering surgery. But when an operation goes disastrously wrong, she regards him with contempt. Becoming more desperate, Emma persuades Rodolphe to run away with her, but he reneges on his promise, whereupon she succumbs to listless depression.

At the opera in Rouen with Charles, Emma encounters Léon. The two start a passionate affair. Emma buys more and more expensive clothes, incurring debts with the unscrupulous haberdasher, Lheureux. As the debts spiral, she persuades her husband to grant her power of attorney over their financial affairs, using their situation to find excuses for visiting Léon in Rouen. The debts are called in and, when they cannot be paid, the town bailiff arrives to repossess the Bovary property. The distraught Emma turns to Léon and Rodolphe, but neither is willing to help her. In despair, Emma poisons herself with arsenic from Homais' pharmacy and suffers an excruciatingly slow death, her uncomprehending husband at her side.

*   *   *

Chabrol's declared intention in filming *Madame Bovary* was 'to make the film Flaubert would have made had he had a camera instead of a pen'. The film received a favourable response from French critics for its fidelity to the original. But what gets lost in adapting a literary classic for the screen is often as revealing as what remains. It's here that the 'Chabrol touch' surfaces in what is otherwise strictly 'filmed Flaubert'.

The beginning and end of the novel have gone – Charles' childhood, the repercussions of Emma's suicide and her husband's discovery of Léon's and Rodolphe's letters to her are elided, which reduces identification with Charles. The director has also transposed the collective narratorial voice of the novel – the Flaubertian 'we' – into the Olympian objectivity of the Chabrol camera. The process of condensation includes reorganising details from the novel; for example, Charles' garbled giving of his name as 'Charbovari' is relocated from his schooldays to his first meeting with Emma. This marks the catastrophic mutual misunderstanding that characterises their marriage.

It is surprising that Chabrol should come to Flaubert so late in his career, since the novel is the Ur-text of themes in his work from *Le Beau Serge* to *Les Biches* and *Masques*: stultifying French provincial life, the self-destructive pursuit of illusory desires and bourgeois duplicity. Isabelle Huppert seems to have replaced Stéphane Audran as the director's *actrice fétiche* – this is her third role for Chabrol following award-winning performances in *Violette Nozière* and *Une Affaire des femmes*. Chabrol has whittled away the viewpoints of other characters to install Huppert centre stage. Her Emma alternates between terrifying self-absorption and Charcot-style *attitudes passionnelles*. At the same time, she displays a combination of petulance and defiance, crystallised in the moment when – having swallowed a handful of arsenic – she turns to the camera, her mouth smeared with the white powder, an image of her final gesture of impetuosity and indulgence.

Fassbinder commented that Chabrol's attitude to his characters resembles that of an entomologist observing them like insects in a glass cage. This particular glass cage is extremely well decorated, a sumptuous addition to the French heritage cycle, superior to the picture-book aesthetic of Claude Berri's Pagnol adaptations and offering a diseased Romantic vision which runs counter to the heartiness of Rappeneau's *Cyrano de Bergerac*. Chabrol's film was only made possible by the last-minute intervention of the television channel FR3, and there are aspects of its formal organisation – its pace and cutting, emphatic punctuation-by-fades and redundant narrative voiceover – that make it suitable for television serialisation.

The irony is that Chabrol has here made exactly the sort of faithful literary adaptation that the *nouvelle vague* once condemned as *le cinéma de papa* – respectful, luxurious and eminently forgettable.

Chris Darke

COMO AGUA PARA CHOCOLATE (LIKE WATER FOR CHOCOLATE)
Mexico 1991
Director: Alfonso Arau

Mexico, 1895. Born, literally, in a flood of tears on the kitchen table, Tita is condemned by family tradition never to marry. As the youngest daughter of the family, she must rather care for her mother. Tita becomes bound to the kitchen, where she learns the secrets of traditional culinary arts from the servants. However, she falls in love with Pedro, a young neighbour who asks for her hand. Elena, Tita's mother, refuses and offers him her eldest daughter, Rosaura, instead. He accepts so that he can be near Tita.

Food now becomes a weapon in Tita's hands. Forced to make the cake for her sister's wedding, she cries into the mixture: those who eat it cry uncontrollably and are then seized by nausea. A year later, she makes quails in rose petal sauce: everyone at the table is seized by sexual desire and Gertrudis, Tita's other sister, is carried off naked to join the Revolution by a soldier attracted from the heat of a battle nearby by the scent of roses.

Aware of the electricity between Tita and Pedro, Elena sends him, Rosaura and their newly born son off over the border to live with a relative in Texas. On hearing of the death of her baby nephew soon afterwards, Tita suffers a breakdown and the local doctor, John Brown, insists on removing her from the household so that he can look after her. In gratitude, Tita agrees to marry him.

Meanwhile the ranch is attacked by bandits and Elena is killed. Tita and Dr Brown return and are joined by the rest of the family. Rosaura gives birth prematurely to a baby daughter and asks Tita if she can be named after her, since she, too, will be condemned to a similar fate in the name of family tradition. Tita refuses and the baby is named Esperanza (Hope). Tita also discovers the reason for her mother's bitterness: a love affair which produced Gertrudis.

Pedro and Tita consummate their long-standing passion and Gertrudis returns, now a general of the Revolution. Tita stands up to the ghost of her mother that has been tyrannising her. Elena now disappears for good and Rosaura dies from chronic indigestion; Esperanza is free. Dr Brown, aware of the situation, tells Tita that he only wants her happiness and that she does not have to marry him.

Years later, Esperanza weds Alex, John's son from a previous marriage. Finally alone, Tita and Pedro make love and Pedro dies in ecstasy. Tita decides to follow him and eats matches. The flames of desire envelop the couple and burn down the ranch: Pedro and Tita are united for eternity. All that Esperanza finds when she returns from her honeymoon is Tita's book of recipes.

*   *   *

Like Water for Chocolate has repeated the success of Laura Esquivel's novel of the same name in both Mexico and the United States. This is quite appropriate for a film whose action takes place at the border between both countries. It is also the most financially successful of the films associated with the much-heralded renaissance in Mexican cinema that has emerged with a new generation of film-makers, independent producers and, perhaps most importantly here – because the director, Alfonso Arau, is not himself part of this generation – a middle-class public interested in local film production.

The main action of the film takes place during the Mexican Revolution and tells the story of a woman's struggle for affective freedom against authoritarian maternal law and tradition. And this is what marks the film off from the majority of films of the Mexican Revolution and the Westerns that constitute their US counterpart. *Like Water for Chocolate* retreats from the masculinised terrains of high politics and the battlefield and concentrates our attention on the so-called private sphere of a household run by women (the men are either dead, like Tita's father, or mere objects of desire, like Pedro himself). It presents itself, apparently at least, as a 'woman's film'.

The most important place in this home is the kitchen, where Tita is born and learns her culinary skills (and weaponry), and which in the context of violent change represents an important site of continuity. Indeed, from the point of view of the Mexican Tourist Board and the National Council for Cinema and the Arts that partially financed the film, the practice of cooking that takes place there probably constitutes a 'national tradition' worth promoting – especially since the relation to food is deprived of all dangerous connotations of excess. The film is told in flashback by the daughter who still possesses Tita's recipe book – and which, no doubt, she will pass on to her own daughter as a safe sign of female solidarity and past rebellion.

Like Water for Chocolate is not an example of Latin American 'third' or 'imperfect' cinema. Rather, it forms part of that international series of films about food fetishism associated most recently with *Babette's Feast, Tampopo* and *La Grande Bouffe*. Even here, however, it lacks the dangerous obsessiveness of these: instead of bringing politics and sex together via food, so as to subject them to visual analysis, Arau's images religiously separate them out and purify each of these activities from mutual contamination. Tita's passionate sister Gertrudis ignites only to leave the household, join the Revolution and return with a husband; whilst Tita herself is born in a flood of tears in a kitchen stinking of onion, only to die in her lover's arms in a barn converted into an altar. The cleanliness of the images, enhanced by good production values, thus serves its function here by domesticating fetishism.

A counter-Western in the form of a family romance, *Like Water for Chocolate* also functions quite explicitly as a national allegory, and it is the place that it accords women here that probably explains its success. There is, however, another reason: the sentimentalised relationship between Tita and the female servants Nacha and Chencha (their names clear signs of social class in Mexico). What is so disturbing about this aspect of the film is that its representation of domestic servitude echoes the classical pre-war Hollywood racism of films such as *Gone with the Wind.*

Despite the violent struggles for power going on both in and outside the household, the servants' own loyalties remain remarkably stable. Moreover, it is they who provide Tita with her culinary skills, their recipes which fill her recipe book. In exchange they come to embody a now tamed tradition and provide the new family emerging from the Revolution with its cultural roots, its links to a mythic past connoted by food. What is so interesting about this film is that it registers this history without, however, acknowledging it.

Like Water for Chocolate is a 'feel-good' melodrama. The fact that the film refuses to reflect on its own social contents may seem remarkable, but is in fact merely a reflection of real social relations in contemporary Mexico itself – and their relative lack of discussion. From this point of view, the film acts as a kind of palliative for the middle-class audiences with which it has been so successful. Despite all the changes brought about in Mexican society by the Revolution and its aftermath, they can still feel comfortable with those things that have remained the same: the servants in their kitchens.

John Kraniauskas

THE SECRET GARDEN
USA 1993
Director: Agnieszka Holland

The 1900s. Mary Lennox lives with her parents in India. After an earthquake in which her parents are killed, she is sent to England to stay with her uncle, Lord Craven, at Misselthwaite Manor. At Liverpool dock, she is met by her uncle's housekeeper, Mrs Medlock, who tells her that Mary's mother had a twin sister, who is also dead. At the gloomy manor, Mary is left to amuse herself. The young maid Martha attempts to befriend the aloof child, but Mary prefers to explore the house and surrounding landscape on her own.

Out in the grounds, she discovers a walled garden. A friendly robin shows her the way to its locked door. Mary rummages through her dead aunt's room and finds the key to this door. Later, Mary returns to the garden and meets Dickon, Martha's younger brother. He explains to her that her aunt died falling off the garden swing and that consequently Lord Craven ordered the garden to be sealed up. In the house, Mary hears a moaning sound and is told that it is the wind. Left to herself, Mary discovers the source of the noise, a young invalid boy in one of the rooms; he is Colin, Lord Craven's son. He explains that he is seriously ill. Meanwhile, Mary and Dickon tend to the garden and plant it for the spring. Mary also secretly visits Colin in his room. One day she is playing with Colin when Mrs Medlock turns up. Mary has to hide, though she is later discovered by Martha. Martha tells Mary that Lord Craven is coming home. Mary is at last presented to her uncle, who is shocked by her resemblance to his wife. Lord Craven is kindly but distant, and soon returns to his travels.

When spring comes, the secret garden blooms. Mary and Dickon visit Colin and tear down the shutters on his bedroom window, to Colin's horror. He throws a tantrum and Mary tells him to shut up. Medlock discovers that the children have been playing together and scolds Martha. Colin decides to get up and bosses the servants around. He is taken by Mary and Dickon in a wheelchair to visit the garden; Mary encourages him to try to walk. During the summer, he grows in strength. Mrs Medlock is convinced that Colin is still not well and continues with his treatments, confining him to his room and putting Mary under lock and key. Mary finds a secret passage leading from her room to the gardens. She makes a wish that Lord Craven will come home, and magically, he decides to return. Finding Colin no longer in his room, Lord Craven goes straight to the garden and finds the children playing hide and seek. He is reunited with his son, but Mary runs off, reminded of her own loneliness. Dickon comforts her and, for the first time, Mary is able to mourn the death of her parents. Lord Craven reminds Mary that she is part of the family, as Dickon looks on.

* * *

Frances Hodgson Burnett's novel *The Secret Garden* was published in 1911, the same years as J. M. Barrie's *Peter Pan*, and also the third edition of Freud's *Interpretation of Dreams*. Indeed, as with *Peter Pan*, there is much more to Burnett's novel than the 'children's classic' tag allows. Another Neverland, the secret garden – a phrase now ripe with sexual connotation – is a landscape upon which the most adult of anxieties can be mapped out. Children on the verge of adolescence losing parents are the staple narrative of the fairy story. Here the story resolves with the finding of a real father, while the mother is manifest as a garden (one thinks of Marvell's 'vegetable love').

Given this, it is appropriate that the director Agnieszka Holland and the writer Caroline Thompson should be hired by Coppola's American Zoetrope to take over the text as part of the children's classics series which started with Carroll Ballard's *The Black Stallion*. Holland's tale of a cuckoo in the nest, *Olivier, Olivier* was a well-aimed crack at the family romance. Thompson, who wrote *Edward Scissorhands* and *The Addams Family*, knows a thing or two about the cobwebbed corners of the imagination: *The Secret Garden* would seem a perfect project for someone who has stated that her two major cinematic influences are *The Black Stallion* and *Carrie*.

The fact that Holland, a Pole, and Thompson, an American, are alien to the English experience is also germane. Though born in England, Burnett went to live in the United States as a child. The England of *The Secret Garden*, as epitomised in the mouldy old manor with its fleet of servants, is the invention of a woman who spent her formative years in Knoxville, Tennessee.

Sex and class with a bit of colonialism thrown in – a heady brew for a family film. Indeed, this story of a young lady from the manor crossing the boundaries and befriending the gardening lad is worthy of D. H. Lawrence. But what is disappointing is that Holland and Thompson, who are obviously not timid of probing the shady side, have been more cautious than an adult might hope for, yet at the same time have created a film that the contemporary children's audience might find not to their taste (with no dinosaurs, turtles or any other opportunities for McDonald's tie-ins, it is hard to see how it will be marketed to them).

Two significant discrepancies between book and film mark the tenor of the project from the beginning. In Burnett's version, Mary's parents die of cholera. There is a vivid account of her left alone in a house full of yellowing death, the only other living thing there being a snake. An earthquake might have more dramatic value, but it seems to provide a more sanitised account of the trauma of separation between child and parent. There is no sense of sickness. The colour yellow manifests itself instead in the golden light that drenches the Indian scenes. This seems to have no other symbolic value other than allowing for a bold contrast with the classically English bleak and rainswept landscape that proves so foreboding when Mary first arrives in her new country. England was never darker, and Misselthwaite Manor has been art-directed to Gothic perfection.

Meanwhile, Burnett's Mr Craven has been upgraded to the status of a lord. This upwardly mobile move does give a certain resonance to Colin's enfeeblement. Here is a sickly child, terrified of following in his father's line (Lord Craven is a hunchback). He is cosseted and protected from the 'spores' in the air, which might just be the smoke churned out from the factories and mills beyond the moors; but, in fact, the source of infection is perceived as coming from the servants, who all wear white linen masks over their mouths when dealing with the young master. When Colin finally comes downstairs, the full complement of masked servants line up to greet him. If this all seems ripely farcical, Holland undercuts any ironic intention in a later scene in which the servants smile and wave from a window at the now walking Colin, happy at his new fortune. See how the aristocracy thrives.

But, conversely, the servants are associated with all that is naturally healthy. The kitchen scenes are brightly lit, bustling with rose-cheeked activity, making a glaring contrast with the gloomy upstairs. Only Mrs Medlock is charmlessly brusque (Maggie Smith on the right side of caricature), but then housekeepers inhabit the miserable limbo between upstairs and downstairs. Proper servants such as Martha melt with heart-cheering goodness, while Dickon is the pastoral boy, trailing with him a menagerie of deer, rabbits, robins and other cute wildlife. With the help of Dickon's green fingers, Mary is able to bring her garden back to life, rousing Mother Nature (she finds the key in her other mother's bedroom).

The film blossoms with stop-frame shots of roots thrusting and flowers burgeoning. The magic of the organic marks an emotionally regenerative process for Mary, and allows her finally to mourn her lost parents and fall a little in love with Dickon. Likewise, Colin is restored to health. But the cultivation of the garden also marks a return to a familiar old order, despite Mrs Medlock's contention that Mary has created havoc. Lord Craven arrives at the manor to take his place as father, Mary and Colin are tentatively aligned (earlier Colin had expressed a desire to marry her), while Dickon is expelled from this new-found paradise and is last seen out on the wild moors. From this, it would seem that the servant class has sown the seeds of their own destruction.

Lizzie Francke

THE REMAINS OF THE DAY
United Kingdom/USA 1993
Director: James Ivory

England, shortly after the end of World War II. The large country house of the late Lord Darlington has been bought by Lewis, a former American diplomat. Lewis finds he has 'inherited' Darlington's old butler, Mr Stevens, a man he remembers from a visit he made to England before the war. Stevens is hard pressed to get the house back in working order before the diplomat's family arrives. Nevertheless, Lewis agrees to Stevens' request for a holiday, and lends him his own Daimler. Stevens plans to travel to the West Country, where he hopes to catch up with the old housekeeper, Miss Kenton, whom he wants to entice back into service following the breakdown of her marriage.

As Stevens sets off on his journey, the action flits back to the 1930s, when Darlington Hall was at its high point. Shortly after Miss Kenton arrives on the staff, Stevens approaches Lord Darlington and asks if he may recruit his own father as the under-butler. Mr Stevens Snr has long experience as a butler, but is getting on in years. Miss Kenton warns Mr Stevens that his father is not up to his tasks, but he ignores her. One afternoon, Stevens Snr slips while carrying a tray of tea. Lord Darlington is solicitous, but worried. He has convened a conference on Anglo-German relations which, he tells Stevens, is vital to European interests: the slightest blunder could have disastrous results. Stevens moves his father to lighter duties.

During the conference, all the delegates except Lewis, the American diplomat, appease the Nazi visitors. Halfway through the event, Stevens Snr falls ill and dies. Although upset, Mr Stevens continues to attend to his duties. Miss Kenton has gradually grown infatuated with Stevens. One evening, she visits him in his private rooms and finds him reading. Momentarily, the couple seem about to kiss, but Stevens recovers his composure and dismisses her. Bitterly disappointed, Miss Kenton eventually leaves Darlington Hall to marry another butler, Mr Benn, and to help him run a boarding house. One night, there is a secret meeting at the house between the Prime Minister and the German Ambassador. Darlington's journalist nephew Reggie writes a piece condemning appeasement, and upbraids Stevens for not paying any attention to politics.

En route to visit Miss Kenton, Stevens runs out of petrol and he seeks assistance in a nearby pub, where the locals mistake him for a politician. The next day, the local doctor gives him a lift back to the stranded Daimler. The doctor is fascinated to learn Stevens served Lord Darlington, who has been discredited in the press as a traitor and had died not long after the war. Stevens defends his former master. At last, he and Miss Kenton have their reunion. They reminisce over tea at a smart hotel, but she refuses to come back to Darlington Hall. Her daughter is pregnant and Miss Kenton wants to stay nearby while she has her baby. As evening falls, Stevens sees Miss Kenton onto her bus and the couple say goodbye, presumably for the last time.

* * *

In Kazuo Ishiguro's Booker Prize-winner, Merchant and Ivory find another novel ripe for their stately brand of adaptation. The book takes the form of an elegiac memoir-cum-travelogue, penned by an emotionally repressed butler who has lived through seismic times without ever quite noticing what was going on. In the 1930s, his 'master' Lord Darlington, a gentleman politician, had been doing his darnedest to appease the Nazis. Many years later, Stevens finally begins to wonder if his own dogged loyalty was misplaced. Worse, he rues his missed romantic opportunity with the housekeeper, Miss Kenton.

Ishiguro is a contemporary novelist, but *The Remains of the Day* is set safely in the past. It thus provides a haven from which the film-makers can continue their excoriation of the English psyche (if *Slaves of New York* is anything to go by, when they stray into modern times, they become seriously unstuck). Here, they go Upstairs and Downstairs, note and observe the absurd rituals of country house living, and even take a few floundering, satirical slaps at the class system. But, as usual, theirs remains a curiously ambivalent project. On the page, perhaps, Darlington Hall may seem a vast mausoleum of a house which keeps servants and toffs alike manacled by propriety. On screen, however, the sheer visual relish with which the place is depicted can't help but undermine the mordant irony in Ruth Prawer Jhabvala's script: we have baying hounds, cheery cooks in the pantry, elegant dinner parties, tea in the conservatory, soirees in the drawing room, rustic pubs, and lots of English autumnal scenes. With most of the story told through flashback, the prevailing mood is one of nostalgia, and it is little wonder *The Remains of the Day* seems more a lament for lost grandeur than an indictment of aristocratic folly.

Only the scenes involving Peter Vaughan as Mr Stevens Senior, a grim, imposing figure who looks as if he has stumbled out of a Charles Addams cartoon, hint at the vein of Gothic comedy the picture might have tapped, or suggest any tension between masters and servants (there is one supreme moment where a little bubble of snot drops out of his nose into the wine just as he is about the pour for his lordship). Counterpointing Vaughan is Hugh Grant as Darlington's journalist nephew, who shows all the cheerful inanity of a P. G. Wodehouse character. The rest of the supporting cast has a mainly decorative role. Christopher Reeve (the spitting image of Albert Gore in his double-breasted suit) plays a far-seeing American diplomat who rails against the Nazi supermen and English amateurs alike; Michael Lonsdale, once a Buñuel regular and a fine Bond villain, is largely wasted as the French Ambassador more concerned about the corns on his feet than the future of his country. The film is full of lookalikes – of Oswald Mosley, Chamberlain and Ribbentrop – but eschews analysis of the rise of fascism in favour of crude caricature.

If much of the picture has an embalmed feel, its ossification turns out to be a positive advantage when it comes to the love story at its core. This is a very British affair, with Anthony Hopkins and Emma Thompson as a latter-day Trevor Howard and Celia Johnson – a couple thwarted by class, convention and the prison house of language. Even at his most monstrous, as Captain Bligh or Hannibal Lecter, Hopkins has always been expert at suggesting a sense of wounded innocence. Here, monolithic, with his hair greased back and hardly a flicker of emotion showing on his face, he still manages to hint at seething inner turmoil. Thompson, in a slightly thankless role, conveys her romantic disappointment effectively enough. Though the film is overlong, taking its plodding, lugubrious pace from Hopkins himself, at least it ends with a fine, tear-jerking flourish, with the last goodbye being said at a bus stop as the rain comes lashing down. Whatever else you may say about it (and it seems unlikely to win round many of Merchant-Ivory's critics), *The Remains of the Day* is a film anybody will be able to go and see with their mother. Whether or not that is a recommendation is a moot point.

Geoffrey Macnab

THE AGE OF INNOCENCE
USA 1993
Director: Martin Scorsese

New York City, the 1870s. Lawyer Newland Archer is engaged to May Welland of the powerful Mingott family. He is anxious to announce the engagement at the Beauforts' annual ball, partly to deflect the gossips' attention from May's cousin Ellen Olenska, who has returned from Europe after the failure of her scandalous marriage to Count Olenski. Archer wants an early wedding, but May is under pressure from her mother to observe the proprieties. Meanwhile, the rumours about Ellen's past proliferate, much to Archer's annoyance. After New York society snubs Ellen by refusing to attend a dinner given in her honour by May's grandmother Mrs Mingott, Archer asks the influential Van der Luydens to intervene. Ellen is invited to dinner at the Van der Luydens', where she asks Archer to visit her at home. Ellen arrives late for their appointment and Archer is disconcerted to see her with Julius Beaufort, a notorious womaniser. Afterwards, Archer orders the usual bouquet of lilies of the valley for May and sends yellow roses anonymously to Ellen.

Archer's boss Mr Letterblair asks him on behalf of the Mingott family to dissuade Ellen from going ahead with her divorce. Ellen is upset, but accepts Archer's advice that the scandal would be too damaging. Archer is increasingly drawn to Ellen and, when May goes away on holiday with her family, responds to a letter Ellen sends him from the Van der Luydens' by visiting her there. Before he can declare his feelings, they are interrupted by Julius Beaufort and Archer leaves angrily. He goes to see May and pressurises her to bring forward the wedding. May is suspicious of his reasons, but Archer assures her there is no one else. When he hears that the count wants Ellen back, Archer visits Ellen to persuade her not to return to her husband. He finally tells her he loves her, but Ellen, who returns his love, refuses him on the grounds that she could never hurt May. A letter arrives from May telling Ellen that her mother has agreed to the wedding being brought forward.

Eighteen months after the wedding, Archer, still obsessed with Ellen, hears that she is visiting Boston and invents an excuse to go there. Ellen explains that she is meeting Rivière, the count's secretary, who is trying to persuade her to return to her husband. Archer begs her not to go back to Europe, and she agrees to refuse the count's offer of recompense. Meanwhile, Beaufort's business collapses and Ellen loses her investments. After Mrs Mingott has a stroke, the impoverished Ellen returns to New York to take care of her. Archer and Ellen decide to meet and make love, but before the rendezvous takes place, May breaks the news to Archer that Ellen is leaving for Europe. Archer is devastated and realises that May's family and friends, believing that he and Ellen are lovers, have conspired to keep them apart. Feeling trapped, he tries to tell May about his feelings and wish to travel, but she forestalls him with the news that she is pregnant. She reveals that she told Ellen about her pregnancy two weeks earlier. Archer finally accepts his fate. Many years later, after May's death, the 57-year-old Archer accompanies his son Ted on a business trip to Paris. Ted has arranged a surprise visit to Countess Olenska, but Archer sends him on ahead, and turns and walks away.

* * *

Scorsese's *The Age of Innocence* might have been subtitled *The Man Who Could Not Love Women*. The poet of impotence has translated Edith Wharton's acerbic scrutiny of the suffocating codes and customs of late nineteenth-century New York into melodrama, centred on a tragic hero incapable of breaking through the social ties that bind. On the face of it, the film is a faithful adaptation of Wharton's book, even allowing the writer herself a voice in Joanne Woodward's narration. The minutiae of the novel's descriptions of decor and fashion have been lovingly re-created, as the matching of image and voiceover testifies. This is a meeting not only of minds, but also of compulsions: the obsessional film-maker has found a fellow fetishist in Wharton, whose fascination with fine detail takes social realism to excess. And, of course, they are both artists who study their society with outsiders' eyes.

The shift that takes place in this adaptation is subtle – as delicate as Wharton's découpage. Newland Archer, with his cultural aspirations and dreams of leaving, is as much the centre of the novel as the film, and Wharton, who was herself an exile in Europe, was clearly in sympathy with her hero's longing to escape. Yet the secret of her success in depicting Archer's psyche is the distance she takes on his attitude to women. For Wharton, Archer is a flawed, contradictory character, as much at the mercy of his own condescending view of the society women who surround him as of society itself. Scorsese has softened the novel's satire of Archer, reserving it instead, through the use of voiceover, for the manners and morals of fashionable New York. For Scorsese, Archer is pure victim – of his background, the claustrophobic matriarchal culture he inhabits – whereas for Wharton, his incapacity plays a key role in the victimisation of Ellen, whose own tragedy as social outcast is given more weight in the novel.

Such distance as Scorsese does take on Archer is realised, characteristically, partly as a problem of vision. His film is literally an art movie in which characters are judged according to their taste and the audience is tested on how many paintings and *objets d'art* it can identify. The camera follows Archer's gaze as he travels from room to room examining acquisition after acquisition. But the connoisseur's eye that sets him apart from most of his peers is also his downfall. Archer's approach to life and love is that of an aesthete – he would rather look than act. To him, May's niceness is a curtain hiding her basic emptiness, but it is his own inability to see beyond surfaces that separates him from the woman he professes to love. His first sight of Ellen after his marriage is from afar as he watches her on the seashore gazing out over the ocean. He promises himself that if she turns round, he will go to meet her, but she does not move and the moment is lost. The scene of Ellen on the shore is reminiscent of an Impressionist painting, with sparkling sunlight and soft colours creating a highly romanticised vista in which the static figure of a woman acts as a kind of guarantee of order and harmony.

Ellen's immobility in this sequence is the mirror image of Archer's passivity and resistance to change. The seashore scene is poignantly replayed at the end of the movie, when Archer, now fifty-seven, sits outside Ellen's flat in Paris, trying to decide whether to go in to see her. As her manservant closes the window, the image dissolves into a thousand particles of light and Ellen is safely locked away as a memory. But then, she was never real, nor did Archer want her to be, in spite of his token defence of women's rights. Archer's aestheticisation of Ellen is reflected in the portraits of women which figure prolifically in the film, as well as in the painterly poses which the characters take up from time to time. And it is there in Archer's fetishism, his fixation on Ellen's shoe, her pink parasol, the whisper of her skirts, revealing that the emptiness or lack he so despises in May is actually at the heart of masculinity. Once again, Scorsese creates a dark, pessimistic vision of male desire in which woman is never more than an alibi.

But what if the woman should move? In 1920, when Wharton wrote *The Age of Innocence*, women were certainly on the move, and the novel registers, in the outcast figure of Countess Olenska, the social anxieties attendant on their economic and sexual emancipation. This clearly struck a chord with Scorsese, whose Archer is both dismayed by Ellen's unconventional behaviour and panic-stricken by May's single-mindedness. In the crucial scene in which his wife tells him she is pregnant, dashing for good his hopes of following Ellen to Europe, she rises from her chair and towers over him, causing him to recoil. Scorsese films her gesture twice, the second time focusing on the bustle-encased lower half of her body and heightening the rustle of her skirt. It is a powerful image of male terror in the face of the maternal body.

Scorsese seems unexpectedly at home with period drama, taking more than one cue from that other saga of social change and doomed love, *The Magnificent Ambersons*. As in Welles' film, the tension between tradition and modernity is signalled by the use of irises and masking, which looks back to silent cinema while at the same time acting as harbinger of the new medium about to take the late nineteenth century by storm. *The Magnificent Ambersons* is melancholic, treating its characters swept up in the tide of history with sympathy and projecting a sense of loss at what is sacrificed in the name of progress. At first glance, Scorsese's movie is less nostalgic, ending on a hopeful note which recognises that Archer's children will achieve the happiness he denied himself. For Scorsese, as for Wharton, Archer's final decision to walk away from love is the last nail in the coffin of the past in which he is entombed. Yet it is clear that the film-maker, more than the novelist, identifies with Archer's desire to live in his memories rather than face reality. Scorsese's *Age of Innocence* is suffused with fear of loss, most notably in its striving for period authenticity (always a lost cause) and in its obsession with faithfully reproducing the novel.

This lends the film a static, stultified quality which is entirely appropriate to Daniel Day-Lewis' frozen stiffness as Archer, but does less justice to the freewheeling body language of more unconventional characters, such as Julius Beaufort, played with vulgar verve by Stuart Wilson, or Michelle Pfeiffer's Ellen, who strides out with an appealing mannish swagger. All the performances are excellent and the production is a visual tour de force; but it really is time to lift the shroud of despair.

Pam Cook

THE THREE MUSKETEERS
USA 1993
Director: Stephen Herek

France, the seventeenth century. Reckless young D'Artagnan is on his way to Paris, determined to join the ranks of the Musketeers. Unfortunately, though, the corps has been disbanded. Cardinal Richelieu, who is plotting to usurp the youthful king, has tricked his Majesty into decommissioning them and sending them off to join the war against England. D'Artagnan, unaware of the fact, heads straight to Musketeers head-quarters to enrol. Athos, one of the three Musketeers who remain at large, is the only man there, and is so offended by D'Artagnan's impudence that he challenges him to a duel. In the course of a busy morning, D'Artagnan also manages to insult Porthos, the portly second Musketeer, and bumps into Aramis, the suave third. Both demand 'satisfaction'.

At the appointed time for the first duel, D'Artagnan is surprised to see his three opponents know each other, and awe-struck to discover they're Musketeers. He gets ready to fence with Athos, but the duellists are interrupted by a troop of the Cardinal's men. A fight ensues. D'Artagnan acquits himself bravely, and all the soldiers are killed. The Musketeers escape, but D'Artagnan is captured by a second wave of the Cardinal's troops. He is thrown into the dungeons, and has his sword stolen by Rochefort, the Cardinal's chief henchman. D'Artagnan escapes from his cell and overhears Richelieu plotting with a mysterious woman. She is being dispatched to England to sign a secret treaty with the Duke of Buckingham. This augurs ill for the King. D'Artagnan is found eavesdropping, pulled before the Cardinal, and when he refuses to say where the Musketeers are hiding, condemned to death. The three come to his rescue, snatching him from beneath Richelieu's nose, and escaping in the Cardinal's own carriage.

Finding out from D'Artagnan about the Cardinal's plan, the Musketeers hurry toward Calais, determined to apprehend the mysterious envoy. There is a price on their heads, and hordes of bounty hunters are close behind them. To ensure greater safety, they split up, resolving to meet at the port. D'Artagnan collapses with exhaustion a few miles short of Calais. He is picked up off the open road by a beautiful woman in a carriage. Although he doesn't at first realise it, she is Milady, the very person he heard the cardinal conspiring with. She nurses him and seems about to seduce him, but then, when she discovers he is associated with the Musketeers, tries to kill him. He escapes her dagger, but is overcome by her guards. She decides to keep him alive a little longer, and takes him as a prisoner to Calais. There, however, she finds the Musketeers waiting for her. It turns out she is Athos' former wife, a convicted murderess. At first, she refuses to reveal the full extent of Richelieu's plot, but then, jut before she is about to be executed, she warns her old husband that there are plans afoot to assassinate the King at his birthday celebrations. She avoids the executioner's axe by throwing herself to her death.

The Musketeers hotfoot it back to Paris. D'Artagnan intercepts the assassin at the very instant he is taking aim to fire at the King with his blunderbuss. There is a huge fight in the palace. Eventually, Athos, Porthos and company, joined by their old comrades, prevail. But the Cardinal escapes into the dungeons with the King and Queen as hostages. As he flees, D'Artagnan is left to fight Rochefort, who turns out to be his father's murderer. With a little help from Constance, the Queen's chamber maid, he beats him in an epic duel.

Just as the Cardinal seems about to escape down an underground river, Aramis stops him in his tracks. The King, grateful to the Musketeers for keeping him on the throne, reappoints them as his bodyguards, and admits D'Artagnan to their ranks. Girard, a pompous upstart whose sister D'Artagnan is accused of insulting, turns up, wanting to revenge the family honour. But on learning that the Musketeer code, 'All for One and One for All', means he will have to fight the entire corps, he turns tail and flees.

* * *

Given memories of the 'Mouseketeers', Uncle Walt's folksy troupe of fresh-faced youngsters who first strutted their way across American television in the 1950s, wearing funny caps and chanting Mickey Mouse mantras while helping hawk millions of dollars worth of merchandise, the prospect of a Disney version of *The Three Musketeers* was hardly one to relish. One of cinema's most exhilarating yarns seemed destined to end up as yet another paean to homely, commercial values, with the chivalric slogan 'One for All and All for One' no doubt converted into a new Disney Club nostrum. This, though, proves to be a surprisingly sprightly swashbuckler.

Admittedly, it is scarcely original, being after all the umpteenth version of the tale. And out latest crop of Musketeers is a little on the callow side. Unlike Oliver Reed, Frank Finlay or even Douglas Fairbanks, they're not worldly-wise, heavy-drinking matinee idol types. Still, if Chris O'Donnell, Kiefer Sutherland, Charlie Sheen and Oliver Platt do lack the element of weary, charming cynicism which sometimes characterises Dumas' heroes on screen, they more than make up for it with their nimble acrobatics and their infinite capacity for duelling. They leap hither and thither, fight on staircases, balustrades and in forests without appearing in the slightest bit fazed by their rather flouncy costumes.

The film-makers take certain liberties with Dumas' original text, rewriting the episode of the Queen's Diamonds, banishing the Duke of Buckingham to an off-screen role, cutting down on the boozing and the wenching, and allowing the usually incorrigible Milady (Rebecca De Mornay) a touch of saving grace; but, in their way, they give as faithful a rendition of the tale as any of their predecessors. Fidelity here lies not so much in keeping to the plot of the novel as in preserving its spirit, in staging the swordfights with grace and élan, and featuring as many chases as possible. It is only to be expected that the villains should be played by English actors. Tim Curry offers an overblown Cardinal Richelieu, not so very far removed from his Dr Frank N. Furter, and Paul McGann is the nincompoop Girard, who is always trying to engineer

D'Artagnan's downfall. They may not be the heroes, but they provide most of the film's comic momentum.

Superficially, this follows in the wake of *Young Guns*: the bankable brat pack, having colonised the Western, rides off into genres new. Nevertheless, there is no sense here that the stars overshadow their vehicle or that this is just another American rites-of-passage yarn transposed to an unusual setting. Director Stephen Herek, whose previous credits include *Bill and Ted's Excellent Adventure*, manages to infuse the film with a little self-reflexive irony without losing that likeable, ingenuous quality so essential to the story. The script incorporates elements of the JFK saga, boasting a denouement which involves a lone sniper with a blunderbuss from the *Indiana Jones* cycle, but never becomes portentous.

On one level, this is corporate, theme-park movie making, guilty of fetishising history. We're presented with the same image of seventeenth-century France as you might encounter in a heritage museum, all dungeons, palaces and vast halls. As the recent GATTS talks illustrated, European sensitivity about Hollywood is at a high pitch. A picture like this, which is based on a French novel, and uses Austrian and English locations, may serve to heighten fears that the Americans, not content with taking most of our box-office receipts, are now pilfering our national myths as well. However, the swashbuckler has always been among the quintessential Hollywood genres. Jeffrey Richards was not far off the mark in his study *Swordsmen of the Screen*, when he placed it alongside the Busby Berkeley-style musical as something so extravagant, colourful and hard to pull off that only the studio system at its best could manage it. True, Musketeer fables are conventional Boy's Own tales, full of derring-do, but they are also highly stylised pieces of cinema, where choreography, costume and music tend to be privileged at the expense of narrative.

Writing in the 1970s, Richards struck an elegiac note. He was convinced that swashbucklers had become prohibitively expensive to make, and worried that their romantic flamboyance was out of synch with the times: he couldn't imagine Clint Eastwood or Steve McQueen in doublet and hose – they were too mean to be chivalric. But he was premature in writing off the sword-and-cape spectacular. Whatever other criticisms might be levelled at it, Disney's *The Three Musketeers*, like *Robin Hood: Prince of Thieves* or the forthcoming *Zorro*, at least suggests there is still mileage in the genre. With Hollywood ever more willing to plunder its past, and the conventional, tough-guy hero on his last legs, the swashbuckler is enjoying an unlikely new lease of life.

Geoffrey Macnab

BELLE EPOQUE
Spain 1992
Director: Fernando Trueba

Spain, 1931. On the eve of the declaration of the Republic, Fernando, a young deserter from the King's army in Madrid, is captured by two Civil Guards. When both of them are killed in a quarrel, the lucky Fernando takes refuge in a brothel. There he meets the elderly libertine and artist Manolo, who invites him back to his large country house in which he lives, separated from his wife. Fernando resolves to return to Madrid incognito, but remains in the village when he catches sight of Manolo's four beautiful daughters as they arrive at the station: the recently widowed Clara, the masculine-identified Violeta, the seductive Rocío, engaged to a local Royalist, and the virginal Luz.

Fernando sleeps with three of them in turn. He is seduced by Violeta when both are cross-dressed at the local carnival; by Rocío when she seeks consolation after an argument with her fiancé; and by Clara, after she has pushed him into the lake where her husband drowned. Meanwhile, Manolo's wife Amalia, an ageing diva of the Spanish operetta, pays an unexpected visit to husband and daughters. The reunion is ecstatic, even though she brings her stage-manager/lover, who reveals that Amalia's career is by no means as successful as she claims. After his amorous experiments, Fernando has finally come to believe that it is the youngest daughter, Luz, who is his true love. They become engaged and Luz visits him in bed on the morning before their wedding. Finally, the three elder sisters leave the station for Madrid, while Fernando and Luz set out for a new life in America, leaving Manolo alone once more.

* * *

In the prologue to *Belle Epoque*, the fortunate Fernando is let off scot-free after the Civil Guards who arrest him as a deserter conveniently kill each other off. In the narrative of transparent wish-fulfilment which follows, director Fernando Trueba seems to be hoping that his audience will be similarly indulgent and will absolve him of the charges of aestheticism and sexism aroused by his film, with its period art design and its multiple seduction plot, with each daughter surrendering herself in turn to the puppy-eyed Jorge Sanz.

As the story develops, *Belle Epoque* nonetheless offers many pleasures. The picturesque decor (filmed in Portugal, not Spain) is beautifully shot by Almodóvar regular José Luis Alcaine, who manfully resists the temptation of soft focus, which ruined so many Spanish period films of the 1980s; and the four young women offer splendidly assured performances. Miriam Diaz-Aroca essays a demure modesty far from the petulant sensuality she lent Almodóvar's *High Heels*; Ariadna Gil does her best to stop Violeta turning into a straight fantasy of a lipstick lesbian; Maribel Verdú (from Vicente Aranda's *Amantes* and currently Spain's hottest young actress) brings intelligence to her customary passion; and Penelope Cruz (from Bigas Luna's *Jamón, Jamón*) pouts prettily as the neglected virgin.

While it comes as no surprise to learn that this lazy plot was cooked up by Trueba and his male collaborators over a series of long lunches, the film's heterosexual wish-fulfilment is partially mitigated by the fact that the passive male is invariably humiliated by the active females before they offer themselves to him. Fernando is pushed into a lake by Clara, and dressed as a maid for the carnival by Violeta, revealing in the process an unnerving likeness to Tony Curtis in *Some Like It Hot*. This episode, in which Gil, cross-dressed, straddles the nonplussed Sanz while quite literally blowing his trumpet, is perhaps the film's most successfully comic and erotic moment. One suspects, however, that the many awards garnered by Gil from the role derive from her perceived courage in Spain in playing a lesbian at all.

More pervasive problems crystallise around Fernando Fernán Gómez's patriarch. The most ubiquitous actor in Spanish cinema, he has been perfecting his crusty old man act for at least twenty years. Here he replays it as an unlikely provincial libertine, freely accepting the lesbianism of one daughter and the lost virginity of the others. The problem is that – as with the film's profane priest or its parodic treatment of political conservatives – *Belle Epoque*'s sunny good humour simply conjures away the real conflicts of Spanish history, encouraging the contemporary audience to adopt the comforting, ironic distance of its anachronistically permissive family.

While domestic audiences clearly appreciated the absence of that po-faced serious-ness with which much state-sponsored cinema of the 1980s addressed the Civil War (making this one of the biggest-grossing Spanish films of all time), *Belle Epoque*'s atti-tude to the past is one of anaesthetic amnesia. Where Merchant-Ivory's films offer a gilded image of a British social order now definitively lost, Trueba's equally aestheticised period piece holds up a mirror to that tolerant, and sometimes indifferent, libertari-anism on which Spain came to pride itself after the death of Franco. At a time when that achievement is threatened by mass unemployment and the rise of the Right, the escapist attractions of such rewriting of Spanish history are all too obvious.

The film ends with a moment of closure and of evasion: Fernando marries the youngest daughter and emigrates with her to America. The chastening of Fernando echoes the domestication of Trueba and his collaborators: one would hardly guess that scriptwriter Rafael Azcona was responsible for some of the most grotesque and bizarre Spanish features of the Franco era, when he worked with directors such as Luis Berlanga and Marco Ferreri. The significance of the extraordinary popular and critical success of *Belle Epoque* is surely in its rejection of that vein of corrosive humour and perverse violence that was once so characteristic of Spanish film. It is Trueba's achievement to have shown that a Spaniard can direct a period picture as polished and inoffensive as any in European art cinema.

Paul Julian Smith

MARY SHELLEY'S FRANKENSTEIN
USA 1994
Director: Kenneth Branagh

The Arctic, 1794. An explorer's ship, commanded by the intrepid Captain Walton, is stranded in frozen sea. A strange, exhausted man comes on board and tells Walton his story. He is Victor Frankenstein, born in Geneva. We see his childhood in a happy house with his parents and adopted sister, Elizabeth. But some years later, his mother dies giving birth to his brother, William. Victor, by now a serious young student, leaves to study medicine in Ingolstadt, promising to marry Elizabeth on his return.

Victor's questioning outlook allows him to befriend a Dr Waldman, who tells him how he once tried to reanimate dead life. When the doctor is murdered, Victor steals his work journal and sets about constructing a living being from body parts he steals, including Waldman's brain and parts of his killer's body. Elizabeth comes to find him. But neither she, nor the cholera epidemic that is raging in the city, can drag him away from his work. Having completed his experiment, Victor is horrified by what he has done. The creature comes to life and escapes. Victor falls ill from pneumonia. When he recovers, he persuades himself that the creature must have died from cholera and decides to go back to Geneva and marry Elizabeth.

Meanwhile, the creature, hounded by the townspeople, runs to the countryside where he shelters in a peasant family's pig pen. The blind grandfather befriends him, but the family, thinking he is harming the old man, drives him out. The creature resolves to take revenge on Victor and journeys across country to Geneva. There he kills William and has the blame pinned on Justine, the housekeeper's daughter. She is hanged by a mob of townspeople. The creature asks Victor to make him a female partner. In return, he will never trouble him again. Victor agrees, but then decides to marry Elizabeth and escape from Geneva instead. The creature finds them and tears out Elizabeth's heart.

Grief-stricken, Victor reanimates a woman using parts of Justine and Elizabeth. The creature claims her for himself, but she sets fire to herself and to the house. Victor follows the creature to the Arctic wastes. Having told Walton his story, Victor dies. The sea melts again and the ship sails off for home, leaving the creature, mourning, to set fire to himself on Victor's funeral pyre.

* * *

Kenneth Branagh continues his apparent quest to turn the works of English literature into adaptations-made-easy with this rip-roaring version of Mary Shelley's novel, probably the most famous Penguin Classic no one has read. Branagh's version of a book mythologised by cinema is easily the most faithful to the original, leaving out the book's more irrelevant departures and adding Gothic moments that Shelley might be proud of. Of course, it should have been obvious that Branagh would do this tale justice: his only non-adapted film so far, *Dead Again*, was another overloaded Gothic drama.

Branagh plays the hapless doctor obsessed as a Marlovian figure, to whom he adds his *Henry V* modus operandi: big, hammy gestures, exaggerated emotions and loud speech. In the context, it works rather well, vying with a thunderous musical score that never lets up for one moment. This Frankenstein also has a dollop of contemporary action hero about him. When he conducts his experiments, the pace accelerates to breakneck speed, with an alarming array of whizz-bang effects. Moreover, at this point, Branagh strips down to a pair of leggings, hoisting a well-toned and certainly well-oiled torso around the screen as he grapples his creation into life. His apparel, or lack of it, adds a sexual dimension to the birthing proceedings – particularly as he only sports this attire again on his wedding night. This quasi-sexual male labour is an alarming contrast to the film's images of women actually giving birth – both bloody, screaming, grim affairs. These could be a nod to feminist readings of the novel, which point to Mary Shelley's own gruesome experience (her mother, Mary Wollstonecraft, died of septicaemia after giving birth to her, and Shelley herself had had a miscarriage just before she wrote *Frankenstein*).

Certainly, the film is full of body horror, the preserve of many contemporary horror movies: not only does this include the monster itself, but also corpse dissection, body parts being cleavered off and sewn together, two hangings and the cholera epidemic that leaves dead bodies strewn everywhere. Elizabeth's murder is a nasty piece of Hannibal Lecter-style heart-ripping. And the whole movie is drenched in blood.

Helena Bonham Carter's Elizabeth echoes Victor's ever-dancing mother in character. Even though neither Elizabeth nor Justine gives birth, both meet a nasty end as a result of Victor's (literal) labour. The dancing of the past is also echoed, to great effect, when Victor waltzes pathetically with his second monstrous creation: the lolling rag doll made from Justine and Elizabeth. These women are born (and reborn) to suffer, and that makes the image of the burning female monster rampaging through the house particularly potent, expressing just as much of the pain of the new-born as the rages of De Niro's male creature.

De Niro is in good form, loping and howling at the horror of his dilemma. His nameless monster, bearing little relation to Boris Karloff, turns from a grunting animal into a pained, articulate psychopath who wants to be 'normal', but cannot help his nature. He ends up a strangely modern creation, understanding psychological conflict where others, including Victor, can only show it. This combination of old and modern permeates the film. The language is colloquially contemporary; the mechanics of the re-animation are fleshed out with intricate-sounding discussions about acupuncture and electricity; and much is made of the scientific nature of Victor's lightning-conducting experiments to convince a knowing latter-day audience who will not be content simply with flashing buttons, sparks and bubbling potions.

The film also seems at pains to get to the heart of the nurture-versus-nature argument. Its conclusion rests on the fact that the monster has been made out of criminals, and must therefore be inherently evil. But the film never asks why Victor, a happy little boy from a happy family, turns out as he does. If his obsession was brought about by losing his mother so gruesomely, then surely there is more to be said about the nature of evil, or of messing with the 'natural state of things'.

Between the crashing opening and closing as the sea ices up then melts again, every episode is a drama in some genre. The only unsatisfactory character is Aidan Quinn's Walton, more of a book end than the glory-seeking explorer he is meant to be. The film is simply not large enough to have more than two big boys in it. Even so, after years of somewhat mistaken identity, it does the job of restoring Mary Shelley's book to its real place in the literary archive, while adding a touch of modernity that embraces its true horror and its sense of the bizarre.

Amanda Lipman

LA REINE MARGOT
France/Germany/Italy 1994
Director: Patrice Chéreau

Paris, August 18, 1572. Marguerite de Valois (Margot), sister of Charles IX, the Catholic King of France and daughter of Catherine de Medici, is to marry the Protestant Duke, Henri of Navarre, in a ceremony arranged to appease the two warring religious factions. Marguerite, forced to marry a man she does not love, acquiesces only under pressure, but insists that she will not share the conjugal bed with her new husband, preferring the attentions of her lover, the ruthless, bloodthirsty Duc de Guise.

Catherine de Medici wishes to neutralise the perceived Protestant threat by killing their leaders. As King, Charles – though indecisive and half-mad – declares that the deaths of the leaders alone is insufficient; he wants all of them dead, so that not a single Protestant survives to blame him. Despite his words being uttered while in the throes of a fit, and under coercive pressure from the Dukes of Anjou, Guise and Tavannes, they are taken as the royal assent to what will become known as the Saint Bartholomew's Day Massacre.

On August 23 and 24, a militia of Catholic courtiers and the Parisian people indiscriminately slaughter more than 6000 Protestants, including many of the Huguenot guests at Margot's wedding. Navarre is saved from the bloodshed by the attentions of Margot and her courtiers. However, she also attends to a badly wounded young Protestant, La Môle, whom she realises is the same man she picked up several days previously when scouring the streets for casual amorous encounters. They fall in love and she helps him escape to Holland.

During a hunting accident Navarre saves the life of Charles and earns the King's trust, friendship and protection. However, Catherine is plotting to have Navarre killed with a slow-acting poison secreted into the pages of a hunting book. She entrusts the task to her youngest son, the Duc d'Alençon. Unexpectedly, the King, rather than Navarre, handles the book. He dies a slow and agonising death, attended to by Margot. La Môle has returned from Holland to find Margot but is charged with regicide and is executed with his friend Coconnas. Margot visits the decapitated body, taking his head to have it embalmed. Reconciled with her husband, sickened by Catherine de Medici's savagery, Margot flees the court to join the Protestant camp.

* * *

Blood, poison and perfume: *La Reine Margot* is a suppurating broth of all three in which the idea of the 'body politic' receives a highly physical twist. Patrice Chéreau has chosen to film the close, hermetic and murderous life of the French court at the time of Catherine de Medici as a scrum of fluid alliances and shifting allegiances. These are negotiated against the backdrop of a coerced marriage of political convenience (Marguerite de Valois to Henri de Navarre), feral, inbred desire (Catherine de Medici for her son Henri, Duc d'Anjou; the brothers for their sister Margot), merciless religious hatred (the court is Catholic, Navarre is Protestant), focused by the growing horror and despair of the young queen.

Despite having failed as the French entry to set this year's Cannes Festival alight – the Best Supporting Actress award to Virna Lisi being widely (and condescendingly) seen as a token bauble – *La Reine Margot* has gone on to reap both critical and commercial acclaim in France. As yet another in the seemingly interminable cycle of heritage films with which Claude Berri – here in the role of producer – has become synonymous, the film arrives here trailing the baggage of expectations associated with others of its genre, but succeeds in satisfyingly short-circuiting them.

Chéreau himself has stressed his desire to avoid reproducing in his own film what *Cahiers du cinéma* has referred to as 'retro-nostalgia', and has spoken in interviews of using a 'prophylactic measure' to circumvent it – 'Every time an image from a TV film on Catherine de Medici came to mind I would think of the three *Godfather* films, of *Mean Streets* and *GoodFellas*.' The Medicis as Mafia clan – it's a nice idea, and one that has clearly shaped the film's depiction of the family as the arena of morbid power-play, while also allowing it to pull clear of the dread gravitational pull of its generic satellites. The heritage film tends to rely on set-ups that maximise its qualities of spectacle – high angles, mid-long shots – to the end of privileging illustrative tableaux, while also placing the spectator in an Olympian and curiously touristic position. (It is no coincidence that the 'heritage film' coincides precisely with the trend for restaging national history and culture in theme parks.) Conversely, the Mafia film comes in close and claustrophobic, uses two-shots, close-ups and privileges interior spaces. That this strategy places the spectator in a more intimate relationship to the action is something that has not been lost on Chéreau, who brings his camera in among the bodies, knitting in and out of the bloodlines and circuits of power. *La Reine Margot's mise-en-scène* is one in which the spectator experiences a physical disorientation to match that of the characters themselves and, interestingly, the few moments when the film does lapse into a kind of painterly academicism (Vermeer, Zurburan) are those when the action shifts beyond the walls of the Palais du Louvre to Holland.

The uncomfortable intimacy that the film encourages brings out some remarkable performances; Lisi, clad in black throughout, plays Catherine as a woman whose mourning is as constant as her venomous affections. When it becomes clear that the poison she intended for Navarre has mistakenly infected her eldest son, the vacillating, bloodthirsty Charles, a low-angle shot has her lurking in the gallery of the Cathedral casting a vampiric shadow – Queen Nosferatu, her hair scraped cruelly back to show a Max Schreck pate. Jean-Hugues Anglade's Charles is one of the film's real revelations; those with memories of his dream-wimp boyfriends in *Betty Blue* and *Nikita* will barely recognise him here. His is a performance of real range and authority, half slobbering dungeon freak barely ennobled by filthy lace and half strangely sympathetic victim of his mother's appalling plots. And at the centre of all the mayhem is Adjani's Margot, her face a set of nested ovals that coalesce to express muted horror, her white robes forever absorbing the blood of others including that of La Môle, her Protestant lover, whose severed head she cradles in her lap after his execution, just as she absorbs into her clothes the sweated blood of the slow-poisoned King.

Grand guignol, cloak and dagger, cruel Mafia claustrophobia: *La Reine Margot* is nothing if not explicit about power and religious hatred. Its currency is blood, its disguises perfume and lace; parricide, regicide and genocide its manifest destiny. Close to the bone, this is the shocking, slightly cold but undeniable powerful apotheosis of the French heritage film.

Chris Drake

CARRINGTON
United Kingdom 1995
Director: Christopher Hampton

Winter, southern England, 1915. Writer Lytton Strachey arrives at the country house of artist Vanessa Bell and her husband. He notices an unusual, boyish-looking character frolicking in the garden. This turns out to be a young artist, Dora Carrington.

As they walk along the clifftops, Strachey attempts to kiss Carrington. She is repulsed, and later retaliates by creeping into his room by dead of night with a pair of scissors to cut off his beard. She decides against it, and the two become fast friends. Mark Gertler, another painter, is obsessed with Carrington and determined to sleep with her. She eventually consents, but not before she has declared her love for Strachey, who is gay. She and Strachey set up house in the country. Carrington takes a lover, a handsome young soldier named Reginald Partridge. Strachey falls for Partridge, suggests he change his name to Ralph and invites him to move in. Carrington, fearful that Strachey wouldn't consent to live with her alone, marries Partridge.

She starts an affair with Partridge's best friend, Gerald Brenan. Partridge, far from a faithful husband himself, is bitter. Carrington cares little about either man's jealousy. It is Strachey she loves. Strachey's book, *Eminent Victorians*, is published to enormous acclaim. With the proceeds, he buys a bigger house, and also starts an affair with a much younger man. Partridge leaves Carrington for another woman but Carrington is still happy to live with Strachey. He helps her cope with an unwanted pregnancy and she consoles him when his love affair breaks up.

In 1932, Strachey falls ill. Carrington becomes his devoted nurse. One day, when he's lying in bed, seemingly talking in his sleep, he confesses that he loved Carrington all along and bitterly regrets not marrying her. Shortly afterwards, he dies. Carrington decides she can't bear life without him and commits suicide with a shotgun.

* * *

Although inspired by Michael Holroyd's celebrated biography of Lytton Strachey, *Carrington* makes no attempt to portray Strachey's world in full. Its main concern is his relationship with Dora Carrington, and events are seen as much from her perspective as from his. The narrowness of focus is one of the film's strengths. Despite occasional glimpses of such sacred cows of the Bloomsbury Group as Duncan Grant, Lady Ottoline Morrell and Vanessa Bell, there is little wallowing in nostalgia, and a merciful absence of dialogue of the 'How do you do, I'm Maynard Keynes' variety. Carrington and Strachey's rejection of aristocratic high-jinks is spelled out early on, both by their caustic reaction to one of Lady Ottoline's hearty mid-war garden parties and by their decision to retreat from London's fashionable salons to the countryside.

Visually, we're in the realm of heritage cinema: country houses, gardens and pictorial English landscapes are foregrounded; costume and production design are intricately detailed. Hampton opts for a literary structure. The film opens with a lengthy intertitle and unfolds as a series of chapters. Much of the dialogue and voiceover narration is taken from Carrington and Strachey's diaries, and from the letters they exchanged. There's occasionally something a little arch about Strachey's gnomic one-liners on such subjects as semen, death or posterity. (Jonathan Pryce claims to have based the voice for the character on a mix of Malcolm Muggeridge and Ned Sherrin, and speaks in clipped, high-pitched tones.) However, despite the literary-heritage trappings that come with the territory, Hampton never loses sight of the love affair at the core of the story.

'His knees,' Carrington once replied when asked what attracted her to Strachey. Theirs was certainly a very unlikely romance. He was a sagacious, owl-like man of letters, a confirmed homosexual who rarely displayed any feeling, while she was an impulsive young artist. On the surface, this seems like another of those quintessentially

English liaisons of the sort celebrated in such recent pictures as *The Remains of the Day* and *Shadowlands*. (Presumably, the success of those films enabled *Carrington*, which was written in the mid-1970s, finally to be made.)

But there is much more comedy here than either James Ivory or Richard Attenborough were able to bring to their stiff-upper-lipped weepies. Strachey's beard as much as his knees is the key to the romance. Not long after they first met, Carrington creeps into his room by dead of night, intending to cut it off as a prank. He wakes up just before she begins to snip, looks into her eyes, and she is mesmerised. As a couple, they're altogether too eccentric to fit comfortably into the stereotype of emotionally repressed lovers.

Strachey is, almost by definition, odd, but, compared to the other examples of English masculinity on display, he seems a paragon of common sense. Hampton takes great pleasure in satirising the behaviour of the various boyfriends who flit through Carrington's life. There's Mark Gertler, the East End painter (played by Rufus Sewell in manic groove) who comes across as a ridiculous caricature of the conventional romantic artist; there's her husband, 'Ralph' Partridge, an upright, unimaginative Englishman with all the conversational ability of the average 'Norwegian dentist', and there's her lover, Gerald Brenan, an intense, D. H. Lawrence-type who wants to run away with her to Spain.

Most of the action takes place in rooms or gardens. There are few big set pieces. Hampton, roped in to direct his own script when Mike Newell withdrew from the project at the last minute, avoids Merchant-Ivory-style grandeur. He places as much emphasis on looks and glances between the characters, on Michael Nyman's score and on Denis Lenoir's lighting, as on his own dialogue. In one telling scene, an excluded Carrington stands outside at dusk, looking in at the windows of the house as the various couples (Strachey with his new boyfriend, Partridge with his new mistress) prepare for bed. Hampton also has an eye for detail: after Strachey's death, Carrington is shown burning his possessions, and there's a little close-up of his round spectacles on the fire.

Ultimately, *Carrington* relies on its two central performances. Both are mannered – given the quiddities of the characters they're playing, they could hardly be otherwise. Pryce, pipe-smoking, swathed in tweed and with that extraordinary beard, may strike an irritating note with his affected diction, but shows such precision of gesture and such gentleness that he manages to make what easily could have been a caricature immensely moving. Emma Thompson is hardly a natural androgyne, but she, too, is effective, capturing both Carrington's fiery non-conformism and her vulnerability, her bafflement at her own all-consuming obsession with a man she has next to nothing in common with. Wipe off the high culture gloss and period sheen, and the film emerges as a delicately observed, very affecting melodrama.

Geoffrey Macnab

LE HUSSARD SUR LE TOIT
(THE HORSEMAN ON THE ROOF)
France 1995
Director: Jean-Paul Rappeneau

Provence, the 1830s. Angelo, a young Italian Hussar and supporter of his country's Nationalist cause, is hiding from Hapsburg agents in a French town. Betrayed by a friend and almost trapped by his pursuers, Angelo flees to the Provençal countryside. In a village ravaged by disease he meets a doctor treating the dead and dying who then succumbs himself. Angelo befriends a governess and her two charges. Despite the town being quarantined, Angelo manages to escape. Arriving at Manosque, he is immediately suspected of well-poisoning by a rampaging lynch mob of paranoid locals. He is pursued through the town both by the locals and the agents who have caught up with him. Taking refuge in what appears to be an empty house, Angelo is surprised to find the house inhabited by a single occupant, a dignified young woman named Pauline de Théus, who feeds him.

Waking up alone, Angelo leaves the town, discovering along the way that the governess and her children have died. He finally meets Guiseppe, his compatriot, who explains that he was coerced into giving away Angelo's whereabouts to his pursuers. Reunited with Pauline, she and Angelo breach a military *cordon sanitaire* and escape into the countryside. They encounter a peasant huckster who guides them. While waiting outside a house, Angelo overhears that Pauline is married and is searching for her husband who is rumoured quarantined in Manosque. Angelo attempts to dissuade her from returning to look for him, but relents and accompanies her. They are both quarantined but, although unable to find her husband, manage to escape. The pair make their way to a deserted household where they rest and drink hot wine. Pauline starts to show symptoms of cholera which Angelo treats by massaging her. Her husband arrives and Angelo returns to Italy. The pair exchange letters and Pauline is seen standing alone facing the mountain frontier with Italy.

*   *   *

Around fifty different locations, 130 days of shooting, over 100 sets, nearly 1000 costumes especially made; these were some of the publicly-hyped elements involved in the making of *The Horseman on the Roof*, reputedly the most expensive French film ever produced, with a budget of FF176 million (at least FF16 million more than Léos Carax's *Les Amants du Pont-Neuf*). Thankfully, its budget is not its only distinguishing feature. Jean-Paul Rappeneau's *Cyrano de Bergerac* effectively revived the sumptuously dressed historical drama as a highly exportable staple of French film production (the last time it had been so central was in the period after the war, before the *nouvelle vague*). Depending on what one thinks of the genre, the director has either a lot to answer for or a lot to live up to. Despite the French heritage film's importance, both financially and in terms of its exportability, there is a longstanding critical hostility to this cinema. This was rooted in the *nouvelle vague*'s assault on the staid overdressed nostalgia of *le cinéma de papa* in the 1950s and has since gained a wider currency in French criticism.

Patrice Chéreau's *La Reine Margot* did its utmost to internalise such criticisms and, while *Horseman* is nowhere near as bloody and brooding, it succeeds by working elements of the Western and the Saturday morning adventure-romp into the French tradition of cloak and dagger films. Figures on horseback set against gorgeous Provençal horizons abound, giving the film's visuals a neo-Western mythic quality. The concentration on horizons, frontiers and borders also relates to Angelo's exile from his Italian homeland. The adventure element generates a confident sense of narrative drive, one that is unashamedly old-fashioned in its disregard for plausibility; while everyone else around them is wracked by pestilence, Angelo and Pauline gallop blithely on undeterred into the next adventure. The cholera catches up with Pauline only when they reach the abandoned château. Angelo's night-long, life-saving *frottage* of Pauline acts as a sexualised healing, a barely sublimated release of the erotic tension between them.

Rappeneau took the calculated risk of casting a relatively unknown young actor against Binoche, but Olivier Martinez is given a fair amount of screen time to establish himself before happening upon Binoche's Pauline. His Angelo is dashing and agile, a mother-obsessed young Italian patriot whose single-minded devotion to the cause of his country's independence is the source of his invulnerability and his obdurate dedication to duty that oscillates between gallantry and petulance. Binoche makes Pauline resourceful and mysterious. More mature than her gentlemanly escort, she gently mocks his peevishness when he learns she is married to a much older man. Developing through encounters with adversity, theirs is a relationship that neatly dovetails into a growing companionship. It is suggested that their final separation will only be temporary. En route some pleasing secondary performances are offered, including: François Cluzet's driven, doomed medic; Isabelle Carré's attractive young governess; and particularly Gérard Depardieu's near-burlesque cameo as a harried magistrate and Jean Yanne as an untrustworthy huckster.

The film's locations alternate between the detail-drenched depiction of enclosed towns and the parched splendour of the Provençal mountains, but particular emphasis is placed on the accurately reconstructed period roofs of Manosque. The town was the much loved home of the original novel's author, Jean Giono, whose prolific literary output rested on an abiding investment in authentic peasant culture. Pantheist, pacifist and fervent believer in the virtues of peasantry, Giono, like Marcel Pagnol, was one of French literature's devoted regionalists. In choosing to adapt Giono's 1951 novel *Le Hussard sur le toit*, Rappeneau taps into two levels of literary patrimony: he inherits not only Giono's own particular brand of peasant fabulation but also a legacy from Stendhal, the nineteenth-century novelist whose intimacy with Italian affairs of the 1820s strongly informed Giono's depiction of Angelo's exile.

The film's headlong narrative thrust derives from the well balanced combinations of Angelo's flight from cholera and his pursuit by Austrian agents, his yearning to return to fight in Italy and his progress as stymied by the cholera. Themes of exile and disease, selflessness and monomaniac dedication propel the story forward through its numerous bottlenecks in a tension-and-release dynamic. The narrative surges through towns teeming either with cholera or a feverish panicked fear of the cholera and bursts out into landscapes patrolled by platoons of soldiers. *The Horseman* can lightly set off disease, death and political terror very effectively against the beauty of Provence, itself a gift to any director with a budget the size of Rappeneau's and assisted by Thierry Arbogast's cinematography. *The Horseman* is a more than capable and entertaining romp.

Chris Darke

LES MISÉRABLES
(LES MISÉRABLES DU VINGTIÈME SIÈCLE)
France 1995
Director: Claude Lelouch

At a grand ball in 1899, an impostor aristocrat is uncovered, and flees. His car breaks down and, while his chauffeur Henri Fortin tinkers with the engine, he shoots himself. Fortin is arrested, convicted of his murder and imprisoned. His wife Catherine and son (also called Henri) find work in a rough bar in a tiny Normandy sea village, but the wife has to prostitute herself to pay for Fortin's lawyer. Fortin attempts to escape, is betrayed and chooses to fall to his death. His wife kills herself. Henri grows up to be a boxer, retaining the championship for thirteen years after World War I, when he becomes a furniture remover.

The Zimans are a mixed-race couple living in 1940s Paris under the Nazis: André is a Jewish lawyer, Elise a Catholic ballet dancer. They have a daughter, Salomé. Jews are under threat, so the Zimans move to Vichy. Fortin drives the truck, helping them evade a checkpoint. As they drive, he asks them about Victor Hugo's *Les Misérables*; he recently saved two men's lives by lifting a piano off them, and people have called him 'Valjean' ever since (Jean Valjean, the central character in Hugo's classic novel *Les Misérables*, is famously strong and saves lives by lifting things). Fortin is illiterate: so the Zimans begin reading him the novel. They arrive at their new house, but are threatened with exposure and decide to flee again, this time to the Swiss border. Fortin, pretending to be Salomé's father, helps place her in a Catholic school. At the border, the Zimans join other fleeing Jews, but are betrayed. Most are shot: André is wounded, but escapes. A farmer and wife help him recover. Elise is captured, recognised as the famous ballet dancer, made to dress up and escort Nazi officers at parties, before being sent to a Polish death-camp. In Salomé's school, the Mother Superior guesses her background and protects her.

Fortin is arrested for transporting Jews, and tortured. He says nothing, escapes, and joins a band of burglars in Paris. André writes regular letters to Salomé from hiding, paying the farmer couple from a secret Swiss bank account. The wife falls in love with him. Her drunken husband, although jealous, tolerates this unrequited passion, but concocts a plan to rob him. Nazi war fortunes are waning, but Ziman is told that his family are dead and he can never come out of hiding. The burglars realise the war is ending, and belatedly join the Resistance. In the Normandy village where Fortin grew up, they blow up a pillbox during the Allied landings. Fortin becomes a hero, and then

Mayor. Salomé joins him there; then Elise, liberated from the deathcamps. His old burglar pals turn up, police in pursuit, among them the ex-Vichy policeman who once tortured Fortin. Fortin helps the burglars, but there's a siege, and they take the policeman hostage. Torn, Fortin rescues him; after a shoot-out, the police arrest Fortin. He confronts the policeman with his Vichy past: the policeman exits the car and shoots himself. Fortin is charged with his murder. Ziman, still hiding, doesn't know the war is over. The farmer couple, planning to poison him, have withdrawn all his money, but they argue and kill one another. After a time, Ziman ventures out, finds the bodies, his money and newspapers proclaiming the Nazi surrender. He arrives in the Normandy village in time to defend Fortin, successfully. Fortin becomes Mayor again, and Salomé marries the grandson of the bar-owners who gave Fortin and Catherine work long ago.

* * *

In part a film version of Victor Hugo's vast, baggy, nineteenth-century social-conscience melodrama, a French-Lit institution reshaped to explore life under occupation during World War II, *Les Misérables* is also a film about the pleasures and power of reading. Both projects risk disaster, and yet Claude Lelouch – though a notoriously manipulative sentimentalist, as the soft-focus vapidity of his not-so-new-wave *Un homme et une femme* (1966) shows – rather unexpectedly wins us over with the second, and thus evades the more egregious pitfalls of the first. After a somewhat creaky start (forty years of plot exposition), and in the teeth of unavoidable narrative unlikeliness, the director has managed something rather impressive.

Much of the Ziman/Fortin plot echoes Hugo's, despite obvious differences of historical context and possibility. But Lelouch also constantly revisits famous scenes in the book itself, with its decades-long plot and miasma of coincidence, using the same actors to dramatise the readings: thus Belmondo plays Fortin *and* Valjean, while Philippe Khorsand plays Fortin's torturer and Valjean's pitiless-but-honourable nemesis Javert. What this achieves, against all odds, is a credible rendering of the way all kinds of people are brought together (or indeed kept apart) by a book they know. Artfully, Lelouch plays as much with readerly impatience as well as readerly devotion – when Fortin and a burglar pal duck into a cinema to hide out, and find themselves watching *Les Misérables* on-screen. Fortin summarises what they've missed, laughing at the over-the-topness of some of the plot. When Ziman summarises the plot, Salomé has always to correct him. At other times, the lush physicality of reading is slyly invoked, a celebration of books as sensuous objects. The implication is that when the world turns sour this great story is all our stories; which Lelouch 'proves' by juggling differences as well as similarities. Unlike Hollywood, he refuses to fawn on literature, which is fun to watch.

Sometimes the deep argument seems awry: unlike scheming French collaborators obeying Vichy laws, Fortin was just a housebreaker, but if he does good because he's illiterate and knows no better, why are we cheering his induction into the Hugo readers' club? Lelouch's argument is probably that *Les Misérables*, as universally loved popular culture, should be distinguished from all literary and art élitisms and legalisms that challenge and distort the good in all of us, however lowly born. Which is a hard row to hoe in discussion of France under Occupation, and we may not be convinced (intellectually) that the forms, devices and assumptions of the classic Hugo novel tell us that much about doing the right thing in the hardest of times: the evil of circumstance was hardly the only peril French Jews faced in the 1940s, and did Victor Hugo readers really make better moral choices than non-readers in this regard?

But Lelouch after all knows two or three things about applied heart-tugging, and deploys his own childhood memories of this period and evacuation, combining them with a genuine gift for striking moments: a huddle of nervous Jews, in their best bourgeois travelling clothes, waiting in eerie blue dawn light to dash across the snow to freedom or doom; a vast school hall full of small French girls banging pianos to cheer their black American liberators; the relentlessly sinister return to a Nazi commandant who is also a brilliant pianist, and whose demonically expressionist playing merges into several of the soundtrack's emotional climaxes. Though Michel Boujenah is something of a cartoon as regards his 'Jewish' look (his make-up not that far from plastic glasses/nose/moustache), the Zimans' husband–wife arguments are well-observed, especially their spats of superficial recrimination (as if each considers the war the others' fault). The drunken banter between farmer and wife is even better, Philippe Léotard, his usual excellent self, weak and villainous yet strangely sympathetic. Belmondo is also well used: his unsurprisable fleshy blankness gradually softening and sunnying up as the written word enters his soul, and as the hardest of times ends around him. When we find ourselves tearfully pleasured at Claude Lelouch's wholly implausible happy ending, at once a giddy hommage to Renoir (painter/*père*, not film-maker/*fils*) and the virtues of uncorked uprush and silly delighted release from the terrors that went before, we realise that the irrational grip of human-scale decency clutches at film reviewers, too, sometimes. And what's wrong with that?

Mark Sinker

SENSE AND SENSIBILITY
United Kingdom 1995
Director: Ang Lee

It is late eighteenth-century England. When their father dies, sisters Elinor and Marianne Dashwood, teenage Margaret and their mother lose their home and inheritance, Norland Park, in Sussex, because it passes to John, Mr Dashwood's son by his first marriage. They are left £500 a year to live on between them. John's socially ambitious wife, Fanny, wastes no time in taking over at Norland, and when Mrs Dashwood's cousin Sir John Middleton offers the four women a cottage to live in on his Devon estate, they reluctantly accept – despite the unspoken attachment growing between the sensible Elinor and Fanny's shy brother Edward Ferrars.

Although Fanny claims that Edward's mother will never allow the match, Elinor is silently disappointed when he fails to visit Devon. Country life is made more of a trial by the crass matchmaking of Sir John and his mother-in-law Mrs Jennings, who try to pair up Marianne with Colonel Brandon, a sombre bachelor twice her age. Mrs Jennings tells Elinor of Brandon's 'tragic past': barred from marrying the woman he loved, Eliza, he later learned she had fallen into prostitution and found her dying in a poorhouse.

Out walking, Marianne twists her ankle and is rescued by the handsome John Willoughby. Mesmerised by him, she rebuffs the smitten Brandon with cruel indifference, but Elinor grows suspicious about Willoughby when he shows an unexplained hostility to the Colonel. Willoughby suddenly departs for London with no plans to return, leaving Marianne distraught. Meanwhile, Elinor is forcibly befriended by a young woman, Lucy Steele, who confides that she has been secretly engaged to Edward for five years, against his mother's wishes.

Sent with Elinor to stay in London, Marianne becomes feverishly obsessed with trying to see Willoughby. Eventually she spots him at a ball, but his snub sends her into shock. A letter stating that his affections 'have long been engaged elsewhere', worsens her condition, and Elinor confides the situation to Brandon. Brandon reveals that Eliza left an illegitimate daughter, Beth, whom Brandon had promised to care for; a year ago, Willoughby made her pregnant. Cut off by his benefactor aunt in punishment, Willoughby abandoned Marianne in order to make a wealthy marriage.

Fanny explodes when Lucy reveals the secret engagement, and Edward – who had been honouring it solely out of duty – is disinherited as a result. Brandon tells Elinor he plans to offer Edward the parish on his estate to make him financially able to marry Lucy, but that the offer must come from Elinor. Alone with Elinor, Edward finally expresses his feeling for her, but she insists he must stand by Lucy. Back in Devon, Marianne wanders in the rain until she collapses on the hill where she met Willoughby. Rescued by Brandon, she almost dies of a fever, but eventually pulls through. News arrives that Lucy and Mr Ferrars are married, but it turns out that when Edward was disinherited, Lucy married his younger brother instead. Edward proposes to Elinor and Marianne happily marries Brandon.

*   *   *

On the face of it, the Taiwanese-American director Ang Lee and England's most-adapted dead lady novelist might seem as perverse a pairing as *Sense and Sensibility*'s threatened union of Lucy Steele and Edward Ferrars – or, indeed, the marriage of convenience at the core of Lee's earlier film *The Wedding Banquet* in which a young gay Taiwanese gets hitched to a Shanghaiese art student in order to deflect his parents' attention from his true sexuality. In practice, Lee's *Sense and Sensibility* is easily the most enjoyable – and, more significantly, the least complacent – of the recent rash of Jane Austen adaptations.

While screenwriter-star Emma Thompson is already a likely Academy Award contender, the film's flavour owes as much to Lee's expertise as an observer of familial and social codes, constraints and conflict as it does to her droll feminist-revisionist script. Described by critic Tony Tanner as 'a society which forced people to be at once very sociable and very private', the world of *Sense and Sensibility* has more than superficial affinities with the world of *The Wedding Banquet* – in which revellers invade the newlyweds' bedroom and refuse to leave until bride and groom are naked in bed together – or the world of Lee's more recent *Eat Drink Man Woman* – in which three young Taipei career women sit down resentfully each night in obedience to the ritual of a meal cooked by their chef father. All three films focus on narrow social worlds in which private desires and emotions are subordinated to strict regulation by tradition, social mores and the law of the parent while at the same time being subjected to incessant public scrutiny.

Sense and Sensibility is about how two sisters of contrasting temperaments, Elinor (who has too much sense) and Marianne (who has too much romantic sensibility) deal – or fail to deal – with such contradictions. Where Elinor entirely conceals her feelings for Edward even as he haltingly tries to declare his love for her, Marianne cannot hide her emotions for five minutes even if this means being rude or cruel. To a modern audience, Marianne's spontaneous directness is more appealing than Elinor's self-repression, but in the society she inhabits, such openness is a transgression – hence the mass shock which greets her reproach of Willoughby at the ball ('Good God, Willoughby! Will you not shake hands with me?'). As Marianne's subsequent psychosomatic illness hints, lone rebellion against such powerful social forces can be a route to madness.

A particular preoccupation in Thompson's script is the problem of female non-inheritance. Where in the novel the tortuous terms on which Elinor and Marianne's father inherited Norland Park from an uncle leave him powerless to pass it on to his wife and daughters, the film tells us that their inheritance is denied them by the law. ('Boys inherit, girls don't,' Elinor bluntly tells Margaret.) The deathbed scene in which Mr Dashwood breaks the news to their half-brother John that his will contains barely any provision for the women gives us every reason to think this law is sanctioned by the father. This feminist sensibility extends to the reinvention of Elinor and Marianne's teenage sister, Margaret, as a tomboy with a taste for tree houses and adventure – Emilie François, who plays her, is as impressive a find as Anna Paquin was in *The Piano*.

Where *Sense and Sensibility* really scores, though, is in a broad, self-mocking satirical energy, pleasingly at odds with both the politeness of older Austen adaptations and the sexed-up patronising 'updating' of the BBC's recent *Pride and Prejudice*. The hunting-and-shooting Sir John Middleton is a figure of Dickensian boisterousness whose ribald prying into Elinor and Marianne's affairs of the heart is intrusive enough to make even the viewer squirm. Edward, on paper one of the dullest suitors in literary history, is here transformed – in a miraculous departure from Hugh Grant's recent form – into a mumbling super-nerd muffled so deep in shyness that when he does speak his meaning stays runically opaque. (One hilarious scene has Thompson trying to coax a baffling sentence from him, while his own horse snorts in disgust.)

On the down side, Grant's performance begs the question of what on earth Elinor sees in Edward – but then this *Sense and Sensibility*'s attitude to romance is tongue-in-cheek. The movie's prime amorous interest, Willoughby (played by Thompson's real-life lover Greg Wise), is unquestionably a sex god in waiting; but Wise's performance – from his entry on a white charger to his smarmy courtship of the breathless Marianne – is bracketed in such colossal ironic quote marks that it's impossible not to laugh even as you swoon. This subversive spirit even enables Lee to pull off the trick the novel never managed, namely persuading us that Marianne really *has* shifted her affections to Brandon – but then, Austen's rheumaticky Colonel has been granted the dry wit of Alan Rickman. *Sense and Sensibility* might just be the heritage movie that girls who like boys who hate heritage movies will get away with taking those boys to see.

Claire Monk

RIDICULE
France 1996
Director: Patrice Leconte

Versailles in the 1780s. The Chevalier de Milletail tells old Comte de Blayac that he ruined his life long ago with a cruel witticism: as a revenge he pees over him and the old man dies of shock.

In the Dombes marshes near Lyons, Ponceludon de Malavoy witnesses the miserable, disease-ridden life of his peasants. He sets off to Versailles to get the King's support for his drainage plans, arriving as his protector, Blayac, has just died. After Ponceludon is mugged in a wood, the Marquis de Bellegarde takes him under his protection and, while warning him about corruption at the court, sets out to help him.

At court, Ponceludon meets the Abbé de Vilecourt and the Comtesse de Blayac. Initially ridiculed for his country airs, he quickly impresses with his wit. Bellegarde's daughter Mathilde announces that she will marry old and rich Monsieur de Montalieri to finance her underwater research. Ponceludon tries to establish his peerage in order to see the King and witnesses intrigue and corruption around him. He and Mathilde are attracted to each other, but she still plans to marry Montalieri. At court, Ponceludon wins a contest of rhymed verse with Vilecourt and secretly discovers that Vilecourt and Madame de Blayac cheat.

In return for his silence, de Blayac seduces him and helps him see the King. The Baron de Guéret hangs himself after being ridiculed by Vilecourt. Madame de Blayac's horse is frightened by Paul (Bellegarde's deaf-and-dumb servant), and she falls. She banishes Paul to the Abbé de l'Epée's institution, despite Mathilde's plea. She agrees to Vilecourt's request to send Ponceludon away, by ridiculing him at a dinner. He returns to his château, to find a child dying from marsh fever. Mathilde gives up Montalieri and Vilecourt disgraces himself in front of the King. Ponceludon comes back to Madame de Blayac, who promises another encounter with the King. The Abbé de l'Epée displays the achievements of his deaf-and-dumb pupils (including Paul) to the court. Ponceludon impresses the King but is provoked in duel by a jealous officer, whom he kills. He joins Mathilde. Furious, Madame de Blayac intrigues so that the King refuses to see Ponceludon again. He and Mathilde go to a costume ball, where he is humiliated, but gets the upper hand by berating the party for their cruelty. He leaves with Mathilde for his château. In 1793, Bellegarde has emigrated to England after the Revolution. Intertitles tell us that the government started draining the Dombes that year.

* * *

This accomplished costume film comes from the eclectic Patrice Leconte, director of numerous popular comedies (from *Les Bronzés* to *Tango*) and psychological dramas

(*Monsieur Hire, Le Mari de la coiffeuse*). But rather than an auteur film, *Ridicule* is better understood as a genre piece, which shares with other French heritage films polished production values, a taste for a popularised version of history, and a delight in the French language.

'Ridicule' is the leitmotif of the film, the emotion which dominates the twilight years of Louis XVI, since, at court, appearance is all. Top courtiers Vilecourt and Madame de Blayac (and by implication the whole regime) rule through inflicting ridicule, while others go to extraordinary lengths to avenge themselves against it: for instance Milletail in the opening scene. Contrary to the popular French saying that 'ridicule does not kill', old Blayac and Guéret die from it.

The lethal weapon in this warfare is language, and more specifically wit, which Bellegarde attempts to record in its multifarious forms (repartees, witticisms, lampoons, humour, and so on) while he conducts his scientific experiments. As in *Cyrano de Bergerac*, language is the principal instrument of seduction and as such, as Bellegarde says, it 'opens doors'. It also provides the film with its most effective comic moments. Linguistic refinement, with its rigid codes ('never laugh at your own jokes' warns Bellegarde) is the verbal parallel of the other cultural refinements of the court and of this type of film, witnessed in the splendid interiors and magnificent costumes of the courtiers.

In a none-too-subtle contrast, the ritualised and corrupt old order of the court is opposed to the new broom of scientific progress arising from the Enlightenment (Voltaire and Rousseau are explicitly referenced to in the film). Powdered wigs and elaborate costumes are contrasted with flowing dresses, long hair and naked skin as well as Mathilde's diving suit. The *mise-en-scène* is visually structured by an alternation between highly decorated indoor sets bathed in filtered light and open location shots of nature: woods, rivers, marshes. This opposition is further projected on to the two main female characters: Madame de Blayac, who powders her entire body, and Mathilde who spends a lot of time under water and collects pollen from the Versailles gardens in her skirts. While the Comtesse shines through her use of language, Mathilde is in tune with the deaf-and-dumb servant. Meanwhile, the male hero may travel between the two worlds and the two women. If this rather systematic and traditionally gendered structure is a weakness of the film, its strength is to show the hero truly torn between the two worlds.

Like the film, and like the whole genre, Ponceludon recognises the exquisite pleasure of performance and ritual, and the knowingness of its seduction, and it does not take him long to transform himself from idealistic *hobereau* (local squire) to sophisticated wit. The point of the framing story is to show how the system perpetuates itself by turning victim into executioner, but also to contrast with Ponceludon's ability to break that particular circle. Reminiscent of the highly structured fairy tales discussed by Vladimir Propp, here Ponceludon is rewarded with the 'pure' woman, daughter of his kindly mentor. For though Mathilde is initially prepared to use her sexuality to further her ambitions (like Madame de Blayac), she is redeemed by true love, by the progressive nature of her ambitions and by the nature imagery in which she is placed throughout the film.

Not so Madame de Blayac. As in *Les Liaisons dangereuses*, the sexually manipulative woman must receive the harshest punishment. She is not disfigured (like Madame de Merteuil in *Les Liaisons*), but one of the last images of the film is a long close-up of her ravaged face. Once she has removed her mask she has, literally, lost face. So had her male partner Vilecourt earlier on, abandoned by all after his philosophical gaffe. But his disgrace is social. Hers is social and sexual, because her deception is conceived as pertaining to her sex. This is graphically illustrated by the rhymed verse contest between Vilecourt and Ponceludon, in which Vilecourt's fraudulent little pieces of paper are literally stuck in her fan.

Yet the femme fatale and the evil characters are, as ever, the most interesting. Fanny Ardant's superb Madame de Blayac and Bernard Giraudeau's wicked Abbé de Vilecourt stand out from the excellent ensemble cast, which includes Jean Rochefort, hero of *Le Mari de la coiffeuse*. And as in many classic French films, they overshadow the central romantic couple played by Charles Berling and Judith Godrèche. This illustrates the central paradox of the film, which sets out to criticise an order and mode of performance which it cannot but help admire and which fundamentally sustains it.

Ginette Vincendeau

MRS. BROWN
United Kingdom/USA/Ireland 1997
Director: John Madden

A grieving widow in 1861, Queen Victoria is joined on the Isle of Wight by her Highland pony and its handler, John Brown. He quickly antagonises her family and courtiers by his abrupt manner and plain speaking, but begins to coax the Queen out of her cocoon of widowhood. Increasingly imperious with the other servants and contemptuous of those around the Queen, Brown becomes her closest personal servant, obsessively concerned about her health and security.

Back in the Highlands, he prises her further out of the court circle and thwarts an attempt by journalists to spy on her. However, persuaded by Prime Minister Benjamin Disraeli that the monarchy is threatened by the Queen's continuing withdrawal from public life and by the rumours casting her as 'Mrs. Brown', Brown influences her to return to public life. Perceiving this as a betrayal of their close friendship, the Queen re-establishes a chilly, formal relationship with him.

His obsession with her security continues and he foils a would-be assassin, but his frenzied dash into the cold Balmoral night to confront an imagined interloper brings on a fatal bout of pneumonia. He and the Queen are reconciled on his deathbed.

* * *

In the rendering of the assured *Mrs. Brown* – the story of Queen Victoria's relationship with John Brown, one of her grooms – experienced television director John Madden (*Inspector Morse*) delivers an acute portrait of the petrified court at Osborne House: vast arrays of servants are frozen into immobility yet ready to jump to the sovereign's merest whim; great swathes of black fabric rustle as the Queen and her attentive entourage sweep through the corridors; and elegantly languid compositions and camera movements provide appropriate formal correlatives of the social milieu depicted. It is into this funereal, Byzantine world that John Brown blows like a great northern gale. Indeed, it is the clash between Brown's values and those of the court that is the centre of dramatic tension in the film. The narrative shift is delivered via Brown's gradual 'rescue' of the Queen from the suffocating artificiality of the court.

Although British film (and television) historical drama is often ideologically pernicious, its virtues are considerable. British set and costume design surpass those of other countries and the quality of British acting training particularly favours historical subjects. *Mrs. Brown* is further proof of this, with the supporting performances by Geoffrey Palmer as the Queen's private secretary Henry Ponsonby and Anthony Sher's shamelessly camp depiction of Benjamin Disraeli, testifying to the depth of talent and tradition in British historical drama. However, their roles also function as embodiments of the effete English establishment against which the Queen and Brown must struggle. Precisely because their roles involve struggle, Judi Dench and Billy Connolly are permitted depths and nuances not available to the other characters.

The narrative requirement of popular cinema that heterosexual love be at the centre of every story is handled with considerable subtlety in the writing, directing and playing here. When the Queen and Brown arrive back at Balmoral from a jolly sojourn at a ghillie's cottage, the royal physician puts down the flush in her cheeks to drink. Ponsonby demurs, but forbids the physician to speculate further about the reason for Victoria's flushed cheeks.

One scene in particular, however, testifies to the film's subtlety. Brown indicates to the Queen that in order to preserve her reputation he should resign and withdraw from her circle. In the course of their verbal exchanges, she utters the words 'I cannot live without you'. In a modern context, such words would carry a heavy erotic charge. Without wholly losing this charge, the film shifts the meaning much more towards the sense that Brown is her indispensable support in the performance of her regal role. Although such nuances spring primarily from Dench, because it is her assignment to make the dramatic transition from atrophied widow to reawakened woman, the film also hints at darkly paranoid depths in Brown's character, indications strengthened by our familiarity with the usually manic quality of Connolly's performances.

So accomplished are *Mrs. Brown*'s writing, directing, acting and technical features that they tend to mask the extent to which it is operating an ideological con trick. Brown is constructed to represent a breath of earthy air entering the musty court of St James. What is obscured, however, is that his apparent irreverence (for example, he habitually addresses the Queen as 'Woman') conceals a deeper servitude which leaves the institution of monarchy unquestioned. Brown is the direct analogue, in those US-made films about the ante-bellum south, of the 'house nigger', whose licensed insolence masks the cruel injustice of slavery. And there is much talk in *Mrs. Brown* of the threat of republicanism, but no hint that it might be rather a good idea. There is another sense in which *Mrs. Brown* is ideologically suspect. Although it is an infinitely superior film to *Braveheart*, it shares with that and the other so-called 'kilt movies' a traditional, indeed hegemonic, conception about Scotland in which the English are portrayed as élitist, repressed and effete while the Scots are depicted as demotic, 'natural' and warm-hearted. Apparently complimentary to the Scots, this is in fact a discourse which confirms their subjection. As is so often the case with British films, *Mrs. Brown*'s excellence as a film diverts attention from its questionable subtexts.

Colin McArthur

WILDE
United Kingdom/USA/Japan/Germany 1997
Director: Brian Gilbert

During his 1882 lecture tour of the United States, Oscar Wilde visits a silver mine in Colorado and flirts with the miners. Back in London, he marries Constance Lloyd; she is soon pregnant with the first of their two children. But when he is seduced by their Canadian houseguest Robbie Ross, Wilde finally admits to himself that he is primarily attracted to men and starts making excuses to his wife so that he can spend time with Ross. His conscience is assuaged by the financial success of *The Picture of Dorian Gray*.

At the triumphant first night of *Lady Windermere's Fan*, Wilde is greatly smitten by Lord Alfred Douglas, known as 'Bosie', a student at Oxford. Learning that Bosie is being blackmailed by a male prostitute, Wilde volunteers his own lawyer to deal with the matter – and gets sexually involved with Bosie. Their affair quickly cools (Bosie is in constant need of new excitements), but they remain close friends and make frequent visits to Alfred Taylor's male brothel in Cleveland Street; Wilde finds himself picking up the bills not only for their meals and excursions together, but also for Bosie's gambling debts and other expenses. They have many rows. Constance, meanwhile, tells Wilde's old friend Ada Leverson that she blames herself for driving her husband away by devoting herself to the children.

Bosie tries to pacify his tyrannical and curmudgeonly father, the Marquess of Queensberry, by introducing him to Wilde in a restaurant; the peer seems charmed, but afterwards threatens to disinherit Bosie if he ever again meets Wilde. The relationship does end after one particularly intense row, but Wilde relents when he discovers that Bosie's brother Francis has died. Queensberry repeatedly tries to catch Bosie and Wilde together, without success. After failing to disrupt the first night of *The Importance of Being Earnest*, he leaves a note at Wilde's club, calling him a 'posing Somdomite'.

Scoffing at the misspelling, Bosie urges Wilde to sue Queensberry for libel. Ross (who has remained close to both Wilde and Constance) foresees disaster if the case comes to court, and is proved right when Queensberry's lawyer produces working-class boys from Taylor's brothel to testify against Wilde. Arrested and sentenced to two years' hard labour, Wilde overnight becomes a 'non-person' in London society. Despite the scandal, Constance stands by him, visiting him in Reading Gaol and promising never to divorce him – on condition that he never sees Bosie again.

On his release, Wilde hands the manuscript of *De Profundis* to Ada. Mourning Constance, who has died, he travels to France with Ross. His resolve to cut Bosie out of his life soon cracks and he goes to Italy to find him. Closing captions explain that

Wilde left Bosie for good three months later, and died in 1900. Bosie himself died in 1945. Ross died in 1918 and his ashes were reinterred alongside Wilde's in 1950.

* * *

The underlying rationale for this biopic – the first since the rival Ken Hughes and Gregory Ratoff versions of 1960 – comes straight from the tabloid press: Now It Can Be Told! 'At last, at the end of the twentieth century,' the press notes helpfully explain, 'it is possible for a film to present a rounded picture of the Irish-born writer, of his hubris and of the consuming passion which brought him down. No longer is there any need to falsify or ignore the sexual elements which are important parts of this story.' The film thus climbs into bed with recent initiatives to reclaim Oscar for Gay Awareness, both radical (Neil Bartlett's book *Who Was That Man?*, Derek Jarman's campaign for a memorial to 'Saint Oscar') and conservative (Maggi Hambling's twee sculpture of Oscar gossiping from the grave).

Wilde may well be the first film to show Oscar in bed with boys, entranced by the Cleveland Street brothel and watching Bosie fuck a 'renter' in a hotel room, but it isn't the first to tell the story of a gay intellectual brought down by a consuming passion for an exploitative slut. Fassbinder staked out this ground in disguised but extremely self-aware autobiographical terms in *The Bitter Tears of Petra von Kant*, and Gus van Sant redefined it in street-level, ethnic terms in *Mala Noche*. More recently, Ira Sachs has finessed the story's 'tragic' elements into something more ambiguous in *The Delta*. *Wilde* is nowhere near this league. It doesn't wonder why men like Oscar fall for boys like Bosie in the first place, let alone why Bosie's increasingly cruel and selfish behaviour keeps Oscar coming back for more; rather than trying to grasp the underlying dynamics of such relationships, it settles for 'heritage' soap opera with a muck-raking spin. This approach, like the visual style, is impossibly dated.

Oscar liked to insist that fictional speculations were more important than mere facts, but the film lacks the courage to ditch its feeble aspirations to historiography. Events with repercussions in Oscar's life – noisy first nights in the theatre, the death of Bosie's brother – hang in the background like a nagging conscience, coming into focus only in the arbitrary precision of dates in the opening and closing captions. As 'rounded' biography, though, the film stumbles at the first hurdle when it shies away from imagining how Oscar functioned as a husband, heterosexual partner and father during the early years of the marriage to Constance. Later, there's little about his endless scrabbling for money (the humiliation of his editorship of *The Woman's World* passes unmentioned) and nothing at all about his engrained superstitiousness or his eventual conversion to Catholicism. The one eccentricity in Julian Mitchell's screenplay is the decision to place voiceover readings from Oscar's fairy tales on top of the montages which gloss the phases of the life no one can be bothered to dramatise: interludes with the family, the melodramatic horrors of Reading Gaol. The implication that Oscar lived out a fantasy, but had to battle real-life ogres such as Queensberry and the Victorian prison system seems, to say the least, tendentious.

Given the overriding emphasis on bad times with Bosie (the rows are dramatised more or less verbatim from Oscar's own recriminatory accounts in *De Profundis*), it's sad that Stephen Fry and Jude Law – both manifestly capable of going deeper – are limited by the film's overall *Masterpiece Theater* approach. The dismal lack of wit behind the camera coupled with the scrupulous avoidance of anything – frontal nudity, for example – which would earn the film an 'R' rating in the United States might win *Wilde* the wide American release the film-makers clearly crave. If so, it's ironic that the film's most up-front bid to catch the interest of the multiplex programmers is also its one and only flash of genuine inspiration. This is the title sequence, in which discreet lettering decorated with the inevitable Beardsley curlicues suddenly gives way to widescreen images of a Colorado mining camp in the early 1880s. (As in the days of Spaghetti Westerns, a Spanish landscape doubles for the Old West.) Oscar's banter with the 'angelic' silver miners – he tells them that the greatest silversmith ever was Cellini, now sadly dead; they ask who shot him – serves no dramatic purpose beyond establishing that Oscar was aware of homosexual feelings long before he married Constance, and has no follow-through in the rest of the film. But the scene is both unexpected and mildly charming, and that's something to be grateful for in a film as dull and superficial as *Wilde* turns out to be.

Tony Rayns

MRS DALLOWAY
USA/United Kingdom/Netherlands 1997
Director: Marleen Gorris

On 13 June 1923, Clarissa Dalloway, middle-aged wife of a politician, prepares for the society party she will host that night at her London home. The day's events send her thoughts back to her youth in 1890. Musing on her close friendship with the radical, mischievous Sally Seton (which might have been something more) and on Peter Walsh, the socialist suitor whom she rejected in favour of Richard, she reflects on the different course her life might have taken.

In the street, Clarissa glimpses a young man, Septimus Warren Smith, a war veteran tormented by delayed shell-shock, reacting in terror to a car backfiring. Peter Walsh unexpectedly reappears after years in India and confides that he is in love with a married woman. Septimus' wife Rezia takes him to see a shell-shock specialist, Sir William Bradshaw, because insensitive treatment by another doctor, Holmes, has failed. Bradshaw dismisses Septimus' suicidal urges, but later sends Holmes to institutionalise him, prompting Septimus to jump from a window to his death.

Clarissa greets her party guests. Present are Peter and Sally, now wife of a knighted mill-owner and mother of five – but hostess duties and the arrival of the Prime Minister keep Clarissa from the two people she most wants to see. Bradshaw arrives late due to Septimus' suicide. Clarissa, repelled by his token concern, is traumatised by the news. Alone on a balcony, she anguishes over her fears of life and old age and admires the courage of choosing death, but returns to her party.

*   *   *

Virginia Woolf's formally revolutionary 1925 novel *Mrs Dalloway* offers multi-perspective inner monologues and leaps back and forth across space (1923 London) and time (between the 1923 'present', scarred by World War I, and a remembered 1890 'past'). It could be argued that any attempt to film this book demands a director committed to finding an equally radical cinematic equivalent.

Judged by such criteria, Marleen Gorris' *Mrs Dalloway* – the Dutch feminist director's first film since her matriarchal epic *Antonia's Line* – counts as a failure. Innocent of the critic-pleasing, audience-pulling devices of some recent literary adaptations (such as the tricksy cinematography and hyped-up raunch of *The Wings of the Dove*), its aesthetic recalls the European art cinema of an earlier, less commercially frenzied decade. Designed as if the fiercely stylised spectacle of Sally Potter's *Orlando* had never happened, its realist, object-crammed *mise-en-scène* implies an unfashionable unconcern to be faithful to the period.

In fact, *Mrs Dalloway*'s success is due to the nonchalance of Gorris (working from a script which actress and Woolf buff Eileen Atkins had already written with Redgrave in mind) about such formal and narrative problems. As she indicated in her debut, the darkly comic radical-feminist classic *De Stilte rond Christine M./A Question of Silence*, Gorris is not a director who plays by the usual rules. *Mrs Dalloway*'s art-film appearances, like those of *Antonia's Line*, harbour a robustly female-centred sensibility; but a conventional period aesthetic also coexists with a ruthless unsentimentality and political bite which few recent British period films have fully achieved.

At the same time, *Mrs Dalloway* marks a further mellowing of the black-and-white gender politics of Gorris' earlier films. In *Antonia's Line*, men were bad, benign or sperm donors. Here, their peripherality to the lives women could lead in an ideal non-patriarchal Utopia remains a theme. (Although the unrealised implicitly lesbian partnership between the young Clarissa and the radical Sally Seton is treated with peculiar restraint.) However, the existence of women who use their power to poisonous ends is also admitted, most clearly via the figure of Lady Bruton. She exploits her status as a 'mere' woman to persuade male politicians to sponsor a scheme to 'encourage' unemployable casualties of war – such as shell-shocked Septimus Warren Smith – to emigrate.

A less commented-upon trait of both films is their atheistic humanism, and it is this which Gorris' *Mrs Dalloway* develops into a broader exploration of freedom and power. Where, in *Antonia's Line*, the aged Antonia's decision to die is presented as a positive step, *Mrs Dalloway* embraces the idea that death – or, here, suicide – may be a positive gesture of autonomy for those made powerless. More ambiguously, the film juxtaposes the young Clarissa's 1890 decision to marry Richard with Septimus' 1923 suicide, suggesting that her choice of a partner who will 'leave me room' in preference to his more politically radical rival Peter is a similar gesture of necessity in the face of constraint.

Ultimately, though, *Mrs Dalloway*'s real bite and significance derives less from its expected feminism than from its stance as one of only two recent period releases, along with Gillies MacKinnon's *Regeneration*, to admit knowledge of the Great War and its traumas. In a pointed departure from Woolf's novel, its opening shot shows Warren Smith (whose final hours of anguish are juxtaposed with Mrs Dalloway's party preparations) in the trenches. As Mrs Dalloway says at the outset: 'The war may be over, but there's still the echo of it.' The presence of this echo in the film, together with its chilling snapshots of the attitudes of the rich and powerful (given a grimly comic edge by a flawless cast which includes Margaret Tyzack and Phyllis Calvert), make nostalgic viewing impossible.

Claire Monk

LE BOSSU
(ON GUARD!)
France/Italy/Germany 1997
Director Philippe de Broca

Paris 1699. Foundling Lagardère, a fine swordsman, meets his hero, the rich and handsome Duc de Nevers, in the presence of Philippe d'Orléans, the future Regent. Nevers demonstrates his famous secret sword 'thrust'. His treacherous cousin Gonzague plots to kill him to inherit his fortune, with the help of his henchman Peyrolles. Nevers hires Lagardère as protector (and ennobles him) and together they set off for Caylus castle, where Nevers will marry Blanche, the mother of his baby. But Peyrolles and his gang brutally murder him and the wedding guests. Lagardère escapes with the baby Aurore, swearing revenge, while Gonzague abducts Blanche. Lagardère and Aurore hide with Italian travelling players.

Sixteen years later, Aurore thinks Lagardère is her father. After an attack by strangers, he teaches her the Nevers thrust and later reveals her true identity to her. At a soirée in Paris, decadent aristocrats molest her. In defence, she kills her host with the Nevers thrust; consequently, Gonzague is aware that she and Lagardère have come back. Gonzague is now a rich banker, speculating on the colonial settlement in Louisiana; Blanche is a recluse. Lagardère infiltrates Gonzague's house dressed as a hunchback, ostensibly to help him with his banking activities but really to reunite mother and daughter. Lagardère and Aurore's mutual love blossoms. Gonzague tries to deport her to Louisiana, but Lagardère frees her, escaping another murder attempt by Gonzague, whose villainy is exposed at the Regent's ball. Gonzague is killed in a duel by Lagardère and Aurore, who are officially united.

* * *

Paul Féval's *Le Bossu* was published in 1875 as a newspaper serial and as a book, and was reprinted frequently after that. In the late nineteenth century, Féval was a prominent author of the popular novel, along with Eugène Sue, Victor Hugo and Alexandre Dumas. Though his star waned in the twentieth century, *Le Bossu* remained a popular classic thanks to many film and television adaptations. The 'botte de Nevers', the lethal Nevers sword 'thrust' which hits people between the eyes, as well as Lagardère's cry – 'If you don't come to Lagardère, Lagardère will come to you!' – are stock French expressions, though few now read the book. Daniel Auteuil, as Lagardère, has illustrious predecessors, especially Pierre Blanchar (in Jean Delannoy's 1944 version) and Jean Marais (in André Hunebelle's one of 1960).

Why another version today? Producer Patrick Godeau, scriptwriter Jean Cosmos (who wrote *Le Colonel Chabert* and *D'Artagnan's Daughter*) and director Philippe de

Broca's explanation that they love swashbucklers is no doubt genuine. De Broca's own *Cartouche* (1961, with Jean-Paul Belmondo) is a benchmark of the genre, and his caper movie *L'Homme de Rio* (1964, also with Belmondo) is in retrospect a contemporary manifestation of it. But on the other hand, the trio's denial that they are riding the current fashion for costume dramas is disingenuous. The late 1990s viewers of *Le Bossu* will think of *Cyrano de Bergerac*, *Ridicule* and *Beaumarchais* rather than of earlier versions of Féval's story. However, this is no bad thing. De Broca's style is classic French heritage with light comedy, a mixture already in evidence in his 1988 French Revolution film *Chouans!*.

Le Bossu's credits and opening scene display the genre's pleasures. Quality casting, classical music, golden lighting, exquisite costumes and decor, promise a polished and historicised reconstruction. This is 1699 and we are at the Paris quarters of fencing masters Cocardasse and Passepoil who, with their Gascon accents and broad humour, clearly recall *Cyrano de Bergerac*. The *Cyrano* theme is reinforced by the casting of Vincent Perez, an actor who looks very good in anything, but particularly so in historical clothing (he dies, alas, half an hour into the film). Loving attention to details and objects and a dynamic *mise-en-scène* also mark *Le Bossu* as contemporary heritage cinema, distancing it from the earlier versions which look stilted by comparison. Lagardère and Nevers' journey to Caylus is invented, while Lagardère and Aurore's trip to Paris is an extrapolation from the book which allows for location shooting. Numerous fencing scenes display camera mobility.

At the same time, *Le Bossu* harks back to the earlier films' delight in an improbably melodramatic plot (though necessarily simplified by adaptation) and mobilises the mythical archetypes of popular literature. Like Cyrano, Jean Valjean and d'Artagnan, Lagardère is an epic, invincible hero who rises from the people to nobility and triumphs over evil (delightfully personified here by Fabrice Luchini as Gonzague). The makeover of the handsome Lagardère as a grotesque hunchback ('bossu') combines *Beauty and the Beast* with the genre's love of disguise. Archetypal, too, is the deployment of the father–daughter relationship, a familiar feature of French narratives. Aurore is in love with Lagardère even as she believes him to be her father (the beautiful and talented Marie Gillain seems destined for the part: she was Depardieu's daughter in *Mon père, ce héros*). *Le Bossu* modernises the theme with scenes of Lagardère changing Aurore's nappies (shades of *Trois Hommes et un couffin*), but essentially the old archetype lives on: the powerful male hero loses none of his virility as he plays mother to Aurore, and sixteen years go by while, conveniently, 'real' mother Blanche spends the story off-screen as a recluse.

Le Bossu did quite well at the French box-office, but not as well as expected or required by its $30m budget. The innocent mixture of swashbuckling and comedy which succeeded in previous versions no longer seems appropriate. The casting of Auteuil is also problematic, as he's neither classically handsome like Marais or Perez, nor charismatically 'ugly' like Belmondo or Depardieu. Though a wonderful actor, Auteuil does not quite have the star presence to carry the film, which works best when Auteuil and Perez are together or in ensemble scenes. Nonetheless, though not ground-breaking, *Le Bossu* is well made and fun, which is exactly what it aims to be.

Ginette Vincendeau

THE MASK OF ZORRO
USA 1998
Director: Martin Campbell

Los Angeles, 1821. Outlaw 'Zorro' saves some peasants from being killed by Don Rafael Montero. He is saved in turn by the young Murrieta brothers, Alejandro and Joaquin. After discovering Zorro is really Don Diego de la Vega, Montero accidentally kills Zorro's wife, steals his child and sends de la Vega to jail.

Twenty years later, Montero returns from Spain with his daughter Elena. De la Vega escapes from jail and Alejandro Murrieta watches Joaquin shoot himself rather than surrender to Captain Harrison Love, Montero's officer. De la Vega is set to kill Montero, but balks when he realises Elena is really his own daughter. A drunken Alejandro fails to kill Captain Love. De la Vega promises to train Alejandro as the new Zorro. The two of them discover Montero plans to create an independent state of California by buying it from General Santa Ana with what is effectively Santa Ana's own money. After taking the gold from a secret mine being worked by enslaved peasants, Montero is planning to blow up both the mine and the peasants. Alejandro, the new Zorro, falls in love with Elena, who finally realises whom her real father is. The two Zorros defeat their adversaries and, along with Elena, save the peasants. A year later, Elena and Alejandro are proud parents.

*   *   *

A dashingly old-fashioned adventure, *The Mask of Zorro* is an old and familiar story which has been turned into a foxy new movie. Ever since the publication of Johnston McCulley's short story in 1919, Zorro's story has been frequently adapted for the screen, ensuring the popularity of the character. Although arguably the part was most memorably played by Douglas Fairbanks (in *The Mark of Zorro*, 1920, and *Don Q, Son of Zorro*, 1940), there has been at least one screen Zorro per decade, including Robert Livingston, John Carroll, Guy Williams, Sean Flynn, Alain Delon and George Hamilton, to mention but a few. *The Mask of Zorro* boasts one of the very best incarnations of the character in Antonio Banderas. He's not the athlete Fairbanks was, but he's a passionately physical actor who moves gracefully. His romantic appeal is at least the equal of Power's, although Banderas, in spite of having played various gay characters, is less sexually ambiguous. It is perhaps significant that missing here is the previous versions' sub-plot in which de la Vega pretends to be a pansy so no one suspects he's Zorro, a device in one of Zorro's literary antecedents, *The Scarlet Pimpernel*. More importantly, Banderas' star persona highlights rather than obscures the ethnic identity of the hero.

Zorro has been done straight and spoofed up (see *Zorro The Gay Blade* for the latter). And the character forms the intertextual lynchpin, endlessly enduring and eminently adaptable like other myths, for a whole array of merchandising, from dolls to masks and whips (particularly during the television show's run in the 1950s). This new version is so successful because the film-makers have wisely left the story's basic elements alone. *The Mask of Zorro* is still a kind of Western featuring an American

Robin Hood, fighting the injustice of an old and despotic aristocracy in order to distribute justice, win the gutsy señorita and pave the way for the utopian civilisation of the new republic to come.

As the audience knows, the Spanish/Mexican pueblo in which the film is set will become Los Angeles. Also, the film doesn't forget that Zorro is a Hispanic-American hero. In fact, Antonio Banderas is the most Hispanic Zorro to date. Because of this, the casting is invariably implicated in complex ideas about ethnicity and national identity. These notions are given an explicit hierarchy in a way relatively rare in US cinema: at one end are the dark-skinned indigenous peasants, the saintly salt of the earth who absolutely belong here; at the other is the cruel and despotic Aryan Captain Harrison Love. In between, the old aristocratic order is split, one half represented by de la Vega (Anthony Hopkins with upper-class Brit accent), whose belongingness is assured by his support of the future American way of life; the other half by Montero and his cronies (darker-skinned, accents tending more towards a Spanish inflection), whose un-American actions forfeit future citizenship. The film's resolution is to have the new swarthy Zorro, son of the people, defeat evil blondie and marry the raven-haired daughter of the old aristocracy. To a much greater degree than any of the previous versions, *The Mask of Zorro* succeeds in creating a hero who is explicitly Hispanic and unarguably American.

Part of the pleasure of the film lies in its joyous embrace of bombast. When Montero defeats de la Vega and is about to steal his baby and cart him off to prison, the house bursts into flames, the music swells, thunder erupts and we get close-ups of Anthony Hopkins emoting pain intensely through the bars of his prison in a vain attempt to reach his baby. It's the full cliché, with every flourish successfully realised. In fact one of the reasons the film is so enjoyable is the obvious craft with which the film-makers maintain the overall action/adventure structure while shifting fluidly between comedy, melodrama and romance, deploying clichés refreshed with irony.

There are some scenes that don't quite work. For example, the choreography of the dance between Banderas and Zeta Jones is awful. And the film does indulge in some of the worst excesses of contemporary film-making – can Zorro not steal a horse without the entire building blowing up? However, like the banter between Banderas and Zeta Jones, *The Mask of Zorro* might be nonsense, but this doesn't make it any less delightful.

José Arroyo

TEA WITH MUSSOLINI
(TE CON MUSSOLINI)
Italy/United Kingdom 1998
Director: Franco Zeffirelli

Florence, Italy, 1934. Mary Wallace, one of a group of elderly expatriate Englishwomen nicknamed the *Scorpioni*, finds herself looking after Luca, the illegitimate son of her employer, after the boy's mother has died. Rather than abandon him to an orphanage, Mary decides to raise Luca, assisted by the other Scorpioni, including their self-appointed leader Lady Hester and the artistic but disorganised Arabella. Hester is dismayed by a visit from Elsa, a rich American Jewish socialite, whom Hester regards as intolerably vulgar. However, Elsa sets up a trust fund for Luca before leaving Italy.

As the fascist regime tightens its hold, public-order disturbances prompt Lady Hester to contact Mussolini himself. He invites her to Rome for tea and reassurances, a gesture Hester attributes to her status as a diplomat's widow, but which is really a publicity stunt. Luca's father sends him away to school in Austria. When he returns years later, Italy is at war with Britain and the Scorpioni have been interned. Elsa secretly pays for the Scorpioni to be moved to more comfortable quarters. Covertly, she helps Italian Jews out of the country and enlists Luca in her mission, though his willingness to help dwindles when he sees Elsa becoming involved with a local lawyer, Vittorio. After Pearl Harbor, Elsa is also interned and Luca discovers that Vittorio is scheming to steal her wealth and send her to her death. Luca and the local partisans help Elsa escape. Allied troops liberate the town and the Scorpioni are freed.

* * *

Submerged under an avalanche of divas, costumed and art-directed to within an inch of its life, swathed in sentimental music and explanatory intertitles which make it feel like the third-best film of 1954, and boasting a moment where Maggie Smith stops a Nazi soldier from shooting Judi Dench by shouting, 'Stop this nonsense at once,' it's safe to say that *Tea with Mussolini* is not uncamp. Not so much a date movie or a chick flick as a film for the perfect evening out with your ageing gay uncle, it serenely glides along as if the past thirty years of cinema history had never happened.

All of which lends it a certain reprehensible charm. Franco Zeffirelli is seventy-six years old after all and to expect him to modify the well-plumped plushness of his early middlebrow hits would be churlish. This is an old man's film, or, to be precise, an old queen's film, awash in a rapt savouring of stellar femininity and endearingly predictable in its casting of inept but decorative young men. The plot takes elements from Zeffirelli's own childhood, but embroiders them into a wider fabric by introducing fictional characters. The figure of Elsa, for example, is an invention, but who can blame Zeffirelli for wanting Cher in his young life, particularly a Cher dressed to the hilt in a succession of beyond-drag gowns?

The difference between Cher and the theatrical British cast's acting registers is deftly turned into a plot device, placing the clash of outlooks between their characters at the narrative's core. Smith does her party piece of pinched imperious haughtiness. Dench floats about twitchily like Sandy Dennis playing Isadora Duncan, and Plowright embodies no-nonsense maternal dependability. Cher has little trouble slipping into the role of glamour personified, prompting an awestruck Italian to ask: 'Are all American women as exciting as you?' 'Alas,' she replies, timing the pause to perfection, 'no.' Her later switch to doughty freedom fighter makes some demands on our incredulity, but she does pull off a to-die-for last scene, gorgeously stoical and irresistibly Garboesque as the partisans' boat rows her to safety.

Buried beneath the film's satin surface are some gestural attempts at addressing questions of sexual politics. The presence of lesbian archaeologist Georgie (played by Lily Tomlin as if she were auditioning for the role of Indiana Jones) signifies this, as does the curious subplot which sees Lady Hester's nephew Wilfred dressed as a woman to escape detection. When the strain of this becomes too much, he strips off, shouts (not with masses of conviction), 'I'm a man,' and runs away to join the partisans, instantly sprouting stubble in the process. The trouble is that he looks immensely more convincing in the first kind of drag than the second, implying perhaps that, while anti-fascist guerrilla subversion may be a fine and noble cause, it's never as important in a Zeffirelli film as the swish of an epigram or the cut of a frock.

Andy Medhurst

THE END OF THE AFFAIR
USA/Germany 1999
Director: Neil Jordan

London, 1946. Writer Maurice Bendrix encounters civil servant Henry Miles on Clapham Common. Maurice recalls how in 1939, just before the outbreak of war, he had begun a passionate affair with Henry's wife, Sarah. It lasted until 1944. One day, when the lovers were in Maurice's flat, a bomb hit the house and knocked him unconscious. Immediately afterwards, Sarah ended the affair without explanation. Now, hearing that Henry suspects Sarah of adultery, Maurice undertakes to investigate on his behalf. He visits a private detective who puts his operative Parkis on the case.

Sarah phones Maurice. They meet for lunch, but his resentment drives her away. They're observed by Parkis and his young son Lance, whose face is blemished by a strawberry birthmark. Parkis learns Sarah regularly visits a man called Smythe who later proves to be a Catholic priest. Parkis enters Sarah's house and steals her journal; from it Maurice learns that Sarah, a lapsed Catholic, had made a promise to God when the bomb fell. Thinking Maurice dead, she vowed never to see him again if his life was restored. She has been seeing Smythe for religious instruction.

Maurice rushes to see Sarah; she tries to evade him, but her desire is too strong. They become lovers again and go away to Brighton together. Henry shows up and confronts them. He tells Maurice that Sarah is fatally ill, and invites him to move into their house. After a long illness, Sarah dies. At her funeral service, Maurice sees Parkis, who tells him Sarah kissed young Lance on his blemished cheek one day; since then his birthmark has vanished.

*   *   *

Should a film adapted from a novel (or play, or whatever) be judged purely on its merits as a film without reference to its source material? Ideally, perhaps, yes. Yet when a film turns out as bland as Neil Jordan's *The End of the Affair*, despite its writer-director's evidently sincere admiration for Graham Greene's novel, it surely makes sense to invoke the original in trying to work out what went so wrong.

It's not just a matter of cinematic prettification, though that enters into it. In a crucial scene in the novel the two former adulterous lovers, Maurice Bendrix (played by Ralph Fiennes in the film) and Sarah Miles (Julianne Moore), meet in a church. It's cold and dark and comfortless. There's a 'hideous statue of the virgin', writes Greene. In the film, the church has become spacious and opulent. The draperies are bright with blue and crimson, the rood screen a glowing expanse of gold. Hazy sunlight streams through the stained glass. This is symptomatic: an awkward, edgy, tormented novel has been upholstered for comfort. Unexpectedly, Edward Dmytryk's plodding 1954 black-and-white version, starring a badly miscast Van Johnson opposite Deborah Kerr, gets closer to the visual feel of it.

But the problem goes deeper than that. The key character in Greene's novel is a jealous, possessive lover. He's devious, underhand and calculating; he lies in wait, takes unfair advantage; he'll pull every trick in the book to prevent the woman he wants from succumbing to a rival. If necessary, he'll even kill her. This schemer isn't the writer Bendrix (a semi-autobiographical portrait by Greene), but Greene's personal and highly unorthodox version of the Roman Catholic God – a character who in Jordan's film has been marginalised, in places almost written out. Much of the power of the novel lies in the sense of God's trap closing inexorably, of every potential exit being quietly shut off as soon as glimpsed. In the film, the trap is sprung open and the mice are out cavorting.

The central turning point, in the film as in the novel, is when Maurice reads Sarah's journal and discovers why she ended their affair so abruptly. He imagined she'd tired of him and, since her marriage to dull civil servant Henry (Stephen Rea) was a sexless shell, found herself another man. Instead, it turns out she believed him killed by a flying bomb and, praying desperately, offered God a swap: bring him back to life and I'll give him up for ever. It's left ambiguous whether Maurice was really dead, or simply unconscious; but the vow is absolute. Greene's petty-minded version of the Deity sees to that. Each time either Maurice or Sarah tries to break the promise, God the supreme chessmaster moves deftly to block them. The lovers are kept apart until Sarah's death. Thereby, Greene implies, her soul is saved for the Church and she even becomes a miracle-working saint.

Whatever you think of this as theology – and many people, believers and non-believers, have found it pretty repellent – it does at least give the story a consistent *raison d'être*. But Jordan's film blows it wide open. A few changes apart, he stays reasonably close to the original until the reading of the journal. He even preserves one of Greene's most Hardyesque ironies, when Maurice's own schemes are turned against him. Sarah, her resistance worn down, is packing to leave her husband at the very time when Maurice confronts Henry with (as he thinks) evidence of her affair with another man. Broken, Henry comes home and implores Sarah not to desert him, and she stays.

All this goes for nothing in the second half of the film. Having read the journal, Maurice rushes to Sarah. She resists briefly, then succumbs and they fall into bed together. Next we find them jaunting off for a dirty weekend in Brighton, where Henry bizarrely pops up to catch them together in the Pavilion. With this episode, the whole fabric of the film coarsens: we even get a clichéd shot of the grinning couple whirled around together at a fun fair. Perhaps Jordan fears modern audiences will find the concept of voluntary chastity incomprehensible, but these tinkerings make nonsense of everything that's gone before. What matters isn't that his film is not true to the book – no reason why a film should have to be, after all – but that the film isn't true to itself.

One or two other changes seem ill thought-out. The facial strawberry birthmark that in the novel afflicts a different character is transferred to Lance, the son of the private detective Parkis (Ian Hart) Maurice hires to spy on Sarah. Since Parkis takes the boy (Samuel Bould) with him in his work, where his aim is to stay inconspicuous, this makes him not simply a pitiable figure but an incompetent fool. And it's scarcely credible that in 1946 an ultra-respectable senior civil servant like Henry would invite his wife's lover to join in a *ménage à trois*, even if the wife was dying. (In the novel, Maurice moves in after Sarah's death, which today might raise eyebrows for a different reason.)

It would be unjust to imply that *The End of the Affair* is some kind of write-off. In the first half of the film Jordan skilfully sustains his three-way time scheme, switching from postwar to pre-war to wartime with deft visual economy and no loss of narrative clarity. At times, too, the performances all but carry it. Ralph Fiennes, fresh from *Onegin*, has perhaps played too many guilt-stricken lovers just recently; but Stephen Rea, with his doleful jowls, makes an ideal Henry, and Julianne Moore gives a vibrantly sensual performance, movingly convincing as a woman so selfless in her passion she would make the agonising bargain to have her lover alive even if forever unattainable.

But nothing can overcome the gap at the heart of the film. The story, Jordan has been quoted as saying, 'is about the question of how far love goes between people. If somebody says, "I will love you forever", do you know how far they will carry that promise through?' At best, this is an oversimplification, at worst a total misreading. The story, at least as Greene conceived it, is about religion, seen not as a solace but as an affliction, presided over by a Deity who, for all Greene's Catholicism, has a lot in common with the grim Lutheran God of Ingmar Bergman: the malignant spider on the wall, watching and spinning his web. There's little place for such an implacable being in the comfortable, sunlit church of Jordan's film.

Philip Kemp

MANSFIELD PARK
USA/United Kingdom 1999
Director: Patricia Rozema

England, the early nineteenth century. Fanny Price leaves her home in Portsmouth to live with wealthy relatives on their vast country estate Mansfield Park. There, she is treated as a social inferior by her aunt and uncle, Sir Thomas and Lady Bertram, and her cousins Tom, Maria and Julia. Only Edmund, the Bertram's second son, treats her kindly.

Fanny grows into a spirited young woman. Sir Thomas departs on a business trip to his plantations in Antigua, accompanied by Tom. The Mansfield routine is disrupted by the arrival of charismatic siblings Henry and Mary Crawford. Henry flirts with Maria, despite her engagement to Mr Rushworth; Mary has designs on Edmund. Tom returns from Antigua, and proposes putting on a play. The rehearsals are a pretext for much unseemly flirtation by the Crawfords, but the performance is prevented by the return of Sir Thomas.

Maria marries Mr Rushmore. A debut ball is held in honour of Fanny, where Henry declares his love for her. Secretly in love with Edmund, she spurns him, enraging Sir Thomas who sends her back to Portsmouth. She is abruptly recalled to Mansfield Park when Tom falls ill. While nursing Tom, Fanny discovers some of his sketches of abuses against the Antiguan slaves. She also finds Henry in bed with Maria, who then runs off with him. Mary's callous behaviour repels Edmund. Soon after Tom recovers, Edmund confesses his love for Fanny, which she reciprocates.

* * *

Given the recent spate of Jane Austen adaptations (notably, Ang Lee's *Sense and Sensibility*, Douglas McGrath's *Emma* and the BBC productions of *Persuasion* and *Pride and Prejudice*), one could be forgiven for anticipating diminishing returns from what is widely viewed as the author's least satisfying and most intractably moralistic work. But that would be to reckon without the contribution of Canadian director Patricia Rozema who, disdaining a purist approach, offers some smart and suggestive variations on the usual Regency rituals.

Rozema's previous features (*I've Heard the Mermaids Singing* and *When Night Is Falling*) have all dealt with meek, repressed female protagonists who are initiated into new social and cultural worlds, before attaining self-sufficiency. In this respect, Austen's Fanny, who arrives at Mansfield Park a timid and socially unsure young woman only to become an indispensable member of the household, would seem to be another variant on Rozema's heroines.

Yet the Fanny of Rozema's film, as incarnated by a radiant Frances O'Connor, is resolutely all the things the Fanny of the novel is not: vivacious, artistic, even sexy – a self-confessed 'wild beast'. This Fanny is, in fact, something of a hybrid of Austen's heroine and the novelist herself (Fanny's stories and her updates to her sister Susan are based on Austen's own early writings and letters). In Fanny, Rozema creates a screen heroine we can root for (more in the mould of *Pride and Prejudice*'s Elizabeth Bennet), and a film that stands alongside the rest of her *oeuvre* as a paean to female artistic and romantic independence.

Rozema's emancipatory agenda is significantly different from the novel's more sober, stoic preoccupation with the upholding of true moral consciousness through abstinence and self-denial. Austen's Fanny, as the unimpeachable repository of older, High Tory values, must strike modern sensibilities as something of a prig. Rozema's heroine, on the other hand, is a modern woman oppressed by an antiquated patriarchal society. To throw this theme into sharper relief, Rozema has chosen to make the slavery issue (fleetingly alluded to in the novel) explicit. At one point, Fanny mortifies her family by raising the subject of abolition. The scene in which she discovers Tom's sketches of atrocities (gang rape included) committed against the slaves on his father's Antiguan plantations is shocking in its deliberate rupturing of the film's predominantly genteel *mise-en-scène*.

Rozema's point is that Mansfield Park and the amorous escapades of its wealthy inhabitants are founded on and sustained by this debased form of exploitation. This is certainly an intriguing opening-out of the novel, but in doing so the film appropriates the moral high ground in a way that further distances it from the delicacy and ambiguity of Austen's insights.

Rozema might shift the moral dynamics of the tale to suit our modern broad-stroke sensibilities, but she also has fun with the novel's romantic conventions. The initial entrance of the glamorous, seductive Crawfords is played as a comic cliché, a languorous camera tilt up their bodies intercut with hot flushes from the assembled onlookers. The central ball scene – filmed with candlelit intimacy and rhapsodic camera swirls – and a couple of fanciful sapphic interludes between Fanny and Embeth Davidtz's serpentine, cigar-smoking Mary Crawford also confirm this as the most overtly erotic of Austen adaptations to date.

Andy Richards

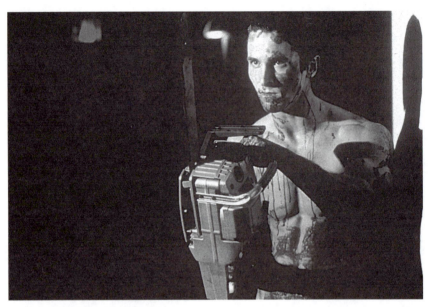

American Psycho (Mary Harron, 2000)

Section 3:
Modern Dystopias
from Book to Screen

Case Studies

The Naked Lunch
THE WRONG BODY

Amy Taubin

Naked Lunch is less an adaptation of William Burroughs' novel than David Cronenberg's fantasy about how it came to be written. The young Cronenberg wanted to be a writer; Burroughs and Nabokov were his models. He claims that he turned to film-making when he realised he'd never write as well as either of them.

Affronts to the 'I married Joan' sit-com consciousness of the Eisenhower era, Burroughs' *Naked Lunch* and Nabokov's *Lolita* each presented a radically different version of subversive male sexuality, modernist reflexivity and expatriate alienation, not to mention a fascination with insect life connected in part to a certain queasiness about the female body. The obscenity trials which surrounded the publication of both novels in the United States marked the beginning of the end of the repressive 1950s. Today, the stuff the authorities claimed was pornographic – homosexuality in *Naked Lunch*, paedophilia in *Lolita* – is the staple of television talk shows. Nevertheless, the context in which these subjects are placed is as poisonously puritanical as it was forty years ago. 'I'm afraid that 1993 is going to be like 1953,' Cronenberg commented. 1953 is the year in which the film *Naked Lunch* is set.

Between 1984, when Cronenberg and producer Jeremy Thomas acquired the rights to the novel, and the film's Christmas 1991 release (just in time for it to win both a New York Film Critics and a National Film Critics award), Burroughs' devotees questioned whether Cronenberg was the right man for the job. There were obvious similarities in the Burroughs and the Cronenberg *oeuvres*: the sci-fi paranoia, the fascination with control and addiction, the definition of subjectivity as unstable, biochemical and hallucinatory, the connection between sex and vampires, sex and disease, sex and mutation, sex and death.

Yet, while sexuality is polymorphous and definitely perverse in the work of both Burroughs and Cronenberg, the trajectory of desire and the specifics of representation is homosexual in the former and heterosexual in the latter. Thus, *The Advocate*, a major American gay weekly, cautioned against expecting much from 'the heterosexual Cronenberg'. The irony is that the gay critics who've attacked the film would have great difficulty recuperating much of Burroughs – the terroristic goings-on in 'Hassan's Rumpus Room', for example, which are among the pages of *Naked Lunch* most vividly inscribed in the collective cultural memory – within their politics of essentialism and positive imagery.

Cronenberg responds to the criticism as follows: 'It wasn't as if there were a dozen directors vying for the rights and they gave it to the heterosexual.' Indeed, when Cronenberg acquired *Naked Lunch*, no one else was interested. 'If *Naked Lunch* were a gay book and that's all, you would have an argument. I wouldn't do *The Wild Boys* [the Burroughs novel that's high on Gus Van Sant's agenda]. But the sex in *Naked Lunch* is beyond gay. It's sci-fi sex; it has metaphorical meaning every way.' Yet, when I ask Cronenberg what he thinks of Kubrick's *Lolita* (1961), an adaptation fraught with similar problems, he answers that, although James Mason's performance is perfect, he didn't like the film very much when he first saw it. 'The actress who played Lolita was too old. She's supposed to be a child, not a teenager. To shift that shifts everything.'

The shift that Cronenberg makes in *Naked Lunch* is to wind it around the body of a woman. He takes as his premise Burroughs' statement in the introduction to *Queer* that, if he hadn't killed his wife Joan, he would never have become a writer. Burroughs, however, goes on to say that he put up a writer's block around her death; women barely exist in his work. Cronenberg, on the other hand, structures *Naked Lunch* as a bare-bones, but not unconventional, noir narrative. The film is driven by the repetition-compulsion of its protagonist William Lee – his need to save and destroy his wife Joan over and over again.

To lift a metaphor from *The Fly* (1986), *Naked Lunch* is less a case of Cronenberg adapting than absorbing Burroughs. That the experiment is not totally successful is proof of Burroughs' stature both as a writer and counterculture myth. Nevertheless, the first half of the film is nearly as intellectually inventive, mordantly witty and visually stunning as Cronenberg's *Dead Ringers* (1988). Pristine and putrid, the decor encompasses every shade of shit and glows as if it were radioactive. Erupting from this controlled, though repellent, visual surface is a diarrhoeic flow of language, thick with puns, threats and obscenities.

The film opens with Lee trying to live the 'straight life'. He's married and has a job as an exterminator. Lee and Joan get addicted to the poison he uses to kill roaches. (For heroin and hashish, Cronenberg substitutes sci-fi drugs – bug powder and the meat of the black centipede. The drugs are not merely agents of hallucination, they are hallucinatory in and of themselves.)

High on bug powder, Lee is contacted by a giant roach whose wings spread open to reveal a talking, all-too-human-looking asshole. The roach tells Lee that his wife, Joan, is an alien and instructs him to kill her. Lee invites Joan to play a game of William Tell. He aims for the glass she's placed on her head, but the roach takes control and the bullet blasts her brain. Lee flees to Interzone with the bug, which now has the body of an old-fashioned Smith-Corona typewriter grafted on to its head.

The film's central image is of Lee alone in his wretched hotel room sitting in front of this insect writing machine, which functions as a combination id and super-ego. 'I'm your case worker,' it tells him, 'your contact to Control.' Control wants Lee to write reports about the death of Joan Lee. The game of William Tell has made it possible for William to tell all, that is, to write *Naked Lunch*.

Lee gets involved with two other American expatriate writers, Tom and Joan Frost (modelled on Paul and Jane Bowles). In an extremely sinister scene, Lee reads Tom's mind and discovers that just as he destroyed Joan Lee, Tom is destroying Joan Frost.

Departing from both the Burroughs' biography and the homoerotics of *Naked Lunch*, Lee becomes obsessed with saving Joan. She invites him to try Tom's favourite typewriter. Messing around in the back of the machine, her hand penetrates a kind of uterine cavity – red, raw and pulsating. The scene is terrifyingly erotic and, given the anal-retentive quality of the rest of the film, flagrantly transgressive. The effect is to stop the film long before it's over. The potentially chilling scenes that follow – Lee selling out Kiki, his boy lover, to the cannibalistic Yves Cloquet; his discovery of the factory farm where the Mugwamps are milked by human sex slaves addicted to their jissom; the revelation of the hermaphroditic identity of the controlling Dr Benway; Lee's shooting of the second Joan in order to prove to the border guards of Annexia that he's really a writer – happen as if by rote.

Brilliant as it is, Cronenberg's *Naked Lunch* never resolves the incompatibility between the heterosexual drive of its narrative and the remnants of Burroughs' homoerotic fantasy. The amazing insect typewriter, which collapses desire for buggery with paranoia about being bugged, could never have produced the encounter between William Lee and Joan Frost. 'It's not the instruments that are wrong; it's the women's bodies,' cries one of *Dead Ringers'* twin gynaecologists as he descends into madness. In terms of *Naked Lunch*, he might just have a point.

THE NAKED DINERS CLUB

Iain Sinclair

In 1959, *Naked Lunch*, a set of junk/sex routines from legendary lie-down comedian William S. Burroughs, was shuffled and edited by a team of friends and collaborators so that Maurice Girodias of Olympia Press could cash in on publicity ensuing from the suppression of the *Chicago Review*, where extracts from the book were due to appear. The author (mouthpiece, stooge, fall guy) for this toxic collaboration between Dante and Lenny Bruce enjoyed what amounted to a posthumous reputation: the first reviews read like obituary notices. Journalists meeting Burroughs behaved as if they were interviewing a zombie. His masterpiece was variously interpreted as Swiftian satire (copywriters have yet to identify any other brand), a masturbatory *aide-mémoire*, or a sequence of coded scripts transmitted by cockroaches from Mars.

It is generally accepted – by the literary pimps who trade in used snapshots – that Burroughs agreed to give his first public reading at the Mistral bookshop, Paris. When the day came, as Harold Norse reports, the man was 'junk-sick'. He sent a tape recording as understudy. The tiny audience was captivated by this entirely appropriate paradigm of all future Burroughs happenings.

Another tiny audience gathered in a preview theatre to enjoy *Naked Lunch The Movie* were victims of the same three-card con Burroughs pulled at the Mistral bookshop. We sat through a chamber piece of modest ambition in which neither

Burroughs nor his most famous work was present. We were offered in exchange a linear narrative composed of a sober critique of the writer's more notorious obsessions, restaged bio-clips (highlights from the lowlife), and a slimy escalation of rubber horror metaphors for the author's fear of the typewriter.

If film in the 1990s is defined as the art of burning somebody else's money, most of its aboriginal tent show impulses remain intact. You want prestige? Buy a good title, then throw away the book. The Beverly Hills rich are still different, but they are far from nouveaux. Taking possession of cult titles has become the ultimate form of book collecting. It's much cheaper than a Matisse or a Chagall. And there are no insurance premiums. They've cracked *Ulysses*, gutted *Under the Volcano*, nibbled at a few lemon-scented extracts from Proust. *Naked Lunch* has to be the choicest titbit left on the shelf. It's impossible. The producers admit it can't be done. A direct translation would devour the national debt of any self-respecting coke republic, and still be banned everywhere. Hanging orgies, dope freaks, vaudeville surgery ... the *Titanic*? Forget it. Director David Cronenberg and producer Jeremy Thomas go for the easier option of tapping 'the spirit of the book' while – get this – maintaining at the same time the discipline of a 'traditional narrative structure ... psychological and emotional develop-ment, the story told through the main character'. In other words, the film disregards and deconstructs every moral and technical decision Burroughs made in assembling his text. Instead of 'an endless novel which will drive everybody mad', we have a film openly representing itself as a promo for a debased cultural artefact. A sentimental journey through an intolerable past.

The film, the finite event that makes it on to the screen, is inevitably the ghost of a much grander concept, a spent rocket dragged back to Earth. The octane is elsewhere. In the deal. That's what excites us. That's the alchemy. Good meetings. Great calls. Epic breakfasts. Networking that finally delivers 'William Seward Burroughs II' as a name above the title. He's been around for aeons on underground back lots as writer and performer. An out-take. Who remembers *Chappaqua*? It's much easier to get scripts published – in signed, numbered editions, with prelims by Ron Kitaj – than to persuade some proper person to shoot them. An anorexic fetish, a decadence: like promoting the rejected outlines of novels straight from the slush pile into hardcovers.

Naked Lunch was the pipe dream, a grail for all the heads in town. They sidled up on it by way of *Junkie*, which optioned its reckless way through some notably shaky hands. Terry Southern and Dennis Hopper, according to Burroughs' biographer, Ted Morgan, 'had the two worst reputations in Hollywood'. Not only would they never eat lunch again, they couldn't even find the restaurant. Hopper 'had a habit so bad that the bridge of his nose was misshapen and discoloured ...'. Southern, the triumphs of *Strangelove* a remote memory, cranked himself into shape on Brampton's Mixture ('which combined cocaine, morphine, alcohol, cherry syrup and water'). Script confer-ences for these boys were Bedlam at sixteen speeds: speaking-in-tongues, blue lip rhapsodies, escalating arias of threat, the magical invocation of hit men, serial muti-lation, cannibalism. How unlike the homelife of our own dear commissioning editors.

Burroughs, the elder statesman, Member of the American Academy of Arts and Letters, affects a good-natured disinterest in these antics. He's far too canny to involve himself in the time-wasting frivolities of script-doctoring. Cash up front. Let 'em pay for the brand name and butcher the rest any way they want. Like a retired frontier veterinarian, he's sitting this one out. 'You write a part for James Coburn and you wind up with Liberace,' he reported to Brion Gysin. But the author of *The Process*, calligrapher and cut-up pioneer can no longer be reached by air mail. He didn't live to see himself impersonated by a white suit with Julian Sands attached to it. He might otherwise have been amused to see his complex relationship with Burroughs elided to a snatch of ambiguous two-shots, before he mutates into a brain-sucking rubber crawly in a parrot's cage.

Whatever palpitations of nostalgia Cronenberg sets in motion by pastiching fandom's Beatnik album (Ginsberg, Kerouac, Paul and Jane Bowles), his film is limited by its costume-design concept of history. Even the cast has been hired like props, because they have a proven heritage pedigree. Julian Sands steps seamlessly out from his *Room with a View*. Ian Holm escapes from *Chariots of Fire* to the frying pan of 'Interzone' and marriage to a Jane Bowles impersonator. The film publicists do not need to point out that 'all the clothes relate to the year 1953'. They relate to 1953 as much as the style postcards of Marilyn Monroe relate to the experience of watching one of her films. If history does indeed operate in cycles, it has the unfortunate habit of returning dry-cleaned by the 'Merchants Ivory'. Burroughs champions a contrary notion: all ages, all crimes, are contactable in present time. We inhabit a shifting concertina of past and future lives, open to us through acts of control and sex magic. The elitism of this hierographic vision is not accessible through the efforts, however well intentioned, of a democratic art form. Cinema, the team game for fat cats, has no business with the hermeticism of the writer/magus.

Cronenberg's *fin de siècle* travelogue gets the suits right, the pinched light, the mustard-dust breath, the photofit faces. Peter Weller bravely attempts the impossible, underplaying the ancient-souled Burroughs. A floater pulled from the river would have more animation. Burroughs was born tired. Weller, although he manages very convincingly the hatchet-cheeked, whipped-cur look that reminded cinematographer Peter Suschitzky of 'a character out of a painting by Otto Dix', can only impersonate. He can never repossess. There is no active contact with a criminal consciousness. You can't set-dress the shabbiness of damaged lives. It's too much like rolling new money in the dirt. We, the audience, know too much. We have been taken too often behind the scenes. The tricks have been explained to us. But time, in Burroughs' own films, is always an optional extra. Anytime is everywhere. The clothing is utterly unmemorable. It would never convince any self-respecting style analyst. Film clothes, unlike real clothes, outlive the people inside them.

Remove Cronenberg's *Naked Lunch* from its spurious association with a great book and you're left with a lean, intelligent and enjoyable movie. One of the few for the grown-ups. But this divorce is impossible. The project came into being as the formal mating of dynasties: *Dead Ringers* meets *Dead Fingers Talk*. The crowd will not disperse until they have witnessed the bloody sheets.

Cronenberg is shortly to extend his collection of designer modernist classics by shooting J. G. Ballard's *Crash*. (These titles, along with *Clockwork Orange*, are what I would define as record company books. Names that decay into albums.) How much better advised talent scouts would be to pillage the canon of the literary underclass, where highly energised source books invite a collaboration of equal patterns. Pulps written for loot, gun to temple, may be painlessly transformed, with no loss of karma, to cash once more. Too much respect kills a film at birth. The nature of contemporary cinema is such that it cannot, by definition, cope with the single most crucial element in the junkie's universe: boredom.

Crash
CRASH

Chris Rodley

They said it wouldn't be done. They said it couldn't be done. They said it shouldn't be done. But the inevitable has happened. In a slow-motion car-smash in the telepod of *The Fly*, director David Cronenberg and novelist J. G. Ballard have finally fused. The result emerged recently at Cannes: *Crash*, a movie destined to do for seatbelts what James Dean did for denim.

If Cronenberg's 1992 adaptation of William Burroughs' *The Naked Lunch* seemed overdue, his filming of Ballard's 1973 novel *Crash* looks and feels as if it was made long, long ago in a parallel universe. For one is forcibly struck by the overwhelming impression that this is early Cronenberg. Unblinking, undiluted, unrepentant and downright provocative.

For those unfamiliar with J. G. Ballard's white-hot, totally original book, it tells the story of James Ballard (James Spader) and his wife, Catherine (Deborah Unger). Locked in a practice of compulsive sex with strangers, they compare notes, seeking any physical experience that makes sense in a bleak, passionless world of multi-lane freeways. Ballard becomes involved with Helen Remington (Holly Hunter), after he accidentally ploughs into her car, killing her husband. Their mutual crash-victim status brings them together, ultimately delivering them into the sump oil-soaked world of the pathological Vaughan (Elias Koteas).

Renegade scientist and leader of a strange subterranean group, Vaughan is only able to achieve sexual release by crashing into people on the motorways surrounding Heathrow airport. His tattered leathers smell of stale semen. His cock only responds to twisted metal, beautifully formed chrome, shards of windscreen glass and blood on instrument panels. He photographs crash sites and victims, and dreams of the ultimate orgasm: ramming into a Rolls Royce carrying Elizabeth Taylor.

In the film, his band of scarred and semi-mutilated crash victims (including Rosanna Arquette) spend their time looking at videos of simulated accidents, fucking in cars or attending Vaughan's own 'illegal' performances – such as his restaging of James Dean's 'Death by Porsche' (a brilliant Cronenberg addition). Ballard, his wife and

Helen Remington are all drawn into Vaughan's crazed orbit, and his dream of a new conceptualised relationship of flesh and metal, man and machine.

The book was (and is) shocking, by any standards. Ballard proudly announced, in his introduction to the French edition, that it was 'the first pornographic novel based on technology', in the days before the word 'pornography' began its own complicated shape-shifting process. Naming the novel's first-person hero after himself seemed calculated to shock the reader into confronting the book's hardcore fantasy/reality. The author was being totally honest about his own imaginative life.

Given the novel's scenario, in which humans realign their minds, bodies and sexuality to dominant technology, it was always perfect Cronenberg material. And it had echoes that might satisfy the director's personal interest in cars (he's an amateur racing driver).

Although the book is set in London, the cars are often American (Vaughan drives a '63 Lincoln, the car in which Kennedy was assassinated). It feels like the future, but is steeped in the present. Ballard's version of science fiction is all too now. The novel's dystopic vision seems as contemporary in the 1990s as it did in the 1970s.

The movie relocates the story to Cronenberg's home town of Toronto, that most archetypal of North American cities. The perfect quasi-sci-fi backdrop. Nowhere. No time. A brilliant solution to the novel's sense of America, and that country's very particular relationship to the car and its development.

Fiercely loyal to its spare, no-holds-barred script, it's structured around a number of sometimes perverse, sometimes joyless, sometimes verbally excoriating sex scenes. Characters pair off in various permutations. Not since actor Udo Kier fucked his own monster in *Andy Warhol's Flesh for Frankenstein* have audiences witnessed the erotic opportunities offered by an open wound: to Cronenberg, a neo-sex organ.

Crash obviously presented very particular problems for any financier. The $9 million budget eventually came from Alliance, one of Canada's biggest producers of film and television. The French company UGC, who had a deal with producer Jeremy Thomas, got out of the kitchen. With the exception of *The Fly*, it has never been easy to find finance for a David Cronenberg film. It's rumoured that certain executives at Fine Line – the film's American distributor – regard the result as 'morally reprehensible'. They won't be alone. *Crash* will be an NC17 in the States, with the added problem that Blockbuster Video – who control 25 per cent of the video market in North America – refuse to stock NC17 tapes. So there will have to be a special video version, which the director estimates will last about forty minutes.

Of course, Cronenberg is no stranger to censorship, economic or otherwise, and with *Crash* looks to be preparing to come out fighting all over again. He's back, and the signal (perhaps a little faint lately) is again loud and clear: 'I want to show the unshowable. Speak the unspeakable.' *Crash* is Cronenberg, Florida orange-juice style. No waste. No mercy. No way out.

* * *

Chris Rodley: Great books often make very bad films. Ballard's *Crash* is so original and so complete a vision in itself that it must have seemed a daunting challenge.

David Cronenberg: It's also hermetically sealed. But there was something about it that I thought really did lend itself to being distilled and transformed into a film. You can only go on your instinct. When I finally started to write it, I was surprised just how directly it distilled. I thought I would be doing a lot more funny stuff, like inventing other characters, changing things structurally. But it distilled in a very pure way. And what was left was not only the essence of the book, but a living thing in its own right.

Chris Rodley: With *The Naked Lunch*, you said it was a matter of choosing exactly when to do a film adaptation. That you had to let it alone until you felt you could assert yourself over the material. Was that the case with *Crash*?

David Cronenberg: I might have put the book away before I finished it, because I was afraid that I was going to want to make it into a movie. That was probably the gestation period: between when I didn't finish it and when I did. But then I didn't think about it for a couple of years. I think it needed that time to settle.

Chris Rodley: Have you managed to make *Crash* the novel into a Cronenberg film?

David Cronenberg: Every day you're making a thousand decisions about what a film should be. It's hard to feel that it's not you. I think this is a lovely fusion of me and Ballard. We're so amazingly in synch. We completely understand what we're both doing. Right down to why he called the main character 'James Ballard'. There was never a question in my mind that I wouldn't call that character James Ballard. I knew why he did it. For some people it might seem strange. It is quite unusual. It might be unprecedented for an author to write a book like *Crash* and name the main character after himself. All of these things just seem so right to me.

Chris Rodley: You and Burroughs are very different as people, in that Burroughs lived his books. Are you closer to Ballard? He has always distinguished between his imaginative life and his 'ordinary' daily existence.

David Cronenberg: I think that's true. Although I don't know if I could live in Shepperton! But, even when you talk to Burroughs, he'll say, 'Look, I spend 70 per cent of my life sitting at a desk, so how adventurous is that?' And now he lives in Lawrence, Kansas. That makes Toronto seem adventuresome! But I do know what you mean. The Ballard character in *Crash* could just as easily have been called David Cronenberg, and it would have the same relationship to me as Ballard the character does to Ballard the writer.

Chris Rodley: The shooting script of *Crash* is only seventy-seven pages. Very short. Was that intentional?

David Cronenberg: Yes. I've been doing that for some time. It's part of what I think is my strength as a producer/director. It's a question of control. I shoot slow, with a lot of attention to detail. I'd rather focus microscopically on seventy-seven pages. I like to have the script really pared down.

It's also an issue of budget. If I'd had a 120-page version of *Crash*, I couldn't have afforded the movie. My shooting schedule wouldn't have been any longer in terms of days, but it would have been almost half the time that I needed to do it right. I remember George Bernard Shaw saying that the length of a play is dictated by the capacity of the human bladder. You've got to get up and pee!

I like things to be taut and intense. To make a two-hour movie of *Crash* would be so draining people would hate me for it! If you're going to do *different* material on low budgets, that's a critical thing. Also, with a 77-page script, I'm building a protection for myself and my actors. I can guarantee them that I have control, that I have final cut. That's part of directing actors.

Chris Rodley: It's very hardcore script. When it was completed, were there any 'worried' reactions initially?

David Cronenberg: My then agent at CAA, who I still like very much, said, 'Do not do this movie. It will end your career.' When I said, 'I really want to do this,' he said, 'OK, then forget I said this. As a friend and business associate I felt I had to tell you.' I changed agents ultimately, and certainly that moment had something to do with it, because he really wanted me to do films like *The Juror* with Demi Moore. So I figured that we weren't talking about the same stuff. We'll see if *Crash* ends my career. I don't think so. I've never been in competition at Cannes before. That's definitely a good career thing!

Chris Rodley: To get this script made, did it have to be low budget?

David Cronenberg: It was always going to be a low budget. There was no question. It was obvious from the word go that under $10 million was really what we were talking about. The question then became how far under ten million.

Chris Rodley: After the big-budget location extravaganza of *M. Butterfly*, was *Crash* intended as a back-to-basics Cronenberg movie?

David Cronenberg: Absolutely. That was very conscious. But it wasn't just the budget. It was also subject matter. My last three pictures have basically been studio pictures. Even *M. Butterfly*, despite the location shooting. Here we were shooting in Toronto locations with available light. There was no way we could afford to light three miles of road. It was very much like shooting *Scanners*. This means you have to absorb and incorporate what's there. It's much more like found art, and that's very exhilarating.

What's interesting is that this extended to the music as well. Since *Dead Ringers*, my composer Howard Shore had gotten into the habit of going to London and recording with an 84-piece orchestra! We didn't have the budget, so he came to Toronto. He hasn't recorded in Toronto since *Videodrome*. So it would be: first day, do the whole movie with three harps; second day, do the whole movie with six electric guitars; third day, do the whole movie with two percussionists. Very much like we did on *Scanners* and *Videodrome*. We had many discussions about returning to the old style, except we felt we were a lot better at it! But the techniques and the parameters were like the old days.

Chris Rodley: Seeing *Crash*, I was immediately reminded of very early Cronenberg. *Shivers* and *Rabid* mainly. Like those two, it is uncompromising, very stark and very bleak.

David Cronenberg: I don't disagree. I was also thinking of the Darryl Revok character in *Scanners*. Vaughan in *Crash* does seem very much like my own creatures, who were emerging at the same time Ballard was writing his creatures.

Chris Rodley: There also seems to be a sci-fi link. Ballard's version of science fiction isn't dissimilar to the worlds of *Videodrome*, *Scanners*, or *Shivers*. Is it or isn't it the future?

David Cronenberg: Yeah. The conceit that underlies some of what is maybe difficult or baffling about *Crash*, the sci-fi-ness, comes from Ballard anticipating a future pathological psychology. It's developing now, but he anticipates it being even more developed in the future. He then brings it back to the past – now – and applies it as though it exists completely formed. So I have these characters who are exhibiting a psychology of the future.

I think that'll be tricky for some people. If they try to apply the normal movie psychology to these characters, they're doomed to be confused, baffled and perhaps frustrated by *Crash*. Where are the sympathetic characters? Where is this recognisable domesticity that is then destroyed by Vaughan?

Some potential distributors said, 'You should make them more normal at the beginning so that we can see where they go wrong.' In other words, it would be like a *Fatal Attraction* thing. Blissful couple, maybe a dog and a rabbit, maybe a kid. And then a car accident introduces them to these horrible people and they go wrong. I said, 'That isn't right, because there's something wrong with them right *now*. That's why they're vulnerable to going even further.' The novel is uncompromising in that way. Why shouldn't the movie be?

Chris Rodley: Ballard loves the film and says it is even more extreme than the book. Do you agree?

David Cronenberg: In the book, you're in the head of the character James Ballard. There's that interior monologue thing that fiction does so beautifully, and which movies cannot do at all. Maybe that would give people more of a feeling of empathy for the character. But not much. When Ballard says that I go even further than the book, that delights me. I don't know how accurate it is, though. I think it might just be a difference in the media. The immediacy of movie reality might do that on its own.

Chris Rodley: Hearing that Holly Hunter was to play Helen Remington, it sounded like radical casting. How did you decide on her?

David Cronenberg: I've had some people saying angrily, 'I don't know what Holly Hunter was doing in this movie!' Outraged. But that's Holly. She wants to outrage those people. She was the first in! I hadn't even sent the script out. Her agent phoned me and said, 'Holly wants to play Helen Remington.' Holly is tough in ways her fans don't realise. She's not afraid. She had let me know as far back as *Dead Ringers* that she liked my movies and wanted to work with me. So you see an actor saying, 'OK, so I've got some power now. I've got some fame and clout and what I want to do is work with these people who always seem to do things that I wish I was in.'

We did have some discussions, but always with the understanding that she was already in. This was a character she wanted to explore. You can imagine the kind of things that Holly must get offered. None of them would be like Helen Remington! So we talked about the function of the character in the script.

Chris Rodley: What about James Spader?

David Cronenberg: Well, I was really surprised that right away he wanted to do it, because he's done so many different kinds of movies it's hard to know. It was obvious he wasn't afraid to play unromantic or strange characters. But I didn't realise the depths to which he was willing to go in terms of exploring the *dark*. He really was an incredible collaborator and buddy once we started. He said that he was afraid of the script, as well as being intrigued, terrified and mystified by it. But he absolutely wanted to do it. So I thought, 'He's my kind of guy.' He did want to know who else was going to be in *Crash*, because he said, 'After all, I do fuck everybody in the movie.' So I thought, 'He's going to be fine.' And by God he was more than fine.

Chris Rodley: How did he cope with doing certain scenes? He has to fuck a wound in Rosanna Arquette's crash-damaged leg!

David Cronenberg: In the character that Rosanna Arquette played, there's a definite humour involved. But people are pretty grossed out by that scene, I must say. But for me and for James it was just, 'Well, it's in the book, and it's in the script.' It made perfect sense and was integral to what's happening with those characters at that time. Being involved in a strange sexuality that is a mutation – not genetically but physically – through scars, car-crashes, and self-mutilation. It was just a question of how to do the scene effectively. The way you would do a dialogue scene.

I did a little rehearsing with this movie because the actors requested it. As Holly put it, it's really a matter of comfort. Getting to know each other, given what everybody had to do. So we sat and talked and told stories, read scenes, discussed what were the nuances of the dialogue and how could we best make them work.

Chris Rodley: There's another very confrontational scene of anal sex between Deborah Unger and Spader. They're in bed, and Unger talks throughout their fucking about Vaughan and his car. How it must smell of stale semen, etcetera.

David Cronenberg: She's very verbal there because what's happening is that they're incorporating Vaughan into their sex life. So the way she talks – getting her husband aroused by talking about him having homosexual sex with Vaughan – means there are really *three* people in that scene. That is very close to how the scene is in the book.

That was a difficult scene to do, but in bizarre ways. You can't get hair to look the same when it's messy! You can't get pillows to scrunch up the same way! I had those agonies, as well as getting the scene to work. For the movement to be sexy, elegant but awkward. And finding the right tone. It's difficult for actors physically, when you're doing a lot of takes.

Chris Rodley: You did a lot of takes on that!?

David Cronenberg: Oh yeah. Several masters, and several of each close-up. We had to take breaks and stuff. One of the ways that I worked in this movie was to let the actors look at tapes of what they'd done. I've known directors who won't tape what they're shooting, or who deliberately use horrible black-and-white monitors so the actors won't look good. I had the *best* colour monitor I could possibly find, and I showed my actors whatever they wanted to see. It was a measure of trust. They could see exactly how they looked naked, how they looked talking, or where their ass was when their skirt was pulled up. If they were going to freak out and be upset then fuck it, they were going to freak out and be upset and we'd discuss it. I found it was well worth the time on the set in terms of just finessing what they were doing.

Chris Rodley: The sex in the movie is rarely face to face. It's usually rear-entry or anal. Why is that?

David Cronenberg: It's the choice I made. I liked the way it looked. It felt right, getting both the actors looking towards the camera and not at each other. It helped that sort of 'disconnected' thing. It's been suggested that I'm obsessed with asses, but I like everything, you know. I don't think I'm too overly obsessed with asses. It's more, 'How do you have sex when you're not quite having sex with each other?' That kind of thing.

Chris Rodley: The movie also begins with three sex scenes in a row. Again, this seems very confrontational.

David Cronenberg: Yeah, it is. There are moments when audiences burst out laughing, either in disbelief or exasperation. They can't believe that they're going to have to look at *another* sex scene. To me that was replicating the tone of the book, which was absolutely unrelenting and confrontational. I thought that was one way I could replicate that.

Chris Rodley: In fact, rarely does a sex scene appear in isolation. They usually come in pairs!

David Cronenberg: And they all mean different things, too. Each one leads to the other one. The first scene is of Deborah Unger with this anonymous guy in an airplane hangar. Then James Spader with an anonymous camera girl. They're parallel of course. And then James and Deborah come together, fuck, and compare notes. That's how they develop their sexuality. In one of my little test screenings, someone said, 'A series of sex scenes is not a plot.' And I said, 'Why not? Who says? It worked for Arthur Schnitzler.' And the answer is that it *can* be, but not when the sex scenes are the normal kind of sex scenes: lyrical little interludes and then on with the real movie. Those can usually be cut out and not change the plot or characters one iota. In *Crash,* very often the sex scenes are *absolutely* the plot and the character development. You can't take them out. These are not twentieth-century sexual relationships or love relationships. These are something else. We're saying that a normal upper-middleclass couple might have this as their norm in the not-so-distant future.

Chris Rodley: I was struck by the desire in the film to merge with metal and technology. It reminded me of ideas like the handgun in *Videodrome.*

David Cronenberg: Yeah, yeah. A car is not of the highest of high-tech. But it *has* affected us and changed us more than anything else in the last hundred years. We *have* incorporated it. The weird privacy in public that it gives us. The sexual freedom – which in the 1950s wasn't even subtle! I mean, the first guy who had a convertible in high school was the guy who had the sex. He could take girls out to the country and do things to them. You'd have to take the fucking bus, and that's not the same. He had a mobile bedroom. That's exactly what it was, and that element hasn't changed. Maybe that's why people still refuse to take public transport! If they had little isolated sleepers in the subways, maybe it would work better.

So we have already incorporated the car into our understanding of time, space, distance and sexuality. To want to merge with it literally in a more physical way seems a good metaphor. There is a desire to fuse with techno-ness.

Chris Rodley: And yet, in *Crash,* doing this seems to lead inevitably to death. The body is destroyed in this process of merging.

David Cronenberg: That's just an acknowledgment of the way it works with humans, which is more disguised than – let's say – with a salmon. After salmon spawn, they're so exhausted they die. Their sexuality and desire leads them to death. But there's a sense in which *Crash* – the book and the movie – are totally above death. They are about how much human control and human will is going to be involved in that.

Chris Rodley: When Ballard claims the dead Vaughan's car at the end, it's as if he's claiming his body. The movie does seem to imply that after a fatal crash, a merging has taken place.

David Cronenberg: Yes. I still remember when Marilyn Monroe's body wasn't immediately claimed. As a kid, I thought, 'Well fuck, *I'll* claim her body. OK, she's dead, but she's still Marilyn Monroe.' I thought, 'Boy, that's very strange. This body that was the most desired body in the history of humankind, and no one will claim it.' Taking the car in that scene is exactly like claiming Marilyn Monroe's body.

Chris Rodley: Is the movie tapping into current obsessions with body piercing and scarification?

David Cronenberg: Oh yeah. I've seen some very middle-class people with eyebrow rings and stuff like that. I think they would be mortified if you said it was self-mutilation, or very primitive, or related to scarification, but without the ritual tribal structures that justify it. It's a huge not-so-far underground culture. And tattooing. That's why I had a Lincoln steering-wheel shape tattooed on Vaughan's chest towards the end. That was my invention. But I'm sure someone somewhere has that – anticipating having a steering wheel buried in their chest in a crash.

Chris Rodley: Can you discuss your view on the characters' desire to explore the sexual excitement of the car crash?

David Cronenberg: It's making very conscious what is already out there. It's not so far-fetched. Apparently, at one of the early LA screenings of *Crash*, they were doing some focus-group thing and a guy came down waving his arm – which was in a cast – saying, 'I've just been through the hell of a motorcycle accident and I broke my arm and there was nothing sexy about it. It was just hell and I think Cronenberg's gone psycho.' I don't think too many people will take the movie on that level and maybe go out and do it. But one of the reasons this movie puts pressure on the unconscious is because this is something that has flitted through everyone's mind on one level or another at some time.

Ballard really touched on those aspects of writing about cars that can really arouse you. Surprise you. You find things arousing that you never thought could be; his descriptions of semen on steering wheels and instrument panels, and of how it got there. It was techno-sex.

Chris Rodley: Vaughan and his motley group reminded me very much of the low-life souls at the Cathode Ray Mission in *Videodrome*. Or the scanners, who were derelicts.

David Cronenberg: In most sci-fi movies, it's usually the elite who are on the cutting edge of whatever's going on, but I think it's quite the contrary. It's going to be a grassroots-type movement. Those are the ones who are not fighting it, not analysing it, not organising it. They're just experiencing it.

Chris Rodley: The characters want to embrace the car crash, a potentially life-threatening event, rather as characters approach disease in your earlier films. In the script, Vaughan actually says that we must see the crash as a 'fertilising' event. Not a destructive one.

David Cronenberg: Yeah. That is a line right out of Ballard. And yet it is so much my line about parasites being a good thing rather than a bad thing. Or viruses being a creative force rather than destructive force, if seen from their perspective. Absolutely.

But it's also about the tension between reality and that whole idea of an idealised life. It's strange to me that we can conceive of a life that possibly no one has ever lived and say that that life is ideal: what we should aspire to and strive to attain. That's always seemed quite odd to me, even though fantasy often precedes reality. You need the fantasy to give shape to the reality you're trying to move towards.

In *Crash*, I'm saying that if some harsh reality envelops you, rather than be crushed, destroyed or diminished by it, embrace it fully. Develop it and take it even further than it wanted to go itself. See if that's not a creative endeavour. If that is not positive.

And the more strange and grotesque the circumstances, the more interesting it becomes. It's also me picking up on some of the philosophical tone of Ballard; trying to figure out once again my own little philosophy of life.

Chris Rodley: About the look of the movie. It's very stark. Simple. Very European in sense.

David Cronenberg: It feels that way to me, too. I like things to be deceptive in their simplicity. But sometimes the simplest things are the most difficult to do. The way I put the camera on the cars, for instance. The framing is not quite normal. I was thinking, 'I'm not going to do the usual tricky stuff. I'm not going to use wide-angle lenses from above and underneath, because it's so distracting.' And yet I *do* want to suggest people wrapped up in their cars: their relationship to their cars. So the framing is unusual, but in a very simple way.

It's really a matter of exactly where you put the camera. Not that simple. Each day, after choreographing the first scene to be shot, that would be the first thing I would do. I put it more outboard of the car body so that the windshield pillar was halfway through the frame, and the other half is looking right down the car body. That meant building rigs. You don't see that much because it takes a lot of time and it's hard to do. Shooting on a platform means you can dolly while the cars are moving. We had six Lincolns; one of them cut in half, one of them made into a pick-up truck so that I could dolly and put lights on from behind.

We got the roads department in Toronto excited about the movie. They closed a lot of things for us that they swore they would never close. Much to the dismay of some politician. We were going to get the Gardner Freeway because they were working on it, but they finished it early. Politicians came out and said, 'Due to the wonderful efficiency of your politicians, we now can open the road *this* weekend.' So we said, 'Sorry. You promised that we would have it that weekend.' So they had to *keep* it closed. Embarrassing.

Chris Rodley: The car crashes are unusual for 1990s cinema in that they're very unspectacular. Why was that?

David Cronenberg: I wanted them to be fast, brutal and over before you knew it. There's not one foot of slow motion. No repeated shots. I wanted to make them realistic in a cinematic way, because it's the *aftermath* that is delicious: that can be savoured and apprehended by the senses. What happens during a crash itself is too fast to feel without slow-motion replay. Most of us don't get replays on our car crashes.

Chris Rodley: Ballard says that *Crash* is a cautionary tale from the eye of the hurricane. Do you think it's timely in that we're approaching the millennium, and this century has definitely been the century of the car?

David Cronenberg: Well, the place of the car in the world economy can't be overestimated. Although people don't think of cars as being very high-tech, every high-tech development is represented somewhere in a car. Whether it's fibre-optic electronics, or in the metallurgy. All of these incredible industries serve the car.

So if suddenly we said, 'There can't be any more cars, we're stopping today,' it would be the end of the world; economies diving, people not knowing what to do with themselves. Our attachment to it, as discussed in the movie, is very primitive indeed. It has become the quintessential human appendage. I think it won't go away easily. It's got a lot of shape-shifting to do before it disappears.

Chris Rodley: What surprised you most about making *Crash*?

David Cronenberg: It has become a very *emotional* movie. In the beginning it wasn't, and certainly I would never have said that about the book. I find that people come away having been really shaken, feeling very emotional, but not knowing why or how. It doesn't push any of the usual buttons. And that's really good. There's going to be a lot of different reactions. I do think we might get a lot of people throwing things. I'm prepared for that. But I don't really like being rejected. You know that. I really do want to make movies that everyone loves!

Chris Rodley: For your last movie you went to the Great Wall of China. Was there a sense with *Crash* that you were – in more senses than one – coming home?

David Cronenberg: Definitely. And I took considerable strength from that. We literally shot the whole movie within half a mile of my house. I like that very much. I'd drive by all the locations every day on my way to the editing room. There's a wonderful sense of this movie being physically and tangibly a part of my life, a part of my daily, mundane life as well as my artistic life. That's very satisfying. Something that I haven't experienced quite that way for some time. It's good.

Short Cuts
IN THE TIME OF EARTHQUAKES

Jonathan Romney

The last word spoken in Robert Altman's film *Short Cuts* is 'lemonade'. We hear it as the camera tracks out over a briefly shaken Los Angeles, as two partying couples toast to survival in the face of a minor apocalypse. As so often happens with Altman, who is famous for his habit of scrambling soundtracks to the limit of comprehensibility, the word is audible but not entirely noticeable, certainly not impressing itself on you as central to the film's meaning. Yet, in an oblique fashion, that is precisely what it is – an operational password for the entire film. For 'Lemonade' is the title of a poem by Raymond Carver, and the poem's subject is also the film's real subject, as well as its structural principle.

Short Cuts is based on nine stories by Carver, who died in 1988 aged fifty, having established himself as the poet laureate of small, desolate, claustrophobic middle American lives. 'Lemonade' itself is not directly adapted in the film, although its theme – What if this had happened, rather than that? What then? – is foregrounded in the episode involving Jack Lemmon, and runs throughout the film, both in the narratives themselves and in the way they interlock. In the poem, a man ponders on his son's drowning; he is convinced he would still be alive if only he had not gone to fetch lemonade that day. The lemonade, he reasons, would not have been there if only there had not been lemons in the shops. So he tries to pick his way back casually to a prelapsarian moment: 'It all harks back to first causes, back to the first lemon cultivated on earth.'

Carver knows there is no first lemon, and Altman knows it, too. There is no way of untangling the mesh of cause and effect, hence the gloriously unruly tangle of chance that governs *Short Cuts*. The credits divide the cast list conveniently into nine family sets of characters, plus supporting players, but in reality the groups are not separated neatly from one another; rather, they intermingle, meeting, playing, straying with seismic effect into each others' lives. Each group has its own story, but no story belongs solely to one group. Altman plays with an illusion of order by framing the narratives between two urban catastrophes during which all the characters are effectively united simply by virtue of being in the same boat. The sense of unity is illusory, though, imposed as it is by narrative contingency. There is no start or finish, no first or last lemon, only the all-pervasive smell of lemonade. Savour it, or baulk at its bitterness, that's all you get in life, and you have to drink it.

There is no first lemon in Robert Altman's career, either. Looking back on the director's exceptionally diverse history, no clear thread is immediately apparent. We can impose an overall narrative on it, but only if we give in to the temptation continually to ask, 'what if?'. There is the fact that after the international success of his 1969 film *M*A*S*H*, Altman went on to make a number of movies whose eccentricity wilfully flew in the face of box-office logic – the flight fantasy *Brewster McCloud* (1970), the dreamlike *3 Women* (1977), the bleak science-fiction vision *Quintet* (1979). He also made some that worked over genres in a way that seemed to tap in directly to the sceptical Zeitgeist of the 1970s – notably his brutal demystifications of the frontier Western and the Philip Marlowe myth in *McCabe and Mrs Miller* (1971) and *The Long Goodbye* (1973) respectively.

But what if Altman's career had been more coherent? What if his 1980 shot at a grandly fanciful comic-book epic, *Popeye*, had been the intended box office smash? (Indeed, what if its star Robin Williams had actually been audible at any point in the film?) And what if the administration at Fox had not suddenly changed just in time to scupper the commercial hopes of his 1980 satire *Health*?

Pure speculation, of course, but all these factors contributed to one of the exemplary adventures in American cinema – the strange situation in which the most ambitious, wayward director of his generation (Altman, remember, preceded the Class of Movie Brats) suddenly found himself having to reinvent his career on a shoestring, having blown his luck not only with the major studios but also with his own ill-fated production company, Lion's Gate. Hence an extraordinary spate of low-budget ventures into chamber cinema, often drawn from theatre: the remarkable one-hander for Richard Milhous Nixon, *Secret Honor* (1984), which did for Tricky Dicky what *Syberberg* did for Hitler; *Fool for Love* (1985), *Come Back to the Five & Dime Jimmy Dean, Jimmy Dean* (1982). There were other off-the-cuff projects for television, such as the adaptations of Pinter's *The Dumb Waiter* and *The Room* (1987), and a version of that creaky tub-thumper *The Caine Mutiny Court-Martial* (1988), a small miracle of a film which testily jump-started that somnolent genre, the courtroom drama.

It's tempting to consider that had Altman's Hollywood fortunes been more consistent, this whole daredevil chapter might not have happened. Altman himself is sanguine about his whole story and aware of just how random can be the elements that impinge on his progress. Visiting Britain for *Short Cuts'* screening at last November's London Film Festival, he cited the example of his *Buffalo Bill and the Indians* (1976), co-written with his protegé Alan Rudolph, and after *McCabe and Mrs Miller* his second scathing debunking of the legends of the Wild West.

'*Buffalo Bill* was released on Independence Day 1976, which was the Bicentennial of the country. Nixon had just resigned in disgrace, and the whole country was licking its wounds, and I come out with this picture and say, "Hi, folks, here I am, let me tell you what assholes you are and how America's myths are blah blah blah blah…" Nobody wanted it. At a different time in history, that film could have been a big hit.'

Short Cuts, too, falls wonderfully into this schema of apparent randomness. Altman first read Raymond Carver's stories on a plane journey. Inspired by them, he started planning a Carver film, and got as far as selecting the locations and signing up a number of actors, including Tim Robbins, Peter Gallagher and Fred Ward. But finally the finance was not available. While pondering his next move, he was offered a project called *The Player*. Those same actors found their way into that film, which in 1992 turned out to be Altman's first commercial and critical success in years – as well as a modish *succès de scandale* among the Hollywood mandarins, at once outraged and flattered to see their world lampooned. *Short Cuts* was financed on the strength of that film.

The Player was notable for playing an extreme version of a trick that Altman had used before, and fully intends to use again – the interweaving of real and fictional universes. In *The Player*, a host of familiar Hollywood faces played themselves, raising the interesting question of what being 'oneself' might mean in a city predicated entirely on performance. But the most cunning variation on this effect came in Altman's television series *Tanner '88: The Dark Horse* (1988), in which real-life US politicos, including Robert Dole and Pat Robertson, were drafted in to be encountered by Michael Murphy's fictional Democrat presidential hopeful. Altman intends to push the method further in his next production, *Prêt-à-Porter*, which he is filming this year in the Paris fashion world.

'In *Prêt-à-Porter*, we're using much more reality. There's not much reality in *Short Cuts*, except the presence of the game show host Alex Trebek [who appears early on in a concert scene]. In *Prêt-à-Porter*, I will probably push the mix between reality and fiction as far as I've ever pushed it. I'm dependent on it, because I can't recreate the amount of people in that world – especially when you get into the fashion shows, the press, the photographers. So I have to use a lot of reality.'

Unlike *The Player*, *Short Cuts* plays less on reality *per se* than on the real. Carver's low-key, minimally stylised portrayals of the doldrums and zero moments in blue-collar living led him to be counted as a leading exponent of that amorphous school known as 'Dirty Realism'. He wrote about dead marriages, dead-end jobs, typhoons in teacups, minor misunderstandings that blow up into little household apocalypses – but apocalypses in aspic. What's remarkable about these stories is the way they merge explosiveness with absolute stillness. A typical story, one of those in *Short Cuts*, is 'Jerry and Molly and Sam', in which a fatigued father contrives to lose the family dog, then has to retrieve it. When he finally finds the dog, he simply contemplates it, and the story ends on a suspended moment: 'He sat there. He thought he didn't feel so bad, all things considered. The world was full of dogs. There were dogs and there were dogs. Some dogs you just couldn't do anything with.'

Altman and his co-writer Frank Barhydt take a very different approach. The episode becomes a source of high farce, the dog a benign comic focus for the chaotic rage of Tim Robbins' blustering cop. There's clearly more meeting the eye – more energy, more incident – in Altman's version than the moments of cold, clear deadness that Carver's original stories are imbued with. Yet Altman claims that he leaves out everything that Carver leaves out – and precisely what that is, he says, is 'judgment, in most cases. I make a little bit more judgment than Carver made. I have a tougher task in a way. It's very hard to do films as minimalism, because the audience is there and they see every square inch of that screen. They see wallpaper and they see rugs and they see shirts and expressions and weather – until all of the descriptive passages that you have in a book are there.

'Carver uses no descriptive passages, so I don't believe a Raymond Carver story can be literally translated to a visual medium. So I just tried to take the feeling from Carver, the type of incident he dealt with, and express that in a way that tells the same story for an audience. I don't think that I could take any one of his stories and make a film out of it.'

How did Altman and Barhydt decide which stories to use, and which ones would led into which others?

'They do it themselves automatically. You take on base story, you throw it up on the wall, and it's like vines – they grow where there's space to grow in and out of one another.' The image of vines perhaps expresses what's most peculiar to the film. It's certainly true that, as some Carver specialists have pointed out, the film does not strictly adhere to the writer's spirit; it's at once too upbeat and too cynical for that. It only rarely displays the stoic empathy that the stories solicit for their characters; instead, Altman's characters redeem the claustrophobic quality of their lives by the energy and charisma with which they perform (to the extent that some of these lives look somewhat glamorous because they're incarnated by the likes of Tom Waits or Frances McDormand). But it is the connections between the episodes that make the film – the sense that they're all bunches of event growing on the same tangled vine. And it's when we become aware of the incongruity of these connections that the film transcends its merely anecdotal base.

There are moments of sublime embarrassment in *Short Cuts*, notably in the sequence where Jack Lemmon, as the estranged father of the son that he hasn't seen for years, turns up at the hospital where his young grandson is in casualty. It's a painful situation in itself, but the film pushes it further by having the father deliver a monologue recounting the banal indiscretion that years ago led to his banishment from the family. Here most of all, the spirit of 'Lemonade' (could Lemmon have been cast purely for a conceptual pun?) makes itself felt. The father's reminiscence represents a crisis in itself, but one that is totally inappropriate to the crisis happening in the hospital ward. It's as if he has wandered from one story into another, suggesting that life's most dramatic moments are the result of inadequate separation between different narratives.

'This is what happens every day of your life,' says Altman, 'but we don't recognise it so much because we can't take the involvement. Somebody gets hit by a car and you stop and look in the street, and you think, 'I don't want to see that,' so you go the other way. But people who don't go the other way see more of that story, and the people who are actually involved in that story have another story. These things go on all the time, and it's the juxtaposition of these lives that makes *Short Cuts* interesting.'

The Carver stories operate on two levels. Each one is very much like a closed box, a miniature in which a single core of event, or lack of event, is to be contemplated – in the tradition of modernist short story narrative since Chekhov, Joyce, Mansfield. At the same time, however, the stories taken together, and the regularity of the themes and styles, make an overall human comedy made up of small mosaic pieces. *Short Cuts*, though, functions only through the concatenation of parts – the clash of micro-narratives sparking ironic parallels and negations off each other.

It's a technique that has formed the basis of what is probably the most celebrated strand of Altman's work. The idea of sprawling ensemble pieces made of varying, decentred dramas is one he famously perfected in *Nashville* (1975). At one point he planned a follow-up, *Nashville, Nashville*, with some of the same characters, and *Short Cuts* could be seen as the pay-off of that aborted project (Altman plans eventually to make *More Short Cuts*). But there are variations to this approach. Nashville derived its unity from having different characters doing different business in one setting – a place that in its iconic status as an anti-Hollywood, America's great other dream factory, opened the film up to an allegorical state-of-the-nation reading. *A Wedding* (1978) similarly used a single setting, this time to follow the conventions of situation comedy to their extreme conclusion.

Short Cuts differs from *Nashville* in its relation to place – it is not primarily the portrait of a specific city, but simply uses Los Angeles as a convenient, anonymous venue to bring its various protagonists together. (As Frank Barhydt points out, 'Apart from the palm trees and the weather, there's nothing indigenous to LA, nothing in the characters of the people.') However, the city's anonymity brings its own meaning to the film. Where the city of Nashville forms an arena in which individuals intermingle, with politics and country music as the uniting factor, *Short Cuts* captures the cellular essence of LA, a city in which separate zones, separate homes, are linked by highways. You can imagine each segment to be equivalent to a family cell – and things start happening when characters step out of their own territory into other people's. The theme is seen in undiluted form in the episode based on the story 'Neighbors'. In the film, there is no life-transforming catastrophe as there is in Carver's story. A couple simply make free with the apartment they're caretaking; but our sense of unease is no less powerful, just because we expect the worst – we know they should not be there. As with the Jack Lemmon episode, we receive a sense of trespass: lines have been crossed.

Despite the sense of impending chaos that is perhaps inevitable in a film that juggles twenty-two lead parts, there are plenty of guide rails in *Short Cuts* to ensure that we know where we are. One is the use of familiar faces in the cast. ('I don't have to tell you too much about these people,' says Altman. 'You do the work for me by recognising them.') Another is the use of a nightclub singer, played by Annie Ross, to act as a chorus, casting a sardonic torch-song commentary throughout the film. And another is the way the diversity of incident is framed between the two minor apocalypses.

At the beginning of the film, the city is sprayed against medfly, a pest which leaves harmless blemishes on fruit (what could be more suggestive of the Californian obsession with cosmetic surfaces?). The end of the film – which, beware, this paragraph reveals in full – is rather more violent. At the very second that Chris Penn's repressed, brooding character Jerry unexpectedly smashes a rock down on a young girl's head, an earthquake erupts. It's a horribly suggestive moment. Perhaps Jerry's pent-up rage is the entire city's; perhaps, because of him, heavenly wrath is being visited on the community. But you could read it more cynically as a self-conscious sleight of hand, a playfully apocalyptic gesture in which Altman plays God and brings all the film's diffuse threads together, packing all his characters back in the narrative toy box.

'That's just coincidence,' Altman says of the ending. 'I'm sure that for every earthquake that's ever happened, some very strong, acute dramatic event has happened in somebody's life – I just happened to be there at this particular incident. I needed to polarise the beginning and end of the film – these people's lives never really came together, they just occasionally crossed in a very haphazard way, so that's something that was a common experience. I wouldn't be surprised if in *More Short Cuts* there'll be another two events. One of them might be the Californian fires.'

This closing image of the all-powerful narrative deity suggests a director who likes to keep a tight rein on his creation. But, Altman says, only one type of control interests him: 'the control to be able to change and let ideas come in from my collaborators. To have the ability to say "Yeah" and turn the piece this way or that. *Not* say, "Wait a minute, you said you were going to do this and you'd better stick to it."'

Altman's list of recent and future projects may suggest a sense of multi-directional crazy paving, but there's a flexibility and ambition there that he's always had, and that directors a third his age rarely evidence. Already chalked up: a stage opera version of the novel *McTeague* (the source of Von Stroheim's *Greed*), with composer William Bolcom; a short documentary recording the hoofers' musical *Black and Blue*; producing Alan Rudolph's new film *Dorothy Parker*, itself a multi-character sprawler in the Altman tradition. Planned after *Prêt-à-Porter*: a Mata Hari project; another collaboration with Frank Barhydt about Kansas City's boomtown years during the Depression; a two-film version of playwright Tony Kushner's AIDS diptych *Angels in America*; a film called *Cork* with Harry Belafonte, 'about blackface and entertainment from the turn of the century'. Altman admits, 'I'll never do all of those. It's like *pommes frites* – you throw the potatoes in and then whichever one pops to the surface is done first.'

Altman also offers another, perhaps more apposite analogy, that applies just as well to his career as a whole – reckless, unruly, wilfully patchy – as it does to particular films such as *Short Cuts*. 'It comes down to what occurs to me. It's like doing art – I'm not doing Rembrandts or Corots. I'm doing Rauschenbergs. I'm doing collages. If suddenly I want to stick into my painting a photograph of a flat-iron, it just goes in.'

Trainspotting
THE BOYS ARE BACK IN TOWN

Andrew O'Hagan

Edwin Muir was an Orkney poet who hardly gets a mention now. You may have heard tell of him as the man who introduced the work of Franz Kafka to Great Britain. He was a great stirrer, a spirited observer of modern European reality, and it is he who comes to mind during the first few minutes of the film *Trainspotting*, an adaptation of Irvine Welsh's 1993 novel.

Muir once described Edinburgh as 'a blank nothing', at the centre of a 'sham nation'. For him, the sound of bagpipes along Princes Street, the smell of guns from the castle, the baronial ornaments of the capital city of the 1930s, were the signals of a nation's inability to be a nation, evidence of its grotty willingness to become a tartanised tourist trap. *Trainspotting* opens with a young razorcut running down Princes Street, some time in the 1980s, pursued by two store detectives. As he barges through the crowd, an assortment of stolen goods falls out of his jacket onto the pavement. There is a look of desperation in his eyes, as well as an odd definition of glee, and we soon hear his voice sweeping through the soundtrack, in a direct quote from Welsh's book: 'Choose life. Choose a career. Choose a family. Choose a fucking big television. Choose washing machines, cars, compact disc players and electrical tin openers ... Choose rotting away at the end of it all, pishing your last in a miserable home, nothing more than an embarrassment to the selfish, fucked-up brats you spawned to replace yourself. Choose your future.'

This is the world of Mark Renton, or rather the world Renton is straining to reject. He and his mates wouldn't be affronted by the notion of Kafka-come-alive in present-day Edinburgh, nor would they feel wronged by ideas about the blankness of their local culture. They know all about that, they sometimes speak of it, but they won't be raising any colourful standard on the ground of these truths, if that is what they are. You come to feel that, whatever else is going on, Muir's worries are not theirs: they appear to have had enough debates, and theories, and choices, and fake opportunities. 'It's all shite.' Everything. Renton holds no allegiances, carries no banner, not even for himself. What he's chosen instead is a 'sincere and truthful junk habit'.

William Burroughs once described the drugs economy as the most pure and lethal form of capitalism. At the bottom end of the scale – in that place Renton and his pals would sneeringly call home – the demand is always greater than the spending power. The supply is increasingly plentiful, shoddy and corrupted, and the economy demands that punters steal or begin to deal themselves in order to keep going. It is a cycle of extremity and hopelessness; and in Edinburgh, as in many places, it is beset with violence and crime and plague. If *Trainspotting* continues by sidelight, a form of hard debate about Edinburgh, about Scotland, about Britain, in ways that wouldn't have been thought strange in the 1930s and the 1960s, it must be added that it brings into focus a world of desperation – of hedonism, heartlessness and wastedness – that has little to do with much besides a definite strain of reality in the Scotland of the 1980s and 1990s.

Renton's pal Sick Boy (Johnny Lee Miller) is a sex pest; he likes impersonating national god Sean Connery and he has quit heroin not because he's especially keen, but just because he wants to annoy Renton. Spud (Ewen Bremner) is a manic idiot, a live wire, who gets so far up on speed that he makes a completely misguided effort to secure work. It is somehow instructive that the most powerful person in the group is not the most attractive or intelligent or fun to be with, but the least in all departments. Begbie (Robert Carlyle) is a complete psycho: they don't like him, they fear him. Carlyle plays Begbie as if he were a cartoon, which he sort of is. He smashes pint tumblers in people's faces. He carries a Stanley knife. It's safe to say (though not in front of him) that there is no line he wouldn't cross. He'd knife women. Renton, you come to think, may be a sort of film hero – not just a man being ruined by all things domestic, but a man so often in exile from his own senses, and from the scabby world beyond them, that he just doesn't care that much. Not much.

But, for all that, the thing is mainly a comedy. It is one of those movies (*Easy Rider*, *GoodFellas*, *The Great Rock'n'Roll Swindle*) whose tone can seem to mimic the personalities of the people it pictures. It is not a buddy movie, nor a road movie, nor what used to be called an underground movie. Though it is angry, it is not an overtly political movie either – but, by virtue of the language and the lives it uncovers, it might be seen to have political ramifications. You seldom see these people on film, or hear this language, and this in itself harbours a political message.

Not long ago, a BBC film crew arrived in the Edinburgh housing scheme of Muirhouse. They were making a film about Welsh. They felt it would be good to film something of the world his books come out of, to offer (as they say) something of the context for the writing – the context being this very real place, full of poverty, and addiction. Just as they were getting going, one of the local residents came sloping along. He wondered what they were doing. Yes, he'd heard of Welsh, and his response was not slow on the heels of that recognition: 'Am dying here, dyn' tae score, and yous cunts are making a film aboot it. Huv ye got any reddies?' The boys from the BBC – sorely in love with Welsh's depictions, and who can blame them – were not so well prepared for the real thing. It's easy to understand their strong feelings about Welsh's renderings, but it's also easy to understand their strong feelings of fear when unexpectedly confronted with Mr Scag Territory himself. Such, you might idly say, is the ambivalence of art, and it is an ambivalence welded to the heart of the *Trainspotting* movie.

It's very stylised and lovingly coloured. Those who were all for the confident splashings of *Shallow Grave*, made by the same people, but set in a very different

Edinburgh, will not be disappointed with this. At its best, the movie adds a surrealist tinge to the novel's most perfectly extreme and disgusting moments. But it's disturbing, from time to time, to see the lives of this troop of addicts and psychos blasted about in pop promo fashion. The speed of it sometimes serves to slide over the novel's darker edges, but, with a soundtrack by Blur, Primal Scream, Pulp and New Order, it is guaranteed to win – as the stage-play did – with young audiences keen on disaffection and anarchy and good music.

The film is also a kind of poem to wayward bodily functions. There is a lot of shite in it, and a lot is made of the shite that appears in single scenes. Renton is at one point seen to be climbing in and out of a toilet. But this is a story of young bodies in a time of addiction and sickness – there is always somebody shiteing themselves, or puking up, or ejaculating into the mud. Whatever the arguments, shiteing and pissing and fucking and bleeding and puking are big parts of their talk, they preoccupy Renton and his mates, and it is hardly ever superfluous, except when made too campy and stylish. At such moments, the film threatens to become some sort of 'Carry On Shitein', Fightin' and Shootin' Up' extravaganza.

But extremities of filth – spoken or depicted – are a crucial part of the world of this film. If the shite is sometimes too much, the coarse language never is. The sad ones who spent their evenings a year or so ago counting the 'fucks' in James Kelman's *How Late It Was, How Late*, will be happily busy again – this time counting 'cunts'. I am just as happy to report that not one of them is out of place. Swearing in *Trainspotting* is a vehicle of affection and camaraderie, as well as of violence and frustration. There could be no other way to do it, and the dialogue's alright. The film is original and brisk in the manner of its confidence: it assaults you, calls you everything and, like the characters themselves, it just doesn't give a fuck. These are lives that are lived through words, and the lack of them. John Hodge's script is replete with good bad usage – and closer to the right places because of that.

The film is really Mark Renton's story. He is one of those guys whose outlook and patter are in large part defined by the outlook and patter of his mates. He really understands what it is to have mates: to have shared drugs, and girls, to have minted between themselves a whole lot of talk. But as time goes on, and adult realities bite in, you can see Mark begin to define himself by what his mates are not. He is more cynical, thoughtful and much cleverer than they are, and he comes round to seeing that he will never get away from himself – his need for drugs, his need to be a prick – until he gets away. Their hardness is most often fear and dread thinly made-up, and they don't really know how to talk to each other any more. There is, of course, a point where the strenuous avoidance of sentiment is itself sentimental, and Renton begins to see that his mates are selfish nutters and sentimental losers. The film then becomes a study of betrayal.

Renton is played by a suitably disobliging Ewan McGregor (*Lipstick on Your Collar, Shallow Grave*), who lost two stone to make way for Welsh's gangly, flat-footed hero. Mainly due to the ambivalence in McGregor's face, you get the feeling that Mark wouldn't say no to a bit of feeling. But he's numb – he can't say yes, and he can't say no. Renton is a different sort of man from the fictional men who have gone before him. Renton's father, his grandfather, would have taken drink, they might have been bad to women but they would have talked a lot about responsibility, about decency, about getting on. They would, perhaps, have been religious bigots – they would certainly have had strong feelings about Scotland. Earlier Scottish fictions, and some films, have given breath to characters like the older Rentons. But we haven't had much of Renton himself, or his scaggy, thieving mates. Their fight – with drugs, with boredom, with who they are – might be harder, it might not be. But bravery is not what it used to be.

There is a scene in the film where Tommy (Kevin McKidd) persuades some of the boys to come for a walk in the country. At the foot of the Pentlands, Renton finally loses his rag. He hates Scotland, it's pure shite. Besides everything else, he hates the fact that it couldn't even be dominated by a decent country, just England, a bunch of poofs. There aren't many Scottish writers – previous to this generation – who could write such a thing, no films have given voice to this before. In the novel, Renton rounds on the very notion of national belonging. 'Ah've never felt British, because ah'm not. It's ugly and artificial. Ah've never really felt Scottish either, though. Scotland the brave, ma arse; Scotland the shitein cunt. We'd throttle the life oot ay each other fir the privilege ay rimmin some English aristocrat's piles.' Welsh and others have taken flight from the older Scottish writers who write about the urban working class. He has accused James Kelman, for example, of sanitising the way people talk – airbrushing out their racism, their sexism, their self-defeating naffness about other people. It's true to say that the characters in the fiction of Kelman and Gray and Janice Galloway speak as people do in the West Coast of Scotland – but they don't say the things that people *say* there. For all their verbal innovations and phonetic wonders, the characters in these books tend to say the sort of things the authors themselves might say. The youngsters, who've learnt much from them but not everything, are more likely to do the opposite and have characters say the virtually unsayable. This bears heavily on the *Trainspotting* script.

Renton's pals are part of himself, and therefore worthy of rejection at some point. You get the distinct impression, for all his furious repudiations of nationality, he feels that whatever is wrong with the country is also wrong with them. Get away from them, get away from here, embrace everything you are not, he seems to mutter to himself. Renton is a hurting, scag-addled, late in the day sort of Alfie. He knows what he needs to keep himself going, he knows where to get it, but he wishes there was a way to stop needing it so much. He goes about his haunts with Alfie-like cruelty, but he is much more subject to the wiles and cruelties of others, especially dealers, or those who tax him in the name of friendship. But, on the surface at least, things were smoother for Alfie. His weekend was a wage-packet-in-the-top-pocket sort of place; his sense of male pride was invested in shoe polish and a well-ironed hankie for the top pocket. Alfie's likeable sin was promiscuity; Renton's is the much more pitiable search for the balm of oblivion. And whatever male pride has to do with Renton's world, it seldom has anything to do with a wage packet.

Over the past year or so, cinema screens have been filled with images of a place called Scotland. *Braveheart* and *Rob Roy*, with their high common purpose and battle fatigues, have opened up, and revisited, vistas of pure romance which have absolutely nothing to do with the lives being lived in that country. Scottish people do not even experience their history in that way. The clash of steel, the sweep of the glens, the flash of the tartan badge – not a chance. It's all just shite. People might well go along with these films, but they won't be waking up to them in the morning. This kingdom is in trouble at the extremities. If there are to be moves in such places towards self-government – and people are looking for reasons to think so – then such moves are unlikely to be hurried on their way by the wits of Mel Gibson. *Trainspotting* is set in a Scotland that has hitherto been without existence for filmgoers. It features places that are little known outside of themselves. It is to the like of *Trainspotting* that people will go for a sense of what life is like there, for a sense of what has gone wrong – and it will offer rousing clues. *Trainspotting*, of course, will carry little of this by itself, and neither would it want to. But it is unusual to see a film pointing to something so tangible and so real. The makers of *Trainspotting*, and the novelist with whom it originated, won't be looking for much more than a few laughs. And they'll get their laughs. But it is laughter in the murk – once the giggling stops, people may start to examine the murk.

American Psycho
SICK CITY BOY

Nick James

In Mary Harron's new movie version of the cult novel *American Psycho*, the first victim is an African-American man sitting in a New York alley with a paper cup in front of him, homeless and hungry and smelling of shit and booze. Wall Street worker Patrick Bateman taunts him with offers of money and food, then hisses into his ear, 'Why don't you get a job?' before stabbing him in the stomach. This is lighter treatment than the same beggar receives in Bret Easton Ellis' original 1991 novel, where Bateman's blade 'pops' his retina, cueing a gruesome description of eyeball matter oozing down his face.

An Irish drunk lying on his back in a tunnel singing songs of the old country gets it first in Stanley Kubrick's adaptation of Anthony Burgess' *A Clockwork Orange* (recently released on UK screens for the first time since 1972, when Kubrick withdrew it after several 'copycat' crimes were laid at its door). Stuck in a dystopian future, his misfortune is to be visited by young British yob Alex and his droogs on the lookout for some ultra-violence. 'I could never stand to see a moodge all filthy and rolling and burbling and drunk,' muses Alex before he and his pals lay in with assorted weapons.

Street people are the hapless victims of this kind of social satire not because they make us feel guilty about our relative wealth and privilege, but because they are out of the loop, beyond the pale, non-participants. They can't be consumers of the critique, only targets of its messenger. Bum-killing aside, these two films otherwise bear little comparison. Both are adaptations of satirical novels about young psychopaths who are meant to represent the ills of their age. Both show women as perpetually available objects for mistreatment (though Harron has them show their contempt for Bateman's inanity).

Thereafter, it's all contrast: *A Clockwork Orange* is a 1960s novel inspired by a 1950s phenomenon (teddy-boy gangs) set in a future which Kubrick renders as a 1970s sex-and-violence fantasy married to a somewhat paranoid vision of brainwashing as a treatment for young offenders. *American Psycho* is a 1990s novel set in the late 1980s which Harron has lovingly re-created as a fetishised hall of mirrors for mirror men. Kubrick's film attacks a Britain of rigid and blind institutions which are no longer recognisable with us. Harron's lampoons the denizens of US finance houses and their rabid boomtown consumer culture. One young male protagonist is at the bottom of the social heap, the other at the top. Is there anything else that links these films other than the vicious survival-of-the-fittest ethos of their central characters? The short answer is yes, but to follow my thread we must do like Mary Harron and revisit the 1980s.

The flaunt-it, goldrush aesthetic of the 1980s was satirised almost from the outset. Culturally, it was a pompous decade that took its fantasies of glamour extremely seriously – think on the one hand of the po-faced New Romantic art crowd straining for a post-Bowie, post-punk, post-gender utopia in clubland, and on the other of the brokers and traders with their anal focus on 'correct' forms of consumption. In the United States, these were two sides of the social coin and the twain met in the clubs of New York. It was a time ripe for ridicule, irony and sarcasm, the heyday of ism. But, being the 1980s, it attracted serious ridicule, irony and sarcasm.

American novels of cocaine abuse and anomie among the well heeled took the zeitgeist limelight. Jay McInerney's 1984 *Bright Lights, Big City* concerned the free-fall of a magazine fact-checker lost in clubland and dumped by his model girlfriend. Its hero's dilemma begins when he finds himself in a club in the early hours where 'the bald girl is saying this used to be a good place to come before the assholes discovered it'. The question here is whether the narrator is one of the assholes. Given the book's self-lacerating tone, maybe he is, but the girl with the shaved head is also 'emblematic of the problem ... Her voice ... is like the New Jersey State Anthem played through an electric shaver.' The usual emblematic bum is not a victim here. He doesn't turn up until the last chapter where he confers a blessing on the repentant hedonist with his bleeding nose, as he staggers back to sane bourgeois comfort and someone more conventional to look at than the bald woman.

Ellis' 1985 fiction debut *Less Than Zero* followed in McInerney's footsteps. It's about a rich West Coast boy trying to decide whether or not to let go of his feckless, coke-addled teen milieu and go back to college. This was satire so discreet it looked like celebration. Both books are firmly and unapologetically set among the well-off. They describe and perhaps promote the anomie of limitless self-gratification and, despite the fall each protagonist experiences, I would guess they were hungrily consumed by the envious. Movie versions of both emerged in 1988, but the novels had been defanged to fit the earnest mould of the Brat Pack movie.

The critique sharpened as the me-decade rolled on and the fiscal grotesqueries of Milton Friedman, Margaret Thatcher, Donald Trump and other 1980s icons became harder to stomach. The keynote movie was Oliver Stone's *Wall Street* (1987), with its anti-slogan 'Greed is good' uttered by its resident ogre, corporate raider Gordon Gekko, the archetype of the 1980s money man. As Gekko, Michael Douglas jutted out his chin and made cobra eyes at the victims of his ruthless workaholism. His other oft-quoted utterance is 'Lunch is for wimps.' Aspects of the Gekko creed have returned to haunt us today with the new boom (and looming bust) in cyber-shares. In the forthcoming movie *Boiler Room*, which is about a judge's son who works in a 'chop shop' (a company that trains people to hard-sell worthless bonds), the team of traders recite Gekko's dialogue word perfect while watching a video of *Wall Street*. Like, say, *In the Company of Men* and *Claire Dolan*, *Boiler Room* doesn't feel like a new take on hard-edged city life, but an 1980s film made now.

In the same year *Wall Street* was released, Tom Wolfe, a scion of 1970s New Journalism who had switched to novel writing, put out *The Bonfire of the Vanities*. Wolfe's ambition was to draw a vast portrait of New York's different social levels on a scale worthy of Dickens or Zola. His 'hero' Sherman McCoy was a 'Master of the Universe', a WASP bond trader who takes his Mercedes down a wrong turning and ends up in the Bronx where, by accident, he finds himself accused of killing a young black man. It's worth quoting a little of Wolfe's prologue, which enters the mind of a Jewish mayor of New York trying unsuccessfully to face down a rebellious televised Harlem crowd, to get the full flavour of his race-paranoid thesis: 'They [the WASPs] won't know what they're looking at [on television]. They'll sit in their co-ops on Park and Fifth and East Seventy-second Street and Sutton Place, and they'll shiver with the violence of it and enjoy the show. Cattle! Birdbrains! Rosebuds! Goyim! You don't even know do you? Do you really think this is your city any longer? Open your eyes! The greatest city of the twentieth century! Do you think money will keep it yours?' If the Brian De Palma movie failed to make Wolfe's novel feel relevant, a more succinct take on WASP redundancy was found in Whit Stillman's 1989 *Metropolitan*, which had its well-heeled gentry go gentle into that good night of acceptance.

What all this 1980s them-and-us social satire reminds me of is the way the spectre of 'the masses' haunted modernist writers in the early twentieth century, as described in John Carey's book *The Intellectuals and the Masses*. The growth in population and literacy that led to the advent of mass culture was greeted by a Nietzsche-inspired vein of disgust and horror in the writings of such highbrow authors as H. G. Wells, T. S. Eliot, F. R. Leavis, W. B. Yeats and Virginia Woolf. Carey argues that 'the principle around which modernist literature and culture fashioned themselves was the exclusion of the masses, the defeat of their power, the removal of their literacy, the denial of their humanity'. But, he concludes, 'What this intellectual effort failed to acknowledge is that the masses do not exist.' Literature constructed the idea of the masses by 'the imposition of imagined attributes' – the consumption of newspapers and tinned food, for instance.

What you consume has been the marker of who you are in literature for the better part of the twentieth century. And long lists of what Patrick Bateman consumes notoriously make up a large amount of Ellis' novel. What we consume is also a part of him – it's impossible to read Bateman fully without knowing who Sherman McCoy and Gordon Gekko are. McCoy gets a brief namecheck in the novel and Gekko a walk-on part, post-modernism now being in full swing. All this self-reference poses problems for the film-maker, however, who can't rely too heavily on an interior voice.

Sufficient distance from the 1980s allows Harron to treat Ellis' gruelling subject matter with a greater sense of fun. She takes a more broadly comic, arm's-length view of Patrick Bateman – there's almost a hint of Austin Powers about actor Christian Bale's willingness to camp it up. He looks unreal in a very 1980s way – a lot like Christopher Reeve as Superman (Nietzsche again?). In the book, mockery of Bateman's status obsession is a sly matter of shifting tone – it leavens the intense babble of blood-lust inside his head. Harron makes lampooning 1980s man as a creature of surfaces her grandstanding play.

For Harron it's about getting the surfaces right. (Like *Claire Dolan*, her film has a cold, metallic, surgical gleam.) Bateman's apartment is a white sepulchre, a plinth for his statuesque 'hardbody'. A mantra-like list of bodycare products is delivered in voiceover as Bateman applies them in his shower: a nominally straight man showing a super-feminine level of interest in beauty care as he prepares for the intensely masculine world of Wall Street. It's as if he's putting on armour. The portmanteau word 'hardbody' is just one of a series of puns to do with the vulnerability of the flesh – for instance, Bateman works for a company called Pierce and Pierce. A 'hardbody' is not only an 1980s creation of Nautilus and Stairmaster, but also Bateman's nickname for the kind of woman he needs to find – one invulnerable to his wish to stab and cut.

Harron refuses any empathy with Bateman. She isn't interested in the causes of his internal crisis. She plays down the violence and plays up Bateman the bore, who likes to explain in detail his musical preferences to uninterested whores. For her, as reported in this magazine (*Sight & Sound*, July 1999), Bateman is 'a symbol' who 'represents the craziness of an era, all its psychoses wrapped up in one person – obsession with clothes, obsession with food, obsession with his skin'. The problem with this approach is that it weakens the satirical attack. You immediately feel her art-crowd contempt for the cityboy. Preaching to the converted, the film panders to the average movie fan's disdain for 'suits' in a way the novel avoids. You'd think the art crowd had no part in this 1980s obsession with clothes and restaurants, that they were untainted by greed and ambition. This is a failure to acknowledge the roots of the novel's cult success, which lie in its complicity with the idea that there's something of Bateman in many young men. You can hear the incomprehension when Christian Bale says of the cityboys he met while researching the role, 'For a lot of them, it's their favourite book. They just don't seem to get that it's laughing at them.' Observations which posit the question, is the novel also a failed satire?

To understand what's missing from Harron's film we need to go back further, to the mid-1970s. Ridicule, irony and sarcasm – the weapons of satire – were the first recourse of UK punk rock, which borrowed its sound but not its lyrical content from US punk rock. Its key slogan was 'no future' and its style was a co-option of Dickensian urchin rags and sex-shop bondage gear – what could be more satirical? The link between the sneering of *A Clockwork Orange*'s Alex and Johnny Rotten's ranting delivery is obvious, and rhetorically they are manifestations of the same voice of British youth discontent, of a generation that realised the manufacturing industry was a dead end many of them could be stuck in. It's hard in the neat and tidy new millennium to remember how large crowds of unruly youth did gather in the 1970s. You only have to watch footage of the pitch invasions that invariably followed soccer matches or the pitched battles between mods and rockers to realise how much things have changed. They've changed, too, in New York, where Mayor Giuliani's 'zero tolerance' policy swept visible evidence of the 'underclass' away from the streets, keeping Tom Wolfe's lurid vision of a Third World invasion at bay for the time being.

With the 1980s came an unprecedented interest in the history of youth style and rebellion that went hand in hand with the new fascination with the rich. Writers who came out of punk in the United Kingdom turned their attention to style. The birth of such style magazines as *The Face* and *ID* coincided with marketing companies' and academics' attempts to understand *Subculture: The Meaning of Style* (to use the title of Dick Hebdige's then-essential book). Links were established between the 1950s teddy boys who inspired *A Clockwork Orange* and the 'gorblimey' brokers, the cockney boys who had been allowed on to the trading floors of the stock exchange. Brash, arrogant, brutal and self-possessed, they were matched by a generation of post-punk writers who would eventually dominate British journalism, creating a new grub street of vicious satirists prized for their irreverence, though eventually used to bolster a very British philistinism.

The UK punk voice had its impact on Ellis, too. *Less than Zero* was named after a 1976 Elvis Costello song from the album *My Aim Is True*. This was the album that defined what was then called New Wave music – the tidier, more intellectual pop that ran parallel with early punk – but Costello had also co-opted the Alex sneer, and some of his lyrics, particularly on the *Armed Forces* album, have the tang of Burgess about them. On the US side of punk, Talking Heads, by their very neatness, were also tidied into the New Wave category, but their most requested song, 'Psycho Killer', came from their early punk moment. Listening to the lyrics, it's easy to imagine it was one of the starting points for *American Psycho*. Indeed, Talking Heads are mentioned more than once by Bateman, somewhat against type since the rest of his musical taste is hilariously outré.

In particular, the middle verse of 'Psycho Killer' – 'You started a conversation/That you won't even finish/You're talking a lot/But you're not saying anything/Well I won't say nothing/My lips are sealed/Say something once, why say it again' – perfectly sums up Bateman's attitude to the social round in New York. He can't say anything because what's burbling on and on in his head is unsayable. Heads singer David Byrne's nervy voice edges to breaking point, then relaxes as he delivers the perfect 1980s epitaph: 'We are vain and we are blind/I hate people when they're not polite'.

The voice in Bateman's head is a fucked-up rich kid's counterpoint to Alex's. It speaks of the collision between smart preppy kids and street-smart punks. It wants to destroy the passer-by, but not because it wants to be anarchy – it already is. Ellis' voice is complicit with Bateman's, its endless riffing on product labels a cry for help you feel the author shares. But effective satire requires the satirist to take up a morally superior position and Ellis, being helplessly of the demi-monde himself, can't find that position any more than Harron can.

If spectres of authority haunt *A Clockwork Orange*, there are none to speak of in *American Psycho*. The only cops we see all die when Bateman, having apparently killed too publicly, shoots at their patrol cars and they explode. Harron treats this on-the-run sequence like a Simpson and Bruckheimer movie, with Bateman an untouchable action hero. It climaxes with Bateman hiding in his own office phoning in a full confession that will later be treated as a joke by his lawyer. It's clear that Harron believes Bateman to be a fantasist, that he may not in fact have killed anyone except in his own mind – and, since Bateman is a notoriously unreliable narrator, there's plenty of evidence to back her up (he tells us things he can't possibly know, experiences ridiculous identity mix-ups, former victims turn up and are polite to him).

Violent movies are fed to Alex by state officials, who have injected him with some new drug as they pin back his eyelids and keep his eyeballs lubricated. The drug means that if he tries in future to become violent his recall of these movies will make him nauseous. Violent movies are a staple diet for Bateman – we know he watches *Body Double* and *The Texas Chain Saw Massacre* and that he always has some videos he needs to return to the store. It's the movie in Bateman's head that's making him sick. And, since the 1990s were, by general consent, a continuation of the 1980s by other means, you have to wonder where Bateman is now, and how he's channelling all that rage and sickness.

Jim Thompson Adaptations
TEN PER CENT OF THE PROCEEDS

Adrian Wootton

Jim Thompson was an American paperback fiction writer, one of the 'hardboiled' school whose heyday, at least in terms of mass-market consumption, occurred during the 1950s. Largely anonymous then (along with peers such as David Goodis), Thompson's resurgence now might be put down to the retro-romantic obsessions of pop culture. Certainly this vogue is in high gear, what with Charles Williams (*Dead Calm, The Hot Spot*), Charles Willeford (*Miami Blues*) and David Goodis (*Street of No Return*) being adapted as well as Thompson. Indeed, when one adds in all the TV 'tecs, not forgetting the ubiquitous *Twin Peaks*, it's very tempting to agree with critic Cosmo Landesman in *The Guardian*: 'We've gone from a cultural puritanism to a post-modern promiscuity where any artefact that can flash its populist credentials is automatically applauded.' Yet, while Thompson's life and work do seem to fit into an orthodox retro-trendy hard-done-by/hardboiled category, the real evidence refutes this and perhaps demonstrates why he is now the subject of so much movie action.

Thompson's life from 1906 until his death in 1977 is still largely uncharted territory. Like many other paperback authors, he held numerous jobs (some of them illegal, such as selling bootleg whiskey), was a reporter for a time, had a brief flirtation with screenwriting (which he hated), undoubtedly drank too much, wrote twenty-odd novels at great speed for classic thriller publishers such as Gold Medal (sometimes being given a title or cover artwork by the publishers and told to come back with a finished novel a few weeks later) and died in relative obscurity without one of his novels being available in the United States at the time. Out of these scraps of information, the typical fast-living legend has been fashioned; a legend Thompson himself gave credence to with his own highly dramatised fictional versions of his life, *Bad Boy* and *The Alcoholics*.

Aside from these full-length excursions, Thompson did occasionally drop comments on the writer's lot into his novels, for example, *Savage Night*: 'And every now and then some lordly book publisher would come down and reap my crop and package it at two-fifty a copy and lo and behold, if I praised him mightily… he would spend three or four dollars on advertising and the sales of the book would swell to a total of nine hundred copies and he would give me ten percent of the proceeds… when he got around to it.' In fact, it's important to remember that much of Thompson's life was his own creation, and the image of a hell-raising wordsmith in reality obscures a much more shadowy figure. Perhaps the facts will finally be established with the forthcoming publication of two detailed and long-researched biographies. Until then, Thompson's life must remain largely legendary terrain, a point at which common pulp-writer mythology and critical interpretation meet.

Thompson wrote twenty-nine novels, mostly published in pulp paperback, but the majority can only be described as 'crime' fiction in the broadest sense. His narratives are complex, his characters' motives unclear; there are no heroes, no believable happy endings, and no obvious cultural references (to music or movies). In other words, Thompson doesn't fit the current pop-retro bill at all snugly because the pleasure principle inherent in certain kinds of genre fiction isn't uppermost in his novels. Of course, Thompson uses typical cliff-hanging plot devices to create suspense, and there is violence and sex aplenty in such novels as *A Hell of a Woman*, *The Getaway* and *The Killer Inside Me*. But nothing is casual or simply gratuitous. Everything is locked tightly into bravura narrative structures, where experimentation of form is combined with intensity of style and grotesque horror of subject matter.

Unlike his peers, the pace at which Thompson wrote didn't prevent him from taking outrageous risks in his storytelling. In *The Kill-off*, he constructs a disorientating tale of deceit and murder out of a multiplicity of first-person narratives, in which each character could be the killer. In *A Hell of a Woman*, Thompson suggests the descent into madness of his central character by having his first-person narration progressively disintegrate with odd images and snatches of random thought piercing the smooth flow of the plot. These devices are given atmospheric flesh through Thompson's pared-down, intense style of writing. Using simple uncluttered language, description is sparse and concentrated (particularly in moments of great tension or extreme violence in *Savage Night*), while conversation is colloquial and fluid. Moreover, Thompson is adept at suggesting varying locales through character accent (*Texas by the Tail* and *Pop. 1280*) or, more significantly, the force of a character's personality from his casual dialogue (the banal monologues of Lou Ford in *The Killer Inside Me* which indicate his concealed sadistic egotism).

Thompson's narrative structures and style allow rapid variations in tone and atmosphere, from edgy suspense and occasional terror to bizarre comedy. His novels unexpectedly inject humour, of the blackest kind, into appalling scenes of violence. This is most obvious in the hick jokiness of sheriff Nick Corey's first-person narration in *Pop. 1280*, where he consistently plays the fool to hide his homicidal activities. If Thompson's formal dexterity illustrates this aesthetic daring, then his characters and their actions provide a large clue to his pessimistic view of the world (or more specifically, America). These people and their sordid schemes might not appear on first consideration to be anything out of the genre ordinary. Yet while Thompson uses some common character and story archetypes, the extremes his protagonists are driven to far exceed those of any comparable 'thriller' author and elevate him – if that's the word – to a position of nihilistic pre-eminence.

Thompson's characters are so smoothly capable of calculating deception and horrifying violence that melodramatic plot strands are buckled and bent out of all recognition. Romance is always short-lived, thefts and con tricks lead to unforeseen, mostly disastrous, consequences, and murder mostly begets more murder. Unhappy, untrusting, homicidal and constantly fearful, if not already psychotic, is a fair description of the average Thompson character's state. On top of this, his novels regularly feature extraordinary narrative dénouements; not so much twists in the tale as switchblades in the back. In *The Getaway*, the fleeing outlaw couple of Doc and Carol end up in El Ray, a fantasy hideout community which does not so much resemble paradise as hell. By way of contrast, in both *The Kill-off* and *A Hell of a Woman*, the main characters simply go crazy with the stress of it all (insanity being one of Thompson's fortes). Last but not least, in *Savage Night*, Thompson pitches the story into mad axewoman horror realms that prefigure the slasher movie.

Like so many authors outside the commercial mainstream, Thompson's relationship to the movies has, until the surprising recent boom, been an erratic and uneasy one. Thompson himself was soured on screenwriting after a painful legal dispute over creative credit for the work he did on two Stanley Kubrick films (*The Killing* and *Paths of Glory*), and his only other contact with Hollywood came a couple of years before his death in, ironically, a cameo role in Dick Richards' nostalgic remake of Raymond Chandler's *Farewell My Lovely* (1975). Making movies out of Thompson novels only began in the 1970s with Sam Peckinpah's *The Getaway* (1972), and continued sporadically with Burt Kennedy's failed version of *The Killer Inside Me* (1975), Alain Corneau's *Série Noire* (1978, based on *A Hell of a Woman*) and Bertrand Tavernier's *Coup de torchon* (based on *Pop. 1280*). Each of these films has its merits, although the best of them (*The Getaway* and *Coup de torchon*) owe much more to their respective directors than to any particular faithfulness to the 'spirit' of Thompson.

Apart from the current enthusiasm for crime fiction, the cynical explanation for the renewed interest in Thompson lies in his unsaleability throughout the past decade. As Maggie Greenwald, writer/director of the film version of *The Kill-off*, has confirmed, no one was interested in him and so the rights to his books for quite a while were going cheap. In creative terms, the time may now be ripe for Thompson because his work, reflecting the repression, paranoia and extremes of wealth of the Eisenhower years, has gained a whole new resonance in the era of Reaganomics/Thatcherism and their successors. Just as in the 1950s, Thompson's downbeat writing was in radical contrast to the prevailing atmosphere of conspicuous consumption, so in recent years his work has been seen by some film-makers as an antidote to Steven Spielberg and the big-screen fantasies of Hollywood's dream machine at its most escapist.

To take the general influence of Thompson first, there can be little doubt that a whole new generation of movie-makers (not 'brats') have drawn on the extremes that his novels exemplify and, along with other powerful subcultural resources (comics, rock music, fashion, horror/s-f movies and soap operas), have used them to create that most chic and subversive movie hybrid, American Gothic. Film-makers such as Eric Red (*The Hitcher, Cohen and Tate*), Kathryn Bigelow (*Blue Steel*), James McNaughton (*Henry Portrait of a Serial Killer*) and the Coen brothers seem to share Thompson's implicitly critical pessimism. Bearing this in mind, one might argue that this is Thompson's real relevance to contemporary cinema, rather than the gradual filming of his books. The recent Thompson adaptations are not particularly trendy or super-ficially glossy, but represent genuinely sharp, intelligent and entertaining independent cinema. Maggie Greenwald's *The Kill-off* (1989) comes across as both pure Thompson and a distinctly modern satire on small-town America. Greenwald achieves this by finding her theme in the warped, tragic women of Thompson's world. She re-feminises the novel by extracting and displaying the strength of Luane Devore and Myra Pavlov, an angle she is now hoping to develop with her proposed movie of *Savage Night*.

The success, at least creatively, of *The Kill-off* highlights something else which attracts film-makers to Thompson: that there are no particular rules, stylistic tics, period detail, stereotypic characters or general film precedents to follow when adapting him. The very variety of his narratives allows plenty of room for manoeuvre and great leeway in plot structure and character development. The parameters of Thompson's world have been recognised and celebrated in the Scorsese/Frears/Westlake version of *The Grifters*, and soon to come is James Foley's pressure-cooker translation of *After Dark, My Sweet*, which demonstrates a different, explicitly sexual slant to Thompson. Finally, the planned films of both *South of Heaven* and *Texas by the Tail* are proof that there is a long way to go before Thompson is exhausted by screenwriters and, hopefully, by public prepared for a dose of rich spice in their mainstream sugar.

Elmore Leonard Adaptations
THE MOUTH AND THE METHOD

Erik Bauer talks with Quentin Tarantino about *Jackie Brown*

The release of *Jackie Brown* represents a watershed for Quentin Tarantino. In the pop-culture terms he himself is so familiar and free with, his third film as director bears the same weight of expectation as any big music act's third CD. There are many jealous of his success who would have been only too willing to savage the film had it been a creative and commercial disappointment. It's not, but the high price of failure may explain how cautious *Jackie Brown* is. Unlike *Reservoir Dogs* (1992) and *Pulp Fiction*

(1994), it's an adaptation rather than an original screenplay, it takes great pains to establish character and experiments with long takes of near-Bergmanesque patience, and it shuffles messy violence off-screen. Yet it is Tarantino's film, if only through its instantly identifiable use of language.

Jackie Brown is based on Elmore Leonard's novel *Rum Punch.* Jackie (Pam Grier), a black air hostess in her forties, is caught by cops and customs investigators smuggling a large cash sum into LA from Mexico. They know she is working for Ordell (Samuel L. Jackson), a slick local gun trader, and she agrees to help them set him up, though she knows he is capable of murder. Playing one side off against the other with the help of bail bondsman Max (Robert Foster), she draws Ordell's live-in beach-bum lover Melanie (Bridget Fonda) and his taciturn prison buddy Louis (Robert De Niro) into her elaborate scheme to save her own skin.

Despite the change of tempo in *Jackie Brown*, Tarantino retains his fevered delight in the world he creates. If you take away the scenes of violent confrontation (which admittedly, in his earlier films, is to remove a lot), you are mostly left with characters who are having a good time most of the time – particularly Samuel L. Jackson. Tarantino's people enjoy hanging out and tend not to be burdened by neuroses. All their negative feelings are directed outwards, and reserved for random bursts of anger or disgust. They are practical people, whose needs are clear and who are not to be thwarted. In terms of pure cinema, they are about action not angst, which makes them immensely appealing, as much as the pop-culture references they tend to drop. And Tarantino backs it up with an extraordinary talent for fantasy casting. No other director is gauche fan enough to cast Bridget Fonda as a washed-up beach bum, Robert De Niro as someone really stupid or Michael Keaton as an over-keen cop. It's outrageous wish-fulfilment, free from the po-faced aura that surrounds the casting of the most ludicrous of major Hollywood projects, and only someone with Tarantino's kudos could get away with it.

Some of the new elements are less successful. The choice of soundtrack songs is as good as you'd expect, cementing the blaxploitation connection made by casting Pam Grier in the lead role. But the emotion of the songs, such as the Delfonics 'Didn't I (Blow Your Mind This Time)', is often used as a lazy prod towards what the inscrutable Jackie might be feeling at any moment. In the end, the qualities of *Jackie Brown* that will attract most praise and criticism reside in the dialogue: it has all the rhythm, fizz and humour you'd expect, but many will be offended by its unapologetic use of words like 'nigger', as our interview with Tarantino confirms.

* * *

Erik Bauer: With *Jackie Brown*, it seems you've gone to great lengths to make the dialogue more naturalistic. It contrasts with the stylised dialogue you're known for.

Quentin Tarantino: I've done two movies before this, so wait until I've done six to start pigeonholing me. *Reservoir Dogs, Pulp Fiction* and my scripts for *True Romance* [Tony Scott, 1993] and *Natural Born Killers* [Oliver Stone, 1994] take place in my own universe, but that doesn't make them fantastical. This movie doesn't take place in my universe – this is Elmore Leonard's universe and it was interesting making a movie outside the little universe I created. Because of that, I wanted it to be ultra-realistic. I used a different cinematographer to get a different look – it still looks great, but it's just a little more down-to-earth, a little less like a movie movie, more like a 1970s *Straight Time*. I like building sets. In *Jackie Brown*, I didn't do that. Every single scene in the movie was shot on location.

Erik Bauer: How have Elmore Leonard's books influenced your writing style?

Quentin Tarantino: When I first started reading his novels, I got really caught up in his characters and the way they talked. As I started reading more of them, it gave me permission to go my way with characters talking around things as opposed to talking about them. He showed me that characters can go off at tangents and those tangents are just as valid as anything else. Like the way real people talk. I think his biggest influence on all my things was on *True Romance*. Actually, in *True Romance*, I was trying to do my version of an Elmore Leonard novel in script form. I didn't rip it off, there's nothing blatant about it, it's just a feeling – a style I was inspired by.

Erik Bauer: *Jackie Brown* doesn't rely as much on plot reversals as your other films, and what twists you do have are often brought about through dialogue.

Quentin Tarantino: I think it works well. It's always unfolding: it's not a movie about Jackie figuring out in the first ten minutes how to get half a million dollars and doing it – no! It's like little by little by little it starts coming to her, as life and situations change and she's being torn in this direction and that. It slowly evolves, and then from that point on, it's straight ahead until she does it. It's very novelistic, in that the first ninety minutes are just about characterisation. Then, it's all execution: the last half-hour is just them doing it, the money switches and all that.

Erik Bauer: There's more exposition in the dialogue of *Jackie Brown* than in your previous scripts.

Quentin Tarantino: That's for damn sure, yeah.

Erik Bauer: Was that a result of the adaptation process?

Quentin Tarantino: Yeah, that's all that happened in the book. That's part of Max's whole relationship with Jackie: talking about their problems, with him acting as a counsel, trying to help her out. In the second half it's her thinking out loud, she's kind of talking to herself. That's the first time I was dealing in exposition in a big way.

Erik Bauer: What goals did you set for yourself for the screenplay?

Quentin Tarantino: I like the idea of following a female lead character. I think I have an extremely unfair rap from people who say, 'Ah, but can he write women?' The only reason they're saying that is because I did *Reservoir Dogs* first. I really love the idea of following a black woman in her forties. It's funny, but I do feel that Jackie Brown is mine. She's the same character as in the book, but making her black affects her because her life experiences are different and her dialogue is different.

Erik Bauer: Did you do any research for her character?

Quentin Tarantino: No. I actually have known a few women who reminded me of Jackie and that's who I used. I just wanted to find her in myself. I joke about it, but I'm very much a Method writer. I really become all the characters when I'm writing them, and I become one or two when I'm not writing. The entire year I was Ordell. He's the one I identified with the most in the piece. I walked around like him. I talked like him. I spent a whole year basically being Ordell. I couldn't shut him off and I didn't want to. And in a weird way Ordell is the rhythm of the movie.

Erik Bauer: What do you mean by that?

Quentin Tarantino: The way he talks, the way he dresses – everything about him is how this movie should play. He's the old school of soul music, he's the personification of that and I completely identify with it. If I wasn't an artist, I would probably be exactly like Ordell.

Erik Bauer: But it's not his movie.

Quentin Tarantino: It's Jackie's movie, but what's so neat about Jackie's character is that she isn't revealing at all. The story requires her to have a poker face. It requires that you don't know what's going on in her head. One of the things I held on to in the adaptation was that every time she got with Ordell, she would tell him everything she knew about the cops. That would surprise me, no matter how many times she did it. It's like, 'I cannot believe she's fucking him so bad!' I was like, 'God, I hope she isn't fucking Max. I think she's playing straight with us, but I don't know 100 per cent.' Max is the audience – you see the movie through Max's eyes. He's the conscience and the heart of the piece and he's definitely the major human link to the film. Max is the audience, but Ordell is the rhythm, the soul of the movie.

Erik Bauer: Ordell is fascinating because he really seemed to change from the book. He becomes a lot smarter in your script.

Quentin Tarantino: I had a lot of prior knowledge of Ordell, Louis and Melanie because I read *The Switch*. That was the first Leonard book I'd ever read, so even before *Rum Punch* was published I knew these characters because I was doing a little adaptation of *The Switch* in my mind when I was fifteen. And there's a lot of me in Ordell.

Erik Bauer: What elements define the Tarantino universe?

Quentin Tarantino: I try not to get analytical during the writing process. I try just to keep the flow from my brain to my hand and go with the moment and go with my guts. To me, truth is the big thing. Constantly you're writing something and you get to a place where your characters could go this way or that and I just can't lie. The characters have to be true to themselves. And that's something I don't see in a lot of Hollywood movies. I see characters lying all the time. They can't do this because it would affect the movie this way, or this demographic might not like it. To me a character can't do anything good or bad, they can only do something that's true or not.

When you're writing, you know every script will have four to six basic scenes that you're going to do. But it's all the scenes in the middle that you've got to write through – that's where your characters really come from. That's how you find them, that's where they live. I think that's how novelists write.

Erik Bauer: Definitely more than most screenwriters, where it's all structure, structure, structure.

Quentin Tarantino: I just don't do that – you know by the first act this has to happen, and so on. I hold no interest in that. It's your voice that's important and I see absolutely no reason why a screenplay can't contain that voice. Now it makes it a hell of a lot easier when you're the writer and the director. But that's not even necessary now, because things are a little more open.

There are a lot of bad screenplays, so if you write a good one people are going to respond to it. But if you're just starting your career, it might take a long time to get your work to people who'll appreciate it. It'll just get shot down by all the readers.

But if you keep persevering, eventually you'll get past that reader and on to the people who are bored to death reading screenplays. These are the people who really appreciate something new. That was the big thing I had against me starting off in my career – I was writing shit differently, and differently meant I was doing it wrong for that whole reader mentality. Before David Mamet was David Mamet, people probably thought he said 'fuck' too much, too. But once they get to know you, once you get that Good Housekeeper seal of approval, it's a whole different story.

Erik Bauer: Do you use repetitions of a phrase or word in dialogue to enhance its power?

Quentin Tarantino: I do that a lot. I like it. I think that in my dialogue there's a music or poetry, and the repetition of certain words helps give it a beat. It just happens and I just go with it, looking for the rhythm of the scene.

Erik Bauer: Some people have criticised your use of the word 'nigger' in *Jackie Brown* and you respond that no one word should have such power in our culture. I'm not sure I buy that. Aren't you using it to electrify your dialogue?

Quentin Tarantino: There is no word that should stay in word jail. It's all language. And if I was doing what you're saying, I'd be lying. I'd be throwing in a word to get an effect. Well, you do that all the time, you throw in a word to get a laugh, and you throw in a word to get an effect too, but it's never a situation where that's not what the character would say. You used the example of 'nigger'. In *Pulp Fiction*, 'nigger' is said a bunch of different times by a bunch of different people and it's meant differently each time. It's all about the context in which it's used. When Richard Pryor and Eddie Murphy do their stand-up acts, and say 'nigger', you're never offended because they're niggers. You know the context it's coming from. The way Samuel Jackson says 'nigger' as Jules in *Pulp Fiction* is not the way Eric Stoltz as Lance says it, is not the way Ving Rhames as Marcellus says it.

Erik Bauer: How is Ordell's use of the word different from that of the characters in *Pulp Fiction*?

Quentin Tarantino: Ordell probably doesn't use it any differently from Jules. And when Jules and Marcellus use it in *Pulp Fiction* they're coming from the same place, but having it mean different things. Marcellus is very much like, 'You my nigger now', and it was Ving Rhames who came up with that. But Ordell's coming from the same place too, he's a black guy who throws the word around a lot, it's part of the way he talks. If you're writing a black dialect, there are certain words you need to make it musical, and 'nigger' is one of them. If you're writing about that kind of guy, 'motherfucker' is another. Sam Jackson uses 'nigger' all the time in his speech, that's just who he is and where he comes from. So that's the way Ordell talks. Also, I'm a white guy who's not afraid of that word. I just don't feel the whole white guilt and pussyfooting around race issues. I'm completely above all that. I've never worried about what anyone might think of me because I've always believed that the true of heart recognise the true of heart.

Erik Bauer: Do you put a lot of thought into the way you juxtapose humour and violence?

Quentin Tarantino: No more thought than I put into anything else. I love it, I think it's like a Reese's Cup, two great tastes that taste great together. I'm not bending over backwards to try and do it, it just happens. And then when it happens, it's like, 'Whoa, that's great. I got something.'

Erik Bauer: The final scene between Melanie and Louis was taken almost verbatim from the book. But you could have written that scene.

Quentin Tarantino: Yeah, I felt that. And it was so cool – when I actually talked to Elmore Leonard about something like that, or like the scene where Ordell kills Louis, I found he writes like I write. He didn't know Ordell was going to do it. He knew one of them was going to kill the other, but until it actually happened he didn't know how it was going to happen or who it was going to be.

Erik Bauer: Leonard had a lot of time to set up Louis' character that you didn't have. In the book, the violence that comes out of him in that last scene seems like an extension of his character, but in your script it comes as a shock.

Quentin Tarantino: Right, sort of the way violence plays out in your life, all of a sudden. Very rarely does violence build up in real life the way it does in movies. It explodes in your face. I think it gives the movie a dose of reality, especially in the scene we're talking about.

Erik Bauer: But isn't it important for all action to be set up, so people understand why it's taking place?

Quentin Tarantino: It is set up, but Louis is only partially on the page – all right? I remember talking to De Niro about the role and saying, 'Look, this is not like most of the characters that I write.' The reason actors like to do my stuff is because they usually have a lot of cool things to say and they feel cool saying them. I told him, 'You know, Louis is a different character than the ones I ordinarily write. He doesn't say a lot. This is a character that truly needs to be gotten across with body language.' I'm talking to one of the greatest actors in the world. That's why I wanted him, all right?

Erik Bauer: Did you know who you wanted for all the characters?

Quentin Tarantino: I normally don't. I'll have some people in mind, but this was one where I pretty much had everybody. The one guy that was open was Louis. I thought about De Niro, but I wasn't sure I'd get him.

Erik Bauer: Do you think the audience has an attachment to Melanie when she dies?

Quentin Tarantino: No. I think the audience has a complete love-hate relationship with Melanie. Audiences applaud when Louis shoots her. It's impossible that someone could be asking for it, but she's asking for it. She's a fucking smartass, treacherous and all these things. But we also like her at the same time; she's a totally fun character.

Erik Bauer: You've voiced concern that your own voice might some day become old hat. Was that one of the reasons you decided to go with an adaptation?

Quentin Tarantino: That wasn't the reason, but it does very conveniently serve that purpose. It's a nice way of holding on to my dialogue, of holding on to my gift. I don't want people to take me for granted. The things I have to offer I don't want wasted. When you watch something David Mamet's written you know you've listened to David Mamet dialogue. I want to try and avoid that. I want people to see my new movie, not my next movie. I want each movie to have a life complete unto itself, yet still when you look at it from a certain perspective you can see it all fits. I don't want to do a Woody Allen or a John Sayles thing where one film blurs into the next. Those guys are doing exactly what they want to do, and I'm not putting them down. I just want to do something else.

Erik Bauer: You've said a number of times that you don't want to be known as 'the gun guy'. But *Jackie Brown* and your future prospects seem to be all crime stories.

Quentin Tarantino: Well, the next one I do, I think as a director, will be a Western.

Erik Bauer: A Western in the mode of *The Good, the Bad and the Ugly*, or *Unforgiven*?

Quentin Tarantino: Actually, it's different. It's a prison Western. It takes place in a prison in Yuma, Yuma Territorial Prison. So it's like a Western *Papillon*.

BLIND DATE

Peter Matthews: Steven Soderbergh's adaptation of *Out of Sight*

It's commonly asserted that pulp fiction is more readily transmissible to the screen than literature. Almost by definition, a major work imposes its own way of seeing, and the adapter – forced to truncate and simplify – usually ends up with a prestige-laden stiff. The second-rate or downright trashy, by contrast, liberates the adapter to improvise freely on its themes and structure, without pangs of conscience that anything too sacred has been violated. But the case of crime novelist Elmore Leonard reminds us that the reverse can also be true: there are writers whose sensibility is so exquisitely minor that finding a screen equivalent is nearly impossible. Leonard ought to be a natural for the movies – his books, after all, consist of page after page of laconic, off-the-wall dialogue alternating with functional descriptions of narrative action. No attempt is made to plumb characters' deeper motives, and even a qualifying adjective seems too much of a compromise. 'If it sounds like writing,' says Leonard, 'I rewrite it.'

It's as if Leonard's thrillers are already movies, with the brevity of language and exteriority a screenwriter is supposed to aim for. But almost without exception the films based on his works (*The Ambassador*, 1984, *Glitz*, 1991, and the recent *Touch*) have been duds – including the three (*Stick*, 1985, *52 Pick-up*, 1986, and *Cat Chaser*, 1989) he scripted himself. It may be that the streamlined ease of Leonard's tone is deceptive – a wealth of concentrated effort has gone into those weightless, zero-degree sentences. There's a true formal rigour in Leonard's approach: he whittles away at words until nothing remains but absolute deadpan – the expression of an attitude as much as a writing style. Leonard's heroes don't let on much, and neither does he. His books aspire to little more than a consummate cool: of style, conception and character. That probably accounts for their enormous cult reputation. Where a major author opens up our perceptions of the world, Leonard narrows it to the articulation of a precise, hip wavelength. For all their lowlife settings and apparent shagginess, Leonard's novels are as neatly self-contained and morally trivial as drawing-room comedies.

Uncorking Soderbergh's id

Perfect shallowness demands its own brand of discipline, and that's where the majority of Leonard's screen translators fail. It's not enough to reproduce the plot twists and zingy one-liners – for something of the spirit of the books to come through requires an exactly calibrated nonchalance in the whole treatment. The breezy, buoyant 1995 film version of *Get Shorty* almost caught it, but faltered ultimately under Barry Sonnenfeld's broad, impersonal direction. Now the screenwriter for that movie, Scott Frank, has teamed up with art-house specialist Steven Soderbergh for *Out of Sight*, based on Leonard's 1996 book and starring George Clooney and Jennifer Lopez.

Out of Sight is just a trifle (though, at $49 million, an expensive one), but it strikes me as one of the best formula pictures in years. In case that sounds like a back-handed compliment, it should be remembered that not a few of Hollywood's most memorable entertainments – films that still please audiences after decades – are, strictly speaking, production-line sausages. It's not that *Out of Sight* feels remotely retro: indeed, the loose-limbed contemporary vernacular Soderbergh and Frank employ is one of the movie's singular felicities. But there's an underlying compactness and elegance that puts one in mind of classic Hollywood at its most exemplary. Studio craftsmen of former days – professionals merely doing their jobs – could take conventional genre subjects and turn them adroitly into vital popular art. It's this quality of self-effacing tact that keeps *Bringing Up Baby* or *Casablanca* fresh when more pretentious efforts have sunk without a trace. And *Out of Sight* is among the few current movies to suggest that honest commercial know-how isn't entirely dead.

Steven Soderbergh is just about the last person you would think of inviting to direct an Elmore Leonard thriller. His debut feature *sex, lies and videotape* (1989) is commonly said to have put Miramax on the map and American indie films into the shopping mall. With an aggressive marketing campaign and that come-hither title, it could hardly miss – but the multiplex audiences who turned out hoping for something kinky may have been startled to find themselves confronting the work of a chilly formalist. His subsequent flops – *Kafka* (1991) and *King of the Hill* (1993) – were almost fanatically perfectionist in their look, as if the director had felt compelled to chew over the crystalline imagery frame by frame. By the time he made *The Underneath* (1995), a glacial meditation on film noir themes, one had the sense that Soderbergh was as stymied by art-consciousness as his hero was by torpor. Shock treatment was indicated, and it was apparently delivered in the self-financed *Schizopolis* (1996) – so far unseen in Britain, but described by *L.A. Weekly* reporter Paul Malcolm as a 'screwball, stylistic freak-out… with [a] pointed disdain for narrative coherence and [an] emphasis on sheer momentum'. Given the title and Soderbergh's previous bottled-up style, it's tempting to read *Schizopolis* as the occasion on which the director finally uncorked his id. In *Out of Sight*, he channels this manic high into a technique at once playful and scrupulously controlled.

The movie would appear to be a special case of synchronicity – of the countless things that could be expected to go wrong, going right. I'm not sure Soderbergh has the toughness to make a full career in the mainstream, but serving as a director-for-hire on a project of no importance, he has done better, richer and racier work than he managed as an auteur. Perhaps Soderbergh needed the external discipline of a big-star vehicle to unclench his tight creative personality; in return, he invests a purely commercial enterprise with a portion of his fastidiousness. It's not unlike the proverbial bargain struck between Fred and Ginger – Soderbergh gives the movie class, it gives him sex appeal. The synthesis is a flip elegance that isn't miles away from Leonard's notion of cool.

It's well known that Leonard's crime fiction has exerted considerable secondhand influence on contemporary American cinema via the work of his number-one fan, Quentin Tarantino. Still, I'm glad it was the meticulous Soderbergh and not the blowhard Tarantino who filmed *Out of Sight*. Judging from the cautious and painfully overextended *Jackie Brown* (based on Leonard's novel *Rum Punch*), when Tarantino approaches his idol too directly he chokes up in bashful reverence. Tarantino's indebtedness to Leonard is more patent in his screenplays for *Reservoir Dogs* and P*ulp Fiction*, and the benchmarks of his cinema – busy but seemingly random plotting, sudden leaps from carnage, 'humanised' criminals who discuss the merits of consumer items, and non-stop references to movies – are certainly all there in Leonard. But where the author aims at an almost minimalist leanness of effect, the director is a hyperkinetic sensualist who wants to knock the audience flat.

The light touch Soderbergh brings to *Out of Sight* is far more appropriate to Leonard's book than Tarantino's inflated nihilist chic. That's partly because the story is a crime caper through which a delicate, reticent love affair has been threaded. Fugitive bank robber Jack Foley (George Clooney) and Deputy Federal Marshal Karen Sisco (Jennifer Lopez) aren't flamboyant lovers-on-the-lam like the couple in the Tarantino-scripted *True Romance*. They don't burn up the track with erotic friction; instead, their courtship is oddly oblique, tentative and experimental. Karen, we learn, has a history of romantic waywardness, choosing married men or guys who turn out to be felons. Ambitious to rise in a male-dominated profession, she nonetheless feels an obscure yen for more glamour and adventure than can be safely warranted by the law. (Being a Leonard heroine, she never says so – but you intuit it from Lopez's leggy, provocative demeanour and such carefully planted details as her Chanel suit and the silvery-pink shade of lipstick she wears on the job). Jack, too, longs for something other. A career criminal with nowhere to go but down, facing a thirty-year prison sentence if caught, he harbours the pipe dream of a regular life where people meet for cocktails, talk about movies, get acquainted. The reciprocity of their desires makes them a perfect fit, like the symmetrical couples (played by Cary Grant and Katharine Hepburn or William Powell and Myrna Loy) in 1930s screwball comedies. Movie love in those days could cause difference to crumble instantly, but Jack and Karen recognise there's no future in their developing rapport: he must continue to dodge the law, and she to hunt him down. The sly conceit of the movie is that these official adversaries choose – now and then, in isolated pockets of the chase – to bunk off from their public roles and find out what could have been.

Inimical lovers

They indulge their caprice in a handful of the most subtly seductive scenes ever filmed. The first suggests a witty extension (or perhaps contraction) of the 'meet-cute' once mandatory in Hollywood romantic comedy. Escaping from a medium-security

Florida prison, Jack is obliged to abduct innocent bystander Karen, whom he bundles into the trunk of a getaway car driven by his accomplice Buddy (Ving Rhames). Then he climbs in himself, and illuminated by the lurid red tail-lights, their bodies pressed snugly back to back, the pair soon fall into an easygoing patter about their respective careers and Faye Dunaway movies they have enjoyed. Soderbergh frames this (literal) blind date the only way he can – in huge close-up – yet his darting camerawork offsets the static situation, charging it with emotional expectancy. That trunk stands a decent chance of being as fondly remembered as the motel room across which Clark Gable and Claudette Colbert string the Walls of Jericho in *It Happened One Night* – and it performs a similar function as a sealed-off free zone where inimical lovers can test their true feelings.

That's the beginning for Jack and Karen, but it's also nearly the end. Since their relationship is untenable, it becomes a utopian space within the narrative – the gateway to a parallel universe where a happier story might be told. In Henry Hathaway's 1935 surrealist classic *Peter Ibbetson*, the forcibly estranged sweethearts (played by Gary Cooper and Ann Harding) spend a lifetime visiting each other in dreams. It's almost the same with Jack and Karen. Through some of the most understated techniques of stylisation I've ever seen, Soderbergh lends their love duets a hypnotic quality that abstracts them from the rest of the movie. The effect is most pronounced in the sequence where they have cocktails. Sitting alone in a hotel bar high above Detroit, Karen is chatted up by three advertising types, each of whom she repels. Then suddenly Jack appears, as if materialised by thought.

Authorial poker-face

Soderbergh composes their ensuing *tête-à-tête* in lustrous two-shots that fill the frame, connoting a self-sufficient world. At the same time, he faintly flattens the image to the dimensions of a comic strip – insinuating perhaps that this world isn't quite real. It's here that the theme of the movie is most explicitly stated. Talking of making eye contact with someone on the street, Jack muses: 'And the next moment, the person's gone … and it's too late to do anything about it, but you remember it because it was right there and you let it go, and you think, 'What if I had stopped and said something?' It might happen only a few times in your life.' To which Karen quietly replies, 'Or once.'

What links Jack and Karen to those flaky 1930s movie couples is their willingness to behave irresponsibly, to leave their hidebound identities and take a chance. What makes them 1990s figures is the limited nature of their romantic project. Neither is willing to give up the solid world they live in for something as chimerical as love. And yet *Out of Sight* becomes possibly even more romantic because that love crystallises in memory as a lost potential, a regret. As Jack and Karen continue to talk, Soderbergh flashes forward to their single act of consummation (and has the taste not to picture it too graphically). Now we understand why the freeze-frames, which in earlier parts of the film seemed an annoying tic, are necessary to its conception – Jack and Karen are storing up images for the long, cold future. The reserved, slightly ceremonial framing contributes to the mood of subdued gravity: we feel the characters are utterly conscious of each moment as it slips away and already view it with sharp pangs of nostalgia.

Aside from the usual condensations and a changed ending, Frank's script stays extremely faithful to Leonard's book. So why does the movie come across as far more vivid and touching? Perhaps the answer lies partly in the 'reality effect' of cinema. Reading the novel, you admire the craftsmanlike way Leonard brings everything to a hard point; but he never gives you the impression of a fully imagined world as a major writer can. That's the downside of his authorial poker-face – the locales lack substance, the people feel disembodied. Yet characters who are ciphers on the page become immediately particularised when actors play them on screen. This can feel like a loss in film versions of literary masterpieces, but in the case of *Out of Sight* the vast gain in concrete physical detail is a compensation. Of course, it isn't merely by virtue of being photographed that Clooney and Lopez elicit our intense emotional involvement – it's because they act together with such unforced charm. And it isn't just that the movie was shot on location in Miami and Detroit that provides a convincing backdrop – it's that Soderbergh, the cinematographer and the production designer succeed in establishing a strong sense of place.

Most commercial directors these days fall back on grandiose aerial views to portray a city. But Soderbergh stays consistently at street level, which keeps the movie looking self-contained and almost suburban. He has said he was after a rough, imperfect feeling, and you can see what he means: outside the formally orchestrated interludes between Jack and Karen, he judders the camera in muted imitation of cinéma vérité. In some of his previous films Soderbergh would practically quarantine the characters in the tight frame; here it's as if this pan-and-zoom is trying to catch up with them as they go their independent ways.

'Out of Sight 2'
The style is certainly suited to the ramshackle sub-plot in which Jack, Buddy and a sprinkling of sociopaths conspire to rob millionaire Richard Ripley (Albert Brooks). It's a storyline seemingly composed of ragtags from such 1970s films as *The French Connection* and Sam Peckinpah's *The Getaway*, and indeed there's a flavour of early to mid-1970s American cinema in the movie's veneer of airiness and spontaneity. But the underlying control is very apparent – for instance in the expressionist use of saturated colour, evolving from pink and green pastels in Miami to blues, browns and blacks in Detroit, that plots the darkening course of the love affair.

There's perhaps only one spot where Soderbergh's debonair technique goes splat. The crudely staged scene between Jack and criminal confederate Snoopy (Don Cheadle) on the stairs of the Ripley mansion is plainly there to satisfy the meatheads in the audience. And, ambiguous though it is, I also object to the new ending in which Karen, tongue faintly in cheek, supplies the *deus ex machina* whereby she and Jack can keep the ball rolling. Frank excises Karen's final words to Jack in the novel – her bleakly realistic: 'I'm afraid, though, thirty years from now I'll feel different about it. I'm sorry, Jack.' The return of Jack and Karen for *Out of Sight 2* feels like a dim possibility – but the melancholy beauty of their romance rests precisely on it being an evanescent flash in their lives, which they will never forget.

The Beach (Danny Boyle, 2000)

Reviews

THE GRIFTERS
USA 1990
Director: Stephen Frears

Los Angeles. Twenty-five-year-old Roy Dillon maintains a front as a salesman. Even his girlfriend, Myra – who uses her body to pay her precarious way through life – doesn't suspect that he is a con artist. Though sex is good between them, Myra yearns for more from the relationship (not necessarily marriage); but Roy, bitterly resentful of his mother's neglect when he was a child, and further warned by Mints – the elderly grifter who taught him his trade – that working solo is safest, is wary of any partnership. When Roy is slugged in the stomach after trying to palm off a ten-dollar bill for a twenty, neither he nor Myra realise that he is dying of internal injuries. It is his mother Lilly – estranged since Roy walked out seven years ago, but in town to work a 'playback' scam at the California racetracks on behalf of Baltimore racketeer Bobo Justus – who whisks him off to hospital, ensuring the best of care at her expense. Guessing that Roy has followed in her footsteps to become a grifter, Lilly tries to persuade him that it is a fool's game. Still resentful (though Lilly pleads that she was only a child when she gave birth at fourteen), Roy is furious when she tries to use 'nice' nurse Carol to break up his affair with the 'unsuitable' Myra. The equally angry Myra, discovering Roy's secret, proposes a partnership, using (mostly) Roy's money to set up a big-time scam taught her by a former lover. When Roy refuses, mindful of Lilly's warnings about the dangers ahead, Myra storms out, accusing him of being in love with his mother; then, aware that Lilly has been steadily skimming the racetrack money she handles, Myra shops her to Bobo Justus. Warned by a friend, and doubly terrified in that Bobo only recently burned her hand with his cigar for merely making a mistake, Lilly flees in her loot-laden car to a motel in Phoenix, followed by Myra. Summoned by the Phoenix police to identify his mother's body (a close-range bullet left the face unrecognisable), Roy does so, though realising from the burn-free hand that it was Myra who died. Lilly subsequently explains how she reflexively shot Myra after waking to find the latter trying to strangle her and steal her money. With the money impounded by the police, the panic-stricken Lilly is caught by Roy trying to make off with his stash. When Roy remains deaf to her appeals, insisting that her only way out is to go straight, recoiling when she despairingly offers to make love with him if he will let her take the money, Lilly lashes out at him, inadvertently breaking the glass he is holding and driving a shard into his throat. Sobbing over her son's body as she gathers up the fallen money, Lilly flees ...

* * *

A little too loosely plotted, unusually explicit in its behavioural explanations, *The Grifters* is not quite in the top flight of Jim Thompson's novels. Superbly streamlined in Donald Westlake's adaptation, equally superbly directed by Stephen Frears as a comedy of manners that spirals inexorably into an infernal *huis clos*, it nevertheless emerges as a superb novel. Bleakly faithful to the spirit rather than the letter of the book, it catches considerably more of the quintessence of Thompson than anything else in the recently proliferating spate of adaptations.

As the film begins, the camera picks up each of its principal characters in turn, moving into split screen to observe as the three grifters go to work, then – coming exactly into line as though walking side by side in their several locations – turn in unison to camera and smile. The effect, beyond the implication that what we are about to embark on might well be an airy Lubitsch comedy, is of a theatrical curtain call in which the three stars of the show, revelling in the certain knowledge and sure display of their skills, acknowledge the audience's applause for their performance.

Almost immediately, of course, Roy Dillon comes a slight cropper, detected in his sleight-of-hand and vengefully punched in the belly. But the complacency remains, shared even by Lilly, who tries to persuade her son that she knows better; this sense that they are in total command of themselves, their scenarios and the stage on which they are performing. What they fail to take into account (in Jim Thompson's disenchanted world, nothing is for nothing) is that even if their own greed doesn't drive them out of their depth – mentally and technically unprepared to meet the bigger theatre challenge of the big-time grift – someone else's will.

Thompson's novel rather obscures the issue with a subplot in which Roy, resentfully inclined to discount his mother's advice to go straight as unwarranted interference in his life, finds his hand forced by a lucrative promotion in his legitimate job which, at first resistant, he comes to find irresistibly attractive. His decision (too late) to abandon the grifter's life is compounded by guilt over Carol, the innocent thrown in his path by his mother, with whom he half falls in love, but alienates by riding – roughshod and uncomprehending – over the unhappy past she trails as a former victim from Dachau.

All this is ruthlessly pruned away in Westlake's script, along with clarifications of motive (at the end, Roy still urges his mother to go straight; in the novel he is patently sincere, in the film he may or may not be). The effect is to keep the action tightly focused on the personal interaction between the three main characters, as they struggle to escape and/or dominate each other, with the Mob-connected racketeer Bobo Justus hovering on the fringes as a sort of *deus ex machina*, an inescapable reminder of the prizes and the penalties awaiting any move into the big time. Pressed by Roy as to why her brief and late-lamented moment of glory in the big time came to an end, Myra admits that her lover/mentor landed in an asylum, now criminally insane. 'But I'm not,' she boasts. It becomes a debatable point, not only about Myra, but also about Roy and Lilly, as the trio drive each other headlong down a road to mutual destruction (Lilly may escape at the end, but a car, surely ominously, is following her).

Westlake's script offers much less unimpeachable information about the characters than the novel does. All we can hang on to for sure about Lilly is that she is concerned, up to an indefinable point, about her son's future; about Roy, that his past experience has made him wary of commitment to any other person; about Myra, so free and easy where sex is concerned, that she feels there must be something more to be had out of her involvement with Roy. Beyond that lies a fascinatingly murky quagmire of ambiguity. It doesn't really matter whether Roy harbours incestuous feelings about his mother or not; what matters is the involuntary *danse macabre* in which the mere suspicion drives all three characters to participate for assorted reasons of revenge, seduction and revulsion. Almost in the manner of a Greek tragedy, the characters are helplessly swept to their fates by circumstances beyond their control. 'I gave you your life twice,' Lilly pleads at the end, 'I'm asking you to give me mine once, I need the money.' Roy's terse 'No!' resounds like a poetic distillation of the entire tragedy, simultaneously encompassing his nascent pity for his mother, his awareness that the money offers her no avenue of escape, his unwillingness to give up his hard-earned cash, and his triumph at having finally avenged his unhappy childhood.

Miraculously, despite the strictly filleted and formalised plot, the film itself never for a moment seems artificial or contrived. This is thanks partly to superb perform-ances from Anjelica Huston (especially), John Cusack and Annette Bening, and partly to the fact that Stephen Frears embeds their performances in a world bleak but teeming naturalistically with life: not just the wonderfully busy but never picturesque locations (racetracks, bars, hotels, hospital, motel), but also the vividly realised subsidiary characters (notably Henry Jones' irrepressibly garrulous hotel clerk), presented in such a way as to trail an existence that extends beyond the immediate needs of the action. A brilliant, immensely seductive mixture of Kammerspiel, film noir and naturalistic slice-of-life, *The Grifters* is certainly Frears' best film to date.

Tom Milne

INTERVIEW WITH THE VAMPIRE: THE VAMPIRE CHRONICLES
USA 1994
Director: Neil Jordan

San Francisco. Louis, a vampire, is interviewed by Malloy, a young man who collects taped reminiscences. Louis reveals he lived in Louisiana in the eighteenth century, the master of a plantation. Grieving for a dead wife, Louis wanders around New Orleans and is saved from a robber by Lestat, who offers him the chance to become a vampire. Louis, drinking Lestat's blood as he dies, is transformed, but rebels against the predatory Lestat's cruelty and tries to subsist on the blood of animals. Louis' slaves are on the point of rebellion when he frees them and burns down the plantation.

In New Orleans, Louis finds Claudia, a newly orphaned child of a plague victim, and cannot resist drinking her blood, whereupon Lestat turns her into an unageing vampire. As decades pass, Claudia resents Lestat for robbing her of the chance to grow up. With Louis' tacit approval, Claudia tries to murder Lestat by tricking him into drinking laudanum-laced blood, cutting his throat and dumping him in a swamp. Claudia prepares to depart for Europe, but the withered Lestat attacks them and Louis sets fire to him, burning down their town house.

Years later, in Paris, Louis encounters other vampires. Armand, 400-year-old proprietor of a theatre where vampire killings are passed off as illusions, recognises Louis as a kindred soul and asks him to be a bridge to the modern world. Santiago, a clownish sadist, suspects Claudia of the murder of a vampire – the only crime among their kind. Claudia, feeling rejected by Louis' interest in Armand, insists Louis turn Madeleine, a woman she has chosen to be her companion, into a vampire. Santiago seizes Claudia and Madeleine, and executes them by exposure to sunlight. Louis destroys Santiago and his brood with scythe and fire, and burns down the theatre. Parting from Armand, Louis experiences the twentieth century through compulsive cinema-going. In 1988, he returns to New Orleans and encounters Lestat, still injured, living as a pathetic recluse. Malloy begs Louis to make him a vampire, but Louis leaves in disgust. Driving away, Malloy is attacked by Lestat, rejuvenated by young blood, who promises to turn the interviewer into a vampire.

*   *   *

Instantly after publication in 1975, Anne Rice's *Interview with the Vampire* was optioned for filming and has been in development ever since. It is easy to see what made the property so attractive, as it is to see the snags that have delayed production for nearly twenty years. The novel has roles uniquely suited to male film stars (defending his controversial casting of Tom Cruise and Brad Pitt, Neil Jordan correctly points out that Rice's glamorous, self-regarding, luminous monsters demand to be played by bigger-than-life name actors) and contains set pieces which read like spectacular movie scenes (several of which Jordan has omitted).

It also has the historic sweep of a television mini-series, combined with perverse material that could never be done on American network television and an all-in-one-night narrative frame that would resist serialisation, even though the straggling plot might provide a working description of the term 'episodic'. The thorniest problem of all, though, is Rice's use of the vampire myth not for horror, but for philosophical enquiry, with Louis maundering on at length about his place in the universe under God.

In the event, after much public argument and kiss-and-make-up between author and film-makers, the film of *Interview* is perhaps as strong as it could be, given concealed but inherent weaknesses in the original material. Sometimes, as it trips through two centuries, the film overdoses on montage: decades are encapsulated with a flurry of impressions that can never convey the changelessness that so frustrates Claudia. However, the kitsch-sounding summation of the twentieth century in terms of movie sunrises (*Sunrise, Nosferatu et al.*) is surprisingly effective, even to the throwaway punch line that has Louis re-encountering Lestat after wasting an evening on *Tequila Sunrise*. Exposed by the adaptation are some astonishingly ramshackle plot transitions, papered over by clever banter in the novel, but shown up for arrant melodrama here. By the time Louis has ended a third episode by burning down the set, the device becomes tiresome.

Fortunately, Jordan's work here is more in keeping with the fantastical *The Company of Wolves* than the *echt*-Hollywood of *High Spirits*. Never allowing make-up effects to swamp character as he did in his werewolf outing, Jordan achieves tiny moments of inexplicable creepiness (the stone eyes of the tomb-image of Louis' dead wife closing as he dies) and genuinely shocking scenes of physical horror (Lestat's blood pouring from his throat in a tide that threatens Claudia's delicate pumps). While the first half sometimes seems cramped for an historical epic, the trip to Paris allows for marvellous full-blooded decadences such as the vampire theatre with its Jean Rollin-like ritual cruelties. Sadly, the last-minute reversal, as Lestat pops up magically in Malloy's car without any narrative justification, reduces the grand vision to just another horror movie.

Though Louis is given an unusual interior life, and Lestat and Claudia remain among the most striking vampire characters in fiction, everyone else who passes through the overpopulated story is stuck with being a one-scene victim or a plot contrivance. Stephen Rea's Santiago, who has a neat Chaplinesque introduction as he teases Louis on a Paris street, suffers especially from an ill-thought-out subplot. He first declares it unforgivable for one vampire to murder another. The he kills Claudia merely on suspicion, incidentally destroying Madeleine and thus violating his own rule. Antonio Banderas' gloomy Armand suffers from playing stooge to tiresome stretches of religious debate, then allows his life work to be wrecked for no real reason and steps out of the story, presumably to sulk for a few more centuries.

The subtitle, which Rice has retroactively stuck on new editions of her book, indicates an ambition to chronicle all of vampire-kind, but the strength of the film is the uneasy, eroticised, disturbing relationship between Louis and Lestat. The elder vampire tries to nudge his prissier pupil into indulging a capacity for sin, and their shared crime – the creation of Claudia – is the event which ends the stasis of their lives, consigning Lestat to the past and pushing Louis out into the world in search of answers.

While the import of *Interview* is in Louis' quizzing of human and inhuman nature, the novel's lasting appeal lies with Lestat and Claudia, and Jordan's film is less likely to be remembered for its philosophy than for its action. Pitt's pouting Louis signals modernity by confessing his confused alienation, which Armand marks as the characteristic of the age, but the devils get all the best tunes. Remarkably, twelve-year-old Kirsten Dunst plays Claudia as an embittered woman in a pre-teenage body, a uniquely childish monster who kills her dressmaker or piano teacher on a whim and then nuzzles up to her 'parents' for approval.

In subsequent, much inferior novels, Rice has recanted her depiction in *Interview* of Lestat as a dashing monster, infusing him with Louis' conscience and introspection, but the character works best as a villain. Using an effeminate version of his *Far and Away* accent, Cruise is a fine narcissist monster. Demonstrating a wit rarely seen in his earlier work, he justifies his atrocities ('God kills indiscriminately and so shall we') and complains after the Louisiana purchase that he dislikes the taste of democratic American blood. By contrast with Pitt, and following Gary Oldman's lovelorn Dracula, it is refreshing to find a screen vampire who truly relishes being a monster.

Kim Newman

A JUDGEMENT IN STONE (LA CÉRÉMONIE)
France 1995
Director: Claude Chabrol

At Saint-Malo station, Mme Lelièvre collects Sophie, a young woman she has hired as a housekeeper and drives her to her large family home, also giving the local post-mistress 'Jeanne' a lift. Sophie proves to be extremely efficient, though there is something odd about her. Finding that Sophie can't drive, the Lelièvre family offer her lessons. One day, Mme Lelièvre leaves a shopping list for Sophie to order over the phone. Sophie takes the list to Jeanne and engineers it so that she has to make the order. The two women become friends. Jeanne guesses that Sophie is illiterate and finds out that she was implicated in the death of her father. Jeanne herself was once accused of killing her child.

Jeanne begins to spend a lot of time at the Lelièvres. M Lelièvre is not happy about this, as he is convinced that Jeanne is opening the family mail. He is further annoyed when Sophie fails to carry out an errand for him. One afternoon, Sophie overhears a conversation between the Lelièvre's daughter, Melinda, and her boyfriend, discovering that Melinda is pregnant. When Sophie attempts to blackmail Melinda, she is unconcerned and later informs her parents about Sophie. They decide to fire her. Sophie goes to tell Jeanne. That evening, the two young women are also dismissed from their church voluntary work by the local priest. Sophie and Jeanne go back to the Lelièvre household to collect Sophie's things. The family are in the drawing room watching an opera on television, which Melinda is also taping. Sophie and Jeanne decide to trash the place. They start to play around with M Lelièvre's hunting guns. When M Lelièvre confronts them in the kitchen, they shoot him and then go into the sitting room where they shoot the rest of the family. Sophie stays behind to clean up while Jeanne drives home, swiping Melinda's tape recorder as she goes. On the way, she is involved in a collision with the priest's car which kills her. Sophie walks off into the night, passing the scene. The police are playing the tape recorder.

*　*　*

In recent years, Claude Chabrol's films with the actress Isabelle Huppert have epitomised the best and worst of his work. *Une affaire de femmes* (1988), based on the true story of a woman who was put on trial for being an abortionist during the Vichy years, was an exceptionally powerful and contentious piece. In contrast, the only positive thing to be said about the lacklustre adaptation of Flaubert's *Madame Bovary* (1991) was that it induced exactly the boredom in the viewer that the eponymous heroine was trying to escape from. With *A Judgement in Stone*, the director reinstates his reputation and, while it might not be a full comeback for the man who made *Le Boucher* or *Les Bonnes Femmes*, it is an apt reminder of what he is capable of. It's easy to see why he might be attracted to the work of Ruth Rendell: her thrillers, like his, are commonly concerned with the prelude to murder, rather than its aftermath, and her interrogations of English class-bound society find their corollary across the Channel on the bleak, slate-grey Brittany coast.

A Judgement in Stone fits nicely with a recent spate of films featuring pairs of transgressive female outsiders, particularly those dealing with class, such as Michael Winterbottom's *Butterfly Kiss* and Nancy Meckler's *Sister, My Sister*. But then Chabrol himself has always been interested in transgressive women, whether in his bleak, bizarrely humoured film about the sundering of a lesbian relationship, *Les Biches*, or the more pedestrian *Violette Nozière*, in which Huppert plays a young woman who kills her parents. Certainly there is a feminist streak pursued throughout his career from *Les Bonnes Femmes* (1960) to *Une affaire de femmes* (1988), one which *Madame Bovary*, had it been any good, would have continued. In *A Judgement in Stone*, Jeanne and Sophie are depicted as isolated, working-class women, who become friends, at the rather pushy behest of Jeanne, because there is no one else around. Jeanne also has another agenda, for crucially these two women also trail ambiguous pasts. In both their cases, the law could not prove conclusively whether they were guilty of murdering their kin.

With darkly hollowed eyes and a severe fringe that makes her face appear more gauntly angular than ever, Sandrine Bonnaire plays Sophie as a haunted woman. Within minutes of the beginning, she establishes an odd presence. The questions of Mme Lelièvre (played with *haute bourgeois* polish by Jacqueline Bisset) meet with perfunctory, clipped replies. Even an event as explicable as her not meeting Mme Lelièvre on the right train platform hints at something more sinister. Asked whether she likes her small, dark attic bedroom, she says, 'I don't know.' It becomes a common refrain to other polite questions. Sophie works for the family with a robotically neat zeal, but, when left in the kitchen on her own, she picks at a chicken carcass like a hungry animal. She plays the servile role without a murmur, but there is something gnawing away inside her. Her illiteracy soon becomes evident and Bonnaire, her face taut with frustration, succinctly expresses the feelings of someone alienated from the written word – and hence viewed, by the Lelièvres at least, as a social problem. One scene finds her in the library, the shot angled so that she looks very small amongst all the books. Sophie is construed as someone who would prefer to dodge what for her is evidently a painful problem, rather than confront it. When M Lelièvre calls and requests her to look for a file for him, she slams the phone down and hides away in her room with the television blaring, gobbling up a bar of chocolate like a petulant adolescent.

Chabrol emphasises the girlish quality in both women – at one point, they sport pigtails. Together they are like teenagers with a slight crush on each other (any lesbian subtext is otherwise ignored). Huppert's Jeanne is brash and nosy. Her garish choice of nail varnish (such is the detailed scrutiny of character here that the colour changes on a daily basis) and her short kilts point her out as someone who wants to cut a dash in a small town and to defy restrained, parochial notions of taste. It is Jeanne who goads Sophie into being a 'bad' girl, defying not just the Lelièvres, but also the parsimonious and snobby priest (Jean-François Perrier, doing a delightfully plummy turn). As such, Chabrol ensures that we are sympathetic to the rebellion.

The two women are set in strong contrast to the Lelièvres. While Sophie and Jeanne are preoccupied with television game shows, the family listens to Elgar and watches *Don Giovanni* on their larger set. As one might expect, Chabrol has fun with these *hautes bourgeois*. At first, they express anxiety at the idea of having a servant and ponder exactly how they might address Sophie, but they warm up to the idea and are soon ignoring her while she serves their elegant dinners. During the denouement, the Lelièvres not only drink champagne while watching the opera broadcast, but dress up for it, too. It is with no uncertain irony that they meet their demise, shot with their own hunting guns. As for the two perpetrators, the script is equally playful with their fate. In the *faux*-religious finale, Jeanne is indirectly killed by the pompous priest, who confirms 'it was fate'. Meanwhile, the wraithlike Sophie walks past the accident, with the blue police lights blurring, into the night to the elegant strains of *Don Giovanni*.

Lizzie Francke

CRASH
Canada 1996
Director: David Cronenberg

Television commercial producer James Ballard and his wife, Catherine, live in Toronto, Canada; they have carefully planned sex with other people, perversely attempting simultaneous orgasm in disparate locations, as an extension of their sex life together. One night, James' car accidentally collides with another vehicle. The driver of the other car is killed, but his wife, Dr Helen Remington, and James survive with injuries. At the hospital, James meets a scarred man named Vaughan coming out of Helen's room.

After being released from hospital, James becomes fascinated with cars and finds himself sexually excited by road accidents. He meets a similarly aroused Helen at the police pound and offers her a lift. At an airport parking lot, they have sex in the car. Helen invites James to a re-creation of James Dean's fatal collision staged by Vaughan. Through Vaughan, James meets Vaughan's strange entourage: Colin (a stuntman), his wife, Vera, and their disabled friend Gabrielle.

After a menacing car chase during which Vaughan almost forces Catherine off the road, James introduces Catherine to Vaughan. While the married couple make love, Catherine fantasises aloud about Vaughan. The three of them encounter a freeway crash which was caused by Colin re-creating Jayne Mansfield's fatal accident. Later, Vaughan has bruise-inducing sex with Catherine in his car while James drives them through a car wash. In another car, James penetrates a wound in Gabrielle's leg with his penis to their mutual satisfaction. Later, Vaughan and he have sex, after which Vaughan threatens to run him down with his car. Vaughan once more chases Catherine, but suddenly Vaughan hurtles off the freeway into a bus and is killed. Afterwards, James buys the wrecked hulk of Vaughan's car and uses it to help Catherine experience the pleasure of her own accident.

* * *

Leaving aside for a moment the howling outrage elicited in Britain by *Crash*, it is striking to note that some Ballard fans condemn the film for the opposite reasons: not violent enough, not extreme enough, not transgressive enough. A no-win scenario, in which a film is denounced as both shocking and dull. However, I would propose that this film is indeed both shocking and dull: any obsession that one doesn't share is undeniably dull, while often shocking. This film turns its medical gaze on an obsession and it does not seduce us into partaking in the obsession, nor does it invite us to identify with the obsessed. Indeed, it refuses to provide us with those narrative trappings such as motivation or personality which would allow us to identify in any conventional sense. Not a pornographic text, *Crash* is rather a text on pornography, a cool, detached look at sexual obsession itself.

People who are into cars are also disappointed – the crash sequences are shot with the same detachment as the sex scenes, they feel strangely unreal, artificial, despite (or because of) the obsessive attention to detail. Again, it's a clinical look, Cronenberg's speciality. In *Crash*, Vaughan's (Elias Koteas) car has mythic dimensions, a black Lincoln Continental, the same as the one Kennedy was shot in, thereby proposing

JFK's assassination as another kind of crash, but James Ballard (James Spader) drives a generic sedan, an American car, while Catherine (Deborah Kara Unger) drives a Mazda Miata, a sexy, diminutive sports car. Still, Cronenberg eschews the conventional formulas; neither television car ad nor Hollywood crash sequence, the cars in *Crash* have a conceptual presence that outweighs their styling. They are representations of technology, imbued with the promise of sex and death, not consumer desirables.

The opening of *Crash*, in a light aircraft hangar, sets the terms for sexuality as an encounter of bodies and technology. Catherine, in high heels and straight skirt, a homage to Helmut Newton, presses her magnificent breast up against a plane, before being fucked from behind by some anonymous man. I was irritated by the Victoria's Secret-style satin bras that keep appearing until I understood the technological parallel: the gleam on the protuberant satin like the shine on the bulging wing of a car or nose of a jet. The topic of *Crash* is the intersection of (sexual) bodies, (automobile) technology, and (catastrophic) medicine, with the cars standing in for modern society, becoming sheer representations of the death drive. It seems Freud's idea that people are driven towards death and destruction as much as towards survival and reproduction is still wildly transgressive.

For J. G. Ballard, the novel *Crash* was a dystopian satire, a counter-blast to consumer-safety advocate Ralph Nader. Ballard saw cars as the totem of American culture: aggressive, wasteful, violent, sexual, with a functional dimension, undeniably, by far the least intriguing aspect. Naderism was an attempt to draw a veil over this reality, to pretend that seat belts and crumple zones and baby seats would make safe this killing machine, domesticate it. But to Ballard, this was a lie, like the lie that home itself is a safe place. A true surrealist, Ballard celebrates those rare moments when the unconcious speaks true, and the American car provides one of those moments, where form follows (unconcious) fantasy, not function.

The sexual obsession in this movie is idea-driven, and while it presents an unutterably bleak and dark view, it also allows for a vein of wit that occasionally moves forwards into outright comedy. Obsession is on some level absurd and, when Vaughan breathes heavily over James' wounds, or Helen Remington (Holly Hunter) fumbles for the remote, at the mercy of an urgent need to see the end of the crash test video she's hooked on, it is a great comic moment. Cronenberg presents Vaughan's cronies as a typical subcultural scene, rolling spliffs on an old sofa in front of the box, while Vaughan plans the next great performance art crash, very Survival Research Lab, very punk. Gabrielle (Rosanna Arquette) is an avatar of punk style, encased in black leather orthopaedic corset, braces, trusses and supports, the back of her thigh revealing (through black net stockings) a fissure, a cleft, the trace of some unspeakable wound. When James gets around to fucking it, it is both shocking and very amusing, because we can't forget the taboos around disability, this ultimate site of the forbidden.

The weakness of the film is in the characterisation of Vaughan, who is the heart of darkness, the black hole towards which all the others are ineluctably drawn. His sexual dynamic is too physical, I think, yet despite this the film does convey the poignancy of this strange relationship, as James and Vaughan first use Catherine as their sexual link, and then finally fuck each other. The car wash scene, with James at the wheel while Vaughan and Catherine do it in the back, is very beautiful, the suds like a psychedelic light show framing James' expressionless face, the clunky convertible roof automatically extending itself as Vaughan descends on Catherine's body.

Crash is a brilliant, brave film – non-narrative, anti-realist, cool as a cucumber, it sticks to its conceptual guns, refusing to situate the audience comfortably, calmly bringing forwards a celebration of sex and death, as if for our consideration. It is this very calm – the stylisation, the use of tableau, the subtle intensity of Howard Shore's score, the emptiness of the characters – that makes the film so disturbing, witty and dispassionate, as it studies an obsession that is itself shocking and, necessarily, as obsession must be, a little dull.

Leslie Dick

L.A. CONFIDENTIAL
USA 1997
Director: Curtis Hanson

Los Angeles, the early 1950s. Police Captain Dudley Smith tells his ambitious, incorruptible protégé, Sergeant Ed Exley, that he will never make detective unless he's willing to kill men he knows are guilty, instead of risking their getting off in court. That same night, officers Bud White, Jack Vincennes and Dick Stensland beat up a gang of Mexicans in police custody. Exley, who tries to prevent the attack, testifies against them, incurring their hatred. White and Vincennes are transferred and Stensland sacked. Exley makes detective.

Stensland and five other bystanders are murdered during a bloody armed robbery at the Nite Owl Café. Exley successfully pins the massacre on three black junkies who have abducted and raped a Mexican woman, Inez Soto. When they escape, he tracks them down and kills them in self-defence during the ensuing shootout. He is decorated with the Medal of Valor. Meanwhile, White investigates another victim of the Nite Owl massacre, Susan Lefferts, and discovers she worked for mysterious millionaire Pierce Patchett, one of whose sidelines is supplying prostitutes who look like movie stars. After spying on another of Patchett's girls, Lynn Bracken, White starts an affair with her.

Exley begins to doubt the guilt of the Nite Owl killers when Soto admits she made up the evidence that implicated them. After agreeing to help Exley find Stensland's real killers, Vincennes reveals his suspicions to Smith, who shoots him dead. Suspicious of White, Exley visits Bracken, and ends up having sex with her. When Smith arranges for White to 'accidentally' see photos of Exley with Bracken. White attacks Exley. But Exley convinces White that Smith is their common enemy: Smith is trying to take over the LA underworld with Patchett, while gang boss Mickey Cohen is in prison.

Exley and White are called to a motel where they are ambushed by police. Smith shoots White and is about to finish off Exley when the injured White stabs him. Knowing he can never prove that Smith was the real killer who committed the Nite Owl massacre (as a cover for killing Stensland over a heroin deal), Exley shoots him in the back. In the ensuing cover-up, Smith is depicted as a hero killed in the course of his duties and Exley receives a second Medal of Valor. White leaves for Arizona with Bracken.

* · * · *

Attempts to compress a 500-page best-seller into a two-hour film often result in hopelessly overcrowded plots peopled with schematic characters. One need only consider the string of recent films adapted from the novels of John Grisham. Doing justice to James Ellroy's *L.A. Confidential* might seem an even more daunting task. For a start, the book is merely one part (the third) in Ellroy's mammoth LA quartet, which traces the secret history of Los Angeles from the 1940s to the 1960s, with recurring characters and themes throughout. Besides, 500 pages of Ellroy are like a thousand of anyone else's: he writes in a fevered shorthand, cramming information onto the page.

So writer-director Curtis Hanson's achievement with *L.A. Confidential* is all the more triumphant. With his co-screenwriter Brian Helgeland (who wrote *Conspiracy Theory*), Hanson hasn't so much condensed Ellroy's novel as filleted it, lifting out characters, incidents and chunks of juicy dialogue and rearranging them into a more streamlined plot. (One hesitates to say a simplified one because the synopsis above only hints at the narrative complexity of the film.)

One inspired decision is to eliminate Preston Exley, the cop-turned-property-developer who in the novel dominates his son Ed and the city as a whole. This allows Dudley Smith to loom more powerfully as Ed Exley's father figure, *éminence grise* and, ultimately, nemesis. In fact, Smith's opening speech to Exley, in which he tests his willingness to plant evidence, rig crime scenes, beat confessions out of suspects and shoot criminals in the back, belongs to Preston Exley in the novel. Also, in the book it is Preston who is destroyed by Ed's investigations, while Smith lives on, guilty but undeterred. If anything, Helgeland and Hanson's devastating ending, in which Exley can only beat Smith by stooping to Smith's cold-blooded, law-bending methods, improves on Ellroy's.

What Hanson has preserved from the novel is the use of three contrasting protagonists: the repressed Exley, the sleazy Vincennes and the explosive White. The way their investigations intertwine, their methods differ and their relationships develop towards the final, grudging collaboration gives the film a richness far beyond the basic thrills of the police investigation. Thanks to Ellroy, *L.A. Confidential* is also peopled with unusually vivid supporting characters, not least the muck-raking gossip columnist Sid Hudgens, whose role is elevated here from colourful (and short-lived) bit player to occasional narrator, spouting Ellroy's magnificent Walter Winchell-inspired tabloid speak.

A thriller specialist, Hanson's previous work has been marked by an old-fashioned, unflashy emphasis on character and tight plots. Here, he manages to capture Ellroy's uniquely raw and brutal tone, but (thanks to Dante Spinotti's luxurious Panavision photography and Jerry Goldsmith's Chinatown-esque score) within a much smoother and more elegant framework than the book provided.

Hanson's real flair, however, is for casting. In the past, he has credibly reinvented Rob Lowe as an evil genius (in the underrated *Bad Influence*), Rebecca De Mornay as a psycho nanny (*The Hand that Rocks the Cradle*) and Meryl Streep as an action heroine (*The River Wild*). Surely no one else in Hollywood would have chosen two Antipodeans, Russell Crowe and *The Adventures of Priscilla, Queen of the Desert*'s Guy Pearce, to play White and Exley, but they are both frighteningly driven, while James Cromwell, the kindly farmer from *Babe*, is equally perfect as the avuncular but lethal

Smith. More conventionally cast, but clearly relishing their roles, Kevin Spacey and Danny DeVito provide some very cynical light relief as the cop and the columnist who collaborate on busting celebrities.

In fact, despite its bleak catalogue of murder, rape and betrayal, and without ever making light of them, *L.A. Confidential* manages to be a very witty film, thanks to Ellroy's gallows humour (at one point, a wry pathologist describes one organ as the 'stomach of the week') and Hanson and Helgeland's inspired interpolations, not least the moment where Exley mistakes the 'real' Lana Turner, on the arm of Mickey Cohen's lieutenant Johnny Stompanato (also a historical figure), for one of Patchett's movie-star lookalike whores.

John Wrathall

JACKIE BROWN
USA 1997
Director: Quentin Tarantino

Ordell Robbie, a gunrunner, goes to Max Cherry's bail bond office to post the $10,000 bail for a henchman, Beaumont, facing time in jail for arms possession. Ordell then kills Beaumont after he's released. Jackie Brown, who smuggles money for Ordell to supplement her stewardess' income, is stopped by cops at LA airport. They find $50,000 and a stash of cocaine in her bag. Ordell bails Jackie out of jail. She realises, after Beaumont's death, that Ordell will kill her too so she strikes a deal: in exchange for $100,000 if she's convicted, she won't give him over to the police. However, Jackie also makes a deal with the cops, saying she'll help them convict Ordell. She tells Ordell of her visit to the cops, but assures him she's thought up a scam to double-cross them when they come after the money.

Jackie tempts Max to come in with her on a $500,000 deal. Having delivered $50,000 of smuggled cash, Jackie wins the cops' trust. But, with a second delivery, Jackie pulls a scam: in a shopping mall changing room, she swaps bags with Ordell's henchwoman Melanie, but hands over a dummy bag containing only some of the $500,000. Louis, an ex-con friend of Ordell's who has accompanied Melanie, shoots Melanie when she irritates him. Ordell realises Jackie has taken the money and shoots Louis. Max, now on Jackie's side, gives Ordell his $10,000 bail bond back and tells him he has the rest of the money in his safe. When Ordell arrives at Max's office, the cops shoot him. Jackie gets away with the bulk of the money. She offers some to Max before leaving for Spain, but he declines.

* * *

Jackie Brown, Quentin Tarantino's adaptation of Elmore Leonard's novel *Rum Punch*, has been on the cards ever since Tarantino and his producer Lawrence Bender optioned the book just after making *Reservoir Dogs*. It feels like a project that's been knocking around for a while, one that's been mulled over, reassessed, changed and finally made. There's something confidently easy-going about it; it's immensely hard to dislike *Jackie Brown*. However, it is not a particularly good film. It's too long and draws out what is essentially a caper movie way beyond its narrative capability. It does, though, make for an interesting auteur piece, eschewing as it does the trademark frenziedness of both *Reservoir Dogs* and *Pulp Fiction.*

As if to signal this difference, *Jackie Brown* opens with an ostentatiously lazy, prolonged profile shot (which lasts for the duration of the opening credits) of Pam Grier, as stewardess Jackie Brown, progressing in stately fashion along an airport conveyor belt. Because nothing much else is going on here, we are lured into becoming obsessively attentive to details, such as Jackie's garish company badge, the cheap blue of her jacket contrasting with the rich browns of her hair and skin, the elegant curve in her nose and her ambiguous eyes, both vulnerable and self-contained. Whereas previously in Tarantino's films, such expansiveness would have been the exception (Mr Blonde's languid torture of the cop in *Reservoir Dogs*, or John Travolta's heroin-fuelled cruise through town in *Pulp Fiction*), in *Jackie Brown* it establishes the defining mood. It's as if the whole film is viewed through the haze emanating from Ordell's girlfriend Melanie's impressive array of dope pipes. At one point, the already monosyllabic Louis, having smoked perhaps a bit too much grass, is rendered catatonic. He's upright, on the telephone, but hardly able to move a muscle. The film is content to grind to a halt with him.

This intriguing, anti-dynamic approach to narration has its drawbacks in what is essentially a 1990s homage to the black-action movies of the early 1970s. The clearest blaxploitation echoes are in the casting of Grier (star of *Coffy*, 1973, and *Foxy Brown*, 1974) and Samuel L. Jackson as Ordell, who with his pimp-look outfits and fast talking is a pastiche of Richard Roundtree in *Shaft* (1971) and the mass of street-smart heroes who followed. Ordell is the antidote to Jackie Brown. While she, a none-too-bothered siren, soaks up and deflects energy, he provokes or perpetrates all the film's action and violence. It is almost an auteurist necessity that he blows out both Beaumont's and Louis' brains at point-blank range. His protracted word-firing sprees function as reminders of the genre Jackie Brown purports to inhabit.

The uneasy discrepancy between generic framework and tone is exacerbated when it comes to Jackie Brown's double-crossing money-swapping ventures. Her final successful attempt at conning Ordell out of his money and the police out of getting hold of it should provide the fast-paced denouement to a twisty plot. Instead, Tarantino elects to film the same changing-room bag-swapping sequence of events from three different subjective angles, thus repeating but also dissipating the tension. Each time new details emerge, such as Louis' half-recognition of Max, the bail bondsman, but the three versions are essentially very similar. Again, the most memorable features of this triptych are the insignificant details such as the fetishistic sight of Melanie's bronzed, sandalled feet pacing around under the changing-room door. Claude Chabrol once wrote of the difference between big-theme and little-theme movies, arguing that just because its story is placed within a more grandiose setting, the biblical epic isn't necessarily about more important things than a film about a domestic argument. Tarantino seems to have learnt a similar love of low-key nuance, but he still can't quite relinquish action and bombastic stylisation.

Jackie Brown is an intriguing failure. Whereas both *Reservoir Dogs* and *Pulp Fiction* were brashly single-minded films, Tarantino's latest meanders constantly off-course, its narrative and mood rarely compatible. Symptomatic of this is the end: as Max lures Ordell into the police trap, the action movie is resolved with a typically excessive vertical shot of Ordell lying on the floor. The actual end of the film, however, is all about a love of faces and character, concluding with a beautiful, caressing close-up of a chaste farewell kiss between Max and Jackie, and then a calm, static shot of Jackie leaving which mirrors her arrival. *Jackie Brown* is an anomaly: an action film that takes us nowhere in particular.

Stella Bruzzi

LOLITA
France/USA 1997
Director: Adrian Lyne

The south of France, the 1920s. Thirteen-year-old Humbert Humbert falls madly in love with Annabel Leigh, who dies shortly after they have sex. Humbert develops a fixation on pubescent girls. 1947. Humbert arrives in the United States to teach at a Midwestern college. Taking a room at the house of Charlotte Haze, Humbert meets Charlotte's twelve-year-old daughter, Lolita. Humbert marries Charlotte to be near Lolita, but Charlotte is killed crossing the road after she reads his diary. Humbert collects Lolita from summer camp and the two of them sleep together. After Humbert reveals that Charlotte is dead, Lolita and he begin an aimless tour of the United States.

Humbert and Lolita settle in the college town of Beardsley. While performing in a school play, Lolita meets the playwright Clare Quilty, an old acquaintance of her mother's. Humbert begins to suspect that she is seeing someone else. When they take to the road again, a car appears to be following him. Ultimately, his suspicions are confirmed when Lolita absconds.

Several years later, Lolita gets in touch. Humbert finds her pregnant and married, in need of money before she and her husband move to Alaska. Lolita reveals that the man she ran off with was Clare Quilty. Humbert tracks Quilty down and kills him. Intertitles reveal that soon after this, both Humbert and Lolita died.

* * *

Adrian Lyne's *Lolita* is a comic romp, an amusing escapade complete with motels – *It Happened One Night* for the 1990s – that turns into a doomed romance, a full-on tragedy – interspersed with quasi-soft porn sequences so tacky they bring tears to your eyes. Nabokov would have liked the motels.

The first time Humbert Humbert lays eyes on Lolita, she is in the garden, lying on the grass under a sprinkler. Long sunbeams angle through the veil of falling water and, needless to say, Lolita is wearing a thin cotton dress, soaked to semi-transparency, which clings to her nubile body. Despite the plentiful droplets, she is reading a magazine, admiring a photo of Burt Lancaster. Lyne adds a childish detail: braces on her teeth, revealed in Lolita's wildly improbable cover-girl smile directed at the stranger. (Later, the dental retainer will perform a key semiotic function, as she gleefully pulls it out, in bed with Humbert Humbert, apparently in preparation for fellatio.)

The initial 'wet T-shirt on a pre-teen' scene gives the game away: no matter how hard the actors work (and they're good actors, doing their job against terrible odds), no matter how crisp the script (and there are only a few real gaffes, such as when Quilty says 'Enjoy!' like a waiter in an LA restaurant), the erotic clichés spoil it all. For example, in the scene where Lolita drops her pyjama bottoms, on her way downstairs to raid the icebox, the unnecessary undressing marks this out as soft-porn fantasy, rigorous in its conventionality – and suddenly it isn't sexy any more.

H. H.'s penchant for little girls goes way back: when he was thirteen, and she was twelve, he loved Annabel by the sea (echoes of Edgar Allan Poe, who married a twelve-year-old), a girl who died three months later. His life is an attempt to rediscover that first love: even the ribbon the youthful H. H. pulled from the ever-so-tasteful broderie anglaise camiknickers of the long-limbed Annabel reappears, fetishistically retained, folded into the leather-bound notebook where he records his secret thoughts. Nabokov does not hesitate to depict his protagonist's furtive masturbation on the bench at the playground, on the couch with Lolita. The movie inevitably romanticises: in place of abject wanking, Lyne gives us tasteful fetishism, a case of arrested development, golden sunlight, sheer romance.

Far more compelling is H. H. in his room, bathroom door ajar, listening transfixed to Lo brushing her teeth, listening to the loo roll spin, as Lolita's collusion – is she aware of him listening? – remains uncertain, ambient eroticism displaced into sound, a sense of bodily proximity, a familiar intimacy. Or when she drops her retainer into his glass of white wine – it's much more plausible, and much more complicated. The unseen presence of Lolita's mother, Charlotte, adds a special frisson, but she's the fall guy, the dupe. She's the fool who thinks Humbert's a disgusting pervert, a despicable criminal monster, when she finds out. She dies, of course, just as all the women in the story do, even Lo.

Lolita's point of view remains necessarily opaque: her isolation, after her mother's wonderfully *deus ex machina* death, is complete and, as a result, she turns to Humbert for comfort, even when he is the cause of her misery. She may be seductive, provocative, voracious even. But she is also a child and, as a child, she has no power in the world. Ironically, Quilty offers her an escape route, yet what he asks of her is even less palatable than H. H.'s embraces: he wants her to take part in an orgy for the camera. But her tragedy is viewed entirely through H. H.'s eyes and the film gives much more weight to his tragedy, his loss, his jealousy.

Given how glib the movie is stylistically, the fact that Jeremy Irons makes Humbert's love for Lolita credible is amazing. When the film tries for the tragic mode, when H. H. runs after her through the rain, the barking dog in the alley, the beautifully preserved 1940s cars, the elaborate lighting and the cinematography recall nothing so much as a very upmarket advert. Lyne's determination to include the whole audience in H. H.'s perverse passion is crucial: we must all partake of the forbidden fruit – a requirement that leads, with inexorable logic, to the wet, transparent dress, among other things – so that subsequently we can buy into Humbert's dubious expressions of guilt, his emotional intensity, so we can indulge him and ourselves. Lyne sets us up to identify with H. H. – maybe he cannot imagine a movie without the central structure of identification. The elaborate edifice of irony, distance, disgust and sympathy that Nabokov so magically sustained is thereby reduced to a story where ambiguity is almost absent, complexity discarded and real transgression evaporates, like so many drops from a sprinkler.

Leslie Dick

THE TALENTED MR. RIPLEY
USA 1999
Director: Anthony Minghella

New York, 1958. As a result of a misunderstanding, Tom Ripley is hired by wealthy American magnate Mr Greenleaf to rescue his son Dickie from a dissolute life in Italy. On the way, Tom meets heiress Meredith Logue and tells her he's Dickie Greenleaf. In Italy, Tom befriends Dickie, who's involved both with Marge, an American writer, and local girl Silvana. Tom and Dickie take trips together and Tom's semi-sexual attraction for Dickie grows. Silvana, pregnant by Dickie, drowns herself. Suddenly bored with Tom, Dickie begins to exclude him. During a motorboat ride, Tom and Dickie argue; he kills Dickie and hides the corpse.

Tom tells Marge Dickie decided to move to Rome. There, Tom assumes Dickie's identity. Problems arise when Dickie's old friend Freddie Miles pays a call. Tom kills Freddie. The police become suspicious, but Tom is saved when a new policeman is assigned to the case. Marge and Dickie's father arrive in town, the latter bringing with him a private detective. Tom bumps into Meredith in Rome. He juggles his two identities, but, when Marge finds Dickie's rings, she's convinced of Tom's guilt. The private detective uncovers Silvana's suicide. Dickie's father, disappointed by his son's bad character, gives up the search. Tom has by now fallen in love with Peter, a friend of Marge's, and they go on a voyage back to the United States, only for Tom to discover Meredith aboard. Tom kills Peter.

* * *

The Talented Mr. Ripley, an adaptation of Patricia Highsmith's 1955 thriller, is a film about the look that cannot speak its name. At one point, the eponymous Ripley sits on a rocking train, gazing at the object of his sexual and economic desire, Dickie Greenleaf. Suddenly, he (and we) realise Dickie knows he's being watched. Director Anthony Minghella keeps the camera fixed on the two men for just that little bit too long, a brilliant move which allows Tom's ambivalent adoration to float queasily before us, while Dickie decides how to react. He finally settles on contempt and (peeping) Tom's body seems to contract with shame. Like that otherworldly moment in *Persona* where wannabe 'double' Liv Ullman steps on to a shard of glass, Tom's expulsion into the land of the single makes us wince.

There are many such episodes in this film. A tense, troubling thriller, marred only by problems of pacing (the middle section drags) and some implausible character-isation (Meredith's obsession with Ripley never convinces), it's full of vivid, miserable life. Philip Seymour Hoffman, for example, burns a hole in the memory as the viciously astute Freddie.

But is this film 'dangerous', as has been suggested by the US press? Minghella has obviously adapted freely from the novel and has been credited with taking more risks, not less. Something has happened, for instance, to the novel's take on class. In the book, the social gap between Tom and Dickie is not as wide as in the film, where Tom is a one-time janitor. Highsmith's Tom is also the more culturally worldly of the two – it's Dickie who's the conventional one. In Minghella's version, the roles are reversed: Tom plays nerdish pauper to Dickie's machiavellian *la dolce vita* prince. Minghella presumably intended to make Tom more sympathetic. He has, but in doing so he's also made him less interesting and drained him of his mercurial power. Instead of identifying with Tom, we feel sorry for him. By the same token, instead of feeling sorry for Dickie, we're intrigued. He, along with girlfriend Marge (no longer a stodgy Ohio bumpkin, but a cut-glass golden girl), now represents a new, enticing moral order.

Dickie and Marge break rules, Dickie with his casual, catastrophic affairs, his 'half-killing' of a boy at school, Marge with her gay friend Peter (in the book, all are horrified by 'queers'). The couple are also bright as buttons. Where Highsmith's Dickie is pitifully limited when it comes to *aperçu* (Tom waits in vain for 'something profound and original from Dickie'), Minghella's charismatic cad manages to impress constantly (he likens his privileged friends to cream, because they're 'rich and thick'). Similarly, while Highsmith pokes fun at Dickie's mediocre paintings, Minghella allows the young man's musical ability to charm not only Tom, but also a crowded room of Italians (the camera, swirling round the room, infects us with the appreciative mood). As for Marge, in the book she remains duped to the end. Here, she's the only one to realise Tom's a murderer. Thus, as in *The English Patient*, Minghella gets to portray certain aristocrats not only as supremely glamorous, but also ahead of their time. Their remoteness, even cruelty, just makes them more attractive. Like Almásy and Katharine, Dickie and Marge are extraordinary, objects of sexual and economic desire perfectly formed to suit middlebrow tastes.

Minghella's other 'radical' break with Highsmith's text involves sexuality, introducing a full-blown homosexual affair into the story, which Minghella has predicted will 'alienate Middle America'. But Ripley does not 'get away' with his sexual/moral deviation. A prisoner of his own device, he ends up a psychologically doomed man. In an afterword to *The Price of Salt*, a.k.a. *Carol*, the 'lesbian novel' Highsmith wrote, she talks about the typical fate of homosexuals in fiction: 'punished for their deviation, they've slashed their wrists or collapsed alone into a depression equal to hell'. Minghella's Tom conforms utterly to this description. By combining sex with an unhappy ending and a contrite beginning ('If I could just go back...' intones Tom), Minghella more than satisfies mainstream requirements.

The Talented Mr. Ripley is worth more than a peep. It's only in comparison with Highsmith's book that its conservatism becomes clear. Minghella cautions that envy won't get us anywhere, even as he makes us giddy with covetous lust for the aristocratic élite. Highsmith teaches that envy gets you everywhere, even as she reminds us how unenviable the rich truly are. What a shame this lesson is available to the reader's eyes only.

Charlotte O'Sullivan

THE BEACH
USA/United Kingdom 2000
Director: Danny Boyle

Richard, an American backpacker in Thailand, alights at a fleapit Bangkok hotel where he meets Daffy, a drug-addled Scotsman. Daffy gives Richard a map to an Edenic island and then kills himself. Richard and a French couple, Françoise and Etienne, set off to find the island. En route, Richard leaves a copy of the map with two fellow Americans, Zeph and Sammy. Richard, Françoise and Etienne swim to the island, navigate an illegal marijuana plantation policed by armed guards and discover an idyllic stretch of beach inhabited by a commune of Western travellers.

The three visitors are inducted into the commune. Later, Françoise dumps Etienne for Richard. On a supply-buying trip with the commune's leader Sal, Richard learns Zeph and Sammy are coming to the island. Sal blackmails Richard into having sex with her. Back on the island, one backpacker is killed by a shark and another, Christo, fatally injured in the attack. Richard is posted to the jungle to watch out for the arrival of Zeph and Sammy. Rejected by Françoise and ostracised from the group, he spies on the plantation guards and is visited by the ghost of Daffy. Zeph and Sammy arrive with two German girls in tow; all four are shot dead by the guards. The guards raid the commune; Sal must either kill Richard or everyone must leave. The gun they give her turns out to have no bullets. Everyone but Sal leaves the island.

* * *

'My name is Richard. So what else do you need to know?' runs *The Beach*'s opening voiceover. It's like *Moby Dick*'s opening 'Call me Ismael' gambit farmed through *Trainspotting*'s blasted 'Choose life' mantra, and effectively sets the film's tone from the start. In adapting Alex Garland's best-selling novel, the film-making troika of director Danny Boyle, producer Andrew Macdonald and writer John Hodge look to be going back to basics. Stung by the poor critical and commercial response to their magic-realist folly *A Life Less Ordinary*, the team appear to be beating a retreat to the misanthropic, twenty-something kicks peddled by the likes of *Shallow Grave* and *Trainspotting*. Strange to report, then, that *The Beach* winds up an oddly wayward and uncertain effort, its tailor-made ingredients only fitfully hanging together.

On the face of it, Garland's source novel is ideally suited to the cinema. First published in 1994, *The Beach* boasted a roster of young, Western characters, a glamorous foreign backdrop, a zeitgeisty flavour (tapping into the 1990s rise in eco-tourism) and a high-concept narrative. Its young author has admitted to feeling more affinity with comic books than traditional literature (his father is *Daily Telegraph* cartoonist Nicholas Garland). Accordingly, Garland writes the sort of zesty, dialogue-driven prose that converts easily into a screenplay format.

But in the event, the film version of *The Beach* has been plagued by problems. First, its original star choice, Ewan McGregor, was dropped in favour of the more bankable Leonardo DiCaprio. Later, the production itself was disrupted by protests that the film-makers had damaged their location. Moreover, the makers have tweaked the original storyline, shoe-horning in two romantic encounters for the previously celibate Richard (reportedly on the direct orders of DiCaprio) and downplaying the book's communal spirit in favour of a loving focus on its hero. So, rising French actress Virginie Ledoyen makes do with a pallid support slot as Richard's love interest, while a steely, tranquil Tilda Swinton struggles to make an impact as the demagogic Sal. Most disconcerting of all is the sight of Robert Carlyle reduced to bug-eyed histrionics in a shamefully underwritten role as the spectral Daffy. In this way, DiCaprio spreads his towel all over *The Beach*. It's a classic example of Hollywood muscle run riot.

It says a lot for the inherent momentum of Garland's story that *The Beach* maintains its trajectory well into the second half. The set-up is efficiently handled, the trip to the island tightly plotted and the multicultural commune sketched out with a minimum of fuss. However, when *The Beach* should be gearing up for a grand finale, instead it nosedives into weary hallucinogenics. With Richard exiled to the jungle and cracking up fast, Boyle substitutes empty pyrotechnics for stringent psychological examination. His direction cannibalises *Apocalypse Now*'s mix of hard light with deep shadow, while a flashy arcade-game interlude (in which a digitised DiCaprio zaps tigers as he runs through the jungle) is a show-off flourish which hints, perhaps, at an underlying desperation.

These moments reveal *The Beach*'s true colours. Compare it to *Trainspotting* and the difference is striking. *Trainspotting* was a low-budget, organic product – properly cinematic, yet generally faithful to the spirit of its source novel. It was, significantly, a film that broke out from its indie niche to find a mainstream audience. By contrast, *The Beach* seems to have sold its soul too early. In pitching for the mass market, Boyle's film has allowed itself to be rebranded as a Hollywood star vehicle, a cynical assemblage that is never more than the sum of its market-researched parts. *The Beach* is set on a tropical beach. It has killer sharks in it. It stars Leonardo DiCaprio. So what else do you need to know?

Xan Brooks

AMERICAN PSYCHO
USA/Canada 2000
Director: Mary Harron

Manhattan, 1987. Patrick Bateman, a 27-year-old Wall Street broker, spends most of his time and substantial income on clothes, dining and clubbing. Notionally engaged to Evelyn Williams, he is having an affair with Courtney Rawlinson, the fiancée of his colleague Luis Carruthers. An avid consumer of drugs, pornography and prostitutes, Bateman fantasises murdering friends, rivals and strangers.

Upstaged at a boardroom meeting by his colleague Paul Allen, Bateman works off his frustration by knifing a street-sleeper and later contrives to murder Allen with an axe. He lets himself into Allen's apartment and re-records the answering-machine message to say that Allen has gone to London. But, when private investigator Donald Kimball begins enquiring into Allen's disappearance, Bateman grows nervous.

Events spiral out of control, at least in his mind. An attempt on the life of Carruthers (who is gay) is misinterpreted as an expression of closeted affection. He is deflected from murdering his secretary, Jean, when Evelyn calls at the crucial moment. A threesome in Allen's apartment with his friend Elizabeth and prostitute Christie turns into a chaotic bloodbath in which both women die. The shooting of an interfering old woman leads to a police chase through the night streets; Bateman kills a cop and at least two others before hiding in his office and calling his lawyer to confess everything. But when he next visits Allen's apartment, he finds it being redecorated and up for sale. In Bateman's absence, Jean checks his private diary and finds doodled evidence of his psychosis. Bateman runs into his lawyer (who takes him for someone else) and learns that Paul Allen is indeed in London.

* * *

Psycho killer, *qu'est-ce que c'est?* The widely shared intuition that lousy books make good movies and vice versa finds a partial corroboration in Mary Harron's long-coming adaptation of *American Psycho.* Bret Easton Ellis' stream-of-unconsciousness novel maps its narrator's befuddled stasis in a miasma of designer labels, hard-to-get bookings in fashionable restaurants and psychotic fantasies. Resting on the thin conceit that a 1980s Manhattan consumerist lifestyle would be the perfect cover for random serial killing and on a series of overplayed gags (identikit personalities lead to recurrent cases of mistaken identity, intense emotional crises are triggered only by fears of losing status in the food chain), the book runs out of shtick around the halfway mark, but dances on the spot for another 200 pages. As a satire of a social phenomenon, it's no more cutting than the caricature of a braying, depraved yuppie in *Naked.*

Against the odds, Mary Harron and Guinevere Turner have succeeded in extracting a viable narrative screenplay from this plotless blank. Almost everything in their film comes from the book, but they have sensibly junked a huge amount: the recitations of designer brands, the taunting of beggars with banknotes, the obsession with a morning television talk show, the 'ironic' ubiquity of *Les Misérables* in the background, the starved rat and most of the sex, violence and sadism. What's left is a brittle and stylised satire of Me-generation values rather conventionally structured as an escalation into madness.

The opening scenes sketch the norms and parameters of Bateman's life: platinum AmEx cards, the workless office, the Robert Longo painting, exfoliating skin creams, that kind of thing. Unsubtle pointers to his psychosis are dropped in sparingly at first, but gradually allowed to take over the film until they climax in the night-time shoot-out with the cops on Wall Street, complete with exploding cars and circling helicopters like something out of a Jean-Claude Van Damme movie. The film presents its psychotic episodes as fantasies from the get-go (Bateman leaves trails of blood on his sheets, his walls and across the lobby of his W. 81st Street building without arousing suspicions), which turns Willem Dafoe's scenes as an investigating gumshoe into dramatisations of Bateman's paranoia and makes the closing scenes – in which Bateman is forced to confront the unreality of his dreams – more interesting than they otherwise would have been.

Thanks to excellent art direction and a set of self-effacing performances from those playing the yuppies, Harron captures late-1980s vacuity better than she captured late-1960s vacuity in *I Shot Andy Warhol.* She flatters the book by playing up its humour:

the decision to turn into dialogue three of the book's interpolated critiques of MOR rock-pop stars (on Phil Collins, Huey Lewis and Whitney Houston, all spoken while preparing people for the slaughter) was sort of inspired, and the sex scene in which Bateman never stops admiring his own prowess in a mirror is genuinely funny. Christian Bale makes a fine co-conspirator in all this, presenting Bateman as a man on the cusp between braggadocio and a barely suppressed awareness of his own insignificance.

And yet the film doesn't work. Late in the game, Harron brings in Ronald Reagan (seen defending the Iran-Contra scandal) to provide an objective correlative for the gap between surface and substance, as found in the yuppie milieu generally and in Bateman in particular. But Bateman has insisted from the moment he started intoning voiceovers that he exists only as a cipher ('I simply am not there'), and so it's hardly a knockout conceptual punch to close the film with a threatening close-up of his eyes and a threatening assertion on the soundtrack that he has gained no insight into himself or catharsis from his experiences. The problem, again, is the book, an insurmountable obstacle. If Harron and Turner had set out to make a real movie on these themes, they would never have started from a script like this. As it is, they've come up with an ingenious adaptation, minimising the book's shortcomings and maximising its intermittent panache. But they remain prisoners of the smug and self-satisfied Bret Easton Ellis.

Tony Rayns

Bram Stoker's Dracula (Francis Ford Coppola, 1992)

Section 4:
The Practice of
Screenwriting and Adaptation

TRUST THE TELLER

Henry Sheehan talks with James V. Hart about *Dracula*

Just about the last person to receive credit for a film's success – down the line after the cinematographer, composer, and producer's brother-in-law – is the screenwriter. It's a phenomenon born from the long-entrenched Hollywood practice of assigning platoons of writers to rewrites, and nurtured by a vulgarised notion of auteurism. James (Jim) V. Hart has managed to stake his own claim to prime authorship as the screenwriter for *Hook*, and for Coppola's new *Dracula*.

'Nobody cares about the writer,' says Hart. In tones from which the bitterness has been drained by success, he recounts the experience of being largely ignored amid the hype surrounding the release of *Hook*. In fact, he was not the only writer to receive credit – Malia Scotch Marmo shared it for screenwriting, while Nick Castle shared it for story. Yet, Hart points out, 'I wrote the original script, my name is in first position. I'm glad Malia shares credit, but the film is still 90 per cent what I wrote. But when you work with Steven [Spielberg], it doesn't matter. Everyone thinks it was his idea and he made the movie, that he dreamed it all up and it all came out of his mind.'

Oddly enough, Hart has robbed himself of some of the credit for the new *Dracula*. Emphatically, he insists that he has written an unusually loyal adaptation of Stoker's tale. And even with *Hook*, he insists that it is his loyalty to the original text – James Barrie's *Peter Pan* – that distinguishes his approach.

It isn't so much that he is attracted to late-Victorian or Edwardian fantasy, Hart explains, as to differences between source material and the adaptations drawn from them. '*Hook* and *Dracula* are both Victorian/Edwardian fantasy adventures,' admits Hart, 'but I think that one of the reasons I was attracted to them was that I discovered books very late in life. I grew up on Disney films, Hammer B movies, the drive-in; I grew up in Texas. I think that *Peter Pan* was burned in me like a genetic code, but when I read James Barrie's novel – the same thing as with Stoker – I was blown away by how different it was from Walt Disney and Mary Martin. I didn't read Barrie's novel until I was thirty-three years old; I didn't read *Dracula* until 1977, when I was thirty years old. It's almost like finding out that the little old man sitting on the street corner begging for food is J. D. Salinger.

'So to rediscover as an adult a new truth in what you have believed for many years to have been the truth immediately attracted me to Stoker. There's a very complex character at the centre of Stoker's novel. It's not about a guy in a tuxedo who wears a red sash and drinks blood, and it's not about a blood-sucking monster; it's about a seductive, powerful warrior prince who fell from grace and is seeking to come back. This is not a *Dracula* I've ever seen.'

But while it's true that Hart's adaptation pays a great deal of attention to Stoker, the story has been altered in crucial ways, even in a way that might have horrified Stoker himself. While remaining faithful to much of the plot and most of the characterisations of the novel, Hart has effected a profound transformation of *Dracula* from horror story to fairy tale. No longer is this the story of respectable English men and women threatened by a foreign ghoul quick to take advantage of any moral lapse. Hart's *Dracula* is the tale of a brave prince transformed into a monster by romantic despair, and how a love which survives the ages starts calling him back to humanity.

'What we brought to the book was a love story that doesn't exist in the novel,' Hart admits. 'I had to figure out a way to tell Stoker in the way Stoker was written, but to make it accessible to a modern audience. Whenever I had discussed *Dracula* in mixed company during the past fifteen years, it was always the women who had read the novel... And then Leonard Wolf, who wrote *The Annotated Frankenstein* and *The Annotated Dracula*, opened a window to the seductive powers of this character.' Wolf's book fills in the historical sources of the novel, examines Stoker's metaphors for their sexual content, and provides biographical analogues. Hart admired Wolf so much that, at one early point, the two collaborated on the screenplay and, Wolf's influence, says Hart, persisted in his own interpretation of the novel, including its autobiographical elements.

Setting Stoker on the couch

'Stoker's writing is like a confession of his fear, a justification of his manhood,' says Hart. 'That's why there are all these great handsome, heroic Victorian men who are going to stamp out the bad guy that's messing with their women. My ending is different, in that it plays into the love story that I try to fit into Stoker's narrative. The novel ends with the birth of the child. And seven years after the birth of that boy-child, Mina and Van Helsing and everybody take him back to the scene where Quincy and Dracula died. When reading that – and the way Leonard set it up – I instinctively wondered what woman would do that unless she was taking her child back to where Daddy died? Now, true, the baby was born thirteen months after Dracula died, but I don't know what the gestation period is for a vampire child. Leonard says it's nine months, but I don't know that for a fact.

'If you look at Mina in Stoker, her whole view of this creature changes once they share blood. Much of what she says in the film is right out of Stoker: she even gets Van Helsing to admit that he respects and admires this creature, which is right out of Stoker, too. So Mina changes, she has sympathy for this creature they're hunting. And that spoke to me when I was trying to figure out what to do with the women characters. It's really licence: maybe we set Stoker on the couch, but I hope we haven't done him an injustice. I feel very strongly that I've tried to support his narrative, rather than mess with it. We certainly haven't messed with it the way everybody else has over the years.'

This notion of loyalty-through-reinterpretation also informs Coppola's direction, which once again plays into the story re-imagined as a fairy tale. Every hint of haunting architecture or ominous costuming is exaggerated through rococo stylisation. Dracula's castle is a pile of towers impossibly perched on a cliff, while the parchment-dry, bouffant-haired Count (grey-haired and distinguished in the book) greets Jonathan Harker at the door wearing a scarlet cape with an enormous train (as opposed to a formal, basic black ensemble in the novel). The film's sense of geography is brilliant, delineating space as a function of emotion, so that a small patio or ruined abbey may include a bewildering number of hideaways, while a whole continent or ocean can be traversed in a panicky flash.

This adornment requires some complementary streamlining, most of which comes at the expense of Stoker's class resentments. Stoker's Dracula is not just a monster, but an imperious employer to the sullenly dutiful Harker. Dracula's assault on Harker's fiancée, Mina, is a further abuse of aristocratic privilege, an upper-class parasite feeding on the hardworking and sexually restrained bourgeoisie. The novel even climaxes with a democratic assault by Harker and his peers on Dracula and his servants.

The characters' class-consciousness is not entirely eliminated in the film and, given the reshaping of the material, its absence doesn't hurt much, except in the figure of Lucy, the high-spirited blonde from an upper-class background who, after an indulgent flirtation with the Count, turns into a child-killing vampire. In Hart's script, Van Helsing, the middle-European vampire hunter, simply dismisses her as a 'devil's concubine' with a predisposition towards satanic sex. Even in fairy tales, sexually aggressive women come to exemplary tragic ends.

Hart jokingly calls Lucy a victim of 'Unsafe vampire sex... and Lucy is a spoiled prattler – Leonard Wolf calls her a prattler, a hoyden – with what is almost a modern approach to her sexuality. I think she says in the novel: "Why can't a woman marry three men or as many men as she wants?" And Lucy is basically a quick snack in fast food for Dracula. I think Lucy pays for her unsafe vampire sex, her brazen attitude towards the world. She's spoiled, she's rich and she can do anything she wants. Mina represents the other side of Victorian womanhood, all corseted up tight. She is suppressing her sexuality, where Lucy is flaunting hers. Lucy pays the price for her wanton ways. Just like any woman today who has sex with multiple partners and is not practising safe sex is going to pay a price.'

It's not the scene I wrote...

Hart's concerns emerge with clarity in this version of *Dracula*, at least in part because they are in harmony with Coppola's preoccupations with the way his protagonists achieve salvation in the face of death and disaster. But his themes didn't sit so well with Spielberg's: in fact, on a fundamental level, they clash, in that Spielberg's heroes are invariably in flight from a strong, loving and demanding woman, while Hart's are crossing heaven and earth in order to find one. 'Listen, I love what Steven did,' says Hart. 'He is probably the only director who could have brought it to life at the scale at which it was brought to life. There are things that he misses, that I miss, things that are not in there that should be. But I've seen the film fifty times and I still love watching it with an audience.

'Tiger Lily and the Indians were in all my drafts and were cut out for political reasons; they were not even shot. I wrote a very specific voice for Tinker Bell... I made her a sniping, feisty, tough task-driver for Peter, who was madly in love with her. But it was rewritten very poorly in my opinion; it took all the edge off her.

'I still think it's Steven's best storytelling, but I wish he had left in the footage he cut out after the preview. I wish people had seen the two-hour-and-twenty-three-minute version. It's a story about mothers and how Wendy became the mother to the Lost Boys, and now that's not there. The other thing I miss sorely is that Peter went to rescue his children, but now he doesn't. It's a complete sequence that wasn't shot because they ran out of time and money. I also miss the battle I wrote: the battle that's there is my battle, but Steven circled all the good moments and gave them to Malia to arrange, who did a great job, but it's not the battle I wrote. It was an amalgamation of the disenfranchised elements of Neverland coming together to free Peter's children. And the flying sequence turns into a joke instead of a celebration of youth and what it would be like for an adult to fly.'

Hart later observes: 'My belief in the material is what every piece of talent in this business is looking for. We spend millions of dollars in the studios every year on producers and actors and directors who don't produce a film. I show up with two scripts that nobody wanted to develop and they attracted Spielberg and Coppola, and amazing casts. Pretty soon it won't be my turn any more, but I still believe that it's the material that is the driving force in this industry, an industry which doesn't look on the writer as even a third-class citizen. I'm trying to change that a little bit.'

Lonely People

Mark Burman talks with Caroline Thompson about *The Secret Garden*

Mark Burman: What drew you to this project?

Caroline Thompson: I had read the book as a child and like every child around and before and after me, I found that it had imagery that I never forgot. What's beautiful about the story is the metaphor of the garden into which the child goes and which she thinks is dead, but which she brings back to life. It's a beautiful little box and it's safe, though it seems frightening at first. It's very pre-adolescent: the idea that you can take this thing you are afraid of and make it bloom. Meaning the sexual and emotional self.

Mark Burman: If you look at images of girls of that period, they are usually very prissy. *The Secret Garden* is quite different.

Caroline Thompson: I think all children think of themselves as hideous and isolated and uncomfortable and difficult. What Burnett has given us is a character who thinks she is a completely unpleasant being, and then discovers the beauty inside herself. It sounds like a horrible cliché, but I think it really is how kids feel. My own memories of childhood are that the table was always too tall or the chair too large; everything was disproportionate to your size. So for a child to be able to enter a world where everything is disproportionate and find her place in that world is something all children yearn for. The story tells kids that they too can do it.

Mark Burman: Did you have to adapt the story to compete with current children's cinema?

Caroline Thompson: It goes for a completely different feeling; it's meant to inspire and give the audience joy, but the riches are not the riches of a rollercoaster ride.

Mark Burman: What is the attraction for you of fairy tales and children's stories?

Caroline Thompson: The attraction of all stories for me is the metaphor. *The Secret Garden* has particularly vivid and lasting metaphors. There is the huge, dark house with too many rooms and places that you can't even begin to explore, and then the garden with its walls and sense of safety where you can make the flowers grow. I'm often invited to seminars for fantasy writers and I doggedly refuse to attend because to me my work is more realistic than so-called realist movies because life is about what things feel like, not about the clock ticking. It is metaphors that express what things feel like: the metaphor in *Edward Scissorhands* of a man who cannot touch or be touched, cannot hold or hug, cannot participate – that's what life feels like.

Mark Burman: There are some wonderful conceits in that film – for example, the castle perched atop pastel suburbia.

Caroline Thompson: To us it was like a memory of our childhood. I had described suburbia, but Tim Burton realised it in such a way that it was of no time and no place, as if it was our memories. That impulse towards honouring my memories is key to the way I approached *The Secret Garden*. When I started to look closely at the book I found that it was heavily plotted and very moralising and repetitive. So my impulse became to honour what I remembered it having felt like when I was a child.

Mark Burman: You've changed the opening, too. Why did you feel the need to do that?

Caroline Thompson: It's simpler dramatically now; it opens with an earthquake rather than a plague. The plague would have given rise to some great images, but the telling of it took too much time. And the earthquake is a strong metaphor for shaking up one's life, as we who live in Los Angeles know.

Mark Burman: Do you think *The Secret Garden* has a different power for women than for men?

Caroline Thompson: Well, you'd know better than I do – you're the man. I think it is a very strong book for women, so I'm always surprised when I meet a man who encountered it as a boy. It is about a girl child and the metaphors are female – the garden is an undeniable womb image. But I hope that boys find things in the movie as well. There's Dickon, who is very much a cipher in the book, but in the film Andrew Knott brings real life to him.

Mark Burman: Did you look at other versions?

Caroline Thompson: No, though I believe that Agnieszka has seen something of each of them. Once I turned on the television and there was the MGM version, but I quickly turned it off. Poor Margaret O'Brien was strapped into some gizmo to make her look flat-chested and they had the world in black and white, and the garden in colour. I guess they got the idea from *The Wizard of Oz*, but there it was a sustained difference whereas here it became a goofy conceit.

Mark Burman: How did you want the garden to appear on screen?

Caroline Thompson: I think that what you see is a result of our collaboration. The garden has a wonderful womblike feel, it's very expansive and extravagant, and feels radically different from the rest of Misselthwaite. There is a feeling of safety there that is key to the psychology of the story.

Mark Burman: How did you get into scriptwriting?

Caroline Thompson: The director Penelope Spheeris wanted to adapt my novel *First Born* as a film and I said she could have it very cheaply if she would teach me how to write the script. The movie was optioned, but never made and, soon afterwards, I was introduced to Tim Burton and wrote *Edward Scissorhands*. While I was waiting for that to get going – because Tim had *Beetlejuice* and *Batman* to do – I did a few other films, one of which, *Homeward Bound: The Incredible Journey*, comes out in January. It's a remake of a Disney movie from 1964 called *The Incredible Journey* – a story based on a Canadian children's book about two dogs and a cat who travel an impossible distance home. The gag here is that though it's a live-action film, we hear what the animals are thinking. Again it's the world through the point of view of creatures who are alienated from the regular rhythms that we think the everyday is composed of. I have another coming out – a musical called *Nightmare Before Christmas*. It's stop-motion animation. The music and lyrics are by Danny Elfman, I wrote the script, Tim Burton produced it and it was made by a young director named Henry Selick.

Mark Burman: When did cinema first get its claws into you?

Caroline Thompson: The first film I ever saw was *The Time Machine*. I was three, I think. The theatre was crowded and there were probably ten little boys at my mother's birthday party. I ended up sitting between two of them, neither of whom I knew. I was terrified and I was between these two strange, smelly little boys and I couldn't hide from the movie; every time I closed my eyes I was utterly petrified. I didn't go back to the movies for years and years. And in one sense that's what draws me to them – they have a real power for me. It's not a safe place to go, it's scary, and I like playing with that.

Mark Burman: What are your plans for the future?

Caroline Thompson: I'm hoping to direct. I think I won't be happy until I take more responsibility for the work. As a writer you don't exactly abdicate responsibility, but you pass on the torch to the next person, and I'd like to be the person to whom the torch is passed. It will be interesting to see if I enjoy it.

Mark Burman: What comes first?

Caroline Thompson: There's a ghost story called *Rouge* which is an adaptation of a Chinese ghost story. It's very, very sad – a story for adults. It's about a couple who kill themselves in order to be together in the hereafter, but they don't meet and so one of them comes back to look for the other and in so doing affects the lives of a contemporary couple. The story has a very sad ending which it would be criminal of me to share. It will be set in LA in the 1920s and 1990s. I love the 1920s – it's a period in which I wish I had been alive. Especially in a place like LA, to which people emigrated to re-invent themselves. There's a lot of sadness and eagerness and excitement and desire in that. I also set the story when I did because there's a period between 1919 and 1923, according to statistics, when women shed twelve pounds of underwear. The idea of taking off your clothes and feeling free has a great appeal. I hope to be exploring some of the feelings that people set themselves free with.

Mark Burman: How much power is there for women in Hollywood?

Caroline Thompson: When people ask me if there's a disadvantage to being female, I laugh. I come from upper-middle-class WASP culture and the men from my particular slice of America have an awful lot of pressures from the start to succeed. It really does them a lot of damage, whereas being a female in the late 1960s and 1970s was a real advantage to me. Nobody told me 'no'. Nobody pressured me or thought I was going to grow up to be a doctor or a lawyer or an Indian Chief. I didn't fall for it. So I've never had a problem being a woman in my business. I know that's not true for others, but for me it was a gift.

THE THRILLER INSIDE ME

Larry Gross on his adaptation of Jim Thompson's *This World, Then the Fireworks*

This World, Then the Fireworks is a short story that the legendary American crimewriter Jim Thompson wrote in the 1950s, but was unable to get published in his lifetime. It tells the story of a grifter named Marty Lakewood, who as well as taking part in the usual minor criminal con games has two striking aspects to his life: he is incestuously involved with his sister Carol, and he has a tendency to murder people, quite abruptly. Though not for profit particularly, nor to advance some other practical agenda. He murders as an avenging angel with a twisted sense of doing what's right.

I read about half of this story and knew immediately that I wanted to try to turn it into a screenplay. The quality that attracted me was this: almost unbearably extreme behaviour, on the part of numerous characters, seemed to arise from a coherent (and therefore credible) set of themes. When a piece of material combines the logical and the illogical in this way, it starts to feel intrinsically cinematic. I write partly to indulge myself – to see almost unimaginable or unthinkable things made real and plausible on screen; things that 'can't happen' somehow happening; behaviour that makes your jaw drop. This story had an abundance of that sort of stuff in it.

For all the violence in cinema, little that we see on screen is genuinely shocking. Killing people in gory ways, for instance, doesn't shock very often. What does, in my opinion, is the vivid, accurate rendering of extreme emotional states of being, states we have all glimpsed in life, but which are rarely represented. This is why it's so scary when Isabella Rossellini holds a knife in proximity to Kyle MacLachlan's underwear-clothed genitals near the beginning of *Blue Velvet*. The expressed ferocity of her fear, suspicion and rage has enormous impact, despite the fact that the action itself is unexceptional, physically. A great deal of Thompson's story had the same emotional power as this scene.

Because hysteria and madness are part of almost the entire surface of the text, there is very little of what you might call a realistically believable element to the story. An insane narrator, surrounded by grotesques distorted by his point of view, makes for an immediate plunge into unrealism. This was the main challenge for the screenwriter.

The critical ambiguity of our movie lies in its relation to thriller machinery. This comes from a split or ambiguity inside Thompson's text. Thompson does three things in his stories that disrupt normal storytelling. First, he focuses on interior psychic states more than external story-oriented thriller writers do. Second, he injects a comic, absurd element that immediately ironises the reader's experience of thriller situations. And third, he exhibits an extreme indifference – whether out of haste, exhaustion or intention – to story logic.

Are Thompson and our movie 'ironic', then, or 'postmodern', in the supposed mode of Tarantino? Are they commentary on genre? In my opinion, no.

There are intentionally ironic authors, but there are more unintentionally ironic ones. I believe Thompson had no intellectual programme to mock the genre tradition he worked in. He ruptured it intuitively, with naive sincerity. I'd make an analogy with the distinction between the primitive or intuitive modernism of Joseph Conrad's novels, say, and the deliberate, self-conscious modernity of Joyce. With Joyce, isn't there a self-conscious, complete separation from realistic convention? But Conrad gropes towards new forms and structures over the bones of the nineteenth-century adventure-novel norms that he never fully repudiates.

Because Thompson's breaches of genre decorum are not systematic, he can at times seem incoherent. That was the danger facing our film. Cinema has a dangerous proclivity for the literal: once you claim to be presenting a story in any kind of real world, then a number of elements of rationality, plausibility and 'realism' have to be taken into account. Part of my job was to make the world of the movie appear a little more real than the world of the story. But if one went too far in that direction, rounding off the mad edges of the Thompson universe to make his world more recognisable, one would just end up with a rather unexceptional and not very terrific crime story. To some degree, this is the flaw of Thompson adaptations such as *The Grifters* or *After Dark, My Sweet*: in both, the decision to move out of Thompson's gothic-degenerate 1950s into the 1990s is intended to make the movies more 'real', and easier to identify with. But it's a choice that is incompatible with the fairytale-like creepiness of the stories.

As compelling 'what-happens-next?' crime drama, there were terrific holes in *This World, Then the Fireworks*. But those holes were more than compensated for by the emotional intensity. In fact, the very disinterest in regular, effective plotting made the piece more compelling. I patched up the holes a bit, but not too much.

I knew that director Michael Oblowitz, who brought me the story to work on, was comfortable with, even in love with Thompson's subversive contempt for conventional moral piety, joined with a certain pessimism about breaking away from conventions. Michael's film-making hero is Fassbinder, who like Thompson utilised commercial narrative forms and then exploded them with his access to unimaginable emotional truth. But Michael is also a great fan of Ridley Scott, who always makes the ugliest realities quite beautiful. The elegance and visual unity that Michael imposed on this material is what makes the screenplay work, to whatever extent it does. Beauty becomes part of the unreality of Marty Lakewood's imagination. The film is shot with a deliberate excess of elegance: the beauty is beyond the functional, and this is the sign of an obsessive universe. In addition to this perverse use of visual beauty, the film's unique quality, taken straight from the story, is how verbally over the top it is. For this to work, the actors (especially Billy Zane, who narrates and who has the most outrageous speeches) had to be at the top of their game. Mostly they are. For this, Michael and I are grateful.

I like art that is aggressive and pessimistic, art that wants to try to assert things about the world, while acknowledging the difficulty of assertion. These are qualities and ambitions of *This World, Then the Fireworks* that I am proud of.

THE ROAD NOT TAKEN

Leslie Felperin talks with Scott Frank about adapting Elmore Leonard

Leslie Felperin: How did you get into screenwriting?

Scott Frank: I studied film at the University of California Santa Barbara. After I graduated I knew I wanted to write screenplays but I didn't know a soul in the film business. I started bartending while I rewrote *Little Man Tate* over and over again. I managed to get it to a friend of a friend of a friend of an agent to another agent. By 1984, I had an agent. By 1985, I was writing my first film, *Plain Clothes*. Martha Coolidge directed it. It's pretty godawful – every time I have 'flu I see it on television. I remember going on the set for a week and watching it all fall apart. My wife said, 'Don't make yourself miserable, just come home and write another movie.' And while I was writing *Dead Again*, *Little Man Tate* was optioned to be directed by Jodie Foster.

Leslie Felperin: How did you develop your art?

Scott Frank: When I was working on *Dead Again*, there was a writer's strike. I read *Red Harvest*, the Dashiell Hammett book, and it taught me how to write the script. I also read *Mildred Pierce* – both James M. Cain and Hammett say a lot with a little, which is the essence of screenwriting. The weaknesses of the *Little Man Tate* screenplay had to do with the fact that it was episodic – I could never get my arms around the material to make it work structurally. I decided that in my next screenplay I would make my weakness my strength.

Leslie Felperin: What was it like working with Kenneth Branagh on *Dead Again*?

Scott Frank: A blast. He was extremely adherent to the screenplay; he kept saying his job was to make my words work. It's because he comes from the theatre – I'll probably never have that experience with a director again. The only thing that came out differently was the tone: he has a very theatrical, almost campy tone, whereas I looked at the script more like *Rosemary's Baby* with a sense of humour.

Leslie Felperin: From there you went on to *Malice*.

Scott Frank: I worked on *Malice* for a couple of years, then Harold Becker fired me and changed the movie into something else. It was an awful experience. It was about

that time that Stacey Sher sent me Elmore Leonard's *Get Shorty*. I read the first sixty
pages and got to the part where the loan shark and the crack dealer are talking
about how to fix a screenplay, and I thought, 'I'm in.' Ironically I'd turned down
Jurassic Park so I could stay on *Malice* – one of those great career moves. There have
been many in my life – I turned down *Forrest Gump*, too.

Leslie Felperin: What does adapting Leonard involve?

Scott Frank: What I like about his books is that there's a freedom to his writing, a real
fluidity and sense of fun. I tend to overthink – I agonise over every word, and the
punctuation. What I have to do is give structure to happenstance – he sits down
and he doesn't know where it's headed, he just lets it unfold. He doesn't think in
terms of theme, so I find a theme, then anything that doesn't play to that theme can
fall away.

Leslie Felperin: What theme were you trying to bring out in *Out of Sight*?

Scott Frank: It's about the road not taken, which is the saddest thing. When I first wrote
the screenplay the character was in his fifties – I thought of Robert De Niro or even
Jack Nicholson. What's so great about George Clooney's performance is that he
conveys that sadness: 'If I hadn't robbed all those banks, I could have been with this
girl.'

Leslie Felperin: Do you usually have a cast in mind when you're writing?

Scott Frank: The truth is, I write everything for Steve McQueen, male and female. He's
the guy you wish you were.

Leslie Felperin: What did the two directors bring to your Leonard adaptations?

Scott Frank: I was on the set of *The Wild, Wild West* looking at video playback – uncut,
unedited, just one camera take – and everything about it screamed Barry Sonnenfeld.
On *Get Shorty*, I found Barry to be very funny and dark, he gets character nuance
very well and he loves texture and detail. Steven Soderbergh has a dry sense of
humour, but he's a much more romantic film-maker, much more adult. Barry sees
things in the material other people can't – he has a unique way of visualising the
world. Steven works from the inside out: he doesn't start with the visualisation, he
starts with the characters.

Leslie Felperin: Did he work closely with you when you were writing?

Scott Frank: Yes, because he's a writer as well. He would come into the office, and if we
had problems with a scene we'd discuss them, act it out, riff on dialogue. And we
were always talking about *The Last Detail*, *The French Connection*. Those were our
favourite sorts of films.

Leslie Felperin: How does the screenplay differ from the novel?

Scott Frank: The screenplay is more romantic, then when you realise the movie with
George Clooney and Jennifer Lopez it gets more romantic still. There are bits that
work better on screen than on the page, too, for instance in the dream – which is
not in the novel – she walks into the bathroom, and when she grabs his hand she
gives a little half-smile. All the emotion is contained in that tiny movement of her
lips – it's wonderful. And George Clooney has a great moment where he does a long
monologue after they sleep together, and she says, 'You're not dumb,' and he has this
laugh when he says, 'I don't know about that.' It's a great moment of self-deprecation.

Leslie Felperin: Do you write stage directions into your scripts?

Scott Frank: I'll put in a nod if it's an answer to a question, but trying to convey much more than that feels like I'm stepping on the actor. Sometimes I'll say someone smiles because that's communicating. But I try to keep it to a minimum because I want room for my dialogue.

Leslie Felperin: Do the actors talk to you about background?

Scott Frank: Not a lot. Sometimes they come up with a bit of business they want to do, like George's thing with the Zippo. I wanted her to give him something in the last scene, and Steven said he'd watched George play with this Zippo and I should find a way to work it in.

Leslie Felperin: Who do you write for?

Scott Frank: I write to amuse myself. I figure I want to tell a good story, but for me the entire plot comes from the characters – you can't just think up a story and then see who's going to be in it. I think about the characters a lot before I start writing – there's a lot of messy getting down impressions then gradually a shape begins to form. Gradually you see things that are more interesting and you focus on those. It's about finding out what makes them different and not just a bank robber.

There was a recent article in *Director's Guild Magazine* where Michael Bay was talking about *Armageddon* and he used the phrase 'shitty script' six times. He's crapping all over screenwriters. 'I turned this pile of crap into something great. I turned straw into gold.' Bay represents a new breed – you start with a concept, then you think about how you're going to shoot it, but it's about nothing. Movies have become totally conceptual: they're all about this blowing up or that blowing up or these guys stealing this. Basically, you hire a screenwriter to make quips; you no longer have characters, you have attitude. You have screenwriters who are twenty years old trying to write a scientist in NASA. We couldn't make *Taxi Driver* today.

Leslie Felperin: Does writing get any easier?

Scott Frank: Anyone can write a script, but writing a good script is one of the hardest things there is. I still haven't learned how to do it – I just stumble my way through. My screenplays are usually a series of happy accidents – I don't know what I'm doing and I thank god I work for people who are much smarter than I am. That's what saves my ass.

BASS HYSTERIA
Benedict Carver examines the Leonard Bass phenomenon

In the power-broking world of the Hollywood studios, screenwriters have until recently always been the bit players. Writers, according to industry lore, are difficult but expendable. They are always making unreasonable demands and they don't know how to play the game. Ron Bass is a thoroughbred power-broker who plays the game to perfection. Over the past twelve years, this former entertainment attorney has sprung effortlessly through a number of hoops to establish one of Hollywood's most successful screenwriting imprints. If being an auteur means being able to make whatever film you want, then Bass is the first auteur screenwriter in Hollywood history and the most powerful penman since Joe Eszterhas, writer of *Basic Instinct.*

The Bass myth is fuelled by his remarkable output – an average of eight screenplays a year – and his controversial working methods, which involve employing a full-time staff of eight as his personal 'development department'. The screenwriting machine himself enjoys an eighteen-hour day, rising at 3 or 4 a.m., working through lunch and rarely going out in the evening. His *oeuvre* has a solid track record at the box-office, and includes such hits as *Rain Man* (1988) and *My Best Friend's Wedding* (1997). In a profile of Bass in *GQ, Variety* editor Peter Bart argued: 'If success were measured purely in monetary terms, Bass is probably the most successful writer Hollywood has ever seen.'

Bass' golden touch is currently so favoured by directors and studio executives that he can be writing or rewriting as many as seven scripts at any one time. At present these include Steven Spielberg's adaptation of Arthur Golden's novel *Memoirs of a Geisha* and a script based on the Pulitzer prize-winning novel *The Shipping News* by E. Annie Proulx, which Sony Pictures wants Bass to polish for star John Travolta. Sceptics of the Bass method allege that his team does more than research and development, that they are, in fact, uncredited writers. And, *Rain Man* aside, Bass' pictures have found little support among critics, who believe them to be sentimental and manipulative. But whether he's a hack carrying out the studio's bidding or a genius with a common touch, unlike most screenwriters Bass has manoeuvred himself into a powerful position in contemporary Hollywood. How did he get there?

The film industry has long harboured what screenwriter Robert Towne calls a 'historic hatred' for writers. And even today, rarely does a week go by without a tale of woe emerging about some budding scribe who has been crushed by a crude and insensitive Hollywood infrastructure. Director John Ford would rip up scripts in front of his writers without even reading them. Jack Warner famously labelled writers 'Schmucks with Underwoods'. In 1988, the failed Writers Guild of America strike over residuals decimated morale in the screenwriting community and arguably worsened writers' working conditions and remuneration. Hollywood has not fully recovered from this conflict. Towne, who won an Oscar for his screenplay of *Chinatown*, believes that writers not only receive little respect from their paymasters, but lack self-respect, too. 'Until the screenwriter does his job, nobody else has a job,' Towne wrote in an essay in *Scenario.* 'In other words, he is the asshole who keeps everyone else from going to work.'

Ron Bass doesn't fit the beleaguered-writer model. Born in Los Angeles in 1942, he attended Stanford University, where he studied political science, and Yale, where he earned a masters in international relations. Bass says that when he was growing up he wanted to be a novelist. He began writing short stories when he was six (he was bedridden between the ages of three and eight). By seventeen, he had written his first novel and was distraught when his English teacher told him it was a 'personal fantasy' that 'could never be published'. A suitably chastened Bass didn't write another word for fifteen years. In an early example of the pragmatism that would govern his career, he turned to law instead, specifically entertainment law. 'If I wasn't good enough to be an artist then at least I could hang around artists,' he says. 'It was vicarious.'

In the early 1970s, Bass returned to his rejected novel and refashioned it in the mornings before starting work. The resulting adventure caper *The Perfect Thief* was published in 1974. After two further novels, he turned his third, *The Emerald Illusion* – a John Le Carré-influenced spy thriller – into a screenplay, *Code Name: Emerald*. 'I insisted on writing the screenplay, just to make money. It was made into a terrible film, written by seven people, that was never even released theatrically. But my then-agent made a bunch of copies of my script, which was good, and sent it to all the studios. They started to hire me. And I realised that writing for screen was not a lesser art form than writing fiction.' After that Bass was on his way, penning Bob Rafelson's *Black Widow* and Francis Ford Coppola's *Gardens of Stone* (both 1987) in quick succession.

Bass' legal background informs his writing regime – most observers point to his unusual level of discipline. He claims that he wakes at 3.15 a.m. and immediately starts thinking about a scene he was working on the previous day. 'Sleeping in is 5.15,' he says. 'That's really indulgent.' Often working outside – in parks, cafés or the homes of his team members – he writes in longhand and keeps a box of newly sharpened pencils by his side. He approaches each scene with the mind set of a methodical problem-solver; the idea that it might defy writing does not occur to him. He even has his own technical vocabulary: he talks about 'blocking' and 'dressing' scenes, to the confusion of studio executives.

Bass put together his development team in the late 1980s. It has turned 'Ron Bass' into a machine that moves with brutal efficiency from one project to the next. And it has led to accusations that Bass is not a writer at all, but a manager of other writers whose ideas and opinions he collects, collates and then passes off as his own work. The first person to join him was Jane Rusconi, a former researcher to Oliver Stone on *JFK*. After Jane came Mimi, and after Mimi came Hannah; and soon there were eight, mostly female team members. (One Hollywood wag has nicknamed the group the 'Ronettes'.)

According to Bass, who funds the entire operation himself, his method is much misunderstood. He insists that he is the only writer in the group. 'It's really sad, people say a lot of hurtful things. If people really understood it then they'd be doing it, too. Not many writers can afford to have eight people, but a lot could afford one or two. And for most people two would be great.' His team, Bass says, carry out research and criticise his ideas. They make suggestions for improvements to scenes and characters' motivations. 'They have to be very courageous because I'll get defensive at times and I'll really fight and get angry.' As if to demonstrate the point he turns to Rusconi, in whose home we are meeting, and says, 'You ought to read the thing I did this morning. You'll find it at 127-A in my notebook...'

Neither Bass' success nor his protestations have convinced Hollywood of the veracity of his claims for his system. 'The line between making "suggestions" and actually "writing" them is a fine one,' notes one colleague. But for Bass film is a collaborative medium and writers should be no exception. 'People say to me, "So, some of the ideas and so forth in your scripts come from other people." I say, "Yeah. That's great. And there's nothing new about it." I don't have to have every idea be my own in order to feel that I've done a good job.'

Bass' team also provides him with a buffer to the studio: their responses replace those of a set of development executives. Like many Hollywood writers he finds little to recommend in the studio development system. 'A studio executive is forced, by the nature of his job, to improve something. So they just take the other side. If the character is angry, the exec will say she should be sweet. If she's imperious, she should be gentle. Right now, as I'm writing *Memoirs of a Geisha* for Steven Spielberg, we give the most recent drafts to executives at Sony. And I say to them: "I don't want to read your memo. I want you to give your memo to Steven. I want to hear from Steven if he wants to incorporate some or all of what you want." I've spent too many years working with competing visions and trying to make it all match. If you do that you end up having no vision at all.'

Rain Man, which Bass co-wrote with Barry Morrow, won him an Oscar for Best Original Screenplay and transported him into the writers' A-list. The other members of this élite club currently include Richard LaGravenese (*The Bridges of Madison County*), Steven Zaillian (*Schindler's List*), Paul Attanasio (*Quiz Show*) and Gary Ross (*Big*). William Goldman (*Butch Cassidy and the Sundance Kid*) lurks in the background, polishing the occasional script such as *Last Action Hero* and *Good Will Hunting*. Like Bass, LaGravenese, Zaillian and Ross have come to prominence by writing melodramatic star vehicles which appeal principally to women (for instance, Zaillian's *Awakenings* and LaGravenese's *The Horse Whisperer*). But, unlike him, they have used their new-found power to move into directing. In fact, LaGravenese (*Living Out Loud*), Zaillian (*A Civil Action*) and Ross (*Pleasantville*) all released films last year which they wrote and directed themselves.

Bass sees LaGravenese, Zaillian and Ross as 'film-makers', but describes himself as a 'storyteller'. But the common consensus about Bass in Hollywood is that he wields so much power with his pen he doesn't need to direct in order to control his material. Bass admits that on some of his projects (such as *My Best Friend's Wedding*), the director or studio couldn't order a rewrite without his consent. But, in general, he says, he defers to the director. 'I've worked with Luis Mandoki, Vincent Ward, P. J. Hogan and Steven Spielberg, who is an extremely open guy. I think they respect me enough that, if I'm really against something, they'll find a solution we both feel okay about. On *My Best Friend's Wedding*, P. J. and I worked together, and producer Jerry Zucker sometimes with us, and P. J. rewrote stuff. There were actors who wrote things, too – Julia Roberts wrote that great toast at the end. And I loved that.'

While he eschews directing, Bass has moved into producing. He earned his first producer credit, which he describes as a 'watershed', on Wayne Wang's 1993 tearjerker *The Joy Luck Club*. Since then he has wanted to be part of the film-making process on almost every film he writes: 'You aren't an island, sending a script off into the sunset and then grumbling when everybody screws it up. I stopped being at war with the process and became part of the process.' Or, as Bart put it in a 1997 profile of Bass for *Variety*: 'Most writers pride themselves on being proverbial "outsiders" railing against the system; Bass has always been an absolute insider.'

Bass has written with some success in almost every conceivable genre – action, comedy, romance, thrillers, drama. But that doesn't mean his screenplays have nothing in common. Nearly all Bass-scripted films, from *Sleeping with the Enemy* (1991) to *Dangerous Minds* (1995), contain strong roles for women. Many in Hollywood credit him with single-handedly inventing the 'women's picture' of the 1990s. (Bass himself notes that 60 per cent of ticket-buying decisions by over-21s are made by women.) Thus Hollywood's leading actresses, at least in box-office terms, are Bass devotees: he has worked three times with Julia Roberts, twice with Angela Basset and once each with Meg Ryan and Demi Moore.

Bass is also an unabashed employer of emotion. In his scathing review of *What Dreams May Come* (1998), the *L.A. Times'* Kenneth Turan wrote: 'Ron Bass never met a tear he didn't like.' (Bass' response: 'When you go through being reunited with your dead children and go through hell to see your wife, if people aren't breaking down it gets totally bogus.') Nearly all Bass' pictures involve humans coming to terms with their 'inner selves', and many with other people – husbands, parents, relatives.

Of course, Bass doesn't hesitate to admit that as a storyteller he manipulates people's emotions. 'I think if someone is going to pay their eight bucks and give me two hours of their time to sit and watch a story, then they don't want to watch something that doesn't engage them emotionally. I go to movies to laugh or cry or to get really involved. The theory that less is more and things have to be very restrained to be truly aesthetic and artful and worthwhile – I think it's a bunch of bullshit.'

In support of his approach, Bass cites the popularity of the Farrelly brothers' *There's Something about Mary*, which he compares to his script for Chris Columbus' *Stepmom* (1998) – starring Julia Roberts and Susan Sarandon – in its combination of street-smart humour, whimsy, and 'heart'. Humour, emotion, romance: it's a formula whose success has already been proved by such film-makers as *Ghost* director Jerry Zucker and James L. Brooks, the writer and director of *Terms of Endearment*, *Broadcast News* and *As Good As It Gets*.

With his willingness and ability to embrace the production process, his empathy with a pre-millennium audience looking to discover their 'inner selves' and his desire to write market-driven pictures, Bass is the quintessence of 1990s Hollywood screenwriting. In July 1997, he signed an exclusive three-year deal to write and produce films for Sony Pictures Entertainment. The deal is thought to be one of the best paid ever for a writer/producer in Hollywood – in his *GQ* article, Bart writes that it is 'virtually impossible for Bass to make less than $10 million a year'. In the 1930s, the contract writer was powerless, at the beck and call of the studio and obliged to pen as many as five generic screenplays a month. Under Bass' 1998 contract, he will earn more than $1 million per screenplay that he writes or rewrites; there is no minimum writing requirement; and he doesn't have to accept studio assignments.

Before February this year, Bass was the exception among Hollywood writers, but now he, along with LaGravenese, Attanasio and Scott Frank, is among the thirty writers involved in a watershed Sony deal that, for the first time, offers a percentage of gross receipts to screenwriters. However, most screenwriters still chafe beneath the studio yoke. Writers say that two issues always come up at WGA meetings: how to limit the number of free rewrites a writer will perform and how to improve his or her chance of staying on a project he or she originated (few writers who start a script are still involved by the time the film goes into production). As John Gregory Dunne explains in *Monster: Living off the Big Screen*: 'Although ritual obeisance is paid to the script, rarely is it paid to the individual scriptwriter. Prevailing industry wisdom is the more writers there are on a script, the better that script will be.'

At Sony, Bass not only writes his own scripts, but also rewrites and produces those of others. Stepmom, for instance, on which he is the fifth (credited) writer, went into production only after it had been given the Bass makeover. It's a process he rigorously defends: 'When you're making a film, there's so much at stake the best idea has to win. On *Stepmom*, we sat at a table in a restaurant in New York – Chris Columbus, Julia Roberts, Susan Sarandon and I. And when you're sitting in the room talking, nobody's wearing a hat with a name on it. It's like four writing partners – we're discussing and arguing and disagreeing and figuring out how to do it right.'

To many of his screenwriting colleagues, therefore, Bass isn't merely a successful writer collaborating with the system; he is the system, and more than that, he's a symbol of the system's triumph. Many upcoming screenwriters say they are turning to television in frustration at the headaches inherent in dealing with producers and executives. 'I don't feel the position of writers in Hollywood has changed much over the years,' says one aspirant, who prefers not to be named. 'We know no script is going to start shooting without some changes being made, but there's this idea in the studios that everybody should be allowed to contribute to the process, that the script should please everybody. So, the writers who are co-operative get most of the work. I think that the idea of a "power writer" in Hollywood is an oxymoron.'

GREAT EXPECTATIONS

Michael Eaton on adapting Dickens

After the success of the Royal Shakespeare Company's eight-hour production of *Nicholas Nickleby*, dramatised by David Edgar, in the early 1980s, the Trickster Ken Campbell sent out letters on meticulously forged notepaper. They purported to be written by the show's co-director Trevor Nunn and to issue from the newly formed Royal Dickens Company. They announced the abandonment of the Bard in favour of the Inimitable, and invited the cream of the literary establishment to pitch for Dickens novels they wished to adapt. That several writers eagerly offered their services to the bewildered artistic director is not surprising – actors and directors have the works of the national playwright to mess about with, but for writers it's the prospect of reinterpreting the output of the national novelist that continues to entice.

It was, of course, ever thus – there were pirated versions of *The Pickwick Papers* playing on the London stage while the serial of Dickens' first book was still appearing. More than ninety silent-film versions of his novels, many of them now lost, were made, followed by the most well-known movie adaptation of them all: David Lean's 1946 *Great Expectations*, which in my view has a better reputation than it deserves. But, in many ways, it's the television serial – its lack of fixed length allowing room for multi-narrative strands and subplot digression – which has proved a more appropriate medium. This was the form through which my generation was introduced to Dickens, though many such serials owe more to the caricatures of Phiz and Cruikshank than to the multifarious characters, active plots and rich thematic concerns of Dickens' text, and now appear more like manifestations of the heritage industry than engagements with the works of a writer whose cinematic style inspired Griffith and Eisenstein.

The comfortable fixity of television's representational codes has recently been fractured, however, most notably by the BBC's *Our Mutual Friend* (1998). This six-hour version mobilised cinematic resources unthinkable before a television ecology of international co-production and assured world sales to re-create the world of the river and the dust heaps (the novel's central metaphors) in all its visual sublimity. It also managed to construct characters imbued with a post-Freudian psychology, which meant they never came across like a parade of unbelievable eccentrics from an old-fashioned rep company, while refusing to abandon the grotesquerie that lies at the heart of Dickensian characterisation.

The BBC's latest venture is the three-hour *Great Expectations*, dramatised by Tony Marchant, directed by Julian Jarrold and produced by David Snodin. Marchant is an obvious choice, since his sprawling, multi-layered eight-part drama of contemporary London life, *Holding On*, with its unexpected connections between people at the top and bottom of today's spoilheap, was itself inspired by Dickens' depiction of the metropolis. *Great Expectations*, though, is something of a poisoned chalice: it is arguably his best-constructed story, so there's little latitude for an adapter to uncover new dimensions in a work so entirely conscious of its purpose and so confident in its manipulation of the effects needed to achieve it.

Marchant's approach seeks out psychological verisimilitude, which has the effect of emphasising the darker aspects of the book. Shades of the prison house – keys, locks, bars and the looming presence of Newgate – continually disquiet Pip (Ioan Gruffudd) even at the height of his good fortune; his adult life can never escape the guilt and fear of the bereaved and abused child. Where John Mills' Pip in the Lean film is allowed several bright and breezy interludes of elation, Gruffudd's is a sombre progress, marked by the snobbery he's learned while becoming a gentleman – unknowingly at the convict Magwitch's expense. Rather than turning Miss Havisham (Charlotte Rampling) into some kind of sex goddess, we are shown that it's the enforced desiccation of her sexuality which motivates the malignity of her actions. And Magwitch (Bernard Hill) seems genuinely perplexed at the double-edged consequences of using Pip as the instrument of his revenge upon 'gentlemen'. Visually, it's dominated by the yellow glow of candelabra on Miss Havisham's blue-veined skin, by the softened focus and sumptuous colours of contemporary portrait painting and by shafts of pale sunlight through dust.

This is a reading of Dickens, rather than a simple illustration. But what is largely abandoned are those elements of bizarre and grotesque humour which co-exist alongside the darker and more plausible psychological verities – the mix Dickens himself compared to 'the layers of red and white in a side of streaky well-cured bacon'. But I would say that, wouldn't I, as I am at the time of writing dramatising *The Pickwick Papers*.

Index

page numbers in italic refer to illustrations or extensively illustrated pieces; int = interview; r = review; sp = screenplay